WOMEN AND CITIZENSHIP IN CENTRAL AND EASTERN EUROPE

For Biljana Lukić (1948–2002),
an outstanding translator, and
devoted sister, friend and a feminist

Donne toujours plus que tu ne peux reprendre.
Et oublie. Telle est la voie sacrée.
René Char

Women and Citizenship in Central and Eastern Europe

Edited by

JASMINA LUKIĆ
Central European University, Hungary

JOANNA REGULSKA
Rutgers University, USA

DARJA ZAVIRŠEK
University of Ljubljana, Slovenia

ASHGATE

Published by
Ashgate Publishing Limited
Gower House
Croft Road
Aldershot
Hampshire GU11 3HR
England

Ashgate Publishing Company
Suite 420
101 Cherry Street
Burlington, VT 05401-4405
USA

Ashgate website: http://www.ashgate.com

British Library Cataloguing in Publication Data
Women and citizenship in Central and Eastern Europe
 1.Women - Europe, Central - Social conditions 2.Women -
 Europe, Eastern - Social conditions 3.Citizenship - Europe,
 Central 4.Citizenship - Europe, Eastern 5.Women in politics
 - Europe, Central 6.Women in politics - Europe, Eastern
 7.Europe, Central - Politics and government 8.Europe,
 Eastern - Politics and government - 1945- 9.Europe, Central
 - Social conditions 10.Europe, Eastern - Social conditions
 I.Lukic, Jasmina II.Regulska, Joanna III.Zavirsek, Darja,
 1962-
 323.6'082'09437

Library of Congress Control Number: 2006926068

ISBN-10: 0 7546 4662 9
ISBN-13: 978 0 7546 4662 4

Printed and bound in Great Britain by MPG Books Ltd, Bodmin, Cornwall.

Contents

List of Figures

Contributors

Anne C. Bellows, Ph.D. (acbellow@rci.rutgers) is a geographer and planner who specializes in gendered community activisms and rights related to food security, environmental management, and health. She is particularly interested in how public voices and civic action work on behalf of economic rights to food, land access, and health. Her research in Poland as well as other countries looks at the health benefits and risks of urban agriculture. She works as a Research Associate in the Food Policy Institute at Rutgers University, US. She is also the author of several articles and reports on food security, community food security, and the right to food. More specific examples of her work include a history of urban agriculture in Poland; an analysis of the gendered aspects of local environmental management under transition in Poland especially as it effects food security, health, and urban agriculture; and the use of the theory and practice of the "women's rights as human rights" movement to reconceptualize thinking in concerns for the human right to food.

Marina Blagojević Ph.D. (marina.blagojevic@chello.hu; marina.blag@beotel.yu) is a senior researcher at the Institute for Criminological and Sociological Research in Belgrade, Serbia, and director of Altera MB – Research Centre on Gender and Ethnicity in Budapest, Hungary. She is a sociologist, with a special interest in the sociology of gender and the sociology of interethnic relations. She has taught gender studies at the Central European University in Budapest and Germany. She has also worked as an expert for the European Commission, the European Parliament, and UNDP, as well as for several governments throughout the Balkan region. Her present research interests focus on institutional and cultural as well as societal mechanisms of women's exclusion with a special emphasis on misogyny. Her work is published in several languages and explores the connection between knowledge, development, and gender politics in the "transition countries," it focuses on the reconciliation process and "positive history" of the Balkans.

Daša Duhaček (dasaduh@sezampro.yu), is a professor of political theory and women's studies, currently teaching women's studies at the Faculty of Political Science, University of Belgrade, Serbia. She is also coordinating the Belgrade Women's Studies and Gender Research Center, which she co-founded in 1992. Her fields of research include political philosophy and feminist theory. She is the author of several articles in Serbian and English, which focus on the position and role of women in South-Eastern Europe and feminist theory. She is the co-editor of *The Captives* *of Evil: The Legacy of Hannah Arendt* (2002) and the co-Director of the Summer School in Dubrovnik, *Feminist Critical Analysis*. She is a peace activist.

Salvatore A. Engel-Di Mauro (Salvatore.Engel-DiMauro@uwsp.edu) teaches environmental geography at the Department of Geography and Geology of the University of Wisconsin / Stevens Point. His research focuses on Eastern Europe and is concerned with the interconnections of gender, class, and environmental dynamics in the world system. His publications range from the gendered history of soil science in Hungary to the development of Menominee forestry in Central Wisconsin. His most recent projects address the social environmental implications of the European Union expansion. Among his recent publications are "The gendered scientific construction of soils in Hungary, 1900–1989" (2006); "USA. Studi di caso" in G. Ricoveri (ed.). *Beni comuni fra tradizione e futuro. Quaderni della rivista* (2005); "The gendered limits to local soil knowledge: macronutrient content, soil reaction, and gendered soil management in SW Hungary" (2002); and "Gender relations, political economy, and the ecological consequences of state-socialist soil science" (2002).

Nanette Funk (NFunk@brooklyn.cuny.edu) is a professor of philosophy at Brooklyn College, City University of New York. Her primary field of interest is political philosophy with a specialization in gender and post-communism. She co-edited *Gender Politics and Postcommunism: Reflections on Eastern Europe and the former Soviet Union* (1993). She has written numerous articles, including "Feminist Critiques of Liberalism: Can They Travel East? Their Relevance in Eastern and Central Europe and the Former Soviet Union" (2004); "Abortion Counseling and the 1995 German Abortion Law" (1996); and "Feminism Meets Post-Communism: The Case of the United Germany" in Susan Weisser and Jennifer Fleischner (eds.), *Feminist Nightmares; and Women at Odds* (1994). She co-directs the Gender and Transformation Workshop at NYU at the Center for European Studies.

Małgorzata Fuszara (mfuszara@isns.uw.edu.pl) is a professor and head of the Center for Socio-Legal Studies on the Situation of Women, and Director of the Gender Studies Program, at Warsaw University, Poland. She teaches courses in the sociology of law, sociology of culture, gender discrimination, and women's rights. Recently, she taught courses on women's rights at Ann Arbor, University of Michigan, US, and at the Institute of Sociology of Law, Oniati, Spain. She is the author of *Everyday Conflicts and Ceremonial Justice* (1998) and *Family in Court* (1995) and is the co-editor of *Women in Poland at the Turn of the Century New Gender Contract?* (2002), co-author of *Civil Society in Poland* (2003) and co-editor of *Polish Disputes and Courts* (2004). Additionally, she is the author of over 60 articles in Polish, English, German, Slovak, and Romanian, as well as a member of the advisory board of *Signs: Journal of Women in Culture and Society* and *The European Journal of Women's Studies*.

Ann Graham Ph. D. (flinthillann@yahoo.com) is Manager of Strategic Planning of the Global Philanthropist Circle at Synergos Institute in New York. She has a Ph.D. in Urban Planning and Public Policy from Rutgers University. During 1992–2002, Dr. Graham was Associate Director of the Local Democracy Partnership, at the Center for Comparative European Studies, Rutgers University where she directed local governance, citizen participation, women's rights, and institutional strengthening projects in the former Soviet Union, and Central and Eastern Europe. She also worked as an independent international development consultant in the Europe and Eurasia region. Her work includes public policy, gender, and anti-trafficking assessments, as well as the development and review of gender and local government training manuals. She is the author and co-author of several articles and chapters on women's political participation, citizen's participation, local government reforms, urban policies, and the transfer of knowledge to countries undergoing political, economic, and social transformation.

Jacqueline Heinen (Jacqueline.Heinen@printemps.uvsq.fr) is a professor of sociology at the University of Versailles-Saint-Quentin and director of *Cahiers du Genre* (CNRS). She is the president of the Conseil National des Universités of France and member of the Group of Experts in Social Sciences of the European Commission. Her research focuses on gender and social policies in Western and Eastern Europe. She directed a comparative research on gender and local democracy in seven European countries, issuing, with F. Gaspard, the *Guide pour l'intégration de l'égalité des sexes dans les politiques locales* (2004). Her recent publications include: *L'égalité, une utopie?* (2002) with L'Harmattan; "Children collective keeping in Poland, yesterday and today" (in Michel and Mahon eds., 2002); "Social and Political Citizenship in Eastern Europe. The Polish Case" (with S. Portet, in Molyneux and Razavi eds, 2002); and "Genre et politiques sociales en Europe de l'Est" (with S. Portet, eds. 2004).

Jasmina Lukić (Lukicj@ceu.hu) is a recurrent visiting associate professor at the Department of Gender Studies, Central European University in Budapest. She is also associated with the Women's Studies Center in Belgrade and the Women's Studies Center in Zagreb, where she regularly gives lectures and short courses. She is co-founder and the first editor-in-chief of the journal of feminist theory *Ženske studije* (1996–1999) and she is an associate editor of *The European Journal of Women's Studies*. Her research interests are primarily related to literary and cultural studies, and South-Slavic literatures. She has published a number of articles and book chapters, as well as critical studies including *Drugo lice* and *Metaproza: čitanje žanra*, and has edited a Special Issue on *Women, Identity, and Identification: "Who are I"* of *The European Journal of Women's Studies* (2003).

Enikő Magyari-Vincze (eni_personal@yahoo.com) is a professor at Babes-Bolyai University. Between 1996 and 1999 she was the coordinator of the M.A. program on

Cultural Anthropology, and since 2003, she is the director of the M.A. on Gender, Differences, and Inequalities. She is also the co-director of the Institute for Cultural Anthropology, and coordinator of the Cultural Analysis Series of EFES. Currently she is teaching courses on anthropology and feminism, identity politics, and nation, gender, and nationalism. Her research topics include ethnic identity politics, women's and men's condition in the multi-ethnic city of Cluj, and Roma women and reproductive health. Her publications include *Diferenţa care contează* (2002), *Diversitatea social-culturală prin lentila antropologiei feministe, Talking Feminist Institutions* (2002), and *Interviews with leading European Scholars* (2002). She also co-edited the volumes, *Breaking the Wall. Representing Anthropology and Anthropological Representations in Eastern Europe* (2003), *Gen, Societate şi Cultură. Cursuri în Studii de Gen*, Volumes 1–3 (2004), and *Performing Identities. Renegotiating Socio-Cultural Identities in the Post-socialist Eastern Europe* (2004).

Irina Novikova (iranovi@lanet.lv) is a professor in the Department of Culture and Literature, and the Director of The Center for Gender Studies, at the University of Latvia, Riga, Latvia. Her research is in the areas of gender and genre in modern textual/visual productions as well as the intersectional analysis of gender, ethnicity, and citizenship in the post-socialist condition. She is the author of numerous articles, chapters, and co-edited volumes, including a collection of essays *Men in the Global World: Integrating Post-socialist Perspectives*, and *European women's social rights* and the author of *Gender and Genre in Women's Autobiography and Bildungsroman*. Currently she is writing a book on gender, ethnicity, and genre in Russian cinema.

Joanna Regulska (regulska@rci.rutgers.edu) is a professor of women's and gender studies and geography, and the Chair of the Women's and Gender Studies department at Rutgers University, US. She is the founder and director, since 1989, of the Local Democracy Partnership Program at Rutgers University. She is the author of numerous articles, chapters, and policy papers for the UN, Council of Europe, and EEC on decentralization, local governance, public administration, women's rights, political activism, and the construction of women's political spaces. She has been a very active supporter of the women's movement in Central and East Europe, and Central Asia. She co-edited *Women's Activism in Public Sphere* (1999), *Being Active* (1998), and edited *Informational Policy at the Local Level* (1995, 2nd edition 1997). Currently, with colleagues in Poland and the Czech Republic, she is working on a book manuscript on the EU, Eastern enlargement, and women's construction of political spaces at the supranational level. She is a Chair of the International Advisory Board of the Network of East-West Women (NEWW).

Kornelia Slavova (formerly Merdjanska) (kornelias@abv.bg) teaches American Studies at the Department of English and American Studies, Sofia University, Bulgaria. Her publications are in the fields of cross-cultural studies, American literature, translation theory, and gender studies. She has edited and co-edited several books on gender theory and literary criticism including: *Women's Time* (1997), *Essays in American Studies* (1999), *Theory Across Boundaries* (2000), *Women's Identities in the Balkans* (2004), and *Gender and Order* (2005). She has also contributed to various magazines and books published in Greece, Germany, the UK, Finland, Canada, and the US. Her most recent book is *The Gender Frontier in Sam Shepard's and Marsha Norman's Drama* (2001). She has translated a number of feminist books into Bulgarian, including *Our Bodies Ourselves* (2001).

Ann Snitow (newwny@igc.org) has been a feminist activist since 1969 when she was a founding member of the New York Radical Feminists. She is the co-editor of *Powers of Desire: The Politics of Sexuality*, a central text in US debates about the historicity of sexual experience. A professor of women's studies and literature at The New School for Social Research in New York City, she has written germinal articles about feminism, among them "Mass Market Romance: Pornography for Women is Different," "A Gender Diary: Basic Divisions in Feminism," and "Feminism and Motherhood". With Rachel Blau DuPlessis, she has collected 37 memoirs written by activists from the early days of second wave feminism, *The Feminist Memoir Project: Voices From Women's Liberation* (1998). She is the founder of the Feminist Anti-Censorship Task Force, of the action group No More Nice Girls, and of the Network of East-West Women (NEWW); her most recent writing and political work is about the changing situation of women in Eastern Europe.

Darja Zaviršek (darja.zavirsek@fsd.uni-lj.si; darja.zavirsek@guest.arnes.si) is a sociologist and professor at the Faculty of Social Work, University of Ljubljana; since 2002 she has also been the vice dean of the faculty. She teaches disability studies, social anthropology, and gender-focused courses. She is the author of several books including: *The Story of Josipdol: An Anthropological Study* (1987) and *Women and Mental Health* (1994). She is the editor of *Sexual Violence. Feminist Studies for Social Work* (1996), *Disability as a Cultural Trauma* (2000), the co-author of *Innovative Methods in Social Work* (2002), editor of *With the Diploma It was Easier to Work: The history of social work education in Slovenia* (2005) and co-editor of *Social Work and Sustainable Development* (2005). She is also co-editor of *The Journal of Social Work* and a member of several international advisory boards. Additionally, she is a member of the Executive Board of the International Association of the Schools of Social Work and an honorary professor at the University of Applied Sciences in Berlin.

Eleonora Zielińska (eleziel@pro.onet.pl) is a professor of law at the Faculty of Law and Administration, at the University of Warsaw, Poland. Her research and practice focus on criminal law, medical law, human rights, and the EU legal framework. She is an active supporter of women's rights in Poland; a co-drafter of the law on the equal status of women and men, and of the proposed changes of the reproductive rights law. She was very actively involved in the process of bringing Polish law into conformity with the international standards of human rights and the EU's *acquis communautaire*. In 1995–1997, she was a Polish delegate to the United Nations Commission on the Status of Women. In 2003, she was a Polish nominee for the "Woman of Europe" award and the Polish government's candidate for the post of the Judge on the International Criminal Court. She is also the author and co-author of numerous books, articles, and chapters on reproductive rights, abortion debates, law enforcement in Poland, and equal opportunities for women and men.

Acknowledgments

The authors would like to thank Nancy Leys Stepan and the many participants of the Inter-regional Seminar on Gender and Culture at Central European University for inspiration and stimulating exchanges. We also would like to thank the participants of the Rutgers seminar, Locations of Gender: Central and East Europe, for invigorating year-long discussions. We greatly appreciate the financial support received from Central European University and Rutgers, The State University of New Jersey. Editorial assistance from Danielle Lockwood and Carol Harrington, and technical assistance from Branislav Kovačević, helped us to finalize the manuscript in its present form. We are grateful to Mary Savigar, our editor at Ashgate Publishing, who offered her support, commitment, and trust in our project. Finally, a word of thanks are due to our families who have supported us during the many twists and turns of bringing this volume to its successful completion.

Introduction

Joanna Regulska, Jasmina Lukić and Darja Zaviršek

Feminist theorists' interest in debates on citizenship is not a recent development; citizenship was "probably the most important single issue to have shaped feminist thought" (Baumeister 2000, 49). The positioning of citizenship discourses within feminist debates has, however, differed over time. Critical attention has been given to reexamining liberal models of citizenship (Lister 2003; Mouffe 1993; Pateman 1988; 1989; Squires 2004; Voet 1998). Feminist theorists have also significantly contributed to the deconstructing and rejecting of the formal universalistic concept of citizenship (Ilić 2001; Lister 2003; Voet 1998). In particular, they have been critical of neoliberal models, where liberal claims for universal rights have been questioned. As Hobson and Lister argue, "to ignore the different needs, claims and situations, the subjectivities and identities of citizens, is to perpetuate exclusionary processes embedded in false universalism" (2002, 47). Feminist scholars have also challenged the socialist models that claimed to liberate women, but in reality only eliminated their subordination theoretically (Ashwin 2000; Funk and Muller 1993; Jancar Webster 1990). As socialist ideology and practices became more rooted, women and men became increasingly subjugated to the aims of the communist state (Ilić 2001; Stites 1978).

The present volume builds upon these debates by placing women's agency at the center of the analysis, and by specifically focusing on the countries of central and east Europe [CEE], thus locating the discussion of women's citizenship practices within the specific context of the post-1989 transformation and its gendered impacts. We are interested in understanding how different forces, generated by recent transformations, instigate women to act and react, in response to political, social, economic, environmental, and cultural opportunities and challenges. We ask how women's agency translates into citizenship practices under the conditions of transformation. How do women accumulate resources, gain access to the political process, confront and challenge state practices, and gain social visibility? How is women's agency shaped not only by material conditions, but also is a result of different experiences and political, cultural, and personal dynamics? How is the process of claiming citizenship conditioned by the local and national contexts, as well as the exposure to global and transnational influences?

Such an approach suggests three important dimensions of the ways through which the notion of citizenship is understood in this volume. First, emphasis is put on the active notion of citizenship. Secondly, the multi-layered conception of citizenship is acknowledged and thirdly, the impact of the transformation period and its locational specificity is recognized as a framing force. We will briefly discuss each of these dimensions and conclude with an outline of the chapters.

Active Citizenship

The concept of active citizenship fundamentally implies that women actively engage in the public sphere. For Voet, this implies not only "being active in the decision making process," but "also of having a political subjectivity, knowing how to play political roles, and being capable of political judgment" (1998, 131, 137). Thus, citizenship becomes linked with certain obligations and requirements. Scholars have long argued that these requirements have been understood too narrowly as only participation in the paid workforce, thereby ignoring a number of the caring and civic contributions that women make on behalf of their families and the communities in which they live (Hobson and Lister 2003; Machado and Vilrokx 2001). In this context, women's participation in political processes was ignored. Although it is not always the case that all citizens participate in decision-making, full citizenship for everybody is an ideal worth pursuing.

Active citizenship is related to the concept of human agency. People have to be able to claim their agency in order to claim their citizenship:

> To act as a citizen requires first a sense of agency, the belief that one *can* act; acting as a citizen, especially collectively, in turn fosters that sense of agency. Thus, agency is not simply about the capacity to choose and act but it is also about a *conscious* capacity, which is important to the individual's self-identity (Lister 2003, 38, emphasis added).

Agency, however, does not operate in a vacuum; rather it is located in a dialectic relationship with social structures and is embedded in social relations (Lister 2003). It also does not act on its own; it can only be enacted when individuals or groups become actively engaged with these structures. Such an act therefore represents a response to specific contexts within which individuals or groups operate and live. Consequently, the "conscious capacity" to act takes place in relation to women's social situations (Goddard 2000). For Dissanayake, this represents a form of resistance that emerges out of the interplay of multiple subjects' positions – in this context the agency of citizens is placed within the larger set of social, cultural, and economic forces, while also accounting for personal desires and interests, where intentionality is recognizable. But McNay warns us that we have to depart from what she calls the "negative understanding of subject formation" paradigm, and recognize the process of the formation of agency as a productive and creative process through which "individuals may respond in unanticipated and innovative ways which may hinder, reinforce, or catalyze social change" (McNay 2000, 4). Since individuals and groups do not operate in a vacuum, the role of institutional mechanisms has to be acknowledged, because it is through them that agency gains power and definition. As our contributors point out, through such interactions, claiming agency is then the political process of subject formation and becoming a citizen.

For many, the arena of civil society provided the space where such a process of subject formation could take place. After 1989, and the creation of civil societies based on democratic practices, the opening of political spaces in civil society was seen as a possibility for the introduction of a new citizenship model (Cohen and Arato 1992). This new understanding of citizenship implied "the active exercise of the responsibilities, including economic self-reliance and political participation.... [and] a dismantling of the 'passive' citizenship associated with the postwar, so-called "statist period" (Schild 1998, 94). Women's responses to the post-1989 neoliberal and free market practices, were to engage in building "alternative spaces" of actions through their involvement in and development of non-governmental organizations [NGOs], where citizenship could be practised beyond the state and market (Fuszara 2001; Lang 1997; Milić 2004; Regulska 2002; Zaviršek 1999). These formal and informal groups, associations, and networks, began to address the immediate needs of the individuals, families, and communities that the new state regimes wanted to restrict or were no longer interested in/or capable of providing for. Many women's and feminist groups then engaged in delivering services that the state often perceived as too costly (such as the (re)training of unemployed women) or too controversial (such as a provision of services to homeless people, AIDS victims, drug users, victims of violence, or people with varying degrees of abilities) (Funk 2004; Hemment 2004).

This process of engagement was not restricted by national state borders, as women began to mobilize across geographical scale, locally as well as transnationally (Einhorn 2003; Jacquette 2003; Jaggar 2005; Regulska 2001). By crossing borders, women and feminist activists accessed new legal, political, and human resources. They also enhanced their skills and knowledge, built new transnational networks, and carried their actions beyond nation-state boundaries. The emergence of NGOs in the post-1989 political landscape was significant because it permitted women to formulate different strategies of survival, engagement, and resistance by opening up new possibilities for women to practise active citizenship in spaces that were outside state structures, but at the same time still controlled by its institutions (Hemment 2004).

Despite their unquestionable accomplishments, women's and feminist NGOs struggled with limited finances, no access to political processes, and the frequent lack of recognition of their voices. In fact, NGOs behaved like the former socialist opposition, functioning parallel to the post-socialist state and free market. While they had the potential to expand the narrow notion of politics, they were relegated to the margins. For women in central and east Europe, Jalušič argues, the notion of civil society was "an important, if not the only" hope for change. However, she also points out that the redefinition of citizenship was only temporary as "we witnessed active citizenship being withered away" (1998, 5; 7). The limited possibility for the reconceptualization of what is meant by political and how politics is practiced by citizens was caused, in Jalušič's view by:

> ...the fact that politics was understood in a narrow institutional sense, and that agency in transitional societies was predominantly prescribed as the activity of a professional, political, and economic elite, which was, from the very beginning, formed by men, [as a result] women had almost no real chance of entering this professional sphere of public engagement (Jalušič 1998, 6).

One of the critical products of the post-1989 changes in the region was the (re)creation of new public private divisions, where public signified a space of action and visibility for men, and private was a space ruled by social constraints and even greater patriarchy for women. This outcome subsequently became an object of women's active mobilizations and resistances, a point that is addressed by our contributors.

Feminist scholars have also argued that the emphasis on civil society and, in particular, on NGOs, has been problematic (Jacquette 2003; Jaggar 2005). Some believe that "grassroots participation and local activism cannot alone solve the problem of political exclusion" (Skjeie and Siim 2000, 353). Others assert that civil society does not exist independently from the state and market, and that the exclusive focus on civil society, in fact, may have inadvertently restricted women's opportunities to shape the contours of citizenship, constrained women's political space, and marginalized feminist voices (Jaggar 2005; Silliman 1999; see also Einhorn 2001). Yet, these new possibilities for engagement signified the recognition of women as flexible and active citizens, who were simultaneously engaged in multiple sites in order to facilitate the mobilization of resources, mount new actions, and address specific needs.

Multilayered Citizenship

The acknowledgment of the varying degrees of women's agency and the diversity of subjects' positions draws attention to a "multi-layered" notion of citizenship and gender-pluralist citizens (Hobson and Lister 2002; Yuval-Davis 1999). These approaches attempt to recognize the multiplicity of contexts within which citizenship is claimed and the multiple identities of its claimants. Thus, citizenship is understood "as a more total relationship, inflected by identity, social positioning, cultural assumptions, institutional practices, and a sense of belonging" (Werbner and Yuval-Davis 1999, 4). The notion of a gender-pluralist citizen reinforces the assertion that it is because citizens occupy different positions and belong to diverse communities that they are able to claim their multiple identities. Such recognition of the plurality of identities challenges gender being privileged as the sole dimension along which citizenship is shaped and demands that different markings such as age, sexual orientation, ethnicity, class, or level of physical and/or mental abilities are also included. The recognition of the multiple subjectivities of citizens implies an understanding that social agents are formed through different subject positions. It also acknowledges the shift away from a simplified and often essentialized understanding of difference as being centered in the opposition between men and women, towards the more diversified and complex understanding of difference seen in relational terms.

Contributors to this volume recognize that the horizontal understanding of difference is key to the acknowledgment of a dynamic and fluid notion of citizenship practices. Such an approach also focuses our attention on the respatialization of power relations between and among individuals, groups, and institutions located across varying geographical scales (local, national, regional, and/or supranational). In that sense, any attempt to conceptualize a "women-friendly citizenship" accommodates differences between women themselves and recognizes the diversity of the locales within which women live, work, and act; citizenship must be understood as an "action practised by people of a certain identity in a specifiable locale" (Jones 1994, 260). As some contributors point out, this redefined citizenship is connected "with people's sense that they are members of a specific community and polity, and have a say in what leaders of that community do and say" (Yuval-Davis 2000, 172).

The reconceptualization of the notion of citizenship evokes another set of questions related to the notion of rights. In general, access to certain rights, guaranteed by the law, has often been understood to be of primary importance for citizenship. Those rights have predominantly been discussed as individual rights, which is in accordance with a social-liberal tradition that understands citizenship primarily as a relationship between the citizen and the state. Rights discourse has been important in constructing a legal set of norms that allow women and other social groups to claim norms and standards that are available to others, but denied to them (Schneider 1991). Feminist scholars and activists have repeatedly pointed out the empowering effects of rights for many women, and their positive impact on women's political mobilization and collective actions. This is especially the case when discriminatory labor practices are challenged or when a case of violence against women is prosecuted (Bunch, et al 2001; NEWW 2005; STOPVAW 2003; Yuval-Davis 1999). At the same time, rights discourse has been criticized for its false universalism and for not recognizing that being a citizen, in plural democracies, means that "the resources and powers that implement and embed the very concept of citizenship are neither equally nor fairly distributed" (Machado and Vilrokx 2001, 149). Such inequalities not only translate into different levels of access to resources, they also shape the process through which individual and collective identities are constructed (Melucci 2001). The numerous barriers and obstacles that women continue to face often result in conditions under which they are simultaneously included because they are citizens (through the right to vote or receiving social services); at the same time that they are excluded because they are women; thereby placing them on the margins and rendering them invisible. Benhabib points to the dialectic of rights and identities, by arguing that, "the meanings of rights claims are altered when exercised by subjects whose legal and political agency had not been foreseen or normatively anticipated in the initial formulations of rights" (2004, 169). Such confrontations, for her, result in contestations that bring "new modes of political agency and interaction" (Benhabib 2004, 169).

Becoming a citizen is both a matter of having access to resources and the means by which to engage in civil actions, and of participating in political processes. However, because resources and possibilities for social participation are unequally shared and distributed, scholars have called for a "renewed commitment to redistributional politics" and the creation of "new forms of representation and social participation" (Jacquette 2003, 332; Machado and Vilrokx 2001, 155). For Machado and Vilrokx, this is a matter of moving beyond the rhetoric of "equal opportunity for all," towards the notion of "equal participation for all" (2001, 155). By focusing on the concept of participation, they argue that "a broader notion of citizenship – 'active citizenship' (as opposed to the more legalistic approach to citizenship)" is then developed. In that sense, as several contributors have pointed out, citizens' participation is critical to counter social exclusion and inequality; however, in order to be able to fulfill that promise, participation has to be expanded beyond the sphere of work and include participation in society at large. Participation also must be understood beyond the right to vote, which is obvious given the fact that in former socialist states, some of which granted women the right to vote as early as 1917, women's equality in political, social, and private spheres never increased. In that sense, "participation and active citizenship are seen as major tools to be used against inequality and exclusion, maximizing people's involvement in their local communities" (Machado and Vilrokx 2001, 157).

Indeed one of the shifts in rights practices after 1989 was the possibility for an active as opposed to a passive claiming of citizenship rights, as was the case under communism. Yet, while the shift from the right to participate to the actual utilization of this right opens up opportunities for an active formation of citizenship practice, authors in this volume point out how, for many, social and economic transformations foreclosed access to such possibilities.

Women's Citizenship in Times of Transformation

The recent transformations, in central and east Europe, demand the rethinking of how the identities and subjectivities of citizens are constructed and articulated during times of rapid political and social changes. As discussed by the contributors, four sets of forces seem of particular significance in shaping the notion of citizenship in the post-socialist state: 1) the collapse of communism; 2) the emergence of neo-liberalism, 3) the resurgence of nationalism and fundamentalism and the creation of non-citizens, and 4) the "European" expansion to the east.

The fact that transformation was not always easy or unproblematic for women has already been observed and discussed by women's and feminist scholarship (see Einhorn 1993; Funk and Muller 1993; Gal and Kligman 2000; Jähnert et al. 2001;

Titkow, Budrowska, and Duch 2003). The decades of socialist, political, and civil restrictions and oppressions, and top-down control of every sphere of daily life, were also decades of widely accessible social and economic benefits that visibly implicated women's positions and status as citizens (Fodor 2004). The liberal notion of ensuring basic rights resonated well with the newly accepted focus on individual freedoms and the market economy. Paradoxically, although 1989 marked the gain of civil and political rights for some, for many it also demarcated the beginning of an erosion of their social and economic rights. Thus, ethnic groups (both old and new), asylum seekers, workers employed under slavery conditions, and/or female sex workers were often denied their basic rights and relegated to the margins of their societies.

In reality, post-1989 states have engaged in an open repositioning, where some groups such as children, the elderly, the sick, women, or people with different degrees of abilities, who had previously been provided with fiscal and service support through state institutions, began to see a rapid erosion of their resources and rights (Hemment 2004). Meanwhile, groups such as private owners, who had formerly been forbidden and located on the margins, gained status, privileges, and access to political processes. In some countries, processes of de-nationalization created, overnight, new economic elites; the "new rich" was comprised of both individuals and special interest groups (such as the Catholic Church who became the biggest private landowner in Slovenia and Poland). This reallocation of state regime interests and its redistribution of resources, which was often further supported by the strengthening of nationalistic, pro-family, and patriarchal values, created new liberal citizen-subjects (Holc 2004). The changed cultural dynamics, which emphasized morality, resulted in new political and social responses on the part of the state and its institutions, and the new crafting of practices of what it means to be a citizen.

While post-socialist states were willing to acknowledge some women's interests, many states have in fact actively restricted women's social, economic, or reproductive rights, or have continued to deny political rights to some groups of women (Bridger 1999; Einhorn and Sever 2003; Fuszara 2003; Jalušič 1998). Thus, as the contributors to this volume stress, the invisibility of women with physical or sensory impairment and their lack of recognition as rightful citizens, as well as issues such as the state's reluctance to address questions of food security and safety, have translated into exclusionary practices whereby some women cannot fully participate as citizens because their rights are restricted, or because they do not posses them at all (the right to choose, the right to vote). In the end, states' practices, whether passively or actively anti-women, often translated into the regimes' persistent refusals to consider women's interests.

The events of 1989 and 1990 were also expected to bring unity to a Europe that had been divided for decades. The reterritorialization of what was to become the "united Europe" brought hope that new centers of power, beyond the nation-state, would be introduced. Given the European Union [EU] policy's commitment to gender equality, this was a promise of new standards and norms, and therefore it offered possibilities for the enhancement of civil, social, and economic rights for women in future member states. Although these hopes for greater gender equality did result in greater political mobilization on the part of some women and women's groups, these hopes never fully materialized (Regulska and Grabowska forthcoming). At the same time, not only have the divisions between "east" and "west" persisted, they have also been reproduced and reinforced. The expansion of the EU has led to new categorizations of central and east European countries into "possible," "doubtful," or "excluded," a division through which west European countries can "preserve for as long as possible the advantages of a division of labor between newly developed zones, and to push the difficulties of a new definition of European identity outside of the frames of thought and action" (Balibar 2004, 167). While questions of economy, competition, and profits had an overriding role in the reconfiguration of the new European divisions, they were not the only relevant ones. The perception of how "west" Europe continued to view the "east" was equally critical. Consequently, while some nations were ready to be partially integrated, "some peoples (always that a bit farther to the East), whether by nature or by history, [were] not 'mature' enough for democracy" (Balibar 2004, 169; see also Funk 2004).

The new division of Europe, which Balibar termed "a cold war after the Cold War" has had profound gender implications (Balibar 2004, 167). First of all, while some women became members of the EU and, at least in theory, could benefit from the strengthening of *de jure* civil, social, and economic rights, others still remain in the "waiting room," and may never experience these rights. Secondly, it is not clear if the promises of new gender-friendly policies and practices will indeed be carried out, and therefore whether they will shape new conditions for women claiming citizenship. The evidence gathered so far, has called these changes into question (Karat 2003; Regulska 2002; Roth 2004). Thirdly, as the EU continues to privilege its economic goals, where women's needs are of interest only as long as they reinforce economic effectiveness, efficiency, and profitability, those who are not recognized as "productive" contributors, are left on the margins, beyond the reach of these promises. There is however, already a noticeable advancement as a result of the European Union eastern enlargement, and that is a more forceful grassroots political subjecthood formation. The increased transnational activities of women's and feminist groups have undeniably resulted in the greater involvement of NGOs in cross-European political activism, nevertheless whether these changes will have the opportunity to translate into new citizenship practices, still remains to be seen (Regulska and Grabowska, forthcoming).

The varying impacts of the European integration, so far, have resulted in women's experiences becoming more diversified. Thus, as our contributors argue, Romanian and Latvian women may have dissimilar priorities and needs, not only because of the great diversity of their own positionalities, but also due to the fact that the transformation took different trajectories in Romania and Latvia. Each country now finds itself at a different stage of transforming its internal institutional policy-making systems, and its external linkages. Therefore, it is not only the class-gender-race-nation matrix, but also the different stages of the transformation processes with their unique social, economic, and political contexts, that mold gendered citizenship's norms and practices. The acknowledgment of this diversity confirms the need to develop a conceptual apparatus that is able to address the multiplicity of the particular positions of women within the diverse contexts of transformation, and construct different intersectional points that take into account already existing categories, while bringing them together to work in different relations. How then do different women across the region craft their citizenship practices under these new conditions?

About the Book

This collection, written by sixteen contributors who represent the multilayered identities of different locations spanning across central, eastern, and western Europe, and the United States, attempts to unpack the complexities of women's citizenship practices. The authors examine past legacies and present conditions, in order to show how, through their experiences, women in central and east European countries are constructing new notions of active citizenship. The subject of this volume is how women's agency, as citizens, is implicated by their multilayered positionalities during times of transformations.

The volume puts emphasis on the diversity of situations in which women have found themselves throughout the region, as a result of the multipositionality of their experiences, agendas, and struggles to assert their citizenship, and as generated by the different forms that the transformation took. The authors discuss the ways in which women, as citizens, are treated in the new, post-socialist realities, and what political strategies they use to address these new circumstances. They also reflect upon the situation of women under past regimes, in order to acknowledge the critical role that socialism played in shaping the present context.

While, both the collective and individual cases acknowledge citizens' agency, the different sites at which the actual engagement takes place points to a variety of circumstances and possibilities for active involvement. In this volume, the authors recognize the diversity of the sites of engagement, calling attention to public political institutions at the national level, local environmental organizations, street protests, local and/or transnational NGOs, and literary texts. This multiplicity of sites is often repeatedly reinforced as citizens' move between them to maximize their intended outcomes and confront the obstacles that they encounter. Not only do these locations vary across geographical scales from local, national, to transnational, they also engage the diverse actors and structures of the state, family, or civil society.

The emphasis on women's agency in this volume has its historical grounding: within the context of the new social reality, women expected to gain a redefined citizenship, which they believed would be brought by the changes they had so strongly supported while living in and opposing the previous regimes. In that sense, the authors include both historical and contemporary perspectives. They draw upon the legacies of the socialist past, and map some highly characteristic points in the gendered transformation processes of the 1990s and early years of the 21st century. As the authors point out, many aspects of the institutional and legal framework already have been subject to major changes, yet, the social reality and the gender relations that generated them still have not advanced substantially. Thus, the case studies presented here, each in their own way, point to the core of the social discrimination between genders, as it is being re-produced once again in the new social realities of post-socialist countries.

The book is divided into three sections: *Regimes, Agency*, and *Transnational Dialogue*. The final chapter of this volume places empirical discussions of women's citizenship, in central and east Europe, within the larger context of neo-liberal discourses and unfulfilled promises.

Regimes

Part One, *Regimes*, examines the roles that diverse regimes such as patriarchy, gender, and the state have played in the past, and how they are presently exercised – in molding the positionality of women citizens. The authors show how traditional patriarchy and the communist system mutually reinforced each other, enabling the surveillance of women, both from a collective point of view (i.e. by the state) and an individual one (at the level of family and home). They assert that, despite the dramatic regime changes, women have continued to confront the challenges brought by neo-liberal discourses and the market economy.

The section begins with a chapter by Enikô Magyari-Vincze who demonstrates how socialism was not able to liberate women from traditional patriarchy; instead, it prolonged the patriarchal gender regime under the hegemony of a paternalistic state. Through the analysis of Romanian gender and state regimes, she demonstrates how, despite awarding women a multitude of rights; the party–state system emptied the power and meaning of these rights (e.g. the right to vote became a formal ritual of expressing loyalty). Women's citizenship was constructed in a way that victimized women by means of severe pro-natalist and anti-abortion policies, and by their representation as desexualized workers. Małgorzata Fuszara and Eleonora Zielińska, continue examining the role of state, and how it constructs the meaning of citizenship for women by focusing on Poland's legal framework and its recent changes. They stress the limits of a one-dimensional approach for achieving gender equality. Their analysis warns us not to assume that changes in the legal framework are sufficient enough to eliminate women's discrimination. They show how *de jure* changes, such as those brought by the EU accession pressures, were insufficient in altering the gender matrix in state institutions, the Polish parliament, and other major decision-making bodies. They argue that little progress is possible without the active engagement of women's and feminist groups, as well as Polish politicians greater political will and further education about gender issues.

Salvatore A. Engel-Di Mauro turns our attention to economic citizenship and its gendered practices in the rural Hungarian town of Ormánság. He examines the significance of the androcentric socialist state in establishing and reinforcing gendered political differentiations through economic policies, and shows how women became constructed as citizens through their status as laborers. In the post-socialist period, a rapid decrease of welfare resources (such as childcare grants), and an increase in women's unemployment, has dismantled women's economic independence and weakened the economic subjecthood that they had previously gained during the socialist period (even though women were still unequal to men). In the following chapter by Jacqueline Heinen, the sexualized notion of citizenship is traced. She argues that the current democratic dynamics, which stress individual and personal autonomy, do not have equal value for men and women in CEE countries. Despite it being criticized for its limited applicability beyond western Europe, Heinen proposes the use of T.H. Marshall's rights framework to unpack the meanings of citizenship for women in the region. By focusing on employment, reproductive rights, and political representation, Heinen demonstrates that women lack full citizenship rights, and reveals how communist policies masked gender inequalities.

The final contribution to this section, by Irina Novikova, takes yet another perspective on how national state and supranational institutions of the European Union use gender equality policy mechanisms, such as gender mainstreaming [GM], and by doing so shape the meaning of being a citizen. She evaluates the results of the gender mainstreaming process during the crucial decade for the Latvian society between Latvia's Letter of Intent to join the EU in 1993, and its membership, in 2004. Novikova shows how outside political pressures and the need to fulfill the EU entry requirements created a pro-GM institutional climate. However, she also points to the significant ambiguities of partially fulfilled promises, and the problems that remain to be solved, both on the part of women themselves as well as on the part of state institutions.

Agency

Part Two, *Agency*, affirms the power of women, both individually and collectively, by showing the diverse strategies through which women map their agendas and shape citizenship practices. Some authors remind us that even if, and when, women exercise their political subjecthood, they often remain marginalized, their voices spoken but ignored. Nevertheless, such engagement is their responsibility, and by exercising it, women's agency is claimed and active citizenship asserted.

Ann Graham and Joanna Regulska's contribution opens this section with the exploration of the degree to which women who are engaged in NGOs, in Poland and Ukraine, define their work as "political." Their study reveals how, for women in both countries, NGOs represent new entry points to active citizenship, and how these interventions are shaped by particular notions of political culture in each country. The authors point out that, while Ukrainian and Polish women subscribe to a different understanding of the "political," in both countries women who participated in the project believed in their own political efficacy. How such political subjecthood is shaped through resistance and political activism, is presented by Marina Blagojević, who examines the gender dimensions and "genderness" of the 1996/1997 citizens' and students' protests against the Milošević regime in Belgrade, Serbia. She explores the protests at two levels: empirically, by analyzing the level of participation, behavior, attitudes, and political representation; and qualitatively by examining their cultural/symbolic representation. She shows how women still remained marginalized from public representation and higher-level decision-making despite their active participation and strong feminist presence during the protests. Blagojević places the protests within the context of the women's movement in Belgrade, in order to examine their mutual influences and interdependence in the process of building civil society.

Anne C. Bellows analyzes the political work of the Polish Ecological Club-Gliwice [PEC-Gliwice] in southwest Poland. By showing how the production of contaminated food violates citizens' human rights, she makes visible the groups that are most vulnerable (young children, pregnant and lactating women, and persons with impaired health, especially the elderly). Although not a feminist organization, the PEC-Gliwice consists mostly of women, who see their work as a form of political activism. Women's work regarding healthy food and a non-polluted environment is not accidental, she argues, rather it stems from traditional gender roles; these practical experiences translate into the praxis of political work and alternative policies. Darja Zaviršek's contribution, addresses another form of women's resistance. She concentrates her focus on women with physical and sensory impairments, intellectual disabilities, and mental health crises. Such women, she argues, have in many respects, remained invisible citizens during the turbulent feminist movement, as well as during the political changes in post-communist countries. Zaviršek shows how sharing the experiences of abuse and violence through "memory work," enables women to become human agents and claim their everyday citizenship rights.

Daša Duhaček's article concludes this section by exploring the notion of responsibility that women have, as political subjects. She provides an analysis of the women's civil society movement in Belgrade during the wars of the 1990s, and shows the necessity for self-reflection and resistance to the totalitarian regime of Milošević in Serbia. Using the political theory of Hannah Arendt, she examines the position of women who have been issuing public calls for responsibility within the political space. One such group, "Women in Black," declared their disloyalty to the governing structure and, through the very act of asking their government for accountability, demonstrated their active citizenship. Although, the state attempted to deny this group active political participation, the groups' activities and written texts successfully reached and addressed the public.

Transnational Dialogues

Part Three, *Transnational Dialogues*, brings together feminist voices that, while separated by geographic distance, speak to issues that connect across borders and boundaries. The authors take a broader look at the character of central and east

European feminist practices and analyze the forces that produce them. While some contributors attempt to interpret the women's movement and women's activism from a collective perspective, others point to the importance of individual responses and personal agency for the recognition and promotion of women's rights.

To examine the intertwined relations between the politics of identification and citizenship rights, Jasmina Lukić offers a close reading of writings by Croatian/Dutch/European author, Dubravka Ugrešić; particularly Ugrešić's resistance to various forms of state, cultural, and political nationalism. Ugrešić's (anti)political essays bring into focus the intellectuals' political responsibility during times of the totalizing state ideology of nationalism. Becoming a social outcast in Croatia because of her writings, and with her own citizenship rights in jeopardy, Ugrešić opted for a voluntary exile and became a Dutch citizen. This change, Lukić argues, shaped Ugrešić writings and influenced her strategies of identification. Nanette Funk takes a different approach and confronts a set of criticisms that have been launched against women's and feminist NGOs in the region of east and central Europe and the former Soviet Union. Using both theoretical arguments and a wide variety of evidence from NGOs' work in the region, Funk dismisses most 'Imperialist Critics', by arguing that it is through NGOs that many women in the region managed to become active agents in the transformation of state and social policies, as well as defenders of women's and human rights. She asserts that the support that they receive from western funding neither excludes nor denies their highly important and positive impact on the promotion of women's rights.

The chapter by Kornelia Slavova brings into focus the relevance of Third World feminist critiques of western feminist thought, for central and east Europe feminisms. She argues that the emergence of CEE feminisms, located in different spatio-temporalities, have produced disrupting effects on some of the "grand narratives" of western feminism. She points to CEE and Third World feminists' similarly ambiguous attitudes towards, and often rejection of, western feminist theories and practices. In her opinion, through the regional histories and women's pseudo-emancipation at the hand of the communist state, CEE feminists have added culturally specific dimensions to their feminist agendas. Similar cross-regional and transnational tensions are also echoed in the writing of Ann Snitow, whose chapter concludes this section. Snitow presents an analysis of the complex relationship between central and east European feminisms, which are rejected and demonized in the region; and western feminisms which, in the post-1989 context, are also looked down upon. She sees both feminisms as currently "homeless"; a condition with potentially positive, as well as negative consequences. She cautions that feminists can make the mistake of using the category of gender to displace equally important sources of oppression such as class, race, and ethnicity. She also warns against abandoning the feminist project – west or east – because of its growing pains or the inequalities it sometimes embodies.

The volume concludes by stressing the fact that despite old and new challenges many women in central and east Europe successfully claim their agency and engage in political organizing. Yet, the revisiting of Lenin's "women's question", with lingering issues such as equal pay for equal work, the equal division of household burdens, and participation in politics and public life, demonstrates that neither states governed by the neo-liberal elites, nor those with Christian conservative, or left leaning governments, have made any significant steps towards gender equality and an empowered notion of women's citizenship. To the contrary, the revitalized masculinity and patriarchalization of everyday life in central and east Europe points to the decline of women's citizenship rights. It can be argued that, for most women, at the end of the first fifteen years of the post-socialist era, the expectation that democracy will bring gender equality still remains an unfulfilled vision and an everyday struggle.

References

Ashwin, Sarah, ed. 2000. *Gender, state, and society in Soviet and Post-Soviet Russia*. London and New York: Routledge.
Balibar, Étienne. 2004. *We, the people of Europe? Reflections on transnational citizenship*. Princeton and Oxford: Princeton University Press.
Baumeister, Andrea. 2000. The new feminism. In *Political theory in transition,* edited by Noel O'Sullivan. London and New York: Routledge.
Benhabib, Seyla. 2004. *The rights of others. Aliens, residents, and citizens*. Cambridge: Cambridge University Press.
Bridger, Sue. 1999. *Women and political change: Perspectives from East-Central Europe*. Basingstoke: Macmillan.
Bunch, Charlotte, Peggy Antrobus, Samantha Frost, and Niamh Reilly. 2001. International networking for women's human rights. In *Global citizen action*, edited by Michael Edwards and John Gaventa. Boulder: Lynne Rienner Publishers.
Cohen, John and Andrew, Arato. 1992. *Civil society and political theory*. Cambridge, MA: MIT Press.
Dissanayake, Wimal, ed. 1996. *Narratives of agency: Self-Making in China, India, and Japan*. Minneapolis and London: University of Minnesota Press.
Einhorn, Barbara. 1993. *Cinderella goes to the market*. London: Verso.
Einhorn, Barbara. 2001. Gender and citizenship in the context of democratization and economic transformation in East Central Europe. In *Gender in transition in Eastern and Central Europe,* edited by Gabriele Jähnert, Jana Gohrisch, Daphne Hahn, Hildegard Maria Nickel, Iris Peinl, and Katrin Schäfgen. Berlin: Trafo Verlag,
Einhorn, Barbara, and Charlotte Sever. 2003. Gender and civil society in Central and Eastern Europe. *International Feminist Journal of Politics* 5 (2):163–190.
Fodor, Éva. 2004. The state socialist emancipation project: Gender inequality in workplace authority in Hungary and Austria. *Signs: Journal of Women in Culture and Society* 29 (3):783–813.
Funk, Nanette. 2004. Feminist critiques of liberalism: Can they travel east? Their relevance in Eastern and Central Europe and the Former Soviet Union. *Signs: Journal of Women in Culture and Society* 29 (3):695–726.
Funk, Nanette, and Magda Muller, eds. 1993. *Gender politics and post-communism: Reflections from Eastern Europe and the Former Soviet Union*. New York: Routledge.

Fuszara, Małgorzata. 2001. Bilans na koniec wieku. [The balance at the end of the century]. *Katedra* 1:4–25.

Fuszara, Małgorzata. 2003. Udział kobiet we władzy. [Women's participation in power]. In *Kobiety w Polsce 2003*, [*Women in Poland 2003*], edited by Urszula Nowakowska. Warsaw: Centrum Praw Kobiet.

Gal, Susan, and Gail Kligman. 2000. *The politics of gender after socialism*. Princeton: Princeton University Press.

Goddard, Victoria Ana, ed. 2000. *Gender, agency, and change: Anthropological perspectives*. London and New York: Routledge.

Hemment, Julie. 2004. Global civil society and the local costs of belonging: Defining violence against women in Russia. *Signs: Journal of Women in Culture and Society* 29 (3):815–840.

Hobson, Barbara, and Ruth Lister. 2002. Citizenship. In *Contested concepts in gender and social politics*, edited by Barbara Hobson, Jane Lewis, and Birte Siim. Cheltenham: Edward Elgar.

Holc, Janine P. 2004. The purest democrat: Fetal citizenship and subjectivity in the construction of democracy in Poland. *Signs: Journal of Women in Culture and Society* 29 (3):755–782.

Ilič, Melanie. 2001. *Women in the Stalin Era*. New York: Palgrave.

Jacquette, Jane S. 2003. Feminism and the challenges of the "Post-Cold War" world. *International Feminist Journal of Politics* 5 (3):331–354.

Jaggar, Alison. 2005. Arenas of citizenship. Civil society, state, and the global order. *International Feminist Journal of Politics* 7 (1):3–25.

Jähnert, Gabriele, Jana Gohrisch, Daphne Hahn, Hildegard Maria Nickel, Iris Peinl, and Katrin Schäfgen, eds. 2001. *Gender in transition in Eastern and Central Europe*. Berlin: Trafo Verlag.

Jalušič, Vlasta. 1998. Gender and political transformation in Central and Eastern Europe. Paper read at the conference Losers of the Wende – Winners of the EU. Participation of Women: Chances and Effects of the Transformation Process, in Vienna, Austria. [cited 6/20/05]. Available from <http://www.mirovni-isntitut.si/ eng_html/ articles/gender_ polit_transf.htm>.

Jancar Webster, Barbara. 1990. *Women and revolution in Yugoslavia, 1941–1945*. Denver: Arden Press.

Jones, Kathleen B. 1994. Identity, action, and locale: Thinking about citizenship, civic action, and feminism. *Social Politics* 1(3):256–271.

KARAT Regional Coalition and NRO Frauenforum. 2003. Expanding rights, creating space for action? EU reform and enlargement from a gender perspective. Position paper presented at the conference Expanding Rights? EU reform and enlargement from gender perspective, organized by NRO Frauenforum and Womnet, Berlin.

Lang, Sabine. 1997. The NGOization of feminism. In *Transitions, environments, translations. Feminisms in international politics*, edited by Joan Wallach Scott, Cora Kaplan, and Debra Keates. New York: Routledge.

Lister, Ruth. 2003. *Citizenship: Feminist perspectives*. New York: New York University Press.

Machado, Carlos, and Jacques Vilrokx. 2001. Tackling inequality and exclusion: Towards dimension of active citizenship participation. In *Inclusions and exclusions in European Societies*, edited by Alison Woodward and Martin Kohli. London and New York: Routledge.

McNay, Lois. 2000. *Gender and agency: Reconfiguring the subjects in feminist and social theory*. Cambridge: Polity Press.

Melucci, Alberto. 2001. Becoming a person. New frontiers for identity and citizenship in a planetary society. In *Inclusions and exclusions in European societies*, edited by Alison Woodward and Martin Kohli. London and New York: Routledge.

Milić, Anđelka. 2004. The women's movement in Serbia and Montenegro at the turn of the millennium: A sociological study of women's groups. *Feminist Review* 76:65–82.

Mouffe, Chantal. 1993. *The return of the political*. London and New York: Verso.

Network of East-West Women [NEWW]. 2005. *Gender and economic justice in European accession and integration* [cited 8/8/05]. Available from <http://www.neww.org.pl/en.php/achivements/projekty/0.html?pro=1>.

Pateman, Carol. 1988. *The sexual contract*. Stanford: Stanford University Press.

Pateman, Carol. 1989. *The disorder of women*. Oxford: Oxford University Press.

Regulska, Joanna. 2001. Gendered integration of Europe: New boundaries of exclusion. In *Gender in transition in Eastern and Central Europe*, edited by Gabriele Jähnert, Jana Gohrisch, Daphne Hahn, Hildegard Maria Nickel, Iris Peinl, and Katrin Schäfgen. Berlin: Trafo Verlag.

Regulska, Joanna. 2002. Der Gleichstellungsdiskurs der Europaischen Union und seine Folgen furFrauen in Polen. [EU discourse on women: Will it matter for Polish women?]. *Yearbook for European and North American Studies* 6:121–151.

Regulska, Joanna, and Magda Grabowska. (Forthcoming). Jumping scale: Polish women's agency in the enlarged Europe. In *Gender issues and women's movements in the European Union*, edited by Silke Roth. New York: Berghahn Books.

Roth, Silke. 2004. One step forwards, one step backwards. The impact of EU policy on gender relations in Central and East Europe. *Transitions* 44 (1):15–28.

Schild, Veronica. 1998. New subjects of rights? Women's movement and the construction of citizenship in the "New Democracies". In *Cultures of politics/politics of cultures*, edited by Sonia E. Alvarez, Evelyn Dagnino, and Arturo Escobar. Boulder: Westview Press.

Schneider, Elizabeth. 1991. The politics of Right politics: Perspectives from the women's movement. In *At the boundaries of law: Feminism and legal theory*, edited by Martha Albertson Fineman and Nancy Sweet Thomadsen. New York: Routledge.

Silliman, Jeal. 1999. Expanding civil society, shrinking political spaces: The case of women's nongovernmental organizations. In *Dangerous intersections: Feminist perspectives on population, environment, and development*, edited by Jeal Silliman and Ynestra King. Cambridge: South End Press.

Skjeie, Hege, and Birte Siim. 2000. Scandinavian feminist debates on citizenship. *International Political Science Review* 21 (4):345–360.

Squires, Judith. 2004. The state in (and of) feminist visions of political citizenship. In *The demands of citizenship*, edited by Catriona McKinnon and Ian Hampsher-Monk. London and New York: Continium.

Stites, Richard. 1978. *The women's liberation movement in Russia. Feminism, nihilism, and bolshevism: 1860–1930*. Princeton: Princeton University Press.

STOPVAW. 2003. Stop violence against women. Available from, <http://www.stopvaw.org/> [cited 8/05/05].

Titkow, Anna, Bogusława Budrowska, and Danuta Duch, eds. 2003. *Szklany Sufit. Bariery i ograniczenia karier kobiet. [Glass ceiling. Barriers and limitations to women's careers]*. Warsaw: Instytut Spraw Publicznych.

Voet, Rian. 1998. *Feminism and citizenship*. London, Thousand Oaks, and Delhi: Sage Publications.

Werbner, Pnina, and Nira Yuval-Davis, eds. 1999. *Women, citizenship, and difference*. London and New York: Zed Books.

Yuval-Davis, Nira. 1999. The multi-layered citizen: Citizenship in the age of globalization. *International Feminist Journal of Politics* 1 (1):119–138.

Yuval-Davis, Nira. 2000. Citizenship, territoriality, and the gendered construction of difference. In *Democracy, citizenship, and the global city*, edited by Engin F. Isin. London and New York: Routledge.

Zaviršek, Darja. 1999. Civil society, memory, and social work. In *Social work and the state. International perspectives in social work,* Brighton: Pavilion.

PART 1
Regimes

Chapter 1

Romanian Gender Regimes and Women's Citizenship

Enikő Magyari-Vincze

The investigation of the cultural dimension of the re–imagining and re–constructing of Romania after the collapse of socialism, has to be considered as a broader framework in which to discuss citizenship, as it is affected by and as it affects gender regimes. In the following pages I first aim to understand how the official/hegemonic ideology of the socialist regime constructed the relationship between the state and the (female) individual; restructured the boundaries between the private and public; redefined traditional gender roles; and re–enforced patriarchy. I will then outline the current trends of how this relationship has been dealt with, in the context of post-socialist transformations. Finally, I will examine the role that feminism plays within these socialist transformations in an effort to offer a more critical approach, which takes into account the influence of the gender order within the analysis of the old and new authoritarian visions of society. Within this context, I will draw upon the work of Fraser, who stresses the need for the development of an alternative vision under the post-socialist condition. Fraser reconnects the problem of cultural difference with that of social equality and "permits us to link an anti–essentialist cultural politics of recognition with an egalitarian social politics of redistribution" (Fraser 1997, 187).

Through the analysis of citizenship, my investigation seeks to contribute to the understanding of how social boundaries and cultural differences are built by the state, both among and between male and female citizens. Citizenship, as the law defines it, plays a role in both the construction of gender differences, as well as the boundaries that are then created between individuals. The ways in which the state ascribes certain duties and rights to women and men through cultural, economic, and political means, also has an impact on gender equality and/or inequality; and, generally speaking, on women's positions and gender relations within a particular society. My aim, within this chapter, is to point out some of the characteristics of how gender differences are influenced by the state. In order to demonstrate this I will draw upon the example of Romania, both during and after socialism.

Principles for a Gendered Perspective in Feminist Research

In order to consider a gendered perspective as a possible entry point through which to understand social realities, we must take into account its benefits and limits, and use it as one of many ways in which issues such as citizenship can be questioned. An analysis informed by a gendered perspective views women and men in terms of their culturally constructed social roles. Rather than viewing women as an isolated group, a gendered perspective analyzes both men and women; it investigates gender relations not only as aspects of social differentiation and stratification, but also as part of power relations in their own right. It distinguishes between the inequalities that affect both men and women, as well as those that affect only men or only women (Rossides 1997, 17). Finally, it deconstructs women's perspectives by identifying differences within the category of women, in order to provide a better explanation of the different ways in which reality is perceived and experienced by individual women.

While examining the ways in which gender structures the social order and inequalities, a gendered perspective considers other factors that are also at work in this process. As Lindsey stresses, its "goal is to understand how gender, race, and class, as social categories, simultaneously work together," and how power relations construct difference (Lindsey 1997, 10–11). However, it should not be forgotten that even if class, race, and ethnicity, as systems of classification, together produce social hierarchies and inequalities, in different places and at different times class, race, and ethnicity can have varying degrees of importance in individuals' lives (Bradley 1993, 53–54). This is why one has to be aware of the political and cultural dynamics responsible for the perception of individuals' multiple identities in particular terms (like ethnicity), and must recognize the need to take into consideration the influence of multiple social divisions, rather than giving priority certain ones (for example, prioritizing ethnicity, while not taking into account other identities).

A gendered perspective enables one to question the ways in which gender is used in classificatory struggles around social positions. It does not reify these differences; instead it examines how they are constructed. As Chodorow emphasizes: "it is crucial for us feminists to recognize that the ideologies of difference which define us as women and as men, as well as inequality itself, are produced, socially, psychologically, and culturally, by people living in and creating their social, psychological, and cultural worlds" (Chodorow 1995, 48).

In terms of the critical potential of such a perspective, I consider that one of its most important contributions, in a country like Romania, for example, is the institutionalization of a new public discourse about social issues. While generating something new, it also deconstructs the grand narratives of the former official socialist ideology such as: the "new society" and the "new man;" the contemporary political representations of the "reform during transition;" and the dominance of male stories about the "central" experiences of everyday life.

A gendered perspective does not necessarily imply a feminist standpoint. While taking into account a gendered perspective, feminism also recognizes the fact that gender is not only an experienced identity and social relation, but also one of the organizing principles of social life. It acknowledges gender as a system of power that structures the order within which individuals are located according to their sex, ethnicity, age, and class. Feminism also does not unilaterally over–stress the gendered dimension of social life, for example, by assuming that sexist oppression and gender stratification is the reason behind all social differentiation, and/ or behind the emergence of social inequalities. Instead, feminism stresses the importance of: "focusing on power relations from the perspective of women located within a variety of social structures who are 'ruled' and who lack the resources to seriously challenge or alter the existing arrangement" (Lindsey 1997, 12). Within my own social and academic context, I envision feminism as a critical approach towards the reproduction of patriarchy across political regimes (in the context of the state socialist paternalism and of the nationalist and/or liberal post–socialist politics). I also consider it an important instrument that can empower the "muted groups," in order to reaffirm the social value of equality through difference, and recognize and transcend the differences between and among women and men.

To conclude, it is important to stress that the analysis of citizenship from a gendered perspective means understanding it as linked to, and embedded in, gender regimes. Such a perspective questions the ways in which gender intersects with racial, class, and ethnic identifications; as well as the ways in which a gender regime that is prescribed by the state and the regimes of peoples' daily lives intersect. Further, the use of a feminist standpoint means that particular values will inform this research, which "involves the opposition to the sexism and patriarchy inherent" in the society under scrutiny, and "provides the ideological framework for addressing women's inferior position and the social, political, and economic discrimination which perpetuate it" (Lindsey 1997, 13).

Understanding Citizenship in the Context of Gender Regimes

As outlined by Connell, I understand a gender regime to be "the state of play in gender relations in a given institution," such as in the family, at school, or in the workplace. A gender regime is also the way in which the state defines the role of women and men, towards its fulfillment of what it considers the "common good" of society. The analysis of a gender regime requires a closer look at the division of labor and the structure of power within these institutions, as well as at the relationships between the gender regimes of different institutions (Connell 1995, 38).

My starting point in conceptualizing the patriarchal gender regime is an idea articulated by Verdery, whereby the "inbuilt" inequalities of a patriarchal gender regime favor the occupants of masculine roles (Verdery 1994, 225–26). Kligman adds that such a social organization constructs hierarchies according to age and sex, and locates men in the public sphere, and women in the private sphere. This defines men's power in the family as formal and delegates them to the position that controls inter–family relationships in public; it considers women to be the administrators of the unofficial problems of their family, and the private mediators of the links between different families (Kligman 1995).

I emphasize that a socio–cultural analysis of a gender regime has to focus its attention on the set of economic, social, political, and cultural mechanisms through which the differences between men and women are transformed into social inequalities. If the differences between the sexes are naturalized and explained by biological terms, then the social inequalities built on these differences also begin to be legitimized, because they are then purported to be the "natural order of things." Therefore, such an analysis considers gender identity as an instrument for the construction of social hierarchies, as well as one of the tools that leads to the social organization of differences in society.

In defining citizenship, I draw upon Voet's proposal to use the term in a broader way, which encompasses the relationship between a state and an individual citizen, the political relationships between citizens themselves, as well as the rights, duties, actions, virtues, and opinions that result from these relationships (Voet 1998). I would like to add to this, that one must also interrogate citizenship not only as a legal process that prescribes certain rights and obligations to members of a state, but also as an everyday practice of playing out and using these rights and obligations within social practices and interactions. Therefore, citizenship is not only a way of defining the rights and obligations of citizens by the state, it is also a way of perceiving one's self in her/his relation with the state, as well as with her/his significant others; the environment in which she/he makes use of the rights and obligations she/he assumes as a citizen. How the rights and obligations assured by the state are played out in people's everyday lives ultimately depends on who controls the chances and limitations of individuals inside different institutions, and how the negotiation of the right to control occurs at different sites. Citizenship is always embedded in power regimes, which ascribe certain rights/duties/attributes to different members of a society, and locates them in particular social positions. This is why citizenship is one aspect of the ongoing classificatory struggle. Citizenship is not only a set of rights and obligations that are circumscribed legally. It is also a whole range of social, economic, political, and cultural practices, through which the state defines the meaning of belonging to a country/society/nation for men and women of different nationalities, professions, ages, and sexual orientations.

In questioning citizenship from a gendered perspective, as produced by gender regimes, I follow Jones' definition of citizenship, according to which "citizenship is defined as a practice of embodied subjects whose sex/gendered identity affects fundamentally their membership and participation in public life" (Jones 1990, 786). I also take into consideration Shola Orloff's assertions about why and how women's opportunities to be full citizens are different from men's. She recognizes that the equality of rights is legislated and formally assured by state "relations of domination," which are "based on the control of women's bodies in the family, the workplace, and public spaces," and that "undermine women's abilities to partici-pate as 'independent individuals' – citizens – in the polity, which, in turn affects their capacities to demand and utilize social rights" (Shola Orloff 1993, 309). With these theoretical dimensions in mind, in the next section, I will examine how the Romanian socialist state shaped women's and men's chances to become the "new man" (imagined as being the ideal–typical citizen) and induced inequalities under the conditions of a shortage economy.

Women's Citizenship in Socialist Romania

Based on the theoretical convictions above, I will now turn to the ways in which women's citizenship was constructed in socialist Romania. I do so without claiming that in relation to men, only women were victimized by the communist practices of defining/using people in what was called "the building up of the multilaterally developed Romanian society." I am aware of the fact that under the surface of the egalitarian ideology of the "homogeneous nation" other social categories endured and at the same time reproduced the hegemonies of the Romanian/Orthodox na-tional–communism and paternalist state. For this reason, my general concern is not as much to understand how women were positioned as second–class citizens by the socialist gender regime. Rather it is to stress how individuals were located in relation to the ideal–type citizen and to the paternalist state (among others) by means of the socialist construction of gender identities and differences.

Understanding the condition of women during socialism, and the impact that this (historically speaking) short regime had on people's way of thinking about gender roles and relations, would not be possible without at least outlining the legacies of the pre–socialist period. Socialism did not liberate women from the oppression of traditional patriarchy but, as many scholars argue, it only exchanged the patriarchy of the male individual for that of the state (for example see, Einhorn 1993; Kligman 1998; Verdery 1994). Because of this kind of "emancipation," women could not learn how to act as autonomous citizens. Rather, they learned how to depend on the paternalist state that "gave" lifetime jobs, maternity support, and pensions to "his daughters;" and experienced how it was to be at the mercy of a state that controlled their bodies and expropriated their reproductive rights.

Pasca Harsanyi is one of many scholars who stress that, before becoming a so-cialist state, Romania was a rural country. In 1938, the agricultural sector employed 80 percent of the working population, and the patriarchal way of life, which was characteristic of the traditional peasant culture, informed gender relations. Until as late as 1948, even the towns preserved many rural values, although especially during the inter–war period there appeared to be a significant number of self–reliant, edu-cated middle–class women (Pasca Harsanyi 1993). This picture changed a great deal during socialism, so that, as Pasca Harsanyi shows, in 1989 only about 28 percent of the labor force worked in agriculture, while 46.2 percent of the total population still lived in the countryside. Therefore, women's new problems were tied to the development of small, agrarian-type towns, rather than to the urbanization of villages (Pasca Harsanyi 1995).

The inter–war period also saw the appearance of feminist movements in Romania – represented by the aristocratic and upper–class Westernized female elite – who were committed to promoting changes in the legislation for the social protection of women and their right to vote. This period was a time when the level of women's education and their involvement in certain public domains grew across the whole population. Despite these changes, the number of economically dependent women was still high. Furthermore, in the pre–socialist rural context the condition of woman was produced and shaped by her place and role in agriculture, by her status inside her family, kinship, and neighborhood, and in the context of different public and private rituals that, in cultural terms, made a great contribution to the construction of the gendered social hierarchies within the rural communities.

If one is searching for the roots of the patriarchal gender regime – that even to-day shapes people's mentalities and practices concerning the "natural" differences between men and women, the conventional rules of the gendered division of labor, and the set of cultural values which are "naturally" attached to women – then one must take into consideration how pre–socialist legacies function in individual and institutional memories. Only when we understand the deeply rooted cultural background of women's inferior position in Romanian society, and the symbolic and cultural means by which this position was/is naturalized and unchallenged, can we interpret the treatment of women as secondary citizens, despite their presence in the socialist labor market.

After observing the legacies of women's positions in socialist Romania, it can be agreed that despite its promise, state socialism did not emancipate women (it did not improve their personal autonomy or their social status). As a project of modernization, socialism did make important changes in women's situation that made it possible for them to participate in mass education and use their right to full employment. However, it is important to remember that the acquisition of these rights did not result from the conceptualization of women as independent subjects, rather it was part of the cultural politics that defined both men and women's subject position as equally subordinated to the paternalist nation–state. When viewed in the dynamics of the entire context, what one might consider to have been women's gains were actually acts in which women were devalued by state policies. Eventually, their meaning was strongly linked to the lived experience of being a female citizen in Romania, to the experiences of the severe pro–natalist policy, and to the burdens of multiple responsibilities within a shortage economy.

As Einhorn observes, what emerged from the linkage between socialist revolution and women's emancipation was the conceptually reductive notion that labor force participation was not only a necessary condition, but also a sufficient one for women's emancipation. In proclaiming women's equality with men, the early socialist constitutions granted women's legal rights – however there was a lack in terms of the recognition of some broader gender issues, such as the domestic division of labor, and sex-based discrimination (Einhorn 1993). One main contradiction in the socialist definition of women's role was generated in terms of their productive and reproductive (and childcare) function. In the context of socialist industrialization and the extensive economic development on the part of the state, women were primarily viewed in terms of their productive potentials; while within the household, they were considered necessary contributors to the family income. However, starting in October 1966, as a result of the recognition of the potential labor shortage (which endangered the Communist Party's long term plans for economic development), an intensive pro–natalist campaign in Romania made abortions and divorces almost impossible to obtain and increased taxes on childless married and unmarried adults (Fischer 1985). Therefore, while women were mobilized into the paid labor force in large numbers, the sectorial segregation typical of noncommunist societies continued under Communist Party rule. As Fischer and Pasca Harsanyi note, the sectors where women worked received less investment and remuneration than more "masculine" areas (and men still tended to hold the positions of power in them). Women therefore became concentrated in jobs with low prestige and remuneration (Pasca Harsanyi and Fischer 1994).

The literature on how women's work was evaluated (as having lesser economic importance and social prestige than that of men) seems to be in agreement that – besides its own contribution to the production of gender inequalities (under the surface of the egalitarian ideology) – the socialist regime strengthened the patriarchal character of the traditional Romanian society. Related to this issue, Pasca Harsanyi speaks about how the gender gap was increased. Harsanyi draws a line between the easy work, considered suitable for women (in sectors such as the textile and food processing industries, services, education, and health care), and the harder, better paid work (in sectors such as metal processing, building, and mining industries), considered more suitable for men. She found that although most of the women worked, and were educated to have a profession and spend their active years in the workforce, they were clustered not only in the feminized sectors of the economy, but also at the bottom of the occupational hierarchy. Consequently, women earned less, and gained less prestige from their jobs (Pasca Harsanyi 1995).

One of the greatest paradoxes experienced by women under socialism is that they became "emancipated" without being valued as such. More than that, they experienced this emancipation as a kind of "punishment" which forced them to carry a triple burden as a worker–mother–housekeeper. The socialist state undervalued the private sphere in favor of the public sphere of work. Despite the fact that at the same time socialist ideology praised the double heroism of women, the system also exhorted them to participate in the labor market, while simultaneously asserting a lower status to women's work. Therefore, far from exposing the gender divisions within the family, the values attributed to the private sphere in state socialist countries both strengthened the public/private divide, and induced solidarity within the private sphere. Socialism did not highlight women's rights or gender inequalities; instead, it discredited any public commitment to the equality of women (Einhorn 1993).

The Romanian project that constructed socialism promised to empower women by considering them both as workers and citizens that were equal to men, as long as they contributed to economic production. This sort of equality was subsumed under the socialist project of industrialization and not invented by a women–friendly way of thinking. Moreover, this situation disempowered women due to the strong pro–natalist policy that expropriated their reproductive rights. Officially, this was presented as part of the "holy" socialist project, subordinated to "higher" aims. Actually, the whole set of arguments that legitimized both the pro–natalist policy and the labor policy were subordinated to the "final" and unquestionable aim of the construction of the Romanian socialist nation. A certain form of collectivism was enforced: a type of traditional community built on kinship that had at its center the Communist Party (a relation in which, women, as "mothers of the nation," were considered as tools of the party, which was defined as "the father of the nation"). It gave collective rights to a de–ethnicized and de–sexualized imagined community, which is how women and ethnic minorities came to be homogenized by the unifying ideology of the working class; and also how they were constructed as economic subjects that lacked any culturally made differences.

If we consider that one of the characteristics specific to socialist Romania was the deep complicity between socialism and nationalism, we may understand how the same state, in its relationship with women, was simultaneously socialist (encouraging women's entry to the public sphere and considering them to be heroic workers); and nationalist (because it subordinated them as objects of the Romanian ethnic nation by instrumentalizing them as heroic mothers). In this framework, the unquestioned politics of national identity came to legitimize the pro–natalist policy; and the politics of social identity came to enforce the sexual equality policy. The system's reason for facilitating women's participation in the labor market was part of the Romanian socialist politics of full employment, which was a result of the politics of rapid industrialization and urbanization. However, the system's reasons for pro–natalist politics were related to the ethnonationalist traditions of Romanian politics, to the ideology of the "historical continuity" of the nation, to the Communist future of the Romanian (ethno)nation, and its autonomy from both the East and West. As Kligman puts it, fertility control was a critical issue around which conflicts of interest between the state and its citizens, especially women, were likely to erupt, and reproduction was "fundamentally associated with identity: that of 'the nation' as the 'imagined community' that the state serves and protects, and over which it exercises authority" (Kligman 1998, 5). Therefore, the participation of women in the public sphere was not equal with men's and did not result in their empowerment.

Generally speaking, the participation of citizens in the construction of socialism was not a process of empowering citizens, but of infantilizing them by means of paternalist politics, while empowering the nation–state against its citizens. It is important to note that Romanian women did not obtain the universal right to vote (without restrictions) and equal citizenship with men until 1946, when these rights, as such, were expropriated by the party–state and turned into a formal ritual of expressing one's loyalty towards the party–state.

Women, as citizens of socialist Romania, were expected/enforced to play a role in the project of building up "the multilaterally developed socialist nation," and by fulfilling this mission were supposed to be emancipated. One has to recognize here the perplexities that result from the celebration of women as heroic workers and as heroic mothers, viewed as subjects who had to build up the socialist economy and procreate the socialist nation. Both burdens were controlled by a central power that monopolized the knowledge about the "common and individual good" of Romania and of Romanians. For a woman to be considered a citizen of Romania she had to participate in the labor market and increase the birth rate. This was not only intended to be a way to achieve common goods, but also a way to experience individual fulfillment. However, the very logic of subjectivity constructed in this way was dominated by deep contradictions that were to be lived out by individual women who had to deal with their everyday problems under the conditions of a shortage economy, while facing the challenge of fulfilling the expectations of the roles of breadwinner and mother.

It was the right to work and the duty to procreate that obligated women to carry this double burden. The ideal–type of socialist woman was a Janus–faced hero. On the one hand, she was a desexualized object equal in the labor market with her male counterpart, a status exemplified by the gender–neutral image of a woman on a tractor. On the other hand, she was a sexualized object in private life, objectified as the patriotic mother, eager to procreate the nation. This situation generated two main patterns of cultural reactions and strategies to address the problems. Sometimes the negative experiences of this double burden were explained as being caused by the state (under the conditions of the state that was also acting as the force entitled to give and take rights and duties). At other times, women's "natural" inability to face the challenges of the labor market was thought to be responsible for the failures experienced in mothering. That is how women's entrance to the public sphere was ultimately considered responsible for the unsuccessful developments of the private life, and why, for many today, this perception is linked to the memories of the socialist experience.

I may conclude that while the policies of state socialism promised to emancipate women and assumed that their participation in the labor force was a sufficient condition of this development, they also reproduced a patriarchal gender regime under the hegemony of a paternalist state. This was a regime in which the occupants of masculine roles were favored, economic sectorial segregation increased the gender gap, where the contradictions between the productive and reproductive function of women were not even questioned, and where women's work was undervalued, despite the fact that the system exhorted them to participate in the labor market.

Aside from the disadvantages and paradoxes mentioned above, the advantages and positive aspects of this system have to be realized as well. Women's entrance into the labor market gave them the chance to learn what it was like to have economic independence in relation to men, while the legislation offered them the formal right to be full citizens. All of this had to have a certain impact on the redistribution of gender roles inside families and on peoples' ways of thinking about women's participation in the public sphere and their authority in the private one. However, one also cannot forget that all of this happened under a political regime where women, lacking private property and at the mercy of the state (like everyone in Romanian society), strongly depended on the paternalist ethno–nationalist regime and the socialist parent–state. As a result, both women and men were expropriated and instrumentalized by the socialist paternalist state which "took upon itself some of the more 'traditional' nurturing and care–giving roles that were the responsibility of women in the patriarchal family," and "expropriated men's patrilinial 'rights' to the sexual and reproductive lives of their wives" (Kligman 1998, 27).

Ultimately, the socialist discourse of the homogenized male and female promised to assure a gender–neutral citizenship by legislating equal rights. However, at the same time, the pro–natalist policy and the paternalist practices of the state already gendered citizenship (and reproduced gender differences as inequalities despite the declared gender–neutrality) because of their links to the legacies of traditional gender regimes. Further, in order to conceal its inability and lack of will to deal with the consequences of such a policy, the regime hid its gender blindness and, most importantly, delegitimized, and ridiculed gender awareness for good. One of the most challenging aspects of the discussion of citizenship, as produced by gender regimes, is the understanding of the relationship between gender–neutrality, gender–blindness, and gender–awareness; as well as how these positions were held simultaneously by the socialist state and how, after the collapse of socialism, their changing meanings shaped the interpretation of the relevance of women's issues.

Gender as a Non-issue in Post-socialist Romania

If one only takes a brief look at the "major issues" that shaped the public discussion about Romania in the beginning of the 1990s – reflecting the hierarchy of urgencies and priorities – it might be easy to observe that problems related to women and feminism were hardly on the agenda. Consequently, we should not be surprised to discover that the topic of citizenship was only debated in ethnic and national terms. This reflects that the only legitimate concern, for both the majority and the minorities, was the redefinition of "our" ethno-national communities under the new conditions of the collapsing Soviet block and the new Europe. That is why, in regards to Romania, the main question is not how gender continues to be a public issue after the collapse of socialism, but why and how it became a non–issue during these times. Rather than being surprised by the lack of feminist consciousness, and by the silence towards and/or the rejection of feminism, we should instead try to identify those structural and cultural factors that have contributed to the emergence of this lack, silencing, and rejection.

One of the most important phenomena to observe is how the anti–socialist rhetoric and practice affects, at least in the first stage of transformations, the way in which gender identities and differences are treated by post–socialist politics and the state. In this context, one can see how the conviction that socialism constructed a gender order contrary to "nature," leading to the belief that the end of socialism should mean the restoration of the "natural order of things." In Romania, this suggests the "need" to restore men's autonomy and authority in public and private life and to drive women back into their "natural"/domestic roles and "re–give" them their reproductive rights, including the right to decide on an abortion. The rejection of socialism sometimes goes hand–in–hand with the romanticization of the remote, pre–socialist past, including the recollection of the traditional ("normal") family. One might observe that, today, there are very many ways in which the "proper" gender regime is defined. Men and women have to deal with the parallel existence of different kinds of gender orders at different sites of everyday life, while also observing the general trends that emerge from the impact of changing state politics.

When taking into consideration the extent to which the participation of women in national level politics was based on a quota system during socialism, and how women in political office were therefore assumed to be there simply because of communist policies, it can be expected that, during the post–socialist era women are likely to disappear from this area, at least for a while. Interestingly enough, men, because they have various connections with the socialist past and have developed their careers quite close to the Romanian Communist Party, are still willing to remain the main actors of politics. That is why one might think that "woman", as a social category, is likely to become one of the main scapegoats during this stage of post–socialist changes, blamed for her relationship with socialist politics and for the "crisis" of the traditional family.

Due to the legacy of socialism one might expect that today's political debates – even if women were to participate in them – would not be developed around women's issues, and that even if they were, they would not overtly assume "feminist" perspectives. The representation of feminist issues is still associated with socialism, and women's "problems" – if they are thought of as problems at all – are already considered solved. The individual or the party/organization that would initiate such a discussion would be ridiculed, and would not be able to compete with the more respected perspectives of nationalism and/or liberalism (whatever individuals' perceptions of this were). In this context, I subscribe to Gal's position, that our effort of discursively constructing the political category of "woman" must be done with an awareness of the meanings that were previously attached to this category. Only then must we try to define it as something else: "not as a worker–recipient of communist entitlements, nor as the naturalized, sexualized private being of civil society, nor as the sacred and inert mother of nationhood, but as an independent subject whose interests and issues can be publicly defined and debated" (Gal 1997, 96).

To the extent to which, during the post–socialist transformations everything is in flux and there is a negotiation around the importance of social problems, women are not supposed to consider their particular interests as a priority. Instead, they are expected to understand the need to reconstruct social solidarities around more "critical" and "urgent" concerns. Previously subordinated to the major causes of the building the "Romanian socialist nation," today women have become subsumed to the ideals of "post–socialist reform." That is how, structurally and culturally, women's particular problems did not have the chance to become an issue (not even discursively) at the beginning of the so–called "transition." It is also why both women and men failed to be motivated to organize around issues that could have uncovered social injustices and inequalities and have been a basis upon which to claim rights. That is how the way in which the socialist gender regime constructed gender differences, and the commonly shared view that the socialist gender order was an un–natural one, still continues to shape the means by which both women and men, as citizens, understand their struggle for rights.

In searching for the ways in which "women's issues" appeared on the political agenda of the new state, one could observe that in December 1989, the severe anti–abortion law was immediately abolished. This, as a rectification of one of the injustices experienced under the old regime, became instrumentalized by the self–legitimizing effort of the new power. Certainly, in Romania, this act was one of the most crucial and direct ways for women to perceive that their life might be changed for the better under the new political leadership. But actually, after "re–giving" women the right to control their reproductive decisions and, at least in these terms, to be liberated from state authority, the new state then considered women's issues as resolved, and therefore struck them off of the agenda of priorities for good. Moreover, because this issue was resolved in such a way, women continued to be subjects of the paternalist state decisions, informed by the needs of the new power, and did not act as autonomous citizens in order to claim their rights.

Another aspect in the political environment that made gender a non–issue during the 1990s, was that politics was reinvented as the space for the politics of national identity. Further, since 1996, political priorities have primarily become focused on issues of economic and administrative reform, battles over corruption, European integration, and other topics considered to be "more serious" than women's rights. In terms of rebuilding a collective identity, political discourses have been concerned with the "Europeanness" of Romania, or, on the contrary, with its national "uniqueness." This leaves the problem of internal social inequalities either missing from the agenda, or debated only in terms of ethnicity, which is how identity and difference have come to be nationalized. As a result, other types of identity politics – such as feminism – have been harder to represent with credibility because of a context in which, "liberalism and nationalism remained the dominant visions" (Kennedy 1994, 44). Under these conditions, feminism will have to struggle for a long time in order to become a force that mobilizes women's and men's efforts of reconstructing political communities following the collapse of socialism.

Signs of Changes

The process of transformation that started at the end of 1989 did not end here. As part of this story, one should also note the emergence of women's non–governmental organizations [NGOs] in the Romanian public sphere. In a way, at the beginning of this process, women's NGOs also had a contribution to the production of the dominant practice (that of re–orienting women to the private life) because they focused on issues related to women's domestic concerns (family planning, maternity, sexuality, domestic violence). It is also important to note that, at the same time, by engaging with these concerns NGOs were raising consciousness about the issues that were most neglected by socialist politics, and, most importantly, were making steps towards the conceptualization of the personal as political. Together with pressure from the European Union, NGOs contributed to the enforcement of various legal initiatives that concerned domestic life. These included, among others, the Law on Paternal Leave (1999), the modification of some articles that defined the punishments for sexual violence (2000), and the Law against Domestic Violence (2003). However, these legal initiatives' impact on everyday life would be another story to tell. One can also observe how, in the case of many of these policies, women are strictly linked to family and children. This is further reflected by the creation of the Department for the Advancement of Women and Family Policies (set up within the Ministry for Labor and Social Protection in October 1995) and that of the Department for Child, Woman, and Family Policies (established by the Ombudsperson institution in 1998).

Another impact of the negotiation process of Romania's integration into the European Union was the re–legitimization of gender equality, which fell under the rubric of the policy of equal opportunities. This is reflected in the governmental ordinance, and later, the Law for Preventing and Punishing All Forms of Discrimination (2000), the Law on Equal Opportunities for Women and Men (2002), the creation of the Sub–Commission for Equal Opportunities (which has had a role in Parliament since June 1997), as well as the creation of the Consultative Inter–Ministerial Commission on Equal Opportunities between Women and Men (set up in November 1999). Yet, despite these legal initiatives, a committed institutional strategy for their implementation was not established.

Meanwhile, citizenship continues to be gendered in a way that disadvantages women. Statistical data published in the booklet, *Men and Women in Romania* (2000), shows that in the post–socialist Romanian context women represent a significant part of the labor force in the poorly remunerated sectors (education, health care, social assistance, and the textile industry). Even those woman that are employed by the well–paid financial and banking sector (where women's presence is 70 percent) receive salaries that are less than 90 percent of those received by men in similar positions. In every domain of labor, women are hired for the positions that pay less, their income is significantly under the average income (by approximately 13 percent), and the percentage of women leaders is almost four times lower than that of men. Moreover, 70.6 percent of the unwaged family workers and 59.1 percent of those retired are women. Additionally, while 42.5 percent of all employees are women, the percentage of women employers is only 24.6 percent.

Further, even if one considers the regain of reproductive rights as a very positive change, one also has to be aware of the fact that a real concern for women's interests would not have turned the respect of women's right to control their bodies into a celebration of abortion as "the gift of democracy". Instead, it should have meant the development of a whole health care and educational system within which women – as responsible individuals – could have decided on the most proper contraceptive methods that would assure their reproductive health. The fact that an interest towards this – again, under the pressure of international agencies and some national NGOs – was only raised at the end of the 1990s, and that the Ministry of Health did not launch its Reproductive Health Promotion Strategy until 2003 prove that the new regime re–gendered citizenship by excluding women's roles as reproducers from its policies.

Tasks for Feminism

I am identifying the possible roles of feminism in Romania in terms of the need for a critical approach towards both the paternalist socialist state, and the post–socialist re–strengthening of patriarchy. A critical perspective must be taken when observing the socialist gender-neutrality (that defined women as equal with men, as public goods having the ability to produce, and naturalized/nationalized women's duty to procreate). If such a perspective is not used, it leads to a post–socialist type of gender–blindness (which refuses to understand the inequalities between women and men as generated by the impact of recent changes, or "explains" them by naturalizing or reifying differences). By making explicit the links between the socialist gender–neutrality and the post–socialist gender–blindness, a critical feminist approach has the analytic power to argue why and how both are/were covering the dynamics of power that construct/maintain the gender order, which place women in a position that is inferior to that of men. It is also able to stress the need for gender awareness that avoids both reifying and naturalizing differences. This standpoint reaffirms gender equality as the opposite of inequality, and not of difference, and promotes the idea of an equality that is based on the recognition of difference. Finally, it enables women to reclaim autonomous subject positions that are no longer subordinated to other forces, like the family, nation, and state.

A feminist endeavor in Romania today might be disturbed, on the one hand, by the naturalization of the link between "socialism" and "gender equality;" and, on the other hand, by the tie that is constructed (again as a taken–for–granted bond) between the post–socialist kind of justice for women, and the return to the traditional (pre–socialist) gender order. Consequently, I suggest that feminism should question these issues by asking questions such as: How was patriarchy practised by means of the paternalist socialist state under the surface of "gender equality"? How was the emancipation of women equalized with their celebration as heroic workers and how did their instrumentalization as heroic mothers produce inequality between women and men, even though both were viewed as two de–sexualized categories of the "new socialist man"? How is patriarchy re–enforced today by the mechanisms of the transition from the centralized to the market economy, as well as by the re–empowerment of the pre–socialist social orders? How is the representation of women's interests equated with "liberating" them from the perplexities of the double–burden, and finally, how is "femininity" re–conquered by women's association with traditional or over–sexualized roles, while "masculinity" is regained through men's empowerment both in the private and public spheres? Obviously, the questioning of these issues has to be processed through different case studies and must avoid generalized statements.

Conclusions

The analysis of citizenship – understood as the relationship between a state and an individual citizen, and as the political relationships between citizens themselves – implies, from a gendered perspective, the understanding of it as affected by, and as it affects gender regimes and explores the ways in which gender intersects with racial, class, and ethnic identifications. A gendered perspective questions the ways in which a gender regime, prescribed by the state, and the regimes of people's daily life intersect; how ideological constructions of gender (performed by state institutions) and the subjective experiences of femininity and masculinity (performed by individuals) constitute each other. Finally, it investigates the ways in which social boundaries and cultural differences are built within and between male and female citizens not only by state ideologies, but also through practices by which citizens play out and use these rights and obligations in their everyday life.

Citizenship is always embedded in power regimes; it is always embodied and gendered. The state is gendering it by policies that have different implications for women and men, and individuals are gendering it by performing their roles in everyday life according to the gender stereotypes that are perpetuated throughout education. Ideologies of gender–neutrality and gender–blindness, as constructed by the mentioned mechanisms, do not alter the gendered nature of citizenship. Instead, they hide gender inequalities between women and men of different ethnicities, sexual orientations, ages, professions, and – by doing so – they naturalize socially constituted (gender) hegemonies, reproducing them as "normal".

The experiences of citizenship acquire different meanings within different social and cultural environments. The right to full employment, access to education, and the chance to participate in the public sphere, are lived differently under the conditions of a socialist type of "egalitarian" society, shortage economy, or centralized political regime. It also differs according to the circumstances of a market economy and a consumerist society structured by class. Again, it is not the same if the "emancipated" women, as a subject position, is a project invented and implemented from above, being imposed as a "patriotic obligation," or if this position is conquered as a result of the autonomous individual's own struggle.

A feminist approach to citizenship within the context of contemporary Romania plays a particular role that has not yet been addressed by any other theoretical, social, or political paradigms. Its importance becomes obvious if we consider the need to reaffirm gender equality while constituting "women" as independent subjects, to critically address both the socialist gender–neutrality and the post–socialist gender–blindness; and to conceptualize gender–awareness as a right and a desire to publicly debate women's and men's changing subject positions within different gender orders.

References

Bradley, Harriet. 1993. Changing social division: Class, gender, and race. In *Social and cultural forms of modernity*, edited by Robert Bocock and Kenneth Thompson. London: Polity Press.

Chodorow, Nancy. 1995. Gender, relation, and difference in a psychoanalytic perspective. In *Polity reader in gender studies*, edited by Polity Press. London: Polity Press.

Connell, R.W. 1995. Gender regimes and gender order. In *Polity reader in gender studies*, edited by Polity Press. London: Polity Press.

Einhorn, Barbara. 1993. *Cinderella goes to the market. Citizenship, gender, and women's movements in East Central Europe*. London: Verso.

Fischer, Mary Ellen. 1995. Women in Romanian politics: Elena Ceausescu, pronatalism, and the promotion of women. In *Women, state, and party in Eastern Europe*, edited by Sharon L. Wolchick and Alfred G. Meyer. Durham: Duke University Press.

Fraser, Nancy. 1997. *Justice interruptus. Critical reflections on the "post-socialist" condition*. New York and London: Routledge.

Gal, Susan. 1997. Feminism and civil society. In *Women and men in East European transition*, edited by Margit Feischmidt, Enikő Magyari-Vincze, and Viola Zentai. Cluj: EFES.

Jones, Kathleen. 1990. Citizenship in woman–friendly polity. *Signs: Journal of Women in Culture and Society* 15:781–812.

Kennedy, Michael D., ed. 1994. *Envisioning Eastern Europe. Postcommunist cultural studies*. Ann Arbor: The University of Michigan Press.

Kligman, Gail. 1995. The rites of women: Oral poetry, ideology, and the socialization of peasant women in contemporary Romania. In *Women, state, and party in Eastern Europe*, edited by Sharon L. Wolchick and Alfred G. Meyer. Durham: Duke University Press

Kligman, Gail. 1998. *The politics of duplicity. Controlling reproduction in Ceausescu's Romania*. Los Angeles: University of California Press.

Lindsey, Linda L. 1997. *Gender roles. A sociological perspective*. 3d ed. Englewood Cliffs: Prentice Hall.

Men and Women in Romania. 2000. Published by the Romanian National Commission on Statistics and the United Nations Development Program.

Pasca Harsanyi, Doina. 1993. Women in Romania. In *Gender politics and postcommunism. Reflections from Eastern Europe and the Former Soviet Union*, edited by Nanette Funk and Magda Mueller. New York: Routledge.

Pasca Harsanyi, Doina, and Mary Ellen Fischer. 1994. From tradition and ideology to elections and competitions. In *Women in politics of postcommunist Eastern Europe*, edited by Marilyn Rueschemeyer. Armonk and London: ME Sharpe.

Pasca Harsanyi, Doina. 1995. Participation of women in the workforce: The case of Romania. In *Family, women, and employment in Central–Eastern Europe*, edited by Barbara Lobodzinski. Westport: Greenwood Press.

Rossides, Daniel W. 1997. *Social stratification. The interplay of class, race, and gender.* 2d ed. Englewood Cliffs: Prentice Hall.

Shola Orloff, Ann. 1993. Gender and the social rights of citizenship: The comparative analysis of gender relations and welfare states. *American Sociological Review* 58: 303–28.

Verdery, Katherine. 1994. From parent–state to family patriarchs: Gender and nation in contemporary Eastern Europe. *East European Politics and Societies* 8 (2):225–56.

Voet, Rian. 1998. *Feminism and citizenship.* London: Sage.

Chapter 2

Women and the Law in Poland: Towards Active Citizenship

Małgorzata Fuszara and Eleonora Zielińska

Introduction

The changes taking place in the political and economic systems of the former communist states of central and east Europe create a unique opportunity to examine how these transformations influence the situation of women in the law, the role of women in influencing new legislation, as well as the interpretation and practical application of existing laws. In Poland, as in other countries of the region, the legal status of women and men was primarily determined by more than forty years of Communist rule. In that system, the law seemed to play an important role in the process of social inclusion of various groups of citizens, including women. Nonetheless, in many cases, and in many spheres of life, women's inclusion was more *de jure* than *de facto*.

Any attempt to evaluate women's impact on the law during that period is futile, since citizens had no real influence on the legislative process because all decisions were made by the Central Committee of the Polish United Workers' Party [PZPR]. Since the representation of women in that body was purely symbolic, it is highly probable that any decisions made were in fact undertaken by men. After the collapse of Communism, the gender distribution of power did not change considerably.

The democratization process, although it created conditions under which citizens could in theory exercise power, did not lead to the increased participation of women in decision–making bodies, which further validates the thesis proposed above. In this paper, we argue that the insufficient representation of women in parliament and other decision–making bodies, the inadequate representation of women's interests by those women who were elected, and the insufficient influence of women's values, priorities, and experiences on legislation are often major impediments to the advancement of their political, social, and economic rights. As has been rightly pointed out, the special role of women in creating legal standards and adjusting the law to fulfill women's needs is particularly vital for post–communist states in the throes of deep social and economic transformation (Lacey 1994). Therefore, the abolition of discrimination is not enough to create the equal status of women and men – the empowerment of women is also a prerequisite. As Kymlicka argues, "Equality demands not only equal opportunities to fulfill male–defined roles, but also [the creation of] women–defined roles . . . this empowerment could radically alter the shape of society as we know it" (1990, 120).

This paper is composed of three parts. The first part will discuss women's participation in institutions of power and the changing social attitudes towards women in politics. The second part will focus on sex discrimination and the level of consciousness of this phenomenon among individual men and women. Finally, the last part will discuss women's legislative activities as well as women's recent mobilizing actions in Poland.

Participation of Women in Power and Attitudes Towards Women's Participation in Politics

In post–war communist Poland, the representation of women in parliament was not high – the percentage never even reached a quarter of parliamentary seats. What should be underscored is the fact that during the years of political thaw, women's share of the seats in the *Sejm* (the Lower Chamber of the Parliament) steadily and rapidly diminished. Such was the case in the years when it seemed that the parliament had real constitutional power (1956), or when it actually obtained constitutional power (1989). In 1956, women constituted an all-time low in terms of their representation within parliament constituting only 4 percent of parliamentary positions. During the long period of communist rule, when the real power was wielded by the PZPR, there were no women among its highest officials and the few that were there only played a symbolic role to "prove" that there was not discrimination. There were also very few women in government positions. The proportion of women in parliament rapidly diminished from 20 percent to 13 percent after the first free election in 1989. Data collected between 1989 – 2004 shows that the percentage of women in the Polish *Sejm* and Senate (the Upper Chamber of Parliament) initially did not exceed 13 percent. However, it did grow drastically after the elections held in 2001, when women's shares of seats grew to 20 percent in the *Sejm* and 23 percent in the Senate. Analyses of parties' election platforms, in the 1990s and 2001, further showed that only a few parties took women's questions into consideration. Many parties did not address women's issues at all, and some did so only in the context of the family and women's roles within the family (Fuszara 1994; 2001).

A variety of research conducted in Poland during the nineties has indicated that Polish society does believe that the representation of women in politics is insufficient and should be greater. The meager representation of women in decision–making bodies was noticed in public opinion surveys, especially by women themselves. A large part of Polish society believed (and still believes) that there should be more women in positions of authority: in 2004, 54 percent believed that there should be more women in the cabinet; 52 percent believed that there should be more women in parliament; and 53 percent thought that there should be more women in local self-government (Fuszara 2004). Research conducted in 1993, 2000, and 2004 shows that opinions concerning the desired level of women's participation in parliament and in local government positions are correlated with the gender and education of the respondents. A higher proportion of women and respondents with a higher educational background thought that women should make up a comparatively larger percentage of the parliamentary and local government positions.

The question of why women are underrepresented is often debated in scholarly literature. The three explanations presented most frequently are not mutually exclusive, but instead are complementary. The first addresses the unequal social status of women and men: in this interpretation, the low number of women in power is a reflection of the economic and social inequality between men and women. This inequality guarantees that men's positions remain privileged, and women's subordinate (Kymlicka 1990; Skard and Haavio–Mannila 1985). The second explanation concerns the diversity of culturally defined roles of men and women in society: this division of roles limits women's access to any positions other than that of wife and mother and leaves men free to access all the roles in what is defined as the public sphere (Siemieńska 1996; Titkow 1993). Finally, the third explanation points to the additional obstacles which women in high positions face because of their gender. For instance, research conducted in France shows that most women mayors talked of the manifestations of misogyny they had to confront in their working environment, which included: the limitation of their activities to certain spheres that were not necessarily chosen by themselves, unfair tactics used against them, constantly being forced to prove their competence and ability, and being hindered in their attempts to reach higher positions of power (Braud 1991). Members of the Poland's Parliamentary Women's Group and women in local government positions gave similar examples of misogyny (Fuszara 2003a; 2003b). What this data indicates then is not only that there are clear gender differences and that women are dissatisfied with the level of their representation, but also that political structures continue to be resistant to the inclusion of women's vocal representation.

The problem, of course, is not unique to Poland. With a few exceptions (most notably Scandinavia, where the representation of women in parliament is as high as 40 percent) in most countries, it can be said that, in general, the representation of women in decision–making bodies is very low. Research from other countries has also shown that members of parliament rarely take initiatives which express women's interests. If these interests are ever going to be addressed, women must be represented in parliament. "It is invariably the women who deal with women's issues to any extent. As far as male MPs are concerned, any initiative in this direction is an exceptional case" (Wadstein 1997). It is therefore certain that despite a slow increase, there is still a low percentage of women in the Polish parliament, which is in turn a barrier to the introduction of legislative changes that would improve the situation of women as well as create equal rights for all citizens regardless of their gender.

In the nineties, an increase in social awareness concerning the need to protect women's rights was observed (Fuszara 2001). Along with the democratization of public life, the women's community, through numerous newly emerged women's non–governmental organizations [NGOs], the Parliamentary Women's Group, and the national machinery for gender equality, became more aware of their ability to exert real influence on legislation, which encouraged women to take more advantage of their political right to active citizenship. This process was crippled after right wing parties came to power in 1997. The phenomenon is best illustrated by the metamorphosis of an agency putatively created as part of the national machinery to promote gender equality.

The Office of Government Plenipotentiary for Women and the Family was established in 1991 as an independent body, directly subordinated to the prime minister. Until that time, the functions carried out by the office had been fulfilled by a plenipotentiary subordinated to the Ministry of Labor, Remuneration, and Social Affairs. The first independent Plenipotentiary for Women and the Family, Anna Popowicz, became involved in defending women's abortion rights and as a result was dismissed in 1992. The office subsequently remained vacant for several years and Poland did not have an independent body for defending women's rights, regardless of its international commitments, the lobbying of women's organizations, or the glaring need for such a body. This also testifies to the fact that the importance of the issue of women's rights was underestimated and the opinion of the women's community was ignored.

It was not until shortly before the United Nations' [UN] Conference on Women, held in Beijing in 1995, that the office was once again filled. Again, the person chosen was the only woman in the Polish government at the time, Construction Minister Barbara Blida. She had to fulfill the responsibilities of her new position in addition to her duties as Construction Minister. As a result, she could not devote all the time and attention that was required for the position and, under pressure from the women's community, she resigned from the office, referring to the job as "harmful to my health." Blida's successor, Jolanta Banach, was appointed before the Beijing conference. She then directed the preparation of the Polish Plan of Action for Women that was based on the outcomes of the Beijing conference.

The Polish government accepted the Plan of Action shortly before the parliamentary election held in September 1997. This election brought a complete change of the parties in power and it very soon became obvious that the new government was not interested in carrying out the action program. The Office of Government Plenipotentiary for Women and the Family was scrapped and was replaced with a Government Plenipotentiary for the Family, which did not take on any tasks for or related to women. The first person appointed to fill the office was a man, Kazimierz Kapera, who in the past had become notorious for preventing a rape victim from getting an abortion and for denouncing homosexuals as perverts. When he was forced to resign in August 1999, a woman was appointed to fill the office; she was, however, a strong activist of the Organization of Catholic Families. She held highly traditional and conservative views on the role of women in society, and opposed birth control and sex education in schools. What becomes clear then is the fact that neither the law nor any other public institution offered protection for women against discriminatory practices nor did it offer any support for gender equality. After the last elections of 2001, the Office of Government Plenipotentiary for the Equal Status of Women and Men was established, directly subordinate to the prime minister. This latter change had little to do with a shift in attitudes; instead, it reflected the pressures stemming from Poland's EU membership, which was still pending at that time.

The active participation of women's organizations in public life took two major forms: complaints about instances of sex discrimination lodged with civic rights protection bodies; and legislative activities, which took the form of either positive actions, initiating changes in mandatory law, or of defensive actions, constituting a reaction against legislative initiatives that limited women's rights.

Sex Discrimination Complaints

Poland's 1986 establishment of the Constitutional Tribunal and, in 1987, of the post of the Commissioner for Civil Rights Protection [Commissioner], created legal avenues for litigating civil rights offences, including gender discrimination against women. Nevertheless, only the most striking infringements of the principle of gender equality had come to the attention of public opinion.

It is significant that the first decisions in which the Constitutional Tribunal ruled statutory provisions as unconstitutional was in a case of sex discrimination in 1987.[1] The decision was made in regards to a regulation that was adopted by the Ministry of Health, which established a 50 percent admission quota for male and female students applying to medical schools. Since there were more female candidates applying to medical schools, several were denied admission even though their scores were higher than those of the admitted male candidates. The Tribunal found that the regulation was contrary to the constitutional principle of equality, which, according to its opinion, "should be regarded as one of the fundamental principles of the Polish Constitution. Any limitations on this principle are prohibited unless they result from an effort to achieve *de facto* social equality" (OTK 1997, item 2).[2]

Another decision, which was reached in 1998, concerned a 1982 pension statute. This statute increased the period of work necessary to acquire the right to disability pensions from five to ten years, specifically in the cases of employees who had begun to work after the age of 40 or who had taken a ten year break in employment. This provision, according to the Tribunal's ruling, violated the constitutional principle of equality since it discriminated against women who began to work after periods of time that were devoted to bringing up children (OTK 1989, item 7).[3]

Additionally, in the 1991 women university lecturers' retirement case, the Tribunal invalidated a provision of the 1990 Universities Act that had established, for certain categories of teachers, a compulsory retirement age of 60 for women and 65 for men. The court decided that while the law may grant certain privileges to women, including the right to an earlier retirement, it must not transform those privileges into obligations, at least for jobs where the "biological and social differences of both sexes" are irrelevant (OTK 1991, item 5).[4]

Most of the sex discrimination complaints reviewed by the Constitutional Tribunal were filed by the Commissioner for Civil Rights Protection. At that time, the office was held by a woman, Professor Ewa Łętowska. It is difficult to say to what extent the sex of the commissioner affected the willingness of the office to pursue complaints lodged by women. It is true, however, that in the annual report she presented to the *Sejm* she always included a separate section on sex discrimination, and that the subsequent male holders of the position of commissioner have discontinued this practice. This fact has special significance. Ewe Łętowska's publicizing of gender discrimination issues played, in our opinion, a significant role in raising the awareness of gender inequalities and contributed to the systemic increase of the knowledge, understanding, and attention given to gender equality and discrimination issues.

The regulations enacted by the Minister of Employment and Social Policy, which obligated employers and employment offices to segregate their job offers by sex, remained in force until 1991, at which time they were forbidden, following the intervention undertaken by the Government Plenipotentiary for Women and the Family, and the Commissioner. Another instance of sex discrimination that was reported by the Commissioner, and settled out of court concerned women divers and miners who were not entitled to the preferential treatment and special benefits that were given to their male colleagues. In the context of this and other complaints regarding employment limitations faced by women, the Commissioner, in his deposition to the Minister of Employment and Social Policy on October 25, 1993, indicated that, among other things, there was a need to include an anti–discrimination clause in the employment code, which would constitute a further development of the appropriate constitutional norms regarding employment conditions and relations.

The best known case of discrimination against both women and men was the Law of 1974, which was later revised in 1994; this law outlined financial benefits in cases of sickness or maternity. It granted child–care benefits (paid leave) exclusively to the mother; the father was entitled to these benefits only when the mother was temporarily outside of her place of residence or was incapable of caring for the child due to sickness or childbirth.[5] In another case, it was found that income taxes discriminated against single parents. This tax regulation primarily hurt single mothers; whereas married couples and families having an employed minor were allowed to consolidate their incomes for taxation purposes, single mothers were not.[6] Yet another complaint concerned a woman who was refused employment as a railroad engineer despite the fact that this occupation was not included in the list of occupations that were forbidden for women. Notwithstanding the criticism, Polish law still includes mandatory protective regulations prohibiting all women from pursuing occupations that require heavy physical labor, forced body position, exposure to high noise or vibration levels, and work either underground or at high altitudes (Nowakowska 2000, 45).[7] Although the law does not state anything about the justification of such prohibitions, it may be assumed that these regulations are, at least in part, an attempt to protect women as potential child bearers.

Sex discrimination was also at the core of the case of a female employee in a central public institution who was forced to retire against her will as soon as she reached the legal age of retirement. Women's legal age of retirement in Poland is five years earlier than men's. This was originally meant, as has been already mentioned, as a privilege, compensating women for their additional duties. However, in today's situation of rising unemployment, the right of retirement at age 60 is increasingly treated as an obligation. This constitutes an instance of unequal treatment of women and men of retirement age that infringes upon the constitutional provision of the equality of women and men and clearly proves that Poland lacks effective mechanisms for combating discrimination. One of the cases related to the gendered differences between retirement ages has been appealed throughout all the courts, including an extraordinary appeal that was filed by the Chair of the Supreme Court, the Constitution Tribunal, and the Commission of Human Rights in Strasbourg. However, for different reasons many of which are a matter of procedure, the case still has not been resolved in a way that satisfies the plaintiff.[8] The issue was taken up by the Commissioner for Civil Rights Protection who lodged a complaint against those provisions that provided different retirement ages for women and men, alleging that they contravened the constitutional principle of equality and the prohibition of discrimination. In its decision of September 29, 1997, the Constitutional Tribunal ruled that the provisions that differentiated between the retirement ages of women and men were unconstitutional because they constituted a legal basis for the termination of an employment contract with a female civil servant, without her agreement, at a younger age than they did for male employees.[9] The different retirement ages established by these laws, in regards to civil service workers, deprived female civil servants the right to work until the same age as male civil servants. Thus, the provisions became a factor that discriminated against female workers by not treating them equal to male workers of the same employment status.[10]

The most striking fact is that the laws that protected women before the transformation are turned against them today. Hence, it is postulated that preferences for women in labor relations be facultative in nature: that is, a woman should be able (but not obliged) to exercise the right to end her professional career earlier than men, and should be able, on par with the child's father, to use child raising leave, child care leave, and other similar benefits.

Despite this fact, and the postulated changes connected with it, there is still a tendency to enact protective regulations, which reduce women's chances for becoming employed in the labor market. Evidence of this was the extension of maternity leave in 1999 which, in its original version was obligatory, and was only eventually reduced in 2001. This means that women's NGOs along with the Commissioner for Civil Rights Protection and Plenipotentiary should vigilantly monitor legislation that is drafted and enacted to make sure that it complies with the principles of gender equality and take firm actions to change those that do not.

Influencing the Legislation and the Role of the Parliamentary Women's Group

Not all the activities that arose from the complaints enumerated above resulted in legislative changes that had a positive influence on the situation of all women in Poland. Therefore, at the same time direct legislative initiatives were also undertaken to assure such changes took place. It should be stressed that some of these were primarily connected with the necessity of adapting Polish laws to the laws of the European Union [EU] and were, in a way, forced by Poland's effort to join the EU. Among these changes we should mention the changes introduced to the Labor Code, particularly the addition of the requirement of equal treatment of women and men in the field of employment (Art. 11.1) and the prohibition of discrimination because of sex, age, disability, race, nationality, union membership, or beliefs (Art. 11.3). The obligation to respect the dignity of employees was also introduced (Art. 11.3), which can be interpreted as an attempt to prohibit sexual harassment in the workplace.[11]

However, the women's community believed that provisions that were worded in such a general way were not sufficient enough for the effective protection of women against employment discrimination, especially because of the difficulties women faced in exercising their rights. Moreover, in discrimination cases the burden of proof should be placed on the employer, who, when accused of discrimination, would have to show what criteria he or she used in making the decision to hire the employee. The provisions on sexual harassment should have been made more detailed and employers should have been obligated to actively prevent harassment. It is worth noting that these postulates were included in the subsequent changes to the Labor Code that occurred on May 14, 2001, and on November 14, 2003, when the legislation that was implemented for the three anti–discrimination directives adjusted Title IIa LC and improved the provision for equal pay and equal treatment (Dz. U. 2001, no. 128, item 1405).[12] In the field of social security, the entire system was amended by an act that was introduced on October 13, 1998 (Dz.U. 1998, no. 137, item 887). However, some months later only one amendment of this act provided a guarantee for equal treatment, which could be attributed to the transposition of the Equality Directives that were already passed by the *Sejm*.

In this context, of particular interest are the many legislative initiatives that were undertaken by women parliamentarians, especially by the members of the Parlamentarnej Grupy Kobiet [Parliamentary Women's Group; Women's Group], established in 1991. The establishment of the Women's Group and more then a decade of its activities is a sign of the conscious creation of parliamentary structures that aim to express the group interests of women and defend their rights. Feminist literature rightly points out that "people should be treated not as individuals, but as members of groups. The discourse of universal citizenship which ignores these differences would just enhance the domination of groups which are already the marginal and oppressed groups" (Yuval-Davis 1997, 17–18). As Yuval-Davis suggests, special mechanisms have to be established to represent these groups.

This is a difficult task. For example, the membership of the Women's Group ranged, during various terms, from one–third to two–thirds of all women deputies and senators, and represented all political parties except the Christian Right. The composition of the Women's Group confirms observations that were made in other countries that only some women parliamentarians see the need for the representation of women's particular interests and believe in their special role in acting to improve their situation. In Poland, the vast majority of the Women's Group consisted of women from the left–wing party Sojusz Lewicy Demokratycznej [Democratic Left Alliance; SLD]. It is difficult to deduce whether their active participation resulted more from their strong belief in such an approach, or if it is related to the fact that the party included gender equality in its program. In regards to other women parliamentary deputies, they still seemed to have greater loyalties to their party lines than to the promotion of gender equality.

The Battle Over Abortion Law

The literature on female representation has often stressed that the most accepted argument for raising the number of women and their group activities is that "women have different experiences and resources than men" (Council of Europe 1997, 13). The activities of the Women's Group members, usually as a result of the prompting by or active participation of women's organizations, proves that the specific experiences of women are clearly reflected in their legislative initiatives and activities. The most spectacular example of women parliamentarians' activities were the attempts to prevent the abortion law from becoming more restrictive (the defensive strategy) and the later efforts to liberalize it (the offensive strategy). These took place several times in multiple forms, including: complaints to the Commissioner, the introduction of counter–bills or, after 1993, the introduction of draft amendments to liberalize the law, as well as initiatives that called for a national referendum to be held on the subject of abortion (Zielińska 2000, 30).

The issue of abortion has appeared on the agenda of the Constitutional Tribunal four times so far, three times as a result of a complaint by the Commissioner, which was instigated by women's organizations who made the claim that anti–abortion provisions discriminated against women, and once as a result of a complaint lodged by a group of Senators, including women from Christian right–wing parties, against the liberalizing amendment of 1996 of the anti–abortion law of 1993.[13] The first case, in 1990, involved a review of governmental regulations (Dz.U. 1990, no. 29, item 178).[14] At that time, abortion in Poland was still legal in a wide variety of circumstances: the 1956 Abortion Act permitted abortions to be performed on the basis of medical, legal, and social conditions. After 1989, numerous attempts to restrict abortion were made. Finally, in 1993, a new law that restricted abortions was passed (Dz.U. 1993, no. 78, item 78).[15]

Meanwhile, in 1990, the Ministry of Health adopted a regulation that allowed a physician to refuse to perform or assist an abortion. The Commissioner (Ewa Łętowska) immediately challenged the regulation before the Tribunal, arguing that the Ministry did not have the authority to regulate this area. She did not question the regulation on its merits: she merely claimed that in the absence of a proper "statutory delegation", a ministerial regulation (namely a "sub–statutory act") was not permitted to regulate matters which clearly were "reserved" for an act of parliament (Łętowska 1992, 76).

The court upheld the regulation on the ground that a physician's right to refuse could be interpreted to be based on the constitutional principle of freedom of conscience, as well as on the Code of Medical Ethics. Therefore, the challenged regulation merely repeated a norm that had already existed within the legal system. Although the Tribunal admitted that such repetition was improper (there was no statutory "delegation clause" permitting the Ministry to regulate this subject matter), it ruled that it was constitutional, because no new legal norm had been established. This decision has been strongly criticized from the legal point of view (Zielińska 1991, 112). It was clear, however, that the Constitutional Tribunal was ready to express its support for anti–abortion policies, even at the expense of its professional reputation.

In the next decision, on October 7, 1992, the Tribunal addressed an abortion provision that was introduced to the Code of Medical Ethics in 1991 (this was an act adopted by the professional self–governing body that represents the medical profession). This provision prohibited physicians from performing abortions unless they were justified by medical or legal reasons. Non–compliance with the Code would warrant disciplinary proceedings. At the same time, the law of 1956, which was still in force, made abortion legal in the case of difficult living conditions (so–called "social indications") and in cases of medical indications (which included a broad number of such indications).

This provision was challenged by the Commissioner on several grounds. She rightly pointed out that although the Code of Medical Ethics was only addressed directly to physicians, it still had a very strong impact on women's access to abortions. Since physicians had the exclusive right to perform abortions, argued the Commissioner, the ban imposed on abortions deprived women the possibility to have an abortion in cases of difficult living conditions or for embryo–pathological reasons. The Tribunal sustained the Code provision by holding that the challenged rules are of a purely ethical (and therefore not legal) character. Finally, in its further decision in March 1993, the Constitutional Tribunal, urged by the Commissioner (Tadeusz Zieliński, successor to E. Łętowska), held that a physician who performs an abortion in conformity with the law, but in violation of the applicable provision of Code of Medical Ethics, could not be subjected to disciplinary action by the medical association.

All these Constitutional Tribunal decisions led to situations wherein doctors, fearing the legal repercussions, refused to abort pregnancies in public health–care centers even before the restrictive statute became law in 1993. However, this did not prevent them from performing abortions privately. What these changes did imply was the marginalization of women's rights, the economic discrimination against indigent women who could not afford private abortions, as well as the increasing power of physicians.

The women's community undertook legislative initiatives that aimed to change the abortion law three times, however almost all were at least partial defeats. The first such an attempt took place in 1989, before the introduction of the anti–abortion law. The draft law on family planning, the protection of the human fetus, and on the conditions of admissibility of abortions was designed as a counter–draft to the restrictive draft law for the protection of the conceived child. As it happened, it was rejected at the very beginning of the legislative process, but some of its provisions, and its title, were included in the final version of the Law of 1993 making this version of the act more liberal than previous ones.

. The Law of 1993 banned abortions in cases of social conditions, even when performed in private physicians' offices. After it came into force, the women's lobby prompted the introduction of deputies' legislative initiatives, which aimed to liberate the already existing legislation on several occasions. In the first instance, in 1995, the bill that overturned previous restrictions (social conditions and allowing abortion in doctors' private offices and clinics) was passed by both houses of the parliament. This law did not, however, come into force, since President Lech Wałesa refused to sign it and the parliament could not muster up the two–thirds majority required to reject the presidential veto.

The second liberalizing amendment was passed by the *Sejm* and the Senate in 1996 making abortion legal again for cases where social conditions deemed them necessary and once again allowed them to take place in private doctors' offices (Dz. U. 1996, no. 66, item 334). It remained in force for less than a year. Its provisions became invalid on December 23, 1997 as a result of the Constitutional Tribunal's verdict on May 28, 1997, which ruled that the 1996 Amendment's provisions contravened the constitutional principle of the protection of life (OTK 1997, item. 19).[16] The old Constitution lacked a clear legal provision on this matter so the Tribunal made a risky interpretation; they extrapolated the protection of the life of a conceived child from the general principle of Article 1 of the Constitution of 1952, amended in 1992, which stated that the Republic of Poland is "a democratic state of the rule of the law respecting the principle of social justice." This verdict did not discourage women's NGOs from continuing to propose liberalizing amendments to the Parliament. The most recent draft of these modifications, which was introduced in the spring of 2005, was also unfortunately rejected (*Parliamentary Print* 2005)

During the almost ten years of conflict over abortion, the women's community, supported by the Democratic Left Alliance, has attempted to hold a national referendum on the issue several times. Hundreds of thousands of signatures were collected and public opinion polls showed wide support for the initiative. However, probably because of the strong influence of the Catholic Church, amongst others factors, the referendum was never formally organized (Zielińska 2000, 34).

Several other attempts at legislative initiatives that served to improve the situation of women were also made, including changes in divorce and child custody regulations, amongst others. However, not one of these initiatives was successful. Instead of liberalizing the divorce laws, the institution of separation was introduced.[17] For instance, instead of changing the family code, Poland, while ratifying the 1989 UN Convention on the Rights of Child, put forward a declaration that all rights guaranteed by the Convention shall be interpreted with respect to parental supervision, in accordance with Polish customs and traditions about the place of the child within and outside the family.

Elaborating the New Constitution

The best example of the fight for women's rights is, however, their work in the creation of the new constitution of the Republic of Poland. From the beginning, the women's lobby opted for constitutional maximalism in regards to women's rights and strongly protested against one proposal that was being supported by legislators, which aimed to limit the issue of equality to an anti–discrimination clause that indicated sex as one of the grounds that was prohibited from being classified. In the opinion of the women's lobby, separate and comprehensive provisions on equality and women's rights were important since they constituted an autonomous basis for individual complaints – this was a new instrument introduced in the draft of the Constitution. The positive impact of such an equality clause was that it would not only constitute an obligation for the state to refrain from interfering with the individual rights that were guaranteed in the Constitution, but also impose on the State the obligation to undertake positive actions to create the conditions needed in order to fully enjoy those rights (Centrum Praw Kobiet 1998).

A separate provision on the equality of women and men was added to the Constitution on April 2, 1997 (Dz.U. 1997, no. 78, item 78).[18] After long discussions that were made, "in a spirit of compromise", the legislators agreed to reject the wording of the provision on equality, because it used "man" as a point of reference for "woman". The initial draft of the Constitution, while declaring equality for the sexes, reiterated the Constitution of 1952's previous formula that women should enjoy rights equal to those of men. As a result of many interventions by the women's lobby, the final wording of Article 33 reads:

> Women and men have equal rights in family, political, social, and economic life. In particular, they have equal rights to education, employment, and promotion, to equal pay for work of equal value, equal social security benefits, equal rights to occupy positions, to perform functions as well as to achieve public honors and awards. (Constitution of the Polish People's Republic, 1997)

This was the only "victory" connected with the feminist lobby. All other women's lobby proposals, for example, the introduction of the right to self–determination in the reproductive sphere of life, or the establishment of a provision that would obligate public authorities to eliminate violence against women, were rejected. Also rejected was the quota that required that 40 percent of the positions within all public nominations (that were not based on general elections) must be occupied by women.[19] The first proposal was aimed to facilitate the change of anti–abortion laws; the second was aimed to sensitize and activate the public authorities to eliminate gender violence; and the third, was to increase women's representation in politics. Under these circumstances, the feminist lobby considered another possible means for the legal regulation of women's rights: the introduction of a special draft law on the equal status of women and men.

The Draft Law on the Equal Status of Women and Men in Poland

The experiences of other states' struggles against sex discrimination, through the use of special legislation, shows many of the possible benefits of a such law. It is surely not by chance that, during the last thirty years, many Western states have introduced legislation that aimed to create equal opportunities and promote equal treatment for women and men. These legislations are based on the assumption that when some groups in society have fewer opportunities of access to valued goods or positions than others, in order to achieve equality, members of disadvantaged groups must be granted preferences in the social division of valued goods. Specifically, if fewer opportunities of access stem from the past discrimination of these groups, the criterion, which had previously been the basis for discrimination, should serve as the criterion for providing advantages, which would then lead to the elimination of the effects of past discrimination. This is the reason why preferential systems are often called "positive" or "reverse" discrimination; their goal is to overturn the dominant pattern of disadvantage and to equalize opportunities by giving an advantage to those who were traditionally disadvantaged (Sadurski 1988). Thus, the introduction of temporary special measures that aim to promote real equality for men and women, which will then be repealed when the goals of equal treatment and equal opportunity are reached, cannot be considered a violation of the equality principle in terms of the understanding of these notions by all relevant international documents (Fuszara and Zielińska 1994).

Obviously, the passing of a special law on equal status will not automatically bring about changes in society or, more vitally, in social awareness. It is, however, also indisputable that without changes in the law, many actions cannot be undertaken. Such legal changes are therefore indispensable for initiating the process of social change. It has been proven that countries that have introduced such laws have experienced a considerable growth in the rate of active participation of women in paid employment and in public life (broadly understood). Germany and the Scandinavian countries stand as the most striking examples. These examples, as well as the failures to achieve gender equality in Poland by other means, encouraged Poland's adaptation of a similar legislative solution.

The first attempt in the *Sejm* to introduce a draft law on the equal status of women and men (prepared by the authors of this paper) took place in 1996 and was supported by 160 deputies' signatures (OŚKa 2001). However, without legal basis the informal opinions that were collected about the draft only recommended the introduction of certain changes instead of starting further legislative steps. These changes were then introduced and the process of collecting signatures began again. The draft was reintroduced, this time bearing more than 140 deputies' signatures. The first reading was held, whereupon the draft was sent to the commission. This occurred immediately before the unscheduled end of the parliament's term. The next election was called for in September 1997, and resulted in the strengthening of the position of right–wing parties. The Women's Group once again submitted the draft for debate. However, this attempt also failed, as did the next in 1998, despite the fact that public opinion favored it (Fuszara and Zielińska 1998, 35). A proposal to create a new parliamentary committee on the equal status of men and women, presented to the *Sejm* in October 2000, was also rejected. However, finally, in 2005 such a committee was created. Unfortunately, the draft of the law on the equal status of women and men, which was supposed to substitute for the Governmentary Plenipotentiary for Equal Status of Women and Men, was rejected in 2005, despite the fact that the present version is limited only to the quota provisions and the establishment of a special equality body.

The first version of the draft, that covered all areas where sex discrimination is most likely to appear, represented the "holistic approach." According to this proposal, the definition of discrimination would be based on Article 1 of the UN Convention on the Elimination of All Forms of Discrimination against Women; however, it would apply to both sexes. The law proposed to outlaw both direct and indirect discrimination. Furthermore, we proposed that the equal status law should not only address discrimination in all possible spheres, but it should also include an exemplary catalogue of rights that were to be accorded protection.

Public authorities were also explicitly obligated to combat the reproduction of the stereotypical roles of men and women throughout the education system, most importantly by eliminating those stereotypes from textbooks and curricula. Additionally, the draft would have banned advertisements that portrayed either of the sexes in an offensive or insulting manner. Equal rights to information and education in the areas of health care, human sexuality, consciousness, and responsible parenthood were expressed verbatim in the act, as well as the right to partake in decisions that concerned sexuality, without coercion, violence, or discrimination. The act also included women's rights to self–determination in reproduction, to decide to have or not have children, to decide on the number of children they did have, as well as the spacing of their children's births. All doubts, according to the draft, should be interpreted to the advantage of the person discriminated against. Public authorities are required to guarantee women and men equal access to legal protection bodies, equal representation of their interests, and equal treatment by those bodies. This includes equal protection against violence, including domestic violence, establishing shelters and assistance for victims of violence, as well as conducting educational programs about the negative effects of domestic violence on public, family, and private life.

The most important part of the law calls for the establishment of authorities to monitor the implementation of its provisions as well as the establishment of procedures to protect and vindicate these rights. For this purpose, we proposed the establishment of an Equal Status Ombudsperson. This office was conceptualized as one that would be responsible for monitoring the execution of the law, negotiating other actions to eliminate specific discriminatory practices, as well as initiating research, gathering and providing information, and informing interested individuals or organizations about the proper procedures for claiming their rights, especially through penal suits, civil suits, or labor court action (Bator 1999, 2; Fuszara and Zielińska 1998, 12).

Conclusion

As was stated earlier, women are insufficiently represented in parliamentary and government bodies. This holds true for all executive positions, only 35 percent of which are occupied by women (who are mostly members of middle management). Women are also less often able than men to take advantage of the new opportunities made possible by the transformation of the political system: they participate in privatization to a smaller extent than men participate and only constitute just over 30 percent of owners of private enterprises. In effect, women received much less power than men did after the change.

The most striking limitation to women's equal status is the above–mentioned anti–abortion law, and in particular the public discussions which preceded its enactment. These discussions demonstrated how the people in power are completely ignorant of the phenomenon of sex discrimination as well as of the role of international instruments, such as the UN Convention on the Elimination of All Forms of Women's Discrimination, in eliminating it. It also proved that, when related to women, fundamental human rights such as the right to dignity, the autonomy of the individual, the right to privacy, or the right to self–determination in important life matters are placed very low in society's value hierarchy. Other areas where the inequality between the opportunities of women and men can easily be observed include the labor market and the social security system.

Similar issues of ignorance and lack of political action can also be noticed in relation to EU legislation. Polish politicians were and, to a large degree, are still not familiar with the legal regulations on gender equality that are in force in the EU. Before Poland was admitted to the EU, the European Commission, in its 2000 Regular Report, concluded that the speed of harmonization of Polish laws that supported the equal treatment of women and men with those of the EU was at an unsatisfactory level. The report pointed out that the issue of the equal treatment of women and men required urgent attention because "against the objective criterion of adoption of the *acquis communautaire* Poland has made no progress in this area over the reporting period" (European Commission 2000). There continues to be extensive evidence that politicians do not realize that all European Union member states have special equality mechanisms which support equality between women and men and which facilitate the actual implementation of the principle of sex equality and non–discrimination. These mechanisms may or may not take the shape of national machinery: such as the Office of the Governmental Plenipotentiary for the Equal Status of Women and Men, special laws on equal status, or both. Recent research indicates that even though Poland is a member of the EU, the level of knowledge among Polish politicians in regards to equal status varies from those that can be seen as EU gender equality specialists; and the "rest" of the politicians who have only a basic understanding of the policy, deny the importance and foundations of this policy, or who simply do not understand it at all. There are, however, also some positive developments in Poland. These include the increased number of women's NGOs and the growing importance of their role in all of these struggles.

The legislative initiatives and feminist lobbying activities outlined above underscore the important evolution of the notion of citizenship; while from a *de jure* perspective Polish women can almost fully claim their citizenship rights, *de facto*, they still have a long way to go. This gives rise to the question of what actions should now be undertaken to defend women's rights. Experience so far, both with the proposed equal status legislation and the efforts by women's NGOs to introduce women's issues to the government and parliamentary agenda, has demonstrated that the parties and people in power only understand or sympathize with these issues and problems to a very limited extent. Taking into account the current composition of power in the parliament after the fall elections of 2005 that resulted in an overwhelming right–wing shift, it is clear that there is no chance of a draft on equal rights for men and women being passed. However, even the left-wing Democratic Left Alliance, after taking over power in the September 2001 election, did little to increase the chances for the passage of such a law, and the recent failed attempt proves that point.

Nevertheless, the very simple fact that attempts were made to introduce a draft law on equal status brought about many positive consequences. First, they gave rise to a public debate on gender discrimination and equality and the previous silence that had surrounded the issue was broken by conferences, discussions, and press, radio, and television interviews. Secondly, such debates increased people's awareness of discrimination, especially of structural and indirect discrimination, and changed their consciousness about this issue, making it possible to stigmatize its most frequent symptoms. Thirdly, these efforts made visible the actual obstacles and arguments used against the draft, which guided the formulation of future strategies.

Indeed these debates pointed out several significant reasons for the continued resistance to the passage of the equal status legislation. The most significant among them are the institutional impediments, connected with, among other things, the insufficient representation of women, who would be the most motivated to introduce changes if in decision–making positions. Another important set of obstacles are cultural: the Roman Catholic Church and the political circles close to it take an oppositional position towards women's emancipation and equality, while promoting a traditional family model that requires women to make considerable sacrifices for the family. Lately, the actions of such groups have tended to appropriate feminist concepts and vocabulary and twist their meaning, while at the same time attempting to annex the areas of social life that were previously occupied by feminism. An example of this is the promotion of a "new feminism", which consists of an affirmation of women in their present roles as wives and mothers, and places particular emphasis on the benefits for women who only pursue these roles. According to this philosophy, the right to choose also includes the right for a woman to choose to stay home instead of pursuing a professional and public life.

A further difficulty is Polish lawmakers' and politicians' insufficient familiarity with the standards of gender equality in other countries, in the EU, and in the resolutions and recommendations of the Council of Europe, of which Poland is a member. This unfamiliarity coexists with the media's promotion of negative portrayals of examples of gender equality in other countries. Such was the situation with the media's promotion of the ruling of the Justice Tribunal in Luxembourg on the interpretation of the principle of equal treatment of men and women in regards to their access to employment, vocational training, and promotions in the case of Kalanke.[20] The Polish press covered this ruling to a much greater extent than any other rulings that concerned gender equality. Similarly, the information booklet *Women in the European Union* issued by the Polish Information Center of the Governmental Committee of European Integration, contained many mistakes, half–truths, and misinformation (Teutsch 2000, 18).

Another obstacle seems to be the false conviction that mechanisms for the promotion of women were characteristic of the communist system and have been dismantled together with that system.[21] Men's fear of having to compete with and make room for women, should any mechanisms that would enable women to occupy high positions be introduced, is also a hindrance. However, one of the strongest barriers is the lack of political will to change the status quo, which is declared openly by right–wing parties, and which also is not, protests notwithstanding, alien to left–wing parties that are dominated by men.

Victory over all of these difficulties necessitates the continuation of actions that have already been started and the initiation of new ones, both by feminist activists and feminist theorists alike. These actions should operate based on a widespread pro–equality education of society, including the organization of informational and propaganda actions, the publishing of appropriate literature, as well as holding decision–makers politically responsible for their declared goals of initiating equality measures. Moreover, it is important that the intellectual movement that is centered on women's issues creates an atmosphere that will enable social change to take place. This intellectual movement can take such forms as the establishment of new women's studies programs and the publication of feminist literature. Finally, educational actions should also target politicians and although politicians will have to change their views about the importance of protecting women's rights, such a change can only occur through the actions and influence of women themselves.

Notes

[1]   For English summaries of Constitutional Court decisions, see Leszek Garlicki, *The Constitutional Court in Poland*, unpublished manuscript, 1995.

[2]   Orzeczenie Trybunału Konstytucyjnego z dnia 3 III 1987 (P.2/87), [Judgment of the Constitutional Tribunal, 3 March 1987 (P.2/87)]. Orzecznictwo Trybunału Konstytucyjnego [Case law of the Constitutional Tribunal].

[3]   Orzeczenie Trybunału Konstytucyjnego z 24 października 1989 r. (K.6/89), [Judgment of the Constitutional Tribunal, 24 October 1989, K.6/89].

[4]   Orzeczenie Trybunału Konstytucyjnego z 24 września 1991 (Kw.5/91), [Judgment of the Constitutional Tribunal 24 September 1991, Kw. 5/91].

[5]   Wystąpienie RPO do Marszałka *Sejm* z 13 VI 1994 – RPO/152826/94/III [Appeal of the Commissioner to the President of *Sejm* on 13 April 1994 – RPO/152826/94/III]. The similar provision, which made the earlier retirement of the father of a handicapped child dependant on whether he is the exclusive custody carrier of the child, has been declared unconstitutional by the Constitutional Tribinal. This provision discriminates against both women and men, because it does not leave the decision of who will take care of a handicapped child to members of the family concerned, rather it gives the father the role of subsidiary custody carrier even if he wishes to be primary. Judgment of the Constitutional Tribunal of 6 July (P.8/98), OTK ZU, no. 5 (27)99. The contents of the judgment have also been published in Dziennik Ustaw. *The Official Journal of the Republic of Poland* cited as: Dz.U. 1999, no. 61, item 679.

[6]   Compared with the motion of Commissioner to the Constitutional Tribunal of 15 the December 1992 RPO/109986/92/VI. The Constitutional Tribunal in its decision of 5 May 1993 (K.19/92) has discontinued the proceeding as a consequence of its entering into force as suggested by the Commissioner amendments.

[7]   The executive order of 10 September 1996. Dz. U. 1996, no. 114, item 545. This executive order substituted the previous regulation, which banned women from over 90 occupations, including those of bus and truck drivers, however it did not fully exclude the "protective" (in other words, discriminatory) approach to women's work (Nowakowska 2000, 45).

[8]   Compare with Paruszewska 2000, 36.

[9]   Compare with (K.15/97) OTK 1991 item 5. The issue of unequal retirement age of women and men has been raised in several judgments of the Constitutional Tribunal. Compare: Judgment of 29 September 1997, K 15/97 OTK 1997, item 37; Judgment of 24 October 1989, K.6/89 OTK 1989, item 7 Judgment of 6 July 1998, KP 8/98, OTK 1999, item 114; Judgment of 12 September 1999, K.1/100, OTK 2000, item 185; Judgment of 28 March 2000 K.27/99, OTK 2000, item 62; Judgment of 6 December 2000, K.35/99, OTK 2000, item 295.

[10] In a recent Judgment of 2000, the Constitutional Tribunal declared that the 1991 act on pharmaceutical devices and medical articles was unconstitutional, since it forbade women

who had already retired from occupying the post of the chief of pharmacy, though they had not reached the retirement age that was provided by law for men. Judgment of 13 June 2000, K. 15/99, OTK 2000, item, 137.

11 These provisions were added by the Act of 2 February 1996 on the amendment of the Act–Labor Code, in addition to other acts. Dz. U. 1996, no.24, item 110.

12 Dz. Act of 24 August 2001, Dz.U. 2001, no. 128, item 1405, according to which the equal treatment in the LC was expanded in a newly added Title IIa headed the "Equal treatment of men and women" was a more or less an exact transposition of the provisions of the EU Directives 75/117/EEC and 76/207/EEC. These provisions entered in force on 1 January 2002. Dz. U. 2003, no. 213, item 1081. Title IIa LC is currently headed "Equal treatment in employment" and was modified in such a way as to enable its application to instances of discrimination on several grounds other than sex. Compare: Labor Code unified text Dz.U. 1998, no. 21, item 94 as modified: Dz. U. 2002, no. 200, item 1679 and Dz.U. 2003, no. 213, item 2081.

13 Compare the Decision of the Constitutional Tribunal of 15 January 1991, Dz.U. 1991, no. 8, item 90; Decision of 7 October 1992, W 1/92, OTK 1992, item 38; Decision of 17 March 1993, W 16/92, OTK 1993, item 16. Decision of 28 May 1997, OTK ZU 1997, item 19.

14 Order of 30 April 1990, Dz.U. 1990, no. 29, item 178, already repealed.

15 Law of 7 January 1993, Dz.U. 1993, no. 78, item 78. In force from March 16, 1993.

16 OTK 1997, item. 19. The judgment has been published in Dz.U. on 23 December 1997 r. (Dz. U. 1997, no. 157, item 1040). With the publication of this Judgment, the provisions considered unconstitutional became invalid.

17 Act of 21 May 1999, which modified the act of 25 February 1964, the so–called Family Code, Dz.U. 1999, no. 52, item 532.

18 Dz.U.1997, no. 78, item 78. The Constitution entered into force on October 17, 1997.

19 See Art. 4 of the Convention. The Convention, hereafter referred to as the anti–discrimination convention, passed by the General Assembly of the United Nations on 18 December 1979, was passed by the People's Republic of Poland in 1980 and ratified in 1982 (Dz. U.1982, no.10, item 72). The Directives of the Council of the European Communities of 12 August 1986, as well as, for example, the recommendations of the Committee of the Council of Europe of 2 February 1985, stress the necessity of implementing state mechanisms that would lead to the enactment of appropriate "equality" laws.

20 In which the Tribunal ruled that the formulation of a regulation of the Brema District in Germany, that provided an affirmative provision that automatically gave priority for the advancement of a candidate from those having similar qualifications, if they belonged to an underrepresented group of sex (described as less than 50%), should be considered as exceeding the limits of a justified exception of the principle of gender equality (case C-450 from 17 October 1995).

21 It has been proved by public opinions polls on the basis of which it can be assumed that the word "quota" is likely to cause most Poles to react negatively out of instinct, without being opposed to the mechanism on reasonable grounds, since so many respondents, and particularly women, believe quotas to be an equitable way of counteracting discrimination.

References

Bator, Joanna. 1999. *Wizerunek kobiety w polskiej debacie politycznej. [The image of women in the Polish political debate].* Warsaw: Instytut Spraw Publicznych.

Braud, Philippe. 1991. *Le jardin des delices democratiques. [The garden of democratic pleasures].* Paris: Presses de la Foundation Nationale de Sciences Politiques.

Centrum Praw Kobiet. 1998. *Równość kobiet i mężczyzn w pracach nad konstytucją RP. [The equality between women and men in the elaborating the Constitution of the Republic of Poland].* Warsaw: Centrum Praw Kobiet.

Constitution of the Polish People's Republic [Dz.U]. 1997. Dz.U. 1997, no.78, item 483. Warsaw, Poland.

Council of Europe. 1997. Declaration and resolutions of the 4th European ministerial conference on equality between women and men. Istanbul: Council of Europe, *MEG* 4 (97):18

European Commission. 2000. Regular Report on Poland's Progress towards Accession. Brussels: European Commission.

Fuszara, Małgorzata. 1994. Rola kobiet w polityce w ich własnych opiniach i programach partii politycznych przed wyborami. [The role of the women in politics in their own opinions and in the political parties programmes before the 1993 elections]. *Bulletin of the Center for Europe* 1:45–60.

Fuszara, Małgorzata. 2001. Bilans na koniec wieku. [The balance at the end of the century]. *Katedra* 1:5–18.

Fuszara, Małgorzata. 2003a. Udział kobiet we władzy. [Women's participation in power]. In *Kobiety w Polsce 2003, [Women in Poland 2003]*, edited by Urszula Nowakowska. Warsaw: Centrum Praw Kobiet.

Fuszara, Małgorzata. 2003b. Równe szanse czy szklany sufit? Kobiety w samorządach lokalnych. [Equal chances or glass celling? Women in local self-governments]. In *Szklany sufit. Bariery i ograniczenia karier kobiet. [Glass ceiling. Barriers and limitations to women's careers].* Warsaw: Instytut Spraw Publicznych.

Fuszara, Małgorzata. 2004. Unpublished results of the research. Warsaw: University of Warsaw.

Fuszara, Małgorzata, and Eleonora Zielińska. 1994. Obstacles and barriers to an equal status act in Poland. *Bulletin of the Center for Europe* 1:14–26.

Fuszara, Małgorzata, and Eleonora Zielińska. 1998. Krótka acz zawiła historia ustawy równościowej. [Short but complicated history of the draft of the act on equal status]. *OŚKa Biuletyn* 4(5):12–15.

Garlicki, Leszek. 1995. Trybunał Konstytucyjny w Polsce. [The Constitutional Court in Poland]. Unpublished manuscript.

Kymlicka, Will. 1990. *Contemporary Political Philosophy. An Introduction.* Oxford: Oxford University Press.

Lacey, Nicola. 1994. Community, identity, and power: Some thoughts on women and the law in Central and Eastern Europe. *UCLA Women's Law Journal* 5:15–48.

Łętowska, Ewa. 1992. *Baba na świeczniku.* [The woman on top]. Warsaw: BGW.

Nowakowska, Urszula, ed. 2000. *Polish Women in the 90's.* Warsaw: Women's Rights Center.

Orzecznictwo Trybunału Konstytucyjnego [OTK, OTK ZU]. 1987–2003. [Case law of the Constitutional Tribunal]. Warsaw: Wyd. Trybunał Konstytucyjny.

OŚKa. 2001. Materialy IV ogólnopolskiej konferencji organizacji i srodowisk kobiecych: Polityka (przyszłego) rządu wobec kobiet. [The materials of the fourth nation-wide conference of women's organizations and communities – OŚKa: The politics of the government (future) towards women]. Warsaw: OŚKa, 13.

Parliamentary Print No. 3215. 2005 [cited 08/14/05]. Available from <www.sejm.gov.pl>.

Paruszewska, Wanda. 2000. Nowy system emerytalny – pułapka finansowa dla kobiet. [The new retirement system – the financial trap for women]. *Prawo i Płeć* 2:36.

Sadurski, Wojciech. 1988. Teoria sprawiedliwości. [The theory of justice]. In *Zagadnienia podstawowe, współczesne teorie polityczno prawne USA. [Basic issues, contemporary politico-legal theories in the USA]*, edited by J. Wróblewski. Warsaw, Państwowe Wydawnictwo Naukowe.

Siemieńska, Renata. 1996. *Kobiety: Nowe wyzwanie. [Women: The new challenge]*. Warsaw: Instytut Socjologii Uniwersytetu Warszawskiego.

Skard, Tortild, and Elina Haavio-Mannila. 1985. Mobilisation of women at elections. In *Unfinished democracy. Women in Nordic politics,* edited by Elina Haavio-Mannila et al. Oxford: Pergamon Press.

Teutsch, Agata. 2000. Program dezinformacji społeczeństwa na temat kobiet w Unii Europejskiej. [The program of disinformation of the society about women in the European Union]. *Kalendarium* 4:18.

Titkow, Anna. 1993. Political change in Poland: Cause, modifier, or barrier to gender equality? In *Gender Politics and Post-Communism*, edited by Nanette Funk and Magda Mueller. New York, London: Routledge.

Wadstein, Margareta. 1997. Evaluation of women's contribution to democracy in Nordic countries. Final Report of Activities, Group of Specialists on Equality and Democracy. Strasbourg: Council of Europe. EG (97)1.

Yuval-Davis, Nira. 1997. Women, citizenship, and difference. *Feminist Review* 57:17.

Zielińska, Eleonora. 1991. Głos do decyzji Trybunały Konstytucyjnego z 15. 01 1991. [Comment on the Decision of the Constitutional Tribunal (CT) of 01.15.1991]. *Państwo i Prawo* 7:112.

Zielińska, Eleonora. 2000. Between ideology, politics, and common sense: The discourse of reproductive rights in Poland. In *Reproducing gender: Politics, publics, and everyday life after socialism*, edited by Susan Gal and Gail Kligman. Princeton, NJ: Princeton University Press.

Chapter 3

Citizenship, Systemic Change, and the Gender Division of Labor in Rural Hungary

Salvatore A. Engel-Di Mauro

Studies from both liberal democratic to state–socialist contexts have demonstrated the debilitating effects of gendered social inequalities on women's ability to engage in the public sphere (among others, Benhabib 1992; Fraser 1995; Friedman 2005; Hegedűs 1971, 90; Heitlinger 1979; Kruks et al. 1989; Lapidus 1978; Lengyel, 1982; Lister 1990; MacKinnon 1989; Molyneux 1984; Mouffe 1992; Pateman 1990; Ryan 1995; Sas 1988; Wolchick and Meyer 1985; Young 1989). Feminist scholars have exposed the masculinist basis of conventional citizenship theory and practice, which is grounded on false dichotomies such as political (legal) and economic realms, public and private spheres, or formal (official) and informal (unofficial) domains (Ciechocinska 1993; Corrin 1994; Ferge 1996; Fodor 2004; Funk and Mueller 1993; Jalušič 2002; Jung 1994; Moghadam 1993; Shola Orloff 1993; Pascall and Lewis 2004; Phillips 1993; Regulska 1994; Szalai 1991). They have thereby challenged the (neo)liberal triumphalism pervading research on the systemic change of the late 1980s in Central and Eastern Europe [CEE].

Whereas a general consensus has emerged among feminist scholars regarding the gendered character of the systemic change, debate has unfolded over the causes of the current paucity of women's political involvement and representation in CEE. Some have interpreted the process of systemic change as further intensifying previous gender inequality (Adamik 1991; Einhorn 1993; Lister 1990; Weiner 1997). Others have pointed to residual cultural and political constraints from the past regime (for example, the solace of the private sphere against state encroachment), viewing the systemic change as a mixture of new gender–based political opportunities and constraints (Brunell 2002; Ferge 1996; Molyneux 1994; Szalai 1998; Tóth 1993). Still others have shown women's active, changing, and widespread participation in the public sphere that was missed by many other researchers, broadening the analytical framework to multiple scales of political activity (Caiazza 2002; Gal 1994; Graham and Regulska 1997; Regulska 1998). While illustrating important processes of systemic change in CEE ignored by mainstream studies, such a discussion has been too confined to the cultural and formal political aspects of citizenship practice. With few exceptions (see, for instance, Fodor 1994; Haney 1999; Regulska 1994), it has thereby largely elided the economic basis of political engagement, which is largely, but not solely, shaped by policy decisions made within state institutions (for example, eligibility conditions and extent of welfare provision). Furthermore, the gendered division of labor that underpins economic inequality has not been linked to the gendered aspects of political exclusion and the specificity of women's political involvement in CEE.

The importance of the gender division of labor lies in the fact that, as a structuring process, it can induce social inequalities through the differential allocation of economic wealth. It thereby effectively preempts long–term, effective participatory activity on the part of citizens lacking the means of political deliberation (for example, funding for publicity of political parties). Such a gendered process applies generally to both state–socialism and liberal democracy, where citizenship is defined through political struggles and state policies that promote both the differential distribution of rights and the consequential exclusion of some social groups as well as the reinforcement of male–dominated elite political power (Andersen and Siim 2004; Arber 1999; Elman 2001; Hagemann 2002; Lister 2002; McDaniel 2002; Wallerstein 2003).

Starting from this viewpoint, conventional notions of public participation, including those recently propounded by Habermas (1999), become superfluous because they ignore the very basis whereby effective participation is even rendered possible; that is, through economic means. This is not to say that such means are attained without political engagement. Economic relations are simultaneously political struggles related to the deployment of force. Economic aspects of citizenship are therefore of paramount importance in understanding the dearth of women's political participation or visibility. More direct coercion, such as sexual violence, is equally important, but will not be discussed here because it is outside the scope of this work (see Corrin 1996, 2005; Elman 2001; Mui and Murphy 2002).

In this chapter, I examine the historical developments in Hungary that contributed to multiple forms of gendered citizenship, specifically in rural areas, focusing on Southwest Hungary in order to exemplify more recent tendencies. Far from being static, these forms of citizenship vary according to shifting social processes within as well as outside state institutions and are enforced through economic means. Changes to gendered citizenship in rural areas are traced below through the analysis of successive regimes and gender divisions of labor beginning from the late 1940s to the late 1990s. During state–socialism, rural women engaged in formal economic sectors by seizing the changing opportunities available in a very constraining set of political arrangements, such as welfare provisions (for instance through motherhood), higher–paying service sector employment opportunities, and household plot production incomes. Following the systemic changes of the late 1980s, rural women's access to economic resources has markedly decreased. As shown through experiences, in Southwest Hungary, rural women have developed coping mechanisms and strategies, in part because of skills and employment experiences gained during the state–socialist period, to adjust to new demands imposed by a reconfigured andro-centric state (van der Lippe and Fodor 1998).

Land Reform and Reindustrialization: 1948–1956

Though characterized by greater state control of economic relations, the dictator-ship of the Rákosi–led Hungarian Workers' Party [HWP] is comparable to those of 1960s–1970s South America and southern Europe. However, employment and welfare policies mirrored or surpassed those of even contemporary liberal states. Large numbers of women entered paid employment for the first time, especially as manual farm workers, thereby attaining some independence from men. In addition to expanding women's political involvement (for example, voting, campaigning), legal provisions were introduced that altered the basis of male privilege. The Family Law granted equal rights in marriage and facilitated divorce, a potential escape from op-pressive family relations. The role of land ownership as a principal source of (male) power and class differentiation was nearly eradicated through land reforms, signal-ing an end to the domination of landed proprietors and propertied clergy over land-less workers and smallholder-peasants. The private property basis of citizenship, mostly a male privilege, was succeeded by one largely based on state employment and party affiliation (Berend 1990; Corrin 1994; Fodor 2004; Gal 1994; Jaquette and Wolchik 1998; Moghadam 1993).

Nevertheless, masculinism was evident in the redistribution of political power. Soon after the systemic change of 1948, the Magyar Nők Országos Tanács [National Council of Hungarian Women] was transmogrified into a perfunctory organ with few decision–making powers (Adamik 1993; Kürti 1991). The period of postwar re-industrialization was based, moreover, on a gendered re–organization of rural labor and land redistribution aimed at controlling and extracting surplus from agriculture to develop an industrial military complex. Economic policies resulted in the develop-ment of a mostly male managerial class, who directed newly formed co–operatives and state farms and whose status was attained through political allegiance. Though more women were officially employed, the work of women, as well as of men that lost their social position, was under the scrutiny and monopoly of the new members of the upper hierarchy, from HWP secretaries to brigade leaders, in a reshuffled se-quence of levels of domination. The governing effectiveness of the male–dominated state's central organs thereby attained at least some popular legitimization, enlisting support of most men and many, especially rural, women by leaving certain patriar-chal ideals of home and family unscathed (Bell 1984; Swain 1985; Völgyes 1980). As actual practices testify, women, consequently, could partake of the public sphere more directly, but largely in a subordinate role.

In 1953, the government granted small land allotments for subsistence and cash crop production by assigning household plots on a family basis. To procure higher salaries, rural families responded by sending most rural young and middle–aged men to factories as commuters, whereas women and the elderly mostly remained in the countryside as agricultural workers, whose co–operative membership secured access to a household plot. Thus, government policy stimulated the emergence of "worker–peasant" households, which increased throughout the late 1950s and 1970s (Swain 1985, 1992). This new basis of rural economic differentiation was essentially a shift in the gendered segregation of labor, whose results were region–specific. In some villages, traditionally "masculine" tasks, such as tending the household plots, vineyards, orchards, and/or gardens, became "feminine" (Huseby–Darvas 1987).

More generally, most rural households survived on women and the elderly's subsistence production and care and reproductive work, which were neither remunerated nor well supported by the state (six weeks of maternity leave with 75 percent of the salary, breast–feeding allowance of one hour per day). The paucity of childcare facilities and welfare provisions, combined with an absence of measures against the unequal sharing of household labor, ensured that women's options would be so confined as to hinder their ability to become more engaged in official politics (Corrin 1994; Hoffman 1982; Lengyel 1982; Sas 1976). The state–socialist road to women's emancipation reinforced, albeit differently, the previous bourgeois system's confinement of housework and social reproduction within the private sphere (Bollobás 1993; Landes 1989).

Greater informal work burdens often impinged on women's abilities to fulfill workplace tasks, thereby contributing to the construction of women as "unreliable" workers (Szalai 1991). However, with the industrialization drive beleaguered by a labor shortage and "Cold War" pressures to increase production, the government required the injection of large amounts of workers. This was accomplished through the uneven integration of women's work into the official economy and the deployment of a political discourse of women's emancipation (although women's workforce participation was not new, especially for lower-class women and girls) (Tóth 1993, 218).

At great savings to state coffers, state enterprises (but also co–operatives) offered paid work to formerly unemployed, primarily rural, women for lower wages relative to men in the same employment category, classifying such women as "semi–skilled" or "unskilled". In the countryside, the mostly female manual farm workers, who received no social benefits, received similarly lower salaries than the mostly male "skilled" farm workers (Corrin 1994; Swain 1985; Völgyes 1980).

In this manner, the androcentric state resolved the "woman question" with the nearly full employment of women. Ignoring job type, income level, and unpaid work, among other processes, served the expansion of industrial productivity while maintaining male privilege.[1] Nevertheless, there was one aspect of women's unpaid reproductive work, giving birth, that gained the attention of the HWP. The state's increasing demand for workers created a need for greater demographic control, which was attempted through the pro–natalist criminalization of abortion (Gal 1994). In other words, unpaid work and public–private dichotomies respectively acquired official relevance and irrelevance only when serving the economic ends of a male–dominated elite. In this case, most women's bodies were to be used to resolve the ironic economic contradictions created by ruling-class men, whose economic privileges defined the state's limits with respect to women's emancipation.

The unevenness of household work distribution and the treatment of reproduction issues betrayed the HWP's androcentric strategies. Various state and enterprise measures ensured the restratification of society according to the new principles of bureaucratic status within the HWP. Masculinity was thereby partly founded upon positioning within Soviet imperial rule through the HWP, and partly, especially in the countryside, within the matrix of previous landholding class differentiation. While, in general, the new source of power became HWP affiliation, in the countryside, the prestige accompanying male proprietor status and farming experience was an occasional source of additional privileges, especially through surviving private family holdings (Bell 1984; Hann 1980; Lampland 1995; Swain 1985). The reorganization of labor under this initial impetus of change succeeded more in extending the duration of daily work for many more women than in emancipating anyone. The policy of gender equality not only remained as superficial as in liberal democracies, but also differentiated women according to class.

Insurrection and Reconsolidation: 1956–1968

The coercive state–socialist system did not succeed in achieving political stability. Tensions resulting from the Rákosi regime's violence erupted with the 1956 uprisings, which the Red Army and the national military suppressed swiftly, leading to leadership change and the incarceration or execution of rebels.[2] In the aftermath, Soviet imperial rule and policies were reaffirmed and draconian political measures were introduced during the first post–insurrection years, though appeasement policies followed through the gradual extension of economic concessions to both industrial and agricultural workers (Berend 1996, 116–126; Hann 1990; Swain 1992). Following a reconsolidation of power and economic reform by the newly–named Hungarian Socialist Workers' Party [HSWP], a new technocratic and managerial class gradually emerged which began contesting party control over the labor force (Swain 1985). A competing masculinity therein arose, based on technocratic status within a hierarchy centered on enterprise management (Asztalos Morell 1999; Fodor 2004).

Between 1959 and 1961, most of the remaining private holdings were absorbed into co–operatives. The "collectivization" campaign achieved widespread success owing to the financial incentives and economic subsidies that were offered to co–operative members. The introduction of pensions also may have motivated people to become members. Moreover, the formerly repressed middle peasantry could finally join co–operatives and even become elected to high posts (Swain 1985).

As farming re–acquired national importance, partly due to a reconfigured Council of Mutual Economic Aid strategy, women's labor came to be gradually excluded from the increasingly remunerative aspects of agricultural labor. This is represented in the continued classification of the majority of women workers as "unskilled" or "semi–skilled," receiving salaries mostly based on in–kind and work–units and mostly within a sharecropping system. Spaces of labor became differentiated according to technocratic principles, where mechanized spaces of work were centers of wealth production, largely the province of "skilled" male proletarians and managers (Berend 1996; Corrin 1994; Répássy 1991; Szalai 1991).

This spatial division of labor could not have been created, however, without the reconfiguration of household production relative to paid work. The extension of social benefits to the countryside increasingly redirected women's and lower–class men's labor to spaces of work near their household, in the case of the "worker–peasant" class (Andorka and Harcsa 1983; Huszár 1974). Women who were married to wealthier male workers worked mostly in or near the household for most of the workday, although the minority of such women that actually partook of industrial jobs were under the control of a mostly male managerial system (Bell 1984; Lengyel 1982).

Wages and benefits for farm workers remained generally lower than for those in the industrial and service sectors. By 1962, 74 percent of the total rural population was officially below the poverty line and 70 percent of those rural poor were divided equally between manual and "semi–skilled" worker households. Meanwhile, agricultural labor continued to decline from 37.7 percent in 1960 to 27.4 percent in 1965 (Corrin 1994). By 1966, farm workers still received only 77.2 percent of industrial workers' wages and benefits combined. As a result of the disparities produced by government and enterprise, women began to join the increasing mass of commuters traveling to industrial centers (although they were still in the minority). Households then came to rely increasingly on incomes generated through household plot production, which greatly depended on the unpaid manual work of women (Lengyel 1982; Sas 1976; Swain 1985).

During the late 1950s and early 1960s central planners became increasingly preoccupied with resolving the problem of labor surplus that was created by the intersection of mechanization, unfavorable world market conjunctures, and demographic trends (Berend 1990; US Census Bureau 2005). Coincidentally, abortion was gradually decriminalized and eventually permitted almost on demand (Gal 1994; Haney 1999). Several policy measures coincided with this new problem which effectively, if not intentionally, pressured households to modify their internal organization of labor without altering their basic structure. The industrialization drive was increasingly attracting and incorporating so many workers as to render childcare logistically impossible for many, especially in urban centers. More state funds were subsequently invested in childcare facilities, but maintaining women within an in–kind and work–unit system of remuneration or providing economic incentives for women to withdraw from wage labor eventually proved a less expensive alternative to the construction and maintenance of childcare facilities, especially in rural areas (Szalai 1991).

Most economists legitimized such reprioritization by citing figures portraying women's employment rate as too "unstable." Women workers' average of 40–50 percent of work time directed at caring for children at home was regarded as disruptive to the production process, rather than intrinsically use–value producing labor. In 1967, the government introduced a Child Care Grant that provided a flat–rate benefit aimed at helping women remain at home beyond the customary five months of paid maternity leave. The grant would last until the child reached 30 months of age and re–employment was assured to the same job, and was contingent upon a one–year minimum term of employment prior to the time at which the grant would be received (Gal 1994; Haney 1999).

Irrespective of such provisions, agricultural households (except worker–peasants) were largely isolated from such developments and the women and elderly who remained adjacent to the household, as in prior decades, still primarily provided the necessary reproductive work. The seasonality of sharecropping work facilitated and reinforced this household division of labor. Paid leave due to illness, paid at 50–75 percent of yearly income, was introduced for agricultural workers. Maternity leave was extended to 20 weeks with full pay, provided 120 work days had been completed during the previous year. The highly seasonal nature of women agricultural workers' employment posed serious obstacles to the fulfillment of this requirement and reinforced susceptibility to male and, rarely, female managerial manipulation (by 1960, women comprised 3 percent of co–operative farm directors and 2 percent of technocrats). That is, control over labor continued in a modified form as a gender– and class–based process (Andorka and Harcsa 1983; Bell 1984; Corrin 1994, 60; Fodor 2004; Hann 1980; Swain 1985). The androcentric state's reorganization of the division of labor created the conditions for new social contradictions and simultaneously reformulated class and gender distinctions that curtailed most women's public sphere participation through the workplace.

Economic Downturns, Reform, and Gendered Systemic Change: 1968–1989

Market–oriented farming had been male–dominated prior to state–socialism, but it became even more so with the introduction of the New Economic Mechanism [NEM] of 1968, which sought to enhance export revenues through a gradual privatization and decentralization of production. Increasingly larger household plots, where profitable labor–intensive crops began to be cultivated, were granted to co–operative farm members. From the mid 1970s to the late 1980s, market–oriented household plot production contributed to 30 percent of total agricultural exports, provided one–third of total agricultural output, and generated more than half of the income of most households, thereby providing the androcentric state with savings on wages (Lengyel 1982; Swain 1985).

These political changes and economic results rested on a gendered re–division of labor. The labor surplus crisis created through the displacement of mostly women's manual farm work by mostly men's machine–aided labor was alleviated by introducing textile and food processing industries in the countryside and providing welfare and regularized wages and benefits to farm workers. Such policies reduced the delegitimizing pressures of unemployment, while increasing output and maintaining upper-class male privileges.

As the total amount of agricultural employment declined after mechanization, displaced rural women increasingly found jobs in the textile and food processing industries as well as in the service sector (Répássy 1991). These workplaces tended to be close to home, so that employment did not interfere with women's fulfillment of unpaid tasks, such as subsistence plot production. Maternity leave and pension programs further created incentives for many rural women and the elderly to remain home (Corrin 1994; Lengyel 1982). In contrast, the 1976 introduction of regularized hourly wages and benefits for household plot production induced more men to work on private parcels for profit. Whereas in 1963 household plots involved both (elderly, lower-class) men and women largely sharing the work, by the late 1970s men began to predominate (Asztalos Morell 1999, 71; Sas 1976, 63; Swain 1985, 78). Yet, women devoted much more work time to household plots in the 1970s and 1980s, especially as officially "inactive" manual workers (Swain 1985, 94–95; Tóth 1993; Vásáry 1987). These processes reinforced men's monopoly of agricultural resources and the lucrative aspects of farming. Men availed themselves of state incentives to bolster their incomes and economic status through business partnerships, while women mainly partook of the same system of incentives through the subordinate role of underpaid manual laborer and mother (Hoffman 1982; Répássy 1991; Sas 1976, 63).

The 1980s featured recurring economic problems connected to global market fluctuations, as Hungary became increasingly integrated and indebted within the sphere of core liberal states (Berend 1996). Paradoxically, the same period was marked by the most generous welfare system in the world. A large number of benefits and welfare provisions were also extended to all women. The provision of these benefits allowed for the further expansion of production in the informal semi–private sector, which was dominated by men since the 1970s. Social benefits also reduced reliance on subsistence, especially for women, during times of crisis or household labor shortages (Moghadam 1996; Vásáry 1987). Women's employment reached 75 percent by 1988, yet wages remained uneven, with higher gender–based wage discrepancies in the countryside (Corrin 1994; Fong and Paull 1993, 219). The bulk of social reproduction continued to be performed by women, in spite of parental leave being extended to men during the last years of state–socialism (Sas 1988; Moghadam1993).

Gender–based employment and educational segregation resulted in a higher proportion of women in the service sector in "low" to "semi–skilled" job categories. Occupational segregation characterized nearly every economic sector where men and women both worked. The state intervened more directly at times in order to segregate the workforce based on gender. For instance, coal mining and similarly dangerous activities were officially proscribed. In agriculture, younger women tended to be employed more frequently as office clerks and older women occupied jobs that mostly involved manual labor. Men, in contrast, predominated in the use and repair of machinery in spite of the large percentage of trained machinists among women workers. Income differentials reached their maximum in the higher "skilled" jobs within the same economic sector (up to 50 percent of men's wages), while lower–ranked employment positions were more even (80–85 percent) but were disproportionately occupied by women (Asztalos Morell 1999; Corrin 1992, 1994; Fodor 2004; Gal 1994; Heitlinger 1979; Landes 1989; Moghadam 1996; Wolchik 1998).

The changing basis of masculinism in rural areas was linked to political struggles at all social levels. Male privilege was initially derived from HSWP connections but, by the 1970s, the importance of party connection competed with the authority acquired through technocratic expertise and managerial position, especially in agriculture. State incentives facilitated the extension of power to highly trained workers and managers who were unaffiliated with the Party, but who were nevertheless regarded as crucial to the effective deployment of economic reforms (Böröcz 1992; Fodor 2004; Swain 1992). Hence, more unaffiliated technocrats, including a minority of rural women, began to occupy managerial positions at co–operative farms and other economic institutions, extensively dominated by male directorship and management (Corrin 1994, 60; Swain 1985).

State–socialist policies mollified some forms of gender inequality, while reinforcing others. Patriarchal agendas persisted throughout the state–socialist period. No policies ever aimed at reducing the unequal share of housework or the salary discrepancies between men and women engaged in similar jobs. Many patriarchal practices established prior to and during state–socialism established the basis for the continuation of patriarchal relations after the systemic change of the late 1980s.

From One Androcentric System to Another: 1989–2000

Throughout the formerly state–socialist CEE, gender relations and economic inequalities, in general, now approach the conditions existing in industrialized capitalist core countries. Gendered economic differentiation developed under state–socialism, especially since the 1980s, has intensified thanks to state intervention. Legal reforms and economic policies have contributed to the rapid dismantling of welfare and legislation that promoted some degree of women's economic independence. The disappearance of welfare resources such as childcare grants has been followed by an increase in women's household work and a larger overall increase in women's unemployment relative to men. Other legal reforms patterned on liberal norms have resulted in a sharp decrease in women's formal political representation at the national scale, while the reduction of protective laws and/or adequate enforcement relates to the emergence of trade in women (Corrin 2005; Einhorn 1993; Jaquette and Wolchik 1998; Moghadam 1993; Molyneux 1984; Regulska 1998).

In Hungary, the welfare system was diminished in 1995 through the Socialist Horn government (1994–1998), under the pressure of the International Monetary Fund. The reforms included the reduction of previous grants for child rearing, the introduction of income testing, and the reduction of maternity leave from three years to 24 weeks. Adding to the gendered character of the new policies, guarantees of re–employment have been scrapped, as they are deemed to hamper the free market. On the other hand, special subsidies related to enterprise and land privatization have been introduced, which benefit the new, mostly male, owners (Fodor 1994, 182; Haney 1999; Makkai 1994; Róna–Tas 1994; Tárkányi 1998).

In terms of employment rates, Hungary, along with Slovenia, constitute exceptions in that, in numerical terms, unemployment discrepancies have actually favored women. Nevertheless, women's relative economic advantage has occurred only through the tertiary sector, where women found more employment possibilities during the latter part of the state–socialist period. In contrast, women working in other economic sectors have been disproportionately affected by layoffs, especially in rural areas. The countryside has been affected more severely by the rapid economic downturn of the 1990s as a result of the restructuring and privatization of a previously successful agricultural sector (exemplified by the process of increasing production prices accompanied by subsidy reduction and market contraction). Land redistribution presently occurs through compensation, direct purchase by a citizen, and quasi–legal contracts with non–citizens. Official land distribution policies grant vouchers to those who owned or who have inheritance rights for land that was confiscated in 1948 (Kovách 1998). Land privatization and the reshuffling of managerial positions have mostly benefited men in terms of ownership and control over farmland and enterprises. Farming women remain poorer and more frequently unemployed in relation to male farmers. Women mainly work as manual farm laborers when older and as low–level office workers when younger. While disappearing from most large–scale agriculture, women farmers have continued to be involved in the retail aspects of agriculture and the running of subsistence plots (Corrin 1994; Répássy 1991; Szent–Györgyi 1993; van der Graaf 1996).

Regional Aspects of Systemic Change

Time–apportionment data from 40 semi–structured interviews conducted in an area of Southwest Hungary (the Ormánság) in the years 1998–1999 also revealed a continuity with past production relations (Engel-Di Mauro 2002). Women contributed the most to housework, care work (for example, tending to the sick), and subsistence agriculture, especially when unemployed, and received less overall wages. The unequal gender division of labor mirrors the uneven distribution of basic farming resources. According to a 1995 survey by the Ormánság Development Association, 24 out of 187 landowners were women. The pattern follows the pyramidal divisions of the early twentieth century, which featured a majority of lower-status peasants owning the bulk of small parcels. Relative to the land distribution among men, there is a larger fraction of women owners possessing less than 20 hectares of land. As I have found through the interviewing process, land titles are occasionally shared, but what is produced and marketed on such shared land is most frequently a male prerogative. As witnessed below, however, a few exceptional circumstances do exist.

The questions of land ownership, employment status, and household production combine with technical expertise to exert further divergence among rural women's abilities to engage in the public sphere. This more nuanced process is well illustrated by the representative experiences of three women, Katalin, Virág, and Linda, which depict the current differentiations of Ormánság women as either marginalized, integrated, and/or advantaged.

Katalin obtained a university degree in law and became engaged in local politics early in her career, while raising two children, the oldest of whom commutes to a Gimnázium [Liceum] in a large nearby city. She still contributes the most to daily housework, though her husband, a local co–operative's agricultural engineer, retired in the early 1990s. Through her spouse, Katalin was well connected to the local prominent managerial class of the 1980s. In spite of her husband's disapproval (which continues to this day), in 1985 she successfully campaigned for the local council leadership and had an influential role in major decision–making processes related to the development of the area around her village. Throughout the systemic change, Katalin continued her prominent political role as mayor. The relative wealth and political clout attained by the family during state–socialism means that she can afford to purchase labor–saving technologies and processed foods, as well as provide various services for her son's and daughter's benefit. Part of what otherwise would be her house and carework time can be thereby freed for political involvement and fund–raising for the association of local mayors and businesspeople she co–founded in 1991. Katalin's connections and successful career, however, have not aided her beyond local politics. In 1998, unable to gain support for her rural development agenda among the main national parties, she ran as an independent candidate for parliament. Unlike other party–supported candidates, who were mostly men, she primarily supported her campaign out of her personal funds. Without staff, much of her campaigning consisted of visiting nearly every village and town in the electoral district just to publicize the fact that she was running. She was unable to pass the first electoral round and regained her position as mayor instead. Her experience of the systemic change, nevertheless, was one of continued prosperity with her consolidation and expansion of her local political influence.

Virág, in contrast, has never sought office but participates in male–dominated farming–related meetings and business expositions. Having lost her father early, Virág's mother, who ran the small private plot that the family obtained through NEM allowances, served both as a role model and as a teacher. Virág thereby developed many farming and business skills, unusual for most women in the area.

Consequently, even though she performs most household chores and subsistence work, she also runs the farm business. Despite the fact that she only received a formal education up to middle school, she was able to informally attain this technical expertise. Virág's career prospects are thereby confined to the status of self–employed, small–scale farmer. The increasing difficulty of maintaining financial stability has already prompted her to seek continuing education courses in word processing offered locally.

Her unemployed husband often cares for their two children and does manual labor on the subsistence plot. He became unemployed as soon as the local co–operative, where he worked as bookkeeper, collapsed in 1997. He receives minimal welfare and occasionally finds temporary employment. Having primogeniture and no male siblings, Virág was able to claim land confiscated from her grandparents in 1948, according to the Compensation Act of 1991. She also inherited pigs and chickens from her extended family, which she uses for both subsistence and market sale. Her vast and pre–existing farming skills allow her to avoid many of the problems facing local farmers, such as dealing effectively with pricing, marketing produce, handling finances, and making contracts. The large, though discontinuous, landholdings that both she and her husband were able to obtain have allowed Virág to diversify her crops to meet the challenge of price oscillations, to derive rent from unused land, and to rely on a subsistence plot to save on groceries. Overall, Virág has benefited from the systemic change and has inserted herself successfully within the new system despite a generally opprobrious economic situation. Unlike Katalin, she has little political influence and she does not express interest in formal politics, in which her participation would be impeded by her lack of rhetorical skills. Her time, moreover, is so completely absorbed by housework and farming that she would have no time to engage in formal politics even if she were to become interested.

Linda's situation reflects the experiences of most rural women in the area. With two children, at first she was involved in farming with her parents and husband until her husband found employment in the local metal processing factory as a metal engineer. After moving to a nearby village in the 1980s, she was able to gain employment as a seamstress in the local co–operative's textile–manufacturing division. Linda engages in all household chores, carework, and subsistence plot production. The plot ceased to be used (her husband never contributed to its maintenance) when it became logistically unfeasible for her, in part because of the new textile plant job she found in 1998.

The systemic change brought much poverty to the family especially when Linda's husband lost his job in 1991 because of the metalworks' bankruptcy. Since then, he has had tremendous difficulty in finding employment and has become a (thankfully non-violent) alcoholic. Though working tenuously at a local non–profit organization, he no longer provides the majority of the family's income. Linda's previous economic dependence on her spouse turned into dependence on her new precarious and low–paying job at the recently re–opened textile factory. The textile company is part of an outsourcing network primarily used by European Union [EU] companies that works through the establishment of short–term production contracts. The working conditions are similar to those of sweatshops, with one ten–minute break given during the ten consecutive hours of production, accompanied by sometimes sweltering heat, crowding, poor ventilation, and exposure to noxious chemicals. All workers are women, whereas the management is comprised mostly of men. Production proceeds intensely until the quota is reached, then Linda and her co–workers are sent home until a new contract is established. The interim period can last more than a week, and even when there is work it is sometimes halted when safety inspectors visit the factory. These become anxious times for Linda, especially if they are protracted for more than a couple of days, as the ability to afford the rising prices for basic utility services, rent, and daily expenses increasingly becomes uncertain. For Linda and the majority of women living in Southwest Hungary, political involvement is a mirage, while their engagement in the public sphere of paid work has become precarious and is potentially deleterious to their health.

Conclusion

The findings discussed above demonstrate that a context–specific scrutiny of economic processes involving multiple scales can more meaningfully address the existing problem of citizenship. Under state–socialism, women's early integration into wage labor, norms purporting to foster gender equality, and the gradual development of the world's most encompassing welfare system substantially altered gender relations insofar as the sources of power and modes of control oscillated within shifting dominant masculinities. Yet, economic citizenship (for example, access to the public sphere of official employment), though shifting spatio–temporally, remained unequal. There was neither any radical alteration of gender–based inequalities nor a necessary reduction in class differentiation among women or in society, as the primacy of upper–class male privilege (differentially constituted through space and time) pervaded state–socialist institutions. Though ignored in this article, the question of race has also acted to differentiate rural women economically, with Rom largely excluded from wealth accumulation throughout succeeding state–socialist regimes. This marginalization continues unabated and needs to be considered in any future analysis of citizenship (see also Stewart 1997).

The androcentric character of state–socialist policies and wider societal responses led to particular forms of rural women's status differentiation, exemplified by the gender relations of production associated with agricultural and worker–peasant households and the unequal distribution of social rights. Basic welfare benefits were introduced later and more gradually to farm workers than proletarians and they had the ironic effect of increasing work in the household plot for many rural women. On the other hand, the eventual extension of maternal benefits to farm workers dichotomized rural women according to their procreative status as mothers and non–mothers, thereby creating additional parameters of economic differentiation among women.

The late 1980s systemic change has intensified economic inequalities previously dividing rural women, with class playing an even more prominent role. Unemployment, rather than underemployment, and the degree and spatial extent of land control, rather than co–operative management position, form the new gender– and class–based sources of economic differentiation. These new sources complement and exacerbate pre–existing inequalities based on skill and education level (for example, technical expertise) and the uneven distribution of housework and other socially reproductive labor.

Examining gendered economic inequalities based on shifting divisions of labor exposes the complexity of past and current gendered asymmetries of political representation. Rural gender relations in Hungary demonstrate that women's social rights were differentiated by successive legislative practices and economic policies through a series of androcentric state–socialist and now bourgeois political regimes. In terms of citizenship status differentiation, these state activities were and are still guided by non–public, non–deliberative practices that occur through the division of labor at both the workplace and the household.

As indicated in other studies, the unequal division of labor directly impinges on the time one has to partake in official politics. "Poverty and gender, lack of money and lack of time, thus combine to curtail the exercise of the political rights of citizenship" (Lister 1990, 458). The increasing amount of time devoted to household plots, for example, detracted from pre–existing unevenness and limitations in time–apportionment, though it simultaneously provided an opportunity to improve access to resources through the higher incomes it generated (Asztalos Morell, 1999; Lengyel 1982; Répássy 1991; Sas 1976). The current erosion of economic stability for rural women exacerbates class differences created through the previous regime and further weakens their overall citizenship status. Gender–based economic inequality especially constrains poorer rural women in the realm of official political participation at all scales, especially at the even less accountable EU level (Bieler and Morton 2001; Bonefeld 2001; Carchedi 2001; McGiffen 2001). Such weakened political status curtails the possibility of partaking in deliberative processes on issues such as workplace discrimination and equal access to farming infrastructure or campaign funds, thus allowing the further development, entrenchment, and/or proliferation of even more intensively gender– and class–biased practices that are intrinsic to capitalism.

Notes

[1] For instance, a 'man question' on the uneven distribution of labor tasks and workplace segregation never arose.

[2] Mainstream accounts have minimized, if not ignored women's roles as fighters, nurses, and agitators and the importance of many rebels' socialist inspiration (Anderson 1964; Bollobás 1993; Jung 1994).

References

Adamik, Mária. 1991. Hungary: a loss of rights? *Feminist Review* 39:166–170.

Adamik, Mária. 1993. Feminism and Hungary. In *Gender politics and post—communism. Reflections from Eastern Europe and the Former Soviet Union,* edited by N. Funk and M. Mueller. New York: Routledge.

Andersen, John, and Birte Siim, eds. 2004. *The politics of inclusion and empowerment: gender, class, and citizenship.* New York: Palgrave.

Anderson, Andy. 1964. *Hungary '56.* London: Phoenix Press.

Andorka, Rudolf, and István Harcsa. 1983. Changes in the village society during the last ten years. *The New Hungarian Quarterly* 24 (92):30–44.

Arber, Sara. 1999. Gender inequalities in European societies today. In *European societies. Fusion or fission?*, edited by Thomas P. Boje, Bart van Steenbergen, and Sylvia Walby. London: Routledge.

Asztalos Morell, Ildikó. 1999. Emancipation's dead–end road? Studies in the formation and development of the Hungarian model for agriculture and gender (1956–1989). *Acta Universitatis Uppsaliensis, Studia Sociologica Uppsaliensia,* 46 Stockholm: Elanders Gotab.

Bell, Peter D. 1984. *Peasants in socialist transition: life in a collectivized Hungarian village.* Berkeley: University of California Press.

Benhabib, Seyla. 1992. Models of public space: Hannah Arendt, the Liberal Tradition, and Jürgen Habermas', in *Situating the Self: Gender, Community and Postmodernism in Contemporary Ethics,* edited by Seyla Benhabib. New York: Routledge.

Berend, István T. 1990. *The Hungarian economic reforms 1953–1988.* Cambridge: Cambridge University Press.

Berend, István T. 1996. *Central and Eastern Europe, 1944–1993. Detour from the periphery to the periphery.* Cambridge: Cambridge University Press.

Bieler, Andreas, and Adam D. Morton, eds. 2001. *Social forces in the making of the new Europe. The restructuring of European social relations in the global political economy.* New York: Palgrave.

Bollobás, Enikő. 1993. Totalitarian "lib": The legacy of communism for Hungarian women. In *Gender Politics and Post–Communism. Reflections from Eastern Europe and the Former Soviet Union,* edited by N. Funk and M. Mueller. New York: Routledge.

Bonefeld, Werner. 2002. ed. *The politics of Europe. Monetary union and class.* New York: Palgrave.

Böröcz, József. 1992. Dual dependency and property vacuum. Social change on the state socialist semiperiphery. *Theory and Society* 21:77–104.

Brunell, Laura. 2002. Cinderella seeks shelter: will the state, church, or civil society provide? *East European Politics and Societies* 16 (2):465–493.

Caiazza, Amy B. 2002. *Mothers and soldiers: gender, citizenship, and civil society in contemporary Russia.* London: Routledge.

Carchedi, Guglielmo. 2001. *For another Europe.* New York: Verso.

Ciechocinska, Maria. 1993. Gender aspects of dismantling a command economy in Eastern Europe: The case of Poland. In *Democratic Reform and the Position of Women in Transitional Economics,* edited by Valentine M. Moghadam. Oxford: Clarendon Press.

Corrin, Chris. 1992. *Superwomen and the double burden. Women's experience of change in Central and Eastern Europe and the Former Soviet Union.* Toronto: Second Story Press.

Corrin, Chris. 1994. *Magyar women. Hungarian women's lives, 1960s–1990s.* New York: St. Martin's Press.

Corrin, Chris. 1996. *Women in a violent world. Feminist analyses and resistance across "Europe".* Edinburgh: Edinburgh University Press.

Corrin, Chris. 2005. Transitional road for traffic. Analysing trafficking in women from and through central and eastern Europe. *Europe-Asia Studies* 57(4):543–561.

Einhorn, Barbara. 1993. *Cinderella goes to market: Citizenship, gender, and women's movement in East Central Europe.* London: Verso.

Elman, R. Amy. 2001. Testing the limits of European citizenship: ethnic hatred and male violence. *NWSA Journal* 13 (3):49–60.

Engel-Di Mauro, Salvatore. 2002. The gendered limits to local soil knowledge: macronutrient content, soil reaction, and gendered soil management in SW Hungary. *Geoderma* 111 (3–4):503–520.

Ferge, Zsúzsa. 1996. Social citizenship in the new democracies. The difficulties in reviving citizens' rights in Hungary. *International Journal of Urban and Regional Research* 20 (1):99–115.

Fodor, Éva. 1994. The political woman? Women in politics in Hungary. In *Women in the politics of postcommunist Eastern Europe*, edited by M. Rueschemeyer. London: M.E. Sharpe.

Fodor, Éva. 2004. The state socialist emancipation project: Gender inequality in workplace authority in Hungary and Austria. *Signs* 29 (3):1–32.

Fong, Monica, and Gillian Paull. 1993. Women's economic status in the restructuring of Eastern Europe. In *Democratic reform and the position of women in transitional economics*, edited by Valentine M. Moghadam. Oxford: Clarendon Press.

Fraser, Nancy. 1995. Rethinking the public sphere: a contribution to the critique of actually existing democracy. In *Habermas and the Public Sphere*, edited by Craig Calhoun. Cambridge: The MIT Press.

Friedman, Marilyn, ed. 2005. *Women and citizenship.* Oxford: Oxford University Press.

Funk, Nanette, and Magda Mueller, eds. 1993. *Gender Politics and Post–Communism: Reflections from Eastern Europe and the Former Soviet Union.* London: Routledge.

Gal, Susan. 1994. Gender in the post–socialist transition: The abortion debate in Hungary. *East European Politics and Societies* 8 (2):256–286.

Graham, Ann, and Joanna Regulska. 1997. Expanding political space for women in Poland. *Communist and Post–Communist Studies* 30 (1):65–83.

Habermas, Jürgen. 1999. *The inclusion of the other. Studies in political theory.* Cambridge: The MIT Press.

Hagemann, Gro. 2002. *Citizenship* and social order: Gender politics in twentieth–century Norway and Sweden. *Women's History Review* 11 (3):417–429.

Haney, Linda. 1999. But we are still mothers: Gender, the state, and the construction of need in postsocialist Hungary. In *Uncertain Transition. Ethnographies of Change in the Postsocialist World*, edited by Michael Burawoy and Katherine Verdery. Lanham: Rowman and Littlefield Publishers.

Hann, Chris M. 1980. *Tázlár: A village in Hungary.* Cambridge: Cambridge University Press.

Hann, Chris M. 1990. *Market economy and civil society in Hungary.* London: Frank Cass.

Hegedűs, András. 1971. *A szocialista társadalom struktúrájáról. [On the structure of socialist society]*. Budapest: Akadémiai Kiadó.

Heitlinger, Alena. 1979. *Women and state socialism: Sex inequalities in the Soviet Union and Czechoslovakia*. Montréal: McGill–Queen's University Press.

Hoffman, Istvánné. 1982. *Háztartás–közgazdaságtan. [Home economics]*. Budapest: Kossuth Könyvkiadó.

Huseby–Darvas, Éva V. 1987. Elderly women in a Hungarian village: Childlessness, generativity, and social control. *Journal of Cross–Cultural Gerontology* 2:15–42.

Huszár, István. 1974. The worker–peasant alliance. *The New Hungarian Quarterly*, 15 (56):8–21.

Jalušič, Vlasta. 2002. Between the social and the political: Feminism, citizenship, and the possibilities of an Arendtian perspective in Eastern Europe. *European Journal of Women's Studies* 9 (3):103–123.

Jaquette, Jane S., and Sharon L. Wolchik, eds. 1998. *Women and democracy. Latin America and Central and Eastern Europe*. Baltimore: The Johns Hopkins University Press.

Jung, Nora. 1994. Importing feminism to Eastern Europe. *History of European Ideas*, 19 (4–6):845–851.

Kovách, Imre. 1998. Hungary: Cooperative farms and household plots. In *Many Shades of Red. State Policy and Collective Agriculture*, edited by Mieke Meurs. Lanham: Rowman and Littlefield, 1998.

Kruks, Sonia, Rayna Rapp, and Marilyn B. Young, eds. 1989. *Promissory notes: Women in the Transition to Socialism*. New York: Monthly Review Press.

Kürti, László. 1991. The wingless eros of socialism: Nationalism and sexuality in Hungary. *Anthropological Quarterly* 64 (2):55–67.

Lampland, Mary. 1995. *The object of labor. Commodification in socialist Hungary*. Chicago: The University of Chicago Press.

Landes, Joan B., 1989. Marxism and the woman question. In Sonia Kruks, Rayna Rapp, and Marilyn B. Young (eds.), *Promissory notes: women in the transition to socialism* (New York: Monthly Review Press, 1989), pp. 15–28.

Lapidus, Gail W. 1978. *Women in Soviet Society*. Berkeley: University of California Press.

Lengyel, Zsúzsa. 1982. Mezőgazdaság, *szövetkezetek, parasztság a hetvenes években. [Agriculture, cooperatives, and peasants in the 1970s]*. Budapest: Kossuth Könyvkiadó.

Lister, Ruth. 1990. Women, economic dependency and citizenship. *Journal of Social Policy* 19 (4):445–467.

Lister, Ruth. 2002. The dilemmas of pendulum politics: balancing paid work, care and *citizenship. Economy and Society 31 (4):520–532.*

McDaniel, Susan A. 2002. Women's changing relations to the state and citizenship: caring and intergenerational relations in globalizing western democracies. *Canadian Review of Sociology and Anthropology* 39 (2):125–151.

McGiffen, Steven P. 2001. *The European Union. A critical guide*. London: Pluto Press.

MacKinnon, Catharine. 1989. *Toward a feminist theory of the state*. Cambridge: Harvard University Press.

Makkai, Toni. 1994. Social policy and gender in Eastern Europe. In *Gendering Welfare States* edited by Diane Sainsbury. London: Sage.

Moghadam, Valentine M. 1993. Bringing the Third World in: Comparative analysis of gender and restructuring. In *Democratic Reform and the Position of Women in Transitional Economics* edited by Valentine M. Moghadam. Oxford: Clarendon Press.

Moghadam, Valentine M. 1996. Patriarchy and post–communism: Eastern Europe and the Former Soviet Union. In *Patriarchy and Economic Development. Women's Positions at the End of the Twentieth Century*, edited by Valentine M. Moghadam. Oxford: Clarendon.

Molyneux, Maxine. 1984. Women in socialist Societies. Problems of theory and practice. In *Of Marriage and the Market. Women's Subordination Internationally and its Lessons*, Kate Young, Carol Wolkowitz, and Rosalyn McCullagh. London: Routledge and Kegan Paul.

Molyneux, Maxine. 1994. Women's rights and the international context: Some reflections on the post–communist states. *Millennium: Journal of International Studies* 23 (2):287–313.

Mouffe, Chantal. 1992. Democratic citizenship and the political community. In *Dimensions of Radical Democracy. Pluralism, Citizenship, Community*, edited by Chantal Mouffe. London: Verso.

Mui, Constance L., and Julien S. Murphy, eds. 2002. *Gender struggles: practical approaches to contemporary feminism*. Lanham: Rowman & Littlefield.

Pascall, Gillian, and Lewis, Jane. 2004. Emerging gender regimes and policies for gender equality in a wider Europe. *Journal of Social Policy* 33 (3): 373–395.

Pateman, Carol. 1990. *The disorder of women: Democracy, feminism, and political theory*. Cambridge: Polity Press.

Phillips, Anne. 1993. *Democracy and difference*. University Park: Pennsylvania University Press.

Regulska, Joanna. 1994. Transition to local democracy. Do Polish women have a chance? In *Women in the politics of postcommunist Eastern Europe*, edited by Marilyn Rueschemeyer. London: M.E. Sharpe.

Regulska, Joanna. 1998. The "political" and its meaning for women: Transition politics in Poland. In *Theorising transition. The Political Economy of Post–Communist Transformations*, edited by John Pickles and Adam Smith. London: Routledge.

Répássy, Helga. 1991. Changing gender roles in Hungarian agriculture. *Journal of Rural Studies* 7 (1–2):23–29.

Róna–Tas, Ákos. 1994. The first shall be last? Entrepreneurship and communist cadres in the transition from socialism. *American Journal of Sociology* 100 (1):40–69.

Ryan, Mary. 1995. Gender and public access: Women's politics in nineteenth–century America. In *Habermas and the Public Sphere*, edited by Craig Calhoun Cambridge. Cambridge: MIT Press.

Sas, Judit H. 1976. *Életmód és család. Az emberi viszonyok alakulása a családban. [Life style and family. The constitution of human relations in the family]*. Budapest: Akadémiai Kiadó.

Sas, Judit H. 1988. Nőies nők és férfias férfiak. A nőkkel és a férfiakkal kapcsolatos társadalmi sztereotípiák élete, eredete és szocializációja. [Womanly women and manly men. The existence, origin, and socialization of social stereotypes for women and men]. Budapest: Akadémiai Kiadó.

Shola Orloff, Ann 1993. Gender and the social rights of citizenship: The comparative analysis of gender relations and welfare states. *American Sociological Review* 58:303–328.

Stewart, Michael. 1997. *Time of the gypsies*. Boulder: Westview Press.

Swain, Nigel. 1985. *Collective farms which work?* Cambridge: Cambridge University Press.

Swain, Nigel. 1992. *Hungary: The rise and fall of feasible socialism*. London: Verso.

Szalai, Júlia. 1991. Some aspects of the changing situation of women in Hungary. *Signs* 17:152–170.

Szalai, Júlia. 1998. Women and democratization: Some notes on recent changes in Hungary. In *Women and Democracy. Latin America and Central and Eastern Europe*, edited by J.S. Jaquette and S.L. Wolchik. Baltimore: The Johns Hopkins University Press.

Szent–Györgyi, Kathryn A. 1993. Embourgeoisement and the "cultural capital" variable: Rural enterprise and concepts of prestige in Northeastern Hungary. *Man* 28:515–523.

Tárkányi, Ákos. 1998. Európai családpolitikák: a magyar családpolitika története. [European family policies: the history of Hungarian family policy]. *Demográfia* 61 (2–3):233–268.

Tóth, Olga. 1993. No envy, no pity. In *Gender politics and post–communism. Reflections From Eastern Europe and the former Soviet Union*, edited by Nanette Funk and Magda Mueller. New York: Routledge.

US Census Bureau. 2005. IDB summary demographic data for Hungry [cited 06/23/03]. Available from, <http://www.census.gov/cgi–bin/ipc/idbsum.pl?cty=HU>.

van der Graaf, Mary. 1996. *Everything and nothing changed. Gender relations in Hungarian agriculture during the transition*. Wageningen: Wageningen Agricultural University.

van der Lippe, Tanja, and Éva Fodor. 1998. Changes in gender inequality in six Eastern European countries. *Acta Sociologica* 41 (2):131–150.

Vásáry, Ildikó. 1987. *Beyond the plan: Social change in a Hungarian village*. Boulder, CO: Westview Press.

Völgyes, Iván. 1980. Dynamic change: Rural transformation, 1945–1975. In *The modernization of agriculture: Rural transformation in Hungary, 1848–1975*, edited by Joseph Held. New York: Columbia University Press.

Wallerstein, Immanuel. 2003. Citizens all? Citizens some! The making of the citizen. *Comparative Studies in Society and History* 45 (4):650–679.

Weiner, Elaine. 1997. Assessing the implications of political and economic reform in the post–socialist era: The case of Czech and Slovak women. *East European Quarterly*, 31 (3):473–502.

Wolchick, Sharon L. 1998. Gender and the politics of transition in the Czech Republic and Slovakia. In *Women and democracy. Latin America and Central and Eastern Europe*, edited by Jane S. Jaquette and Sharon L. Wolchick. Baltimore: The Johns Hopkins University Press.

Wolchick, Sharon L., and Alfred G. Meyer, eds. 1985. *Women, state, and party in Eastern Europe*. Durham: Duke University Press.

Young, Iris M. 1989. Polity and group difference: A critique of the ideal of universal citizenship. *Ethics* 99:250–274.

Chapter 4

Clashes and Ordeals of Women's Citizenship in Central and Eastern Europe[1]

Jacqueline Heinen

The transformation of the political and economic systems of the countries of Central and Eastern Europe has been accompanied by processes whereby women have become marginalized from both an economic and political point of view. Even though women are underrepresented in the corridors of power, how many times have (male) politicians proposed to send women workers back to their homes to resolve the problems of (male) unemployment? The tendency to confine women to the private sphere illustrates the denial of women's full citizenship.[2]

After examining just how these new rights are linked to the establishment of the democratic system and mediated by a construction of a sexed model of citizenship, which confers rights differentially according to gender, I will analyze the specific relationship between the public and the private which prevailed under "real socialism" (socialism in our time) in order to better understand the place that was made for women, as well as the manner in which past experiences influence today's actions and aspirations. Finally, I will examine the conditions of women's participation in the political sphere, referring to the recent debates on citizenship in Western feminist scholarship.

The workplace is where the marginalization of women is the clearest and particularly visible. With rare exceptions (notably Hungary), the female workforce has been by far the most affected by unemployment in the first phase of the so–called 'transition'. This is expressed most clearly by the proportion of women who are among the long–term unemployed and individuals who are no longer eligible for unemployment benefits.[3] Most studies show the existence of discriminatory hiring practices against women, especially when they are married and have children. The priority granted to male heads of households is predicated upon the well–known discourse concerning the "natural" place of women within the family and society, and the most trenchant arguments are invoked in order to justify women's primary assignment to domestic tasks. Practices, such as making it more difficult for women to qualify for loans in their attempts to become independent, further reflect the unequal employment policies and specific obstacles that inhibit the female gender's exercise of rights, particularly civil rights.

However, what is true of civil rights is equally true in the case of social rights. The expansion of the economic crisis has incited new governments to drastically reduce the budget expenditures for the social sector. Additionally, a number of legal dispositions and structures that have been judged to be either too expensive or contrary to market–economy logic have been put into question. This applies to protective laws that confer a privileged status for mothers with young children (parental leave, child–sickness leave) and for single mothers (priority for childcare and nursery access, doubling of family or care allowances). It also applies to childcare facilities which have been reduced and suppressed. All of these measures have primarily affected women and limited their mobility which has simultaneously reduced the number of possibilities for them to regain employment. Further, even increased access to the European Union (in those countries concerned) has not changed these processes (Watson 2000; Roth 2004). Consequently, the process of pauperization, which has taken on unprecedented dimensions in Central and Eastern Europe, strikes women more than men, legitimating talk of a veritable "feminization of poverty."

Simultaneously, since 1989, the proportion of women representatives elected to national parliament has diminished substantially: from figures of 25 percent to 30 percent during the communist regime down to the present day figures of 5 percent and 20 percent. At the same time, there are also very few women in governmental institutions— both in administrative and appointed positions. The exiguous presence of women in Parliaments that were writing new constitutions and completely remodeling the laws that strongly influence how social relations are being restructured is paving the way for the construction of a political world dominated by males (Sloat 2004). The attempts to ban abortion, that have occurred in multiple countries and, in Poland, have resulted in an almost total proscription of voluntary pregnancy interruption, illustrate the difficulties women face when defending their own interests.[4] Presently, democratic practices that emphasize individual and personal autonomy do not have equal value for men and women in Central and Eastern Europe. Although post–communist countries endeavor to restore those civil rights that were denied or largely emptied of meaning under the Soviet regime, the negation of personal liberty for women shows the sexualized character of the concept of citizenship.

While preoccupations abound regarding the extent to which the legacies of the past affect the present situation, one becomes struck *a posteriori* by the paucity of attention that social scientists have given to the private sphere when analyzing processes in "Soviet–type" societies. It should be recognized that as much as the deprivation of democratic rights were at the heart of the crisis of communism, the problems relating to everyday life were also equally relevant. Aside from a few acts of visible social resistance, only a small number of which occurred outside of Poland, the embryonic tensions that countries of Central and Eastern Europe came to know during the course of the years were generally related to prosaic questions such as: the cost of food, lack of housing, supplies, special services, and so on. The inability of these governments to keep the promises to improve consumption which they had made during the 1970s have played a significant role in the loss of credibility in the eyes of those who did not belong to the opposition movement, which was the majority of the population. If economic questions relative to the private sphere have received such little attention on the part of economists and sociologists, has it not been as a result of its reference to a domain that is, above all, synonymous to the "feminine universe"?

The Community vs. the Individual?

Prevailing discourses that magnify women's reproductive role also necessitate an argument that draws upon the rhetoric of nationalist and religious currents which occupy a significant place on the political scene. After an initial phase marked by strong disappointments regarding the future awaiting these countries, the collapse of communism has effectively left room for a political and social climate characterized by a lack of anchoring on the cultural plane and a general floating of identities, which explains the infatuation with these insisting on myths of the nation of the past. It therefore becomes clearer how, even within intellectual circles, nineteenth–century theories of "communitarism" and religious beliefs that define women's place as within the home find a resolute echo in the countries of Central and Eastern Europe. Supporters of this idea often refer to Ferdinand Tönnies' theories, which valorize the natural right of community, where tradition is central, by emphasizing groups united by blood, land, and language. Placing the mother on a pedestal, they consider women's emancipation a salient and disgraceful trait of "so–called" socialist societies. The nationalist beliefs of Valentin Rasputin in Russia, of the extreme Catholic right in Poland, or of nationalist parties in Serbia, Croatia, or Bosnia, all illustrate the reproduction of this idea (Heinen 1992; 1995; Papić 2004).

Nevertheless, the ideological valorization of family and community is conjoined in Eastern Europe with the development of a market economy that extols the values of liberal individualism, associated with individual initiative and competition. An obvious tension results from this between values presented as mutually opposing (nationalism, community, dependence, and family on the one hand, and capitalism, the individual, and autonomy on the other), regardless of whether the manner of posing such terms as antagonistic is full of ambiguities. Linda Nicholson rightfully notes:

> As the majority of such types of oppositions, individualism and community share a similar logic underlying their polarity, that which authorizes each to define the other in negative terms. Each of these notions tends to negate difference and to reduce the multiplicity and heterogeneity for one more than through some opposing biases. Liberal individualism is accompanied by formal ethics of the juridical type that rejects difference in postulating that all individuals are equal under the law. Community, for its part, rejects difference in making a social ideal out of fusion (1990, 14).

Nevertheless, the tension mentioned above is bearing disorder. This is indirectly noticed in the numerous electoral results that were favorable to political formations connected to the old Communist Parties in the first half of 1990. These votes primarily translated into the disenchantment of the majority of Central and Eastern European populations with the market economy, in addition to a deep dissatisfaction simultaneously manifested towards the social policies of the new governments. These fears have been visibly manifested through strikes and other forms of protest as well as through the fear of not knowing what could happen next. The hope of filling the void of values created by the disappearance of the former political system has translated into a tendency on the part of many individuals of embellishing the past by bestowing it with romantic virtues. In addition, it is precisely this that provides the basis for those movements advocating the turn to the "secure" values of the family and the nation, which are often explicitly opposed to the rights of the individual.

For those who admit that individual rights constitute one of the important dimensions of citizenship (the other one, which refers to political action, I will return to below), the approach of T.H. Marshall proves heuristic for attempting to hem in the course of changes in Eastern Europe and for analyzing the status conferred to women in these countries that are in a process of full transformation (Marshall and Bottomore 1992). Marshall's typology has been applied in diverse contexts. It was formulated in 1949 and was strongly influenced by the juridical and social history of Great Britain, in a period of full employment when the development of welfare appeared secured.[5] Feminists, in particular, have criticized this theoretical model by underlining that it is predicated upon a periodization which exclusively concerns men. Many of the rights specifically concerning women (particularly maternity protection and the proscription on night shifts at the workplace) were, in fact established before women had the right to vote, and many civil rights (particularly related to marriage) continued to be refused to women until the 1970s. The category of citizen is therefore much less universal than it would appear. Elsewhere, the delimitation that Marshall traces among the different categories of enumerated rights is not always clear. As Bérengère Marques–Pereira stresses, reproductive freedom, where the right to an abortion constitutes a central element, is related to civil rights as much as political or social rights.[6] In my view, the pertinence of these observations does not weaken the interest of Marshall's approach, despite the dated character of his reflections.

Not all individuals have the same status. Not everyone is considered a full–fledged citizen: one thinks of immigrants, deprived of political rights, or of women, for whom civil rights are often truncated. From this point of view, the articulation established by Marshall among three types of rights, civil, political, and social, can serve as an initial model for locating those rights that are lacking for a particular social category. Regarding Central and Eastern European countries, Marshall's typology facilitates the recognition of those rights that existed under the communist regime and the analysis of the content of the new citizenship rights that are emerging at the present time.

Old Rights and New Rights

Based on the fact of their systemic framework (abolition of private property, negation of the freedom of expression, of organization, of circulation, and so on) the essence of civil rights had a purely formal character in "Soviet–type" societies, as did political rights, to the extent that all organs of power were pervaded by the powerful Communist Party. Nevertheless, some social rights did exist that ensured a minimum amount of protection for the individual (for example: employment guarantees, a subsidy system in matters of food and housing, extremely modest pricing for an array of services, among others). Up to a certain point, these rights recalled one of the dimensions of the Welfare State.[7] One could even say that some of these policies were much more generous than those prevailing in the West during the same period, although they were not perceived by many as such. To many, these policies appeared as due or were even negatively interpreted as coercive acts of the state (in the discourse, for instance, the accent was on the obligation to work more than on the right to employment).

The collapse of the Soviet system involved the restoration of democratic liberties negated under communism and the construction of a rule of law based on civil and political rights as well as on certain social rights which were not needed under the previous regime (especially protection against unemployment). During the first period of the phase referred to as "transitional," hopes, not to mention illusions, regarding the expected benefits of a market economy were such that for the majority of people, social rights were going to be extended, thanks to the improvement of the quality of services such as education and health.

The rejection of the notion of egalitarianism, associated with that of communism, contributed to a minimizing of the risks of an increase of social inequalities, which numerous social scientists of the East had underlined as a major threat, before the inception of this period (Deacon 1992; Mink and Szurek 1992; Ringen and Wallace 1993; OECD 1994). However, events have proved them right, since for the great majority of the population the take–off of the privatization process has mainly translated into the threat (or the reality) of unemployment. Additionally, the strict policies demanded by creditors of international finance, such as the International Monetary Fund [IMF], have undermined most of the social advantages that allowed communist power to establish its domination. It has proven to be the case that free enterprise has not necessarily coincided with the extension of individual liberties, but that, on the contrary, it has engendered strong tensions between civil and social rights.

A glaring illustration is provided by parental leave, one of the rights specifically accorded to women under communism. This was a right that, although strongly appreciated (as opposed to other social measures), was also not divested of ambiguity, which the East Germans did not fail to underline when they spoke about its status in the autumn of 1989.[8] Some authors have spoken of "false rights" in regards to those laws aimed at protecting maternity, in the sense that they constituted little more than rights for the infant (Del Re 1994). Similarly, Carol Pateman has stressed that those rights that women specifically enjoy within the welfare state, in fact, have condemned women to second–class citizenship because they have contributed to situating them within a sphere outside the public one, which is the sphere that these rights purport to make accessible to women (Pateman 1988; Lamoureux 1989; Siim 1994).[9]

Beyond the ambiguity that effectively characterizes such a measure, particularly in the segregation of the workplace, it is important to mention that the suppression of the right to recover one's employment position at the end of parental leave, in Central and Eastern European countries, constitutes an additional barrier for women already penalized in the job market. Many women have therefore ceased to rely on such a benefit for fear of unemployment. In a period where the number of childcare facilities is continuing to decrease, having a young infant becomes an obstacle when looking for or safeguarding employment (Heinen 2002). Thus, in the ex–German Democratic Republic [GDR], where the demographic curve evinces an appreciable decrease, many women have now opted for sterilization. Similarly, in other countries, another practice has gained currency, whereby women are only hired if they sign a contractual agreement that they will avoid having children or risk losing their job (Heinen 1994; Krizkova 2004). The undermining of women's rights by practices that inhibit women's ability to exercise their rights, further limits women's autonomy and constitutes an impediment for the exercise of individual freedoms.

It is on this topic that I find Marshall's typology useful, because it aids us in distinguishing rights from each other, the way in which they are modulated through public–private relations, and the extent to which they interfere with the dimensions, as much social as political, of the definition of citizenship (Heinen and Portet 2002). Marshall's proposal, that each historical or political period produces an "ideal image of citizenship which allows already achieved results to be measured and to which standard aspirations define themselves" is also relevant to this argument. [10] Jane Jenson believes that this theory helps locate the process of the sexualization of citizenship and capture the dynamics of women's movements in Europe and North America during the 1970s (Jenson 1992). "Western" women have not only struggled for juridical equality and against discriminatory laws, but also for the extension of rights to the private sphere and the questioning of traditionally acceptable categories. Marshall invokes more than develops the idea of an "ideal citizenship." The notion of ideal citizenship, as understood by Marshall, can at the same time help us in considering the question of citizenship in post–communist societies because it prompts us to reflect upon those factors that engender social exclusions and imbalances, and upon those policies which disallow women from being considered "full–fledged citizens."

Seen from this point of view, the brave struggle of those small groups of women, who formed themselves during the bustle of events that resulted in the fall of the Wall, and that called themselves feminist, cannot mask the lack of reaction on the part of the very great majority of those affected by the discriminations of which women are the object. The feeble investment of women in the political field does not help in this respect. This can partially be explained by the difficulties of daily life which, although they may have taken different forms, are still retained. In addition, the hostility towards feminism, evoked in any way, both within the ranks of communists as well as dissidents, presents a further barrier. Finally, the experience of a majority of women has not yet provoked them to question the unequal relations between the sexes.

It would be a mistake to attribute the feeble presence of women, within the branches of democratic representation elected since 1989, uniquely in terms of discrimination or to analyze this as only the fruit of the exclusive practices of a political microcosm essentially comprised of men. This state of affairs reflects much of women's ambivalent attitudes towards political life in Eastern Europe, a phenomenon that inscribes itself through the context of the past, where, more so than in the West, their familial functions have been stressed in order to distance themselves from the spheres of power. Certainly, women were massively present in some independent movements that contributed to the creation of a veritable civil society before 1989 (for example, the peace movement in the ex–GDR, Solidarnosc in Poland, Charter 77 in Czechoslovakia). When any feminist dimension was lacking, a number of women in such movements acquired a sense of action and thereby had the experience of direct confrontation with the state. However, it should not be forgotten, that most of these women, including those that played leading roles, were also pushed out in order to leave room for men when issues of equality and the constitution of official political parties were raised.[11]

As different inquiries on the topic of unemployment have demonstrated, we are not witnessing a questioning of social roles based on the function of sex. In the vast majority of cases, women workers, emphasized that they encounter many more obstacles than men in finding employment and most considered it normal that men had priority in employment.[12] They also did not indicate any problems with discrimination. Their point of view remained ostensibly marked by the public–private relations that were established under communism.

The Specific Dimension of Public–Private Relations Under Communism

The examination of the situation of the economic and political position of women, that prevailed under communism, immediately raises a double contradiction. The first is traceable to the ideological and political inconsistencies of power in regards to women's status in a society. In contrast to the official orientation to emancipate women through employment and to socialize education from the youngest age, the actual policies implemented in Central and Eastern Europe diverged substantially from the objectives proclaimed. These policies tended to place emphasis on the role of maternity and reinstated almost all responsibility for the care of children and dependent persons to women. The second contradiction, which partly derives from the first, touches upon the question of representation concerning the place and importance attributed to the family. The communists initially attempted to minimize the function of the family by reducing it to an entity that would above all define itself through women's obligations to society, beginning with their obligations in regards to reproduction. During the time under communism, far from responding to such expectations, individuals had a tendency to valorize the family, which they considered a place of refuge marking the boundary between "us" and "them" (the other, the state) and as the only space allowing the development of personal initiative and autonomy.

Hannah Arendt's *Origins of Totalitarianism* offers a framework for approaching problems concerning the place of women in society and their relationship to politics that have manifested themselves in Central and Eastern Europe since 1989. Let us recall that Arendt established a very clear distinction between a totalitarian regime, on the one hand, and a single–party dictatorship, tyranny, and despotic regime, on the other.[13] Under totalitarianism, she surmises that no concerted actions are possible that do not place one's own, or someone else's, life in peril. Therefore, the isolation of the individual emerges within the political sphere, which simultaneously results in loneliness in the private sphere. Hannah Arendt therefore attributes a central role to the private sphere, particularly the family, as a place where solidarities are forged that enable resistance to a totalitarian regime.

In "Soviet–type" societies which are characterized, to differing degrees, by the elimination of private property and by the absence of the freedoms of association and organization or, according to Arendt, in national societies of single party dictatorships, the private sphere corresponded with the familial sphere, or intimate sphere (in the Arendtian sense of the term). The family appeared therein as a rampart against adversity. Kith and kin networks occupied a central role in what was conventionally called "civil society."[14] However, the situation was not homogenous because particularly among women, social origin, education level, or job type had a significant impact on attitudes about salaried work and, hence, on the importance given to their familial responsibilities. Differences in the relationship between public and private also varied between countries. While the image of the mother–bride remained dominant in Poland, the notion of worker–mother was firmly established in the GDR. In the case of Poland, this was directly related to the family policies that were applied, specifically in relation to the development of parental maternity leave, and in the case of the German Democratic Republic, in relation to state institutions of childcare.

In Central and Eastern Europe, for reasons as much economic as political, the private sphere's valorization has increased with time, in parallel to the growing rejection of the state and its intervention in the life of the individual. In the economic sphere, this tendency has been stronger because of the ruling strata's incapacity to satisfy the most immediate needs within the domain of consumption. This incapacity favored the development of a parallel economy as a response to those needs that were left unmet. The functioning of this parallel economy rested above all on the nucleus of the family and circles of friends. The weight conferred to the domestic universe was much more important than the relative well–being of the individual depending on it. At the same time, this process induced an accentuation of the sexual division of labor because generative activities, related to revenue, were undertaken by men, while women tended to undertake bartering activities.

On the political plane, one will recall that movements resisting the authoritarian regime could not have formed without a strong anchoring within the private sphere. Numerous clandestine and private networks existed that played a significant political role. Similarly, as the reading of multiple dissident testimonies indicates, family solidarity was critical because it provided a much needed "haven" within the private home. The circulation of ideas that contested the power of the state directly depended on the support of friends and neighbors, on their political adherence to the struggle conducted, or at least on their solidarity with people braving the territory of political action. The clandestine structures that gave their form to the inchoate civil societies of the 1970s and 1980s could not have emerged without the support of the familial sphere. This is true for all these countries regardless of the degree to which opposition movements were developed or the degree to which the state oppressed its citizens.

The recollection of this context is very useful for understanding the rather generalized rejection in Central and Eastern Europe of the notion of feminism that was associated with the slogan "the personal is political." This expression was understood by some as a will to efface the limits between the public and private (even if those who initially proposed the term did not share this meaning). This recollection is equally useful to avoid the pitfalls of theories that tended to generalize 20th–century Western women's experiences and did not consider the historical and socio–political dimensions of the society to which they are applied and upon which they are contingent.[15]

It is notable that official policies, whether economic or political, have had the primary effect of raising the prestige of the private sphere, and the secondary effect of masking gender inequalities. These movements have also illustrated the importance of avoiding portraying women solely as "victims." At the same time, it is important to examine how past social policies had responded to this (for example, the leave system which was originally maternal before becoming paternal), although it was only a partial response to some more or less explicit attempts on the part of the women affected. In making them theirs, women have contributed to the consolidation of a host of familial and social norms, which ease the division between the private and the public, and between the social and the political.

The Social/Political: a Much Hazier Demarcation than Would Appear

This split is due as much to the liberal as to the republican tradition. Chantal Mouffe's proposition clearly summarizes the problem:

Liberalism has contributed to the formulation of a notion of universal citizenship based upon the assertion that all individuals are born free and equal, but it has equally reduced citizenship to simple legal status, assigning the rights an individual possesses in front of the state. Moreover, the public sphere of modern citizenship has been constructed in universalistic and rationalistic terms that exclude any recognition of divisions and antagonisms and that relegate any particularity and difference to the private sphere. The public/private distinction, central as it was for the affirmation of individual liberties, has therefore functioned as an important factor of exclusion. In fact, the identification of the private with the domestic sphere has played an important role in the subordination of women (1993, 84).

Mouffe adds that the republican tradition, which emphasizes an active concept of citizenship and can appear attractive for overcoming the limits of liberalism, possesses its own limits as well. Republicans insist on participation in collective deliberations concerning urban affairs, but the notion of "the common good" that is so important to them is presented in universalistic terms as incompatible with the pluralism that characterizes modern democracy (nevertheless minimizing the notion of rights, the importance of which must be admitted, when the very same must be perfected by a more active sense of political engagement).

Numerous feminists have developed the same theme by demonstrating that the "universal" is all too often identified with an individual of the masculine sex (preferably white) and that, in a context marked by unequal power relations (*rapports de force*) between social groups, interests presented as "universals" nearly always serve the interests of the dominant groups. When republicans, for example, demand the individual to transcend her/his immediate situation in order to act as a citizen, it generally implies leaving aside trivial questions of daily life in order to launch oneself into "big" politics. Republicans, as liberals, generally remain silent when encountering the private dimension, namely the domestic.

The notion of citizenship, in its most current meaning, has therefore contributed to the further complication of what takes place in the home. The consequences of such an approach are most evident at present in Central and Eastern Europe, at a moment when the countries of the eastern part of Europe are reappropriating the notion of citizenship for themselves through a rather traditional liberal lens. Some new rights, both civil and political, have been established and they have been defined in identical terms for both men and women. However, the questioning of the reality of gender inequalities, and some eventual means to bring about gender equality, has never been posed, be they in politics, at the workplace, or within the home. This apparent neutrality goes hand in hand with the "natural" assignment of women to the domestic sphere, which results in an automatic marginalization from the political sphere (even if it is not always thought explicitly as such). Thus, by incorporating critiques advanced by social theory, the social movements of years past, especially women's movement, have asserted that the notion of citizenship cannot be abstracted from substantive inequalities within the economic, social, and domestic domain without the risk of remaining purely formalistic and multiplying exclusions.

The Importance of Grasping Citizenship in its Social as Much as Political Components

The example of Central and Eastern European countries is relevant to this discussion. I have already underlined that problems of daily life (for example, health, housing, provisioning) were at the heart of the crisis of the regimes of "real socialism." It is also evident that the absence of democratic practices that granted people the freedom of expression also led to the demise of these regimes. In other words, the refusal to attribute the problems of everyday life, particularly when people were witnessing a deep malaise about the Communists' "social project," directly contributed to the collapse of the Soviet bloc in 1989 (and I would further argue that this refusal was largely related to the fact that they were associated with the private, or "feminine" sphere).

The boundary between the social and the political is contestable for more than one reason; the social can be the bearer of more than mere economic needs, and the domestic is similarly traversed by the economic and by labor, particularly in relation to reproduction. One cannot treat the private and public as if they were two separate worlds without first considering the fact that, for example, there are a number of public policies (for example: in matters of health, housing, and education) that directly interfere with family relations. Conversely, the relations prevailing in the economic and political spheres are modulated by sexual/gender relations which find their basis in the family.[16] The lines of demarcation between these different domains are therefore dynamic and dependent upon the definitions that political and social actors ascribe to them during different periods, according to their historical context. One characteristic of the women's movement has rightfully been to propose an enlargement of the categories. It also prompted the discussion that some problems, which until then were considered as private, and often as taboo, acquire a political dimension when a group of individuals seizes the political process collectively and bring arguments into the public discourse that such problems have a direct affect on groups' statuses as oppressed or marginalized. Since then, it has become clear that relations of domination are not limited to what is conventionally considered the public sphere or to the tasks of democracy.

The issues of abortion and violence against women are paradigmatic examples of questions that had previously been confined to the intimate sphere and how they are now being recognized by some individuals who had previously denied their existence as actually relevant to the political sphere (even if the argument that insists on the fact that a society that obliges women to give birth at any cost is not democratic, is far from being recognized as a valid one). The struggle for defining exactly what depends upon public order is a struggle for justice and democracy because it tends to spur the recognition that some questions "of the private order" are constraints that most often impede females from participating in society with equal status. This is particularly true in relation to the unequal time that women have at their disposal as a result of the "double shift." It is also true in relation to the uneven distribution of domestic tasks in the private sphere, which is a central question within the arguments presently adopted by women of the East and is drawn upon to explain their non–investment in the public sphere (Corrin 1992; Einhorn 1993).

To pose the question of time, in order to demonstrate that it has a direct impact on the very weak presence of women in the political sphere, is to postulate that it is important to discuss problems as collective interests in order to find solutions. Solutions could occur through the diminution of professional work hours (especially for men), or through the improvement of certain public structures that allow the weight of domestic tasks to be lifted. This is not a case of denying that the public and private assume spheres that have their own separate dimensions. It is a case that, on the one hand, problematizes the sexual connotation of that separation and of re-thinking the articulation between the domestic, the social, and the political, and, on the other hand, postulates that such demarcations depend upon the action of affected individuals and groups within a determined period.

If we admit that the sphere of the political, far from summing up those state or political party institutions that constitute the kernel of the matter, encompasses the diversity of citizen initiatives that confer a particular profile to the political life of a specific locale or country, we still have difficulty discerning between the domains. To take an example that is directly tied to the relationship between gender and citizenship, how do we define the action of the associations intervening in family planning in Central and Eastern Europe today. Such groups contribute to filling in for the deficiencies of political authorities in this domain through training specialists, distributing contraceptives, or providing sexual education in schools. At the same time, they directly act within the political terrain of abortion legislation, confronting the parties that are hostile to women's rights to decide about their own bodies. In practice, the distribution of contraceptives is directly connected to the thought and action related to the right to an abortion and abortion rights undeniably refer to the political because negating this right denies women their autonomy and their rights to full citizenship.

Certainly, these types of associative activities do not cover the political entirely, but they form an integral part, which argues in favor of an articulation rather than an opposition between the social and the political, and between public and private. I agree with Ruth Lister when she revolts against the systematic refusal of according the label of "political" to such initiatives under the pretext that they do not belong to an established political structure, that they do not relate immediately to the circles of power, or because they run the risk of falling into reductionism when they concern themselves with determinate social groups:

> Such a refusal implies, in turn, a reactivation of the very processes of exclusion that have characterized republican practices of citizenship, ... of underestimating the dynamic effect, for women at the individual level, of this type of political engagement that can inspire confidence, in itself indispensable, in the exercise of citizenship, ... and ignoring as well the larger and more political and social impact that such initiatives can have. (Lister 1994, 9)

In this sense, one cannot prescribe, in advance, the contours of public space. Not just the content, but also the forms that this action takes and the structures within which it involves itself can vary greatly, which adds to the complexity of the distinction between different spheres.

According to the evidence, the institutional frameworks put in place in the "East", these past years, reproduce some essential traits of the parliamentary systems of the "West" that create an obstacle to some truly democratic practices. Of course, the processes of differentiation that are in operation as much on the political as the economic plane among the different countries that were once designated by the term "bloc" (and this was a hyperbole) more than ever represent globalizing considerations in regards to this part of Europe. One need do little more than to compare the situation in the Czech Republic and Russia today, as much from the point of view of reform as the functioning of institutions. On the precise point that concerns us, nevertheless, there are many similarities. While the political parties born of the wave of democratization that overthrew the communist regimes in 1989 may still be very unstable and poorly socially anchored, they most often seem to have inherited all the blemishes of their counterparts in the West. The incapacity of the newly elected members to clearly communicate current political debates has led to an abstentionist phenomenon.

As one could, or as one must have expected, transformations in mentality appear to require much more time than structural changes. Under communism, the centralized decision–making system, which relied upon a strict adherence to hierarchy, had the effect, and goal, of weakening and even eliminating all individual initiative. "The expectations, values and behaviors, in brief the habitus of Eastern Europe have been forged by nearly a half century of institutions called 'socialist' that continue largely to determine the reaction to the reforms" (Boyer 1994, 3). Most individuals are reticent to engage themselves actively in the field of politics. This is especially true for women, who were particularly deprived places in the public sphere as a consequence of social transformations. The valorization, in the past as well as in the present, of women's activity within the home therefore easily explains why those who become involved in politics are usually men. Moreover, political difficulties, as much as economic uncertainties, bode badly for the adoption of energetic measures aimed at surmounting discriminations of which women are the objects at every level. This type of question is secondary in the eyes of the great majority of politicians and decision–makers in general. It would suppose a radical change in the perception of gender inequalities, which is proportionately less probable, on the part of the authorities.

Therefore, we cannot be overwhelmingly optimistic in terms of the possibilities women will have, in the short term, to affect public affairs and define the type of democracy that is to be established. However, such a view is not incompatible with the existence of resources for action and the mobilization that is liable to modify the course of events. We only need to see the rapidity with which the notion of rights has regained its sense in conjunction with the re–establishment of civil and political liberties, and in regards to what sort of force social advantages, undermined by the passage to a market economy, have been claimed in the present. In this sense, irrespective of the contextual difference between Central and Eastern Europe today and Great Britain in the 1950s, it appears that "the image of the ideal citizen" of which Marshall speaks retains all its actuality.

Certain signs can be discerned in the behavioral changes witnessed among many young women in Eastern Europe about that which concerns their relationship to work and employment.[17] Does not the wish, frequently expressed, to gain positions of responsibility to ensure a higher salary and have prospects of advancement, constitute an indication of a change in regards to the importance accorded to professional activity, concomitant with a refusal to remain constrained within the private sphere?[18] Similarly, debates and mobilizations which have occurred as much in Slovenia and Poland as in Hungary or Russia on the question of the right to abortion have induced the beginning of the realization of the importance of women's rights to decide on this issue themselves.

Therefore, all the attention needs to be given to the initiatives of local associations that have recently emerged and that aim to defend the collective and/or autonomous individual interests of some categories of citizens. As to their exact nature, Jean Leca asserts that:

> Citizenship does not exist other than in a social space between public and private spheres … The intermediate sphere between private and state spheres is perhaps the most strategic. It concerns a sphere of altruistic participation in benevolent associations; although these latter entities have no directly political characteristic, they are no less the citizenship reserves (1992, 21).

I find this definition reductionist, however, since it is too saturated with the traditional distinction between public and private, and I would rather think that the action of a number of associations can be categorized as political. Nevertheless, the idea that they serve as reservoirs for citizenship seems pertinent to me. I think here of the intervention of some associations in Poland, Russia, Albania, and elsewhere, which struggle, often with novel means, for the reinsertion of the unemployed into the job market. Other political and social organizations, taking part in debates concerning the question of unemployment, focus on the introduction of a change of attitudes in regards to gender relations, despite the difficulties that they meet (Sloat 2005). In spite of the fact that relatively few organizations undertake such actions, they make progress towards the defense of the groups that they represent. These activities are then part of the larger process of participation in public debates that are of extreme importance for the future of the societies within which they act. Their activities inscribe themselves within that which signifies the exercise of a social and political citizenship (understood in the larger sense of the term). In other words, they conform to a citizenship that does not solely rely on the retention of rights, but that includes the actions involved in the defense or enlargements of these rights. These actions, as have been noted, are often located at the interface of the social and the political. This is a citizenship that associates the need for equal civil, political, and social rights for all, to the recognition of ineluctable differences that traverse the social body, and are founded on a dynamic understanding of individual participation in the affairs of a community.

Through their activity, these associations touch upon some social problems directly connected to the immediate preoccupations of women, in the same vein as those that intervene in the domain of family planning which also place a high priority on the immediate preoccupations of women. Not only do they have the merit of breaking the attitudes of passivity that was inherited from communism, the fact that they fix objectives for themselves, which are often tied to social policies, constitutes a trump to allow them to assert themselves as full protagonists in negotiations with the state:

> The reforms in the realm of social policies, when they become valid, can contribute to the reconstruction of civil society by relying on local groups for their actualization and the management of social services ... An active civil society depends on the effective organization of institutions and of groups whose sectoral interests can be presented and integrated within the political process (Wallace 1993, 21).

Conclusion

The impact of feminist groups, especially local feminist groups, remains rather weak. However, these are the only structures that can induce a challenge to the public–private dichotomy. Such a notion is crucial in order to break with the restrictive and gendered conceptions of citizenship by virtue of which women find themselves at the margins of power, excluded from the forum of political debates that decide the future of their respective communities. Some time will be necessary before the emergence of public debates such as those that have already occurred in a number of countries of Europe and North America, and before the formation of certain group actions which deserve the term "movements".[19] Nevertheless, I would argue very exactly that the type of associative activities, mentioned earlier, which focus on the rights of unemployed women or on reproductive rights, fall within the idea of democracy from the bottom up and they can serve as a springboard for the fulfillment of the need to enlarge women's representation within the structures of power. This, I would argue is the only way through which to bridge the present phase, characterized by the retreat to the self, and the eventual development of collective aspirations regarding the future of a society in general.

Notes

[1]   This article is partially taken from the French version published in *Sextant* 7, 1997 and includes many of the ideas developed in my *thèse d'habilitation à diriger des recherches* [thesis under entitlement to research management] from which an article has appeared (Del Re and Heinen 1996).

[2]   Space limits a full treatment of the differences existing among the diverse countries of Central and Eastern Europe in the past and even more so in the present. Analyzing women's citizenship in the countries of the "East" risks the development of abusive generalizations. Only the existence of durable traits inherited through the older regime's systemic framework, particularly concerning the status of women in society, justifies such an approach, with all the limits it implies.

[3]   For more on this topic, see also, Corrin, ed. 1992; Einhorn 1993; Heinen 1994.

[4]   On the present situation concerning abortion in Poland, see the interview with Wanda Nowicka, president of the Federation for Women and Family Planning in Warsaw (Heinen and Portet 2004).

[5]   T. H. Marshall examines the evolution of the content of citizenship through time and proposes a terminology that is articulated in three types of distinctive rights, the crystallization of which, according to him, corresponds more or less to three different historical moments. It is in the eighteenth century that civil rights, consisting of a series of liberties (of speech, of thought, of creed, the right to a job of one's choice, the right to ownership, of making contracts, etc.) were established. Political rights (the right to vote, to participate directly or indirectly in government) can be traced to the nineteenth century. In terms of social rights (insurance against illnesses and accidents, retirement pensions, a national education system guaranteeing a certain level of instruction, social services, etc.), which he proposed to be introduced gradually, were not formalized until the twentieth century, and are directly tied to the notion of social citizenship.

[6]   They can be considered at the same time "as political rights, since reproductive freedom can be related to the struggles of women's movements, that is to say, the affirmation of a new political subject that struggles and negotiates in order to render recognizable a collective identity founded upon the visibility of gender relations. As civil rights, in so far as reproductive liberty refers to the principle of individuation dear to classical liberalism which allows the individual to dispose of her/himself freely. They are also social rights, since reproductive freedom refers to public health policies. In brief, reproductive freedom crystallizes within itself the rights–liberties against the state and the rights–trusts regarding the state" (Marques–Pereira 1995, 4).

[7]   Nevertheless, despite the existence of a certain number of social measures belonging to the welfare category, the analogy that is occasionally drawn between Soviet–type regimes and the welfare state is fallacious. One of the distinctive features of the welfare system, in the West, is the fact that the installation of social compensation systems was translated into the sensitive increase of salaries and the conjoining improvement of consumption in the aftermath of WW II, which was anything but the case under "real socialism," as could be seen further in time.

[8]   They have then taken to the paternalism of the East German State, expressing the irony of the *Mutti–Politik* [mama–politics] developed by the Sozialistische Einheitspartei Deutchlands [SED], the communist party of the German Democratic Republic. Such

measures have contradictory effects, in the same way that leaves of absence for caring for sick children or for domestic work (sic) have both been exclusively reserved for women. For more on this, see Heinen, 1990.

9   Pateman develops this idea in reference to that which she calls "the Wollstonecraft dilemma," which relies on the fact that women have in turn claimed their belonging as citizens because the principle of equality transcends social relations that are based on sex, at the same time that they insist on the necessity for women's representation as distinct from men. According to Pateman, the patriarchal notion of citizenship continues to render impossible any reconciliation between these two dimensions (see Lamoureux 1989, 124; Siim 1994, 287).

10   One finds a similar point of view in Claude Lefort when he asserts: "[The symbolic dimension of rights allows] one to comprehend the meaning of claims whose finality is the inscription of new rights, in the same way as the changes made in society under the effect of the dissemination of these claims and, not least, in the social representation of difference for the mode of legitimate existence." (1981, 184)

11   On this topic, there is explicit evidence from the women leaders of Solidarnosc, without whom the union would simply not have existed during the clandestine period. They justify their obliteration by arguing that women fulfilled these tasks "because it was necessary since men were in prison." The women assert that there was no injustice in the fact that they were relegated to oblivion afterwards, since they were never perceived themselves as political militants. (See particularly numbers 2 and 3 of the Polish feminist review *Pelnym glosem* [*In full voice*] (1993 and 1994); Kondratowicz 2001; Penn 2005).

12   This is illustrated by several relevant articles addressing different countries of Central and Eastern Europe that appeared in the *GEDISST papers* (Heinen 1995). Also see Krizkova (2004) and Radimska's work on the Czech Republic.

13   In her eyes, when one can speak of totalitarianism, it is necessary that different factors exist concomitantly – the atomization of society, a single party dominated by one dictator, a totalitarian ideology, propaganda, and terror, that result in the destruction of all solidarity, within the family as well, and therefore the latter's dislocation (for instance, the institutionalization of informant systems that force members of a family to inform against each other).

14   This term is quite different from that with which it is invested in the West.

15   Since the early 1980s, black feminists or those of ethnic minorities in the US and the UK have formulated several critiques regarding the ethnocentrism of Western feminism in that the family, far from uniquely representing a structure of domination, often constituted a haven against the repression of white society.

16   The theory of the social and sexual division of labor has the merit of having rendered evident the interweaving of reproductive and productive labor in the same way that the implications flow from there through the entirety of social relations.

17   I have remarked on this evolution on the occasion of my enquiry into the Polish context regarding women's employment and unemployment, in 1992–93 (Heinen 1995), but various studies in other Central and Eastern European countries support these conclusions (Heinen and Portet 2004).

18   In the 1980s it was noticed that, on the contrary, there was a strong tendency among younger women to seek refuge within the family, and this tendency was substantial, although of less frequency, among those of a higher level of education and who could thereby hope to develop a career.

19   I am thinking of the debates on the various modalities susceptible to facilitating the development of a massive presence in politics, and particularly of the debates concerning parity in France (Mossuz–Lavau 2002). On the debate at the European scale, see Vogel–Polsky and Vogel 1994.

References

Arendt, Hannah. 1972. *Les origines du totalitarisme – Le système totalitaire*. [The Origins of Totalitarism: Totalitarian system]. Paris: Seuil.

Boyer, Robert. 1994. Quelles réformes à l'Est? Une approche régulationniste, [What reforms in the East? A regulative approach]. *Problèmes Economiques* 2 (374).

Corrin, Chris, ed. 1992. *Superwomen and the double burden: Women's experience of change in Central and Eastern Europe*. London: Scarlet Press.

Deacon, Bob, ed. 1992. *Social policy, social justice, and citizenship in Eastern Europe*. Averbury: Aldershot.

Del Re, Alisa. 1994. Droits de citoyenneté: Une relecture sexuée de T.H. Marshall. [Citizenship rights: A gendered rereading of T.H. Marshall]. In *Women's Studies – Manuel de ressources*. Brussels: Université libre de Bruxelles.

Del Re, Alisa, and Jacqueline Heinen. 1996. *Quelle citoyenneté pour les femmes? La crise des Etats–providence et de la représentation politique en Europe*. [Which citizenship for women? The crisis of state–providence and political representation in Europe]. Paris: L'Harmattan.

Einhorn, Barbara. 1993. *Cinderella goes to market: Citizenship, gender, and women's movements in East Central Europe*. London: Verso.

Heinen, Jacqueline. 1990. The impact of social policy on the behaviour of women workers in Poland and East Germany. *Critical Social Policy* 29:79–91.

Heinen, Jacqueline. 1994. The re–integration into work of unemployed women. In *Unemployment in transition countries: Transient or persistent?* Paris: Organization of Cooperation and Economic Development [OECD].

Heinen, Jacqueline. 1995. Unemployment and women's attitudes in Poland. *Social Politics: International Studies in Gender, State, and Society* 2 (1):91–105.

Heinen, Jaqueline, ed. 1995. Transitions en Europe de l'Est: Main–d'oeuvre et citoyennes de seconde zone. [Transitions in Eastern Europe: Labor and second–class citizens]. *Cahiers du Gedisst* 12.

Heinen, Jacqueline. 2002. Ideology, economics and the politics of childcare in Poland before and after the transition. In *Childcare care policy at the crossroad. Gender and welfare state restructuring*, edited by Sonia Michel and Rianne Mahon. London: Routledge.

Heinen, Jacqueline, and Anna Matuchniak–Krasuska. 1992. Right to life versus women: Religious fundamentalism in Poland. In *Women and citizenship in Europe. borders, rights and duties: Women's differing identities in a Europe of contested boundaries*, edited by Anna Ward et al. London: Trantham Books.

Heinen, Jacqueline, and Stéphane Portet. 2002. Social and political citizenship in Eastern Europe. The Polish case. In *Gender justice, development, and rights*, edited by Molyneux Maxine and Razavi Sharah. Oxford: Oxford University Press.

Heinen, Jacqueline, and Stéphane Portet. 2004. Egalité des sexes en Europe centrale et orientale: Entre espoir et déconvenues. [Gender equality in Central and Eastern Europe: Between hope and disappointment]. *Transitions* 44 (1):188.

Jenson, Jane. 1992. The model citizen? Women in the new Europe. Paper read at the Social Science Research Council Conference at the Center for European Studies, at Harvard University.

Kondratowicz, Ewa. 2001. Szminka na sztandarze: Kobiety Solidarności 1980–1989. [*Lipstick on the banner: Solidarity women 1980–1989*]. Warsaw: Wydawnictwo Sic!.

Krizkova, Alena. 2004. Entre transition et stéréotypes de genre. Les femmes tchèques sur le marché du travail. [Between transition and gender stereotypes. Czech women on the labor market]. *Transitions* 44 (1):108.

Lamoureux, Diane. 1989. *Citoyennes? Femmes, droit de vote et démocratie.* [*Citizens? Women, the right to vote, and democracy*]. Montréal: Remue–Ménage.

Leca, Jean. 1992. Questions of citizenship. In *Dimensions of radical democracy*, edited by Chantal Mouffe. London: Verso.

Lefort, Claude. 1981. *L'invention démocratique – Les limites de la domination totalitaire.* [Democratic Invention – The limits of totalitarian domination]. Paris: Fayard.

Lister, Ruth. 1994. Dilemmas in engendering citizenship. Paper read at Crossing Borders: International Dialogues on Gender, Social Politics, and Citizenship, at Stockholm.

Marques–Pereira, Bérengère. 1995. Citoyenneté et liberté reproductive: L'approche de T.H. Marshall est–elle pertinente? [Citizenship and reproductive rights: is the approach of T.H. Marshall relevant?]. Paper read at Conférence de l'ESA, at Budapest.

Marshall, T.H., and Tom Bottomore. 1992. *Citizenship and social class*. London: Pluto Press.

Mink, Georges, and Jean–Charles Szurek, eds. 1992. *Cet étrange post–communisme – Rupture et transitions en Europe centrale et orientale.* [A strange post–communism: Rupture and transitions in Central and Eastern Europe]. Paris: Presses du CNRS, La Découverte.

Mossuz–Lavau, Janine. 2002. La partié en politique. Histoire et premier bilan. [The parity in politics. History and the first balance sheet]. *Travail, Genre et Sociétés*. 7:41–57.

Mouffe, Chantal. 1993. *The return of the political*. London: Verso.

Nicholson, Linda J. 1990. Introduction. In *Feminism/Postmodernism*, edited by Linda J. Nicholson. New York: Routledge.

Organization of Cooperation and Economic Development [OECD]. 1994. *Unemployment in transition countries: Transient or persistent?* Paris: OECD.

Papić, Žarana. 2004. Ex–citoyennes de l'ex–Yougoslavie. [Ex–citizen of ex–Yugoslavia]. *Cahiers du Genre* 36:207–18.

Pateman, Carole. 1988. *The sexual contract*. Stanford: Stanford University Press.

Penn, Shana. 2005. *Solidarity's secret: The women who defeated communism in Poland.* Ann Arbor: University of Michigan Press.

Ringen, Stein, and Claire Wallace, eds. 1993. *Societies in transition, East–Central Europe today.* Prague: Central European University.

Roth, Silke. 2004. One step forwards, one step backwards. The impact of EU policy on gender relations in Central and Eastern Europe. *Transitions* 44 (1):15–28.

Siim, Birte. 1994. Engendering democracy: Social citizenship and political participation for women in Scandinavia. *Social Politics: International Studies in Gender, State and Society* 1 (3):286–305.

Sloat, Amanda. 2004. Where are the Women? Female political visibility in EU accession states. *Transitions* 44 (1):45–58.

Sloat, Amanda. 2005. The rebirth of civil society: The growth of women's NGOs in Central and Eastern Europe. *European Journal of Women's Studies*, forthcoming.

Tönnies, Ferdinand. 1944. *Communauté et société*. [*Community and society*], Paris: PUF.

Vogel–Polsky, Eliane, and Jean Vogel. 1994. *Les femmes et la citoyenneté européenne.* [*Women and European citizenship*]. Brussels: European Commission.

Wallace, Claire. 1993. Citizenship and social policy in East–Central Europe (working paper). Prague: Central European University.

Watson, Peggy. 2000. Politics, policy and identity: EU eastern enlargement and East–West differences. *Journal of European Public Policy* 7 (3):369–84.

Wolchick, Sharon L., ed. 1985. *Women, state and party in Eastern Europe.* Durham: Duke University Press.

Chapter 5

Gender Equality in Latvia: Achievements and Challenges

Irina Novikova

Context

From the perspective of gender, Latvia underwent a dramatic transitional period after the restoration of its political independence in 1991 and en route to its membership in the European Union [EU] in 2004 (Aasland et al. 1997; Ruminska-Zimny 2002; Feldhūne and Mits 2004). During this period, its national legislation had to be conformed to the EU *acquis communautaire*, which included the introduction of both gender equality policies and proactive gender mainstreaming measures. This chapter will examine the adaptation of the EU's gender equality framework in Latvia during the nine–year period between the Europe Agreement signed by The Republic of Latvia and the EU (1995), and the time at which Latvia became a member of the EU, in 2004; it will focus on the successes and obstacles encountered in the process of adopting gender policies.

Several factors must be taken into consideration when reflecting upon the achievements and challenges to gender equality and gender mainstreaming policies in Latvia. When gender equality measures were first introduced in Latvia, there was still a great gap between the equality of men and women, especially in regards to their social citizenship rights and the social benefits that they were entitled to (Corrin 1999; Gal and Kligman 2000). The Soviet provision, which associated women's rights with their social entitlements, was accepted universally and was securely financed by the state budget. Within Soviet policies, women were identified as both mothers and workers. As a result, women were entitled to productive and reproductive benefits, and were granted welfare protection and social security. Women's social identity was thus shaped by this legislation. Despite these benefits, the Soviet labor market was still structured according to gender, which meant that women were primarily employed in what were considered "female-type" jobs. Even with the formal legislation on "sex equality," women's salaries were lower than men's, and the economic independence and security of women, either before or after retirement age was never secure.

The Latvian market's radical economic changes during the 1990s exposed women's disadvantages under the socialist economic model of citizenship. The 1990s brought more than just the reclaiming of patriarchal gender ideology and the nostalgia for the reconstruction of the pre-socialist gender order; women also became the principal target of the patriarchal discourse connected to the masculine bias of the political restructuring. The aim of this partiality was to construct a "bedrock" of male identity during the political rebuilding process (Connell 2002, 58–59). Additionally, as both providers and workers, women were interlocked with, and affected by the unprecedented gendered economic transformations (Trapenciere et al. 2000; UNICEF 1999.) As a major part of the aging population, women also suffered detrimental cuts to their pensions. As a substantial segment of the working force, women had to adapt to what the national labor market could offer them – at the expense of their social and economic mobility, resulting in the feminization of poverty (Aasland 2000; Coleman 2004; EC 2001; Gassmann 2000; ILO 1999; *Latvia Human Development Report* 1995; Neimanis 1999). Professional women and university graduates of all ages had to confront the deterioration of the economic and professional opportunities available to them. This resulted in women's increased vulnerability to low–paying, transnational labor migration, and human trafficking (EC 2001; IOM 2001; EC 2004; Foundation of Women's Forum 1998; Hazans et al. 2003; Huland 2001; Stukuls Eglitis 2002; Van der Molen and Novikova 2005; Wennerholm 2002).

Another crucial component of the Latvian socio-economic situation was the introduction of a new welfare regime (Pascall and Manning 2000). This change demonstrated a shift of a more general character, "from universal to selective, means-tested social protection schemes and a trend towards 'residual' welfare states" (Alber and Standing 2000, 101; see also Deacon 1998; 2001). The liberal model of economic transformation that was implemented was viewed as a panacea that would prevent poverty and alleviate its negative social consequences. Not all the parties in power during the 1990s and early years of the 21st century considered it important to elaborate and implement an integrated, socially oriented, policy. Instead, some preferred the residual model of welfare, which provided benefits only to those who were unable to manage otherwise (Esping-Andersen 1990). Within the framework of residual welfare, occupational welfare was reduced to a minimum.

The social impacts of these systemic changes in politics, the economy, and social and gender relations had a visible effect on women as a group. Since the new regimes were not very sympathetic towards women's concerns, women were also not able to see the opportunities that were opened for them as a result of the process of restoring independence, in the 1980s and early 1990s. If they had, it could have provided the motivation they needed to bring their agenda to the social and political debates that were occurring at the time. The lack of women's active participation can also be attributed to several other factors. First, women's political marginalization was one of the major gender inertias after the Soviet's so-called "sex equality" policies. Secondly, the nationalist discourse of the early 1990s obligated women to fulfill the duties of mothers and wives during the restoration of the nation. Thirdly, the political citizenship regime divided Latvian society into "citizens" and "aliens." Under this provision, only those who were born in Latvia before 1940, the year of the annexation of the Baltic countries by the USSR, and their offspring, became citizens of Latvia. The rest received the status of "aliens." This citizenship model divided the society into two ethno-political communities, paving the way for mainstream politicians to capitalize on the politics of nationalist emotions among the Latvian-speaking and Russian-speaking community (Dawson 2001; Novikova 2002; Zake 2002).

This citizenship legislation and its practice became a significant instrument that divided Latvian-speaking and Russian-speaking women according to state ascribed ethno–political categories, thereby weakening women's NGOs' ability to form solidarities across differences of class, citizenship, and ethnicity. In the early 1990s, when women's rights and/or entitlements were threatened, it also prevented them from being able to develop effective political pooling. In the second half of the 1990s, these differences also significantly determined women's ineffective feedback during the national introduction of the EU policies for the integration of gender equality and gender mainstreaming.

Thus, the developments of the 1990s, and the more recent challenges to gender equality policies and gender mainstreaming, must be understood at the crossroads of several legacies and processes. The patriarchal attitudes of the cultural and social domains, and the transformation of women's social roles, versus the celebration of their traditional roles in the family during the Soviet period, provided a legacy of knowledge that shaped the experiences, practices, attitudes, and legislation of women's rights and entitlements in society. All of this overlapped and interacted with the post-Soviet marketization process and the establishment of the social welfare regime, with its clear corporatist profile. This interaction was "successful" due to the radical marginality of women in politics, the academy, grass-roots movements, trade unions, and individual activism.

In June of 1993, the Copenhagen European Council established three criteria for central and east European countries that wished to enter the EU, they included: 1) the establishment of stable national institutions that guaranteed democracy, the rule of law, and human rights; 2) a market economy and the ability to compete in the economic space of the EU; and 3) the incorporation of the community's *acquis communautaire*. In addition, as a part of the accession process for the Baltic States, the EU community prioritized the promotion of gender equality and gender mainstreaming (*Regular Report on Latvia's Progress Towards Accession* 2002; EWL 2002).

In 1998, gender mainstreaming was constitutionalized through the treaty that established the European Communities (the Amsterdam Treaty). This treaty established that the *elimination of inequalities and the promotion of equality between women and men* was part of a double-track strategy for gender mainstreaming and positive actions (Art. 2 and 3).[1] Gender mainstreaming principles were then incorporated into the Framework Strategy for Gender Equality (2001–2005) (Commission of the European Communities 1996; 2000). This strategy was supported by the Community Action Program, which coordinated, supported, and financed the implantation of numerous means of intervention, as part of the EU Community's Framework Strategy for Gender Equality and Equal Opportunities for Men and Women in the Labor Market.

The next section will examine the changes in Latvia's national legislation in accordance with its harmonization with the EU *acquis communautaire*. The subsequent two sections will then focus on the achievements of the integration of gender equality and gender mainstreaming within Latvia; including the challenges that emerged for Latvia both en route to and after its official membership in the EU. The empirical data and information used in this chapter is based on my past research, which examined how gender equality policies and gender mainstreaming procedures were implemented in Latvia. The empirical data was gathered, in 2005, as a part of a survey conducted with governmental officials, non-governmental agencies, and research institutions.

The National Legislation of Latvia: Gender Dimensions

Prior to the Fourth World Conference on Women, in Beijing, in 1995, Baltic countries knew little about the global achievements and strategies for the advancement of equality between men and women. Furthermore, because there had been no research on gender or any gender-disaggregated analyses, there was a dramatic lack of data concerning the situation of women in these countries. Another challenge for Latvia was that there was no national gender equality or gender mainstreaming machinery that addressed the integration of gender concerns at all levels of decision-making, policy formulation, and implementation. Additionally the national legislation was still influenced by the socialist policies that promoted the protection of women's entitlements. Even more importantly, the existing national legislation did not address the inequalities in social and power relations that developed within the post-socialist context, or those that resulted from the restructuring of the economic system. The decisions, policies, and resources of mainstream politics neglected and excluded all disadvantaged groups, including women.

Following the preparation for the Fourth World Conference on Women, women's issues and gender equality began to be addressed in Latvia. As a result of the Beijing Platform for Action, the Convention on the Elimination of All Forms of Discrimination Against Women [CEDAW], UN treaties and conventions, and EU legislation on gender equality, gender equality policies in Latvia gained greater visibility by the mid-1990s.[2]

The incorporation of gender equality and gender mainstreaming measures into the national legislation of Latvia became a priority during Latvia's process of harmonizing its national legislation with that of the EU's *acquis communautaire*, and were made in accordance with the EU directives on equal pay, equal treatment at the workplace, equal treatment with regard to statutory and occupational social security schemes, and equal treatment for the self-employed and their assisting spouses.

Directives in the area of maternity leave, the organization of working time, parental leave, sex discrimination, and the framework for an agreement on part-time work were taken into account as well.[3] Soft law instruments were used to define gender equality in the fields of employment and social policy. These instruments included the European Employment Strategy, the European Social Policy, and the Community Framework Strategy on Gender Equality (2001–2005) (Commission of the European Communities 2000). According to the European Women's Lobby [EWL], which monitored the progress of gender equality and the enlargement of the EU, these general regulations provided a "comprehensive framework" that would ensure that gender equality would be integrated at all stages of the process.

The pressure of the harmonization process resulted in the formulation of equal opportunity legislation, as well as the adoption of an action plan and program for the implementation of gender equality. Since 1999, the Ministry of Welfare has been the institution responsible for the coordination of gender equality developments at the national level; with all major national gender equality policy-integration activities coordinated by the Unit of Gender Equality of the Department of European and Legal Affairs, at the Ministry of Welfare.[4] Their activities included the establishment of *The Conceptual Paper on the Promotion of Gender Equality* (1999), and The Inter-ministerial Coordination Working Group (2003), responsible for the development of The Program for Gender Equality Implementation in 2005–2006. In 2003, the government signed an Understanding Memorandum of their participation in the European Community program's Community Framework Strategy on Gender Equality, thus, initiating and securing Latvia's participation in multiple subprograms. Additionally, in 2004 the Cabinet of the Ministers accepted The Program for Gender Equality Implementation and established The National Gender Equality Council.

Latvia's required harmonization with the EU *acquis communautaire* had a significant impact on the state's promotion of gender equality legislation. The *acquis* contained a separate sub-chapter on the equal treatment for women and men, which focused on equal pay, the equal treatment of women and men in hiring and employment practices, and the balanced distribution of work and family–related duties. For the first time, the national legislation defined such terms as "gender equality," "equal treatment," "equal opportunities," "gender analysis," and "sexual rights." They also introduced key gender concepts and new approaches for implementing gender equality within national legislation. The EU accession process contributed to the promotion of gender equality in Latvia by requiring that it become part of the national agenda, and guaranteeing that all directives were transposed into the national gender equality legislation.[5]

In 2002, the most important gender equality laws came into force, the Labor Law and the Law on Labor Protection. EU directives, particularly the European Employment Strategy, which included all the standards of the EU's directives on gender equality principles in employment, influenced the revision of the Labor Code. A new law on sexual and reproductive health also entered into force on July 1, 2002, guaranteeing women the right to an abortion (a right that was previously only granted through the Welfare Ministry Regulation of 1993). Also in 2002, Parliament amended the Criminal Code, and strengthened the laws against the trafficking of human beings. In order to adjust the legal framework for the promotion of gender equality policies, the Cabinet of Ministers accepted amendments to the Instruction for the Preparation of Legal Acts (2002), which initiated obligatory preparation of annotations for legal acts. The annotation had to provide an *ex-ante* impact assessment of the compliance of legal drafts with the national gender equality principles and legislation, as well as with the EU documents and legal acts concerning gender equality. One of the most recent changes made in order to promote the reconciliation of work and family life was the paid fatherhood benefit, established in 2004. In 2004, amendments to the Labor Law, which prohibited discrimination and all forms of harassment, were also accepted by the Parliament. Finally, together with the European Commission, the national government prepared the Joint Social Inclusion Memorandum where the long-term goals for gender equality activities were set.[6]

Gender Equality and Gender Mainstreaming: Achievements

The most important achievements of the implementation of gender equality in Latvia were the introduction of legal definitions for and the acknowledgement of gender inequality; the creation of national legislation on gender equality; the introduction of gender mainstreaming principles in policymaking developments; and the subsequent emergence of the public's awareness regarding their rights to gender equality within the new democracy. The EU gender equality policies had an enormous influence on the legitimization of gender equality as a political topic within the national discourse. Without pressure from the EU legislation and institutions during the accession process, it is unlikely that local activists and organizations would have been able to have any impact on the inclusion of gender issues within political debates.

According to the national gender equality legislation, all state and local authorities and institutions in Latvia were obliged to apply a gender equality mainstreaming strategy. The first phase of this strategy included increasing the focus of gender equality units and related ministries in order to efficiently implement the concepts of gender equality within national programs. Training courses on gender mainstreaming for the personnel of the ministries and NGOs, organized by The Gender Equality Unit of the Ministry of Welfare, were held on a regular basis. Civil servants were offered these seminars and training courses to increase their awareness of gender equality and gender mainstreaming. Additionally, groups of civil servants were sent to different countries to familiarize themselves with other countries' national machineries for the promotion of gender equality.

As part of this strategy, the Ministry of Welfare also elaborated guidelines for policymakers as well as for the ministry employees who were responsible for the various spheres of policy. These guidelines assisted policymakers in evaluating the importance of gender for policymaking within their spheres, and educated them about the necessity of individual policies' compliance with new national legislation. Additionally, since 2004, the State Administration College in Latvia has established a lecture course on gender equality mainstreaming and its promotion in the civil service sector.[7]

The promotion of gender equality relied upon foreign-funded research on the economic and social situation of women and men in Latvia. This resulted in new legislation at the national as well as the municipal levels, orientated towards awareness-raising and knowledge dissemination. Tactics included publications, seminars, conferences, and round-tables on such topics as legislative norms for the equal treatment of women and men, violence against women, sexual harassment, human trafficking, and equal pay. Additionally, a number of projects supported women returning to work after childcare leaves or promoted women's entrepreneurship. Other projects attempted to encourage women to take part in political and public life, facilitate family and work reconciliation, improve women's ICT skills, or foster rural women's activism. For example, the Women's Resource Center, Marta, one of the most influential national women's NGOs in Latvia conducted projects such as The Prevention and Rehabilitation Efforts to Combat Human Trafficking (2004–2005), The Protection and Rehabilitation of Victims of Human Trafficking (2004–2005), or Opening the Labor Market to Women (2005–2007).[8]

Gender Equality: Exam Passed?

Formally, Latvia has fulfilled all the requirements for the integration of gender equality and gender mainstreaming within its national policies. However, many challenges were confronted in order to change the social attitudes towards gender issues in Latvia. These challenges included the inadequate commitment to gender equality amongst policy designers, the urgent need to strengthen existing gender equality mechanisms and mobilize the public to put pressure on the national and local government officials to promote gender equality within their daily responsibilities, and the lack of any comprehensive gender training framework. On a nationwide basis, gender equality issues are not taught in higher education or in the training institutions that prepare civil servants. Further, guidelines, handbooks, and manuals on gender mainstreaming and gender equality have yet to become more widely available to the public.

Mainstream politicians did not consider the gender equality measures, outlined above, as necessary, rather they viewed them as an "exam" that had to be passed in order to join the EU. Therefore, instead of a comprehensive policy, the mainstream political actors and governmental agencies responsible for the harmonization of national legislation with the EU *acquis communautaire* reduced gender equality and gender mainstreaming primarily to a management equality tool (Van der Molen and Novikova 2005).[9] Formal operational objectives and activities that had to be changed by May 1, 2004, as part of the obligatory "entry package," were "smoothly" integrated into the national legislation and filtered throughout the national social policy regime.[10] What we have to remember is that these policies and new laws were implemented within a specific socio-economic context of changes, which themselves had gendered effects on women. As a result, the positive action track of gender mainstreaming was marginalized. In order for it to become more effective, it has to become a priority; strategies must be developed for all areas of the issue. The positive action track must be promoted in order to develop political collaborations among women and women's organization with diffuse interests, opportunities, and to aid them in the mobilizing of their resources, and in strategically framing their concerns. Through such a process, women can gain multiple points of access to policymaking and secure their role in policymaking processes.

My own research further exemplifies some of these issues. In the surveys I conducted, respondents made no mention of any awareness of gender equality and gender mainstreaming, or of any projects that were aimed at social/ethnic/gender inclusion, particularly those targeting minority women. In fact, no minority women's NGOs participated in the equality and mainstreaming process; and "alien" women were not visible at the level of women's grassroots activism at all. The reasons for this are two fold. On the one hand, minority and "alien" women do not see themselves as full-fledged participants of women's NGOs. On the other hand, the existing pool of women's NGOs operate through the reductive lens of the general equality principle between men and women, thereby ignoring the intersectionality of women's interests and agendas. There are only rare examples of any attempts to increase the visibility of "alien" women. One such example, are the young female journalists who represent the mainstream Russian-speaking media (such as the newspaper *Vesti*, or the radio channel, *Domskaya Ploschad*) and who, over the last two years, have tried to at least marginally integrate the gender equality agenda into their coverage.

The incorporation of the principles of gender mainstreaming is still very problematic at this stage, because men and women of different social groups and ethnicities, who have not been involved in gender issues until now, still do not see the relevance of the matter to their daily lives. Thus, although a gender perspective has increasingly been written into projects, there have been very few signs of their actual implementation at the levels of policy or practice. The main challenge continues to be increasing people's awareness of the pervasiveness of gender throughout social life, which is necessary in order to move beyond the formal exploitation of the term and enable its actual consideration and application.

The major funding sources for the projects in Latvia have primarily come from outside sources such as the United Nations Development Program [UNDP] and the Nordic Council of Ministers; with other funding agencies offering only partial co-funding. There are also numerous programs that operate with support from the European Union; most prominent are campaigns that target media stereotypes, women's leadership, violence against women, trafficking, prostitution, as well as recent additions such as the training of gender mainstreaming experts by local governments. These programs have promoted gender equality in a variety of ways including training members of women's organizations and civil servants, as well combating poverty, human trafficking, and violence against women.

Additionally, the European Community Program is a key contributor of funding and resources for projects in Latvia. One such project's task was to raise the level of awareness of gender mainstreaming for key actors within the political process; as well as equipping stakeholders with effective methodological tools.[11] In the future, the EU plans continued support for the creation and capacity building of institutions that reinforce the principles of gender equality.

Although projects funded by international and supranational agencies have been important and have had positive effects, they have not yet led to a broader awareness, on the part of the public, about the positive aspects of the national goal for gender equality. Therefore, work within this area must continue as it has proven to be important for many national goals, such as guaranteeing equal pay for equal work, or ensuring a more harmonious relationship between work and family. Since national policy goals for gender equality are often phrased in very broad terms, most projects have already achieved the set goals of the national strategies. Further, because most of the projects are initiated by NGOs and institutions with various backgrounds, it is hard to claim that they act based on a shared perspective. Therefore, the main challenges include increasing the public's awareness of the necessity of gender equality, strengthening support for programs and initiatives that focus on gender-sensitive education/research, and the formulation of clearer joint objectives (Ministry of Social Welfare 2005).

No less important is the obvious fact that there is no direct or even partial governmental funding for projects that implement gender equality principles or address the procedures for gender mainstreaming. The absence of state-funded actions/projects, designed to improve gender equality on a regular and integrated basis, reflects the indifferent, if not reluctant and even hostile, attitude of the political powers towards taking the additional steps that are necessary to move gender equality policies beyond the "accession exam."[12] This kind of "negligence" in mainstreaming gender on the national level should be viewed in connection with the question of how gender equality was dealt with by the EU during the enlargement negotiation process. For example, as both Bretherton and Steinhilber point out, during the enlargement process the complexity of the implementation of women's rights was "subordinated to dominant and deeply embedded neo-liberal values associated with privatization and market opening" and therefore was simply ignored (Bretherton 1999; 2002, 4; Steinhilber 2002).

What Next?

As I indicated at the beginning of this chapter, in the 1990s, the position of women in Latvia's labor market was characterized by discrimination and a strong occupational segregation. Gender asymmetry has since become explicit because of the increasing proportion of women in part-time employment. These discriminatory practices have had an effect on young women who entered the labor market, as well as women of pre-retirement age, who were particularly vulnerable to employment in part-time jobs or impoverishment. The labor market in Latvia has exposed how the "happy marriage" of a neo-liberal economic framework and neo-conservative gender ideology in reality is only a restatement of women's political, social, and economic disempowerment; as exemplified by the politics of exclusion that it enacts in terms of age, ethnicity, and/or class. The economic transition processes have demonstrated that the familiar concepts of the liberal democratic state are:

> ... neither neutral nor impartial in the way in which they operate. Instead, they work in favor of some interests and against others. One of the groups to suffer disproportionately is that of women and it is because of this that the use of mainstreaming can be justified in order to redress this balance (Beveridge et al. 2000, 386).

However, the post-socialist context of tremendous social losses and membership in the EU has exposed "the relative indifference of the European Commission in the transition process which contracted out expertise and failed to push a European vision of social policy and a good society" (Alber and Standing 2000, 110). Gender mainstreaming must be conceptualized as a horizontal policy, a thread that runs through all other agendas. In the EU accession process, however, it was repackaged as a separate "appendix" required in order to join the EU. The implementation of the commitments made during the EU accession process influenced the ways in which the "contracted out expertise" streamlined gender equality and gender mainstreaming in Latvia. This is demonstrated by the fact that gender issues were not addressed in areas other than labor market policies and only recently, in social policies. Therefore, they avoided the cross-sectional effects of gender inequalities. Rather than being a comprehensive policy, integrated into all areas of policy intervention, the experiences of Latvian society have indicated that mainstreaming is mostly viewed as the latest management equality tool.

The mainstreaming strategy was devised to address the perceived needs of women and to prevent gender discrimination in the future labor markets of European member states (Booth 2002, 440). Yet, the mainstreaming strategy has been unable to expose and address the needs of women outside the formal labor market and formal economies of the European Member States. It also does not affect those women who have migrated to work in the lower–paying sector in other western European countries or those who are exploited by the sex industry. These failures are in many ways the result of political and cultural attitudes about women's social status. They are also the result of the interpretation and implementation of gender mainstreaming according to the principle of subsidiarity, which assigns the implementation of programs and projects by member states, to the lowest competent authority (Van der Molen and Novikova 2005).

Finally, as I have shown and argued, in Latvia, the national level governing structures have clearly manifested political preference for what Fiona Beveridge defines as the "integrationist" approach to gender equality policies and gender mainstreaming. Latvia made a clear political choice by selecting an expert-bureaucratic model for implementing gender mainstreaming:

> Under the expert-bureaucratic model, assessing gender impact is regarded as a task to be performed by specialists. Those specialists might be gender experts with specialized training as well as a sophisticated understanding of gender relations. Alternatively, mainstreaming might be seen as the prerogative of administrators. While they may be thoroughly familiar with the policy-making process and the policy area in question, they are unlikely to possess a highly developed understanding of gender relations or a proper appreciation of the exact purpose of gender impact assessment. Under the alternative participatory-democratic model a range of individuals and organizations are encouraged to contribute to any gender impact assessment. This model promotes participation and access to policy-making and emphasizes the accountability of experts and officials (Beveridge et al. 2000, 390).

In Latvia, the "integrationist" approach was welcomed, and based on this approach the national government prioritized the expert-bureaucratic model (Rees 1998; Shaw 2000). However, this was undermined by the absence of gender experts who had specialized training or a sophisticated understanding of gender relationships. Further, what remains at the core of the failed implementation of this model is the absence of any accountability to the stakeholders on the part of the experts and officials in charge of implementing it. No less important a challenge for the successful implementation of gender equality policies is the tension between gender equality policy as a comprehensive policy integrated in the larger policy field–European social policy, and the constructed welfare regime model according to which gender equality policies are mainly "motivated by the desire to more efficiently match demand and supply in the labor market rather than by a concern for social justice, fairness, social sustainability, or diversity in the labor market" (Vanags 2004). The effective mainstreaming of gender has also been hampered at the political level by the rapid changes in national governments; political and individual ideologies of the role of women; perceived threats to identity; the lack of information, training, and expertise within the newly established gender-equality units; and a lack of networking with women's organizations and activists (Van der Molen and Novikova 2005).

In my view, the alternative participatory-democratic model, or "agenda-setting" approach, although not as rapid, would have promoted more active participation amongst different stakeholders. This could have led to the cumulative growth of women's advocacy NGOs and increased their capacity to become influential partners in policymaking. It also could have promoted the introduction of gender equality to the social dialogue (Beveridge et al. 2000). Although the national machineries formally tried to strengthen the lines of communication between women's organizations, women's advocacy organizations (even though they were involved stakeholders in the gender equality and gender mainstreaming processes) were not considered to be key players in the mobilization of agenda-setting for achieving greater gender equality.

Conclusion

As I have argued throughout the chapter, the parity among stakeholders is still not efficient enough to secure a politically productive resonance between the proposed gender mainstreaming framework/policies on one hand, and the relevant accumulation of retroactive actions to assure the sustainability of the double-track strategy on the other (including proactive and retroactive projects and initiatives). In my view, women's opportunities in the arena of political power, women's mobilization, advocacy structures and networks, should be strengthened so women's NGOs networks can attain the resources and capacities necessary to secure their own sustainability and continue their agendas, thus enabling them to have a more active role in the implementation of gender mainstreaming and equality processes.

Thus far, gender equality and gender mainstreaming measures have only been undertaken by certain agencies. There is a continued absence of independent monitoring and public "feedback" on gender mainstreaming processes despite an urgent need to make the public more aware of the benefits of the gender equality projects funded by the EU. Today, in order to become a critical mass that has political influence upon future developments in gender equality, women's NGOs need to focus on building their capacity. They need to operate based on what can be called "cross-sectoral knowledge," and the trans-European expertise of gender inequalities in the capitalist welfare society of the transnational age. They should use the transnational networking opportunities to build up their own mobilization and solidarity so that they can then invest in the structural changes that are expected from gender equality and gender mainstreaming policies and measures. Another issue that must be kept in mind in the future is the fact that local level initiatives primarily originate from women's NGOs, rather than from local municipalities and that there are no structural units responsible for the implementation of gender equality principals at the local level.[13] Local women's NGOs are nevertheless trying to fill in the gap, but because they do not have sufficient funding from local or national authorities, they are still not strong enough to do it alone.

Initially, for example, the scale of trafficking and the relationship between social exclusion or marginalization and an individual's vulnerability to trafficking were not seen as priorities by those Latvian authorities whose responsibilities included enacting gender equality measures (Van der Molen and Novikova, 2005). Despite Latvia's integration of provisions, such as the special criminal provision against trafficking, which prosecutes those who traffic a person for the purpose of sexual exploitation, there is still a limited capacity among gender mainstreaming agencies to address these issues. This is related to a lack of information, expertise, and coordination on the part of the agencies involved. In light of this, it becomes clear that trafficking is not yet an integral part of the mainstreaming process in the national context:

> At first glance, there seems to be almost an over-abundance of international and European instruments and measures relating to trafficking. Yet the instruments form an incoherent strategy and there are actually a few recommendations that recur over and again: multi-disciplinary approach, effective criminalization, proportionate penalties, protection, and non-prosecution of victims (IOM 2001, 5).

This, of course, raises important questions concerning the suitability of the general institutional-legal approach towards gender mainstreaming.

Several aspects of the mainstreaming process have not received sufficient attention yet, including issues such as women's citizenship and the visibility of minority women either individually or collectively in the gender equality process. Minority women have not been involved in positive actions, projects on gender equality, or the overall development of the gender equality framework. The political exclusion of a sizeable number of Russian-speaking women in Latvia and their invisibility in women's NGOs' work is another serious challenge for the strategists and practitioners of gender mainstreaming and gender equality (Novikova 2003; Stukuls Eglitis 2002; Zake 2002).

Prioritizing gender mainstreaming in national state agencies is vital for the progress of gender equality in Latvia. However, it cannot be forgotten that, historically, gender equality and gender mainstreaming as operational categories within the EU have been brought into the social policies agenda by the activism of European women, in politics, academic institutions, grass-roots movements, trade unions, and individual activism. It is not only the EU that is bringing gender equality to the Baltic countries, it is also through the experiences of women in the countries of Europe, with their achievements, losses, and controversies, that Latvian women's realities, losses, achievements and challenges are becoming realized.

Notes

[1]   In this document *gender mainstreaming as a proactive principle* concerns the (re) organization, improvement, and the development and evaluation of policy processes, so that a gender equality perspective can be incorporated into all policies, at all levels, and at all stages by the actors normally involved in policymaking. Gender mainstreaming is a policy-making method, with *soft law* instruments such as sex-disaggregated statistics, gender impact studies, benchmarking, gender audits, etc. *Positive actions (reactive actions)* are specific measures preventing or compensating for specific disadvantages linked to sex.

[2]   However, as one of the respondents to my research on gender equality stated (and in contrast to the opinions of governmental employees responsible for gender equality) "the Beijing Platform and process has been of very limited influence. Most people who are

not closely connected with gender equality are not aware of the content of the Beijing Declaration and although, on the level of national politics, the Beijing process has helped to claim legitimacy to gender equality initiatives and policies, it would be very hard to identify specific developments that would have proceeded from it." (Respondent # 1 to Gender Equality survey (GE#1). Also see UN 2003.

3   For an overview of the main instruments of the EU enlargement process, please see EWL 2002; OSI 2002.

4   All documentation with regard to gender equality and gender mainstreaming implementation is available at the webpage <http://www.gov.lm.lv>.

5   The national legislation, gender equality program and gender mainstreaming initiatives have been implemented in Latvia with regard to the following documents: The Beijing Declaration and Beijing Platform for Action of the United Nations Fourth World Conference on Women; Women 2000: Gender Equality, Development and Peace for the 21st Century" (Beijing + 5). The Final Document of the Twenty–third Special Session of the UN General Assembly of the United Nations; The EU directives, resolutions, and recommendations on the matters of equal opportunities for women and men; Recommendations from the Committee of Ministers of the European Council to EC Member States; Recommendations of the European Council Parliamentary Assembly to Member States; Conclusions and recommendations of the International Follow-up Conference, Equal Opportunities for Women and Men in the Democratic Society, Reykjavik–Vilnius; and conclusions and proposals of the Baltic States Conference, Beijing + 5; among others.

6   Please see EC 2005.

7   Projects run by The Ministry of Welfare included: Strengthening the Multi-Sectoral Cooperation to Prevent Violence (2005); Mass Media in the (Re)Distribution of Power (2003–2004); Gender in Politics in Latvia (2003–2004); Women Towards Leadership in Business and Agriculture (2003–2005); Gender Mainstreaming Development and Implementation at the Municipal Level in Latvia (2002–2004); Administrative Capacity-Building of Governmental Bodies and Social Partners in Gender Mainstreaming Development and Implementation (2003–2004); and the Promotion of Gender Mainstreaming in National Policies of Latvia (2002–2003). For more details, please see the website: <http://www.lm.gov.lv>.

8   Please see the website: <www.marta.lv>.

9   See also Women's NGO Network in Latvia 2005.

10   Latvia was not unique in that sense, as Ostner and Lewis pointed out this was the case in other national contexts (Ostner and Lewis 1995).

11   Capacity of women's NGOs was strengthened by the Access program grant for Empowering Women in the Latvia Network. There have recently been several projects financed by the Action Programme in the Field of Gender Equality between Men and Women, such as: the Promotion of Gender Mainstreaming in National Policies (Latvia); Women Towards Leadership in Business and Agriculture (Latvia); and Mass Media in the (Re) distribution of Power (Ministry of Welfare of Latvia, promoter; Ministry of Social Affairs of Estonia, partner).

12   Only the Ministry of Agriculture has financially supported the Latvian Rural Women's Association.

13   See also Women's NGO Network in Latvia 2005.

References

Aasland, Aadne1. 2000. *Ethnicity and poverty in Latvia.* Latvia: UNDP, Ministry of Welfare.

Aasland, Aadne, Knud Knudsen, Dagmar Kutsar, and Ilze Trapenciere, eds. 1997. *The Baltic Countries revisited: Living conditions and comparative challenges. The NORBALT Living Conditions Project.* Oslo: Fafo.

Alber, Jens, and Guy Standing. 2000. Social dumping, catch-up, or convergence? Europe in a comparative global context. *Journal of European Social Policy* 10 (2):99–119.

Beveridge, Fiona, Sue Nott, and Stephen Kylie. 2000. Mainstreaming and the engendering of policy-making: A means to an end? *Journal of European Public Policy* 7 (3):385–405.

Booth, Christine. 2002. Gender mainstreaming in the European Union. Towards a new conception and practice of equal opportunities? *The European Journal of Women's Studies* 9 (4):430–446.

Bretherton, Charlotte. 1999. Women and transformation in CEE: Challenging the EU women's policy? In *Pushing back the boundaries: The European Union and Central and Eastern Europe,* edited by Mike Mannin. Manchester: Manchester University Press.

Bretherton, Charlotte. 2002. Gender mainstreaming and enlargement: The EU as negligent actor? (National Europe Centre Paper no. 23). Paper read at Conference on the European Union in International Affairs, at the National Europe Centre, Australian National University. [cited 05/05]. Available from <http://www.anu.edu.au/NEC/bretherton.pdf>.

Coleman, David. 2004. Facing the 21st Century. New developments; Continuing Problems. Paper read at the European Population Forum, Geneva. [cited 05/30/05]. Available from <http://www.unece.org/ead/pau/epf/present/ks1/ coleman.pdf>.

Commission of the European Communities. 1996. Communication from the Commission: Incorporating equal opportunities for women and men into all community policies and activities, COM (96)67. Brussels.

Commission of the European Communities. 2000. Towards a Community Framework Strategy on Gender Equality (2001–2005); Communication from the Commission to the Council, the European Parliament, the Economic and Social Committee, and the Committee of the Regions. Brussels, 7.6.2000, COM (2000) 335 final 2000/0143 (CNS).

Connell, Robert W. 2002. *Gender: An introduction.* Cambridge: Polity Press.

Corrin, Chris. 1999. *Gender and identity in Central and Eastern Europe.* London and Portland: Frank Cass.

Dawson, Jane I. 2001. Latvia's Russian minority: Balancing the imperatives of regional development and environmental justice. *Political Geography* 20:787–815.

Deacon, Bob. 1998. *Globalization and Social Policy.* [cited 6/14/05]. Available from <http:// www.globalpolicy.org/socecon/un/unglobe2.htm>.

Deacon, Bob. 2001. *Prospect for equitable social provision in a globalising world.* [cited 5/30/05]. Available from <http://www.ceu.hu/cps/eve/globconf/papers/ deacon2.rtf>.

Esping-Andersen, Gosta. 1990. *The three worlds of welfare capitalism.* Princeton: University of Princeton Press.

European Commission [EC]. 2001. *Trafficking in women. The misery behind the fantasy: From poverty to sex slavery. A comprehensive European strategy.* [cited 03/28/04]. Available from <http://europa.eu.int/comm/justice_home/news/8mars_en.htm#a1>.

European Commission [EC]. 2002. *Regular Report on Latvia's Progress towards Accession.* European Commission: Brussels.

European Commission [EC]. 2004. *European Conference on Preventing and Combating Trafficking in Human Beings: A Global Challenge for the 21st century.* European Commission: Brussels.

European Commission [EC]. 2005. *The Joint Social Inclusion Memorandum Latvia.* [cited 09/01/05]. Available from <http://europa.eu.int/comm/ employment_social /social_inclusion/jmem_en.html>.

European Women's Lobby [EWL]. 2002. *Gender mainstreaming in the structural funds: Establishing gender justice in the distribution of financial resources,* 6/10/2002. [cited 05/14/02]. Available from <http://www.womenlobby.org>.

Feldhūne, Gita, and Mārtiņš Mits. 2004. *Implementing European anti-discrimination law: Latvia.* [cited 03/27/04]. Available from <http://www.humanrights.lv/hri_l/diskrim.htm>.

Foundation of Women's Forum. [Stiftelsen Kvinnoforum]. 1998. *Trafficking in Women for the purpose of sexual exploitation: Mapping the situation and existing organizations working in Belarus, Russia, the Baltic, and Nordic States.* [cited 03/28/04]. Available from <http:// www.qweb.kvinnoforum.se/papers/traffickingreport.html>.

Gal, Susan, and Gail Kligman. 2000. *The politics of gender after socialism: A comparative historical essay.* Princeton: Princeton University Press.

Gassmann, Francisca. 2000. *Who and where are the poor in Latvia?* UNDP Ministry of Welfare: Latvia.

Hazans, Mihails, et al. 2003. *Determinants of earnings in Latvia, Lithuania, and Estonia in OECD. Labor market and social policies in the Baltic Countries.* [cited 03/15/05]. Available from <http://www.oecd.org/dataoecd/18/10/ 2493411.pdf/#search='occupational%20segregation%20Latvia%20Lithuania>.

Huland, Annette. 2001. *Western standards for post-communist women?* [cited 03/28/04]. Available from <http://www.eonet.ro/>.

International Labour Organization [ILO]. 1999. *Employment and labor market policies in transition economies.* [cited 03/28/04]. Available from <http://www.ilo.org/public/english/employment/strat/lmpol/publ/nesporov.html>.

International Organization for Migration [IOM]. 2001. *Trafficking in women and prostitution in the Baltic States, social and legal aspects.* Helsinki: IOM.

Latvia Human Development Report 1995. 1995. [cited 03/28/95]. Available from <http:// www.un.lv/down/1995_e/saturs.htm>.

Ministry of Social Welfare. 2005. *Situacijas analize izglitibas sistema par dzimumu lidztiesibas jautajumiem.* [*Report analysis of the situation with gender equality questions in the national system of education*]. Ministry of Social Welfare: Riga.

Neimanis, Astrida. 1999. *Gender and human development in Latvia.* UNDP: Riga.

Novikova, Irina. 2002. Gendering post-socialist "reason": Borders of nation, boundaries of identity politics and women in Latvia after 1991. In *Sukupuolitetut rajat,* [*Gendered borders and boundaries*], edited by Katri Komulainen. Joensuun yliopisto. Psykologian tutkimuksia 22. University of Joensuun, Department of Psychology.

Novikova, Irina. 2003. "And they have lived happily ever after" in Riga. Keynote paper presented at The First Christina Conference on Women's Studies: Rights and Representations: Visual representations of Gender and Women's Law and Rights, at the University of Helsinki, Finland.

Open Society Institute [OSI]. 2002. *Equal Opportunities for Women and Men in the European Union Accession Process [EOW]. Joint program of the Network Women's Program of the Open Society Institute and the Open Society Foundation Romania.* [cited 05/14/05]. Available from <http://www.eonet.ro/>.

Ostner, Ilona, and Jane Lewis. 1995. Gender and the evolution of European social policies. In *European social policy: Between fragmentation and integration.* Edited by Stephan Leibfried and Paul Pierson. Washington DC: Brookings Press.

Pascall, Gillian, and Nick Manning. 2000. Gender and social policy: Comparing welfare states in Central and Eastern Europe and the Former Soviet Union. *Journal of European Social Policy* 10 (3):240–266.

Rees, Teresa. 1998. *Mainstreaming equality in the European Union: Education, training, and labor market policies.* New York: Routledge.

Ruminska-Zimny, Ewa. 2002. *Gender aspects of changes in the labor markets in transition economies* (UNECE issue paper). [cited 03/28/02]. Available from <http://www.unece.org/commission/2002/Ruminska-Zimny.pdf>.

Shaw, Jo. 2000. Importing gender: The challenge of feminism and the analysis of the EU legal order. *Journal of European Public Policy* 7:406–431.

Steinhilber, Silke. 2002. *Women's rights and gender equality in the EU enlargement. An opportunity for progress* (WIDE Briefing Paper). [cited 05/14/02]. Available from <http://www.eurosur.org/wide/EU/Enlargement/EU%20_ Enlargement_Steinhilber_Oct.2002.htm>.

Stukuls Eglitis, Daina. 2002. *Imagining the nation. History, modernity, and revolution in Latvia.* University Park, PA: Pennsylvania State University Press.

Trapenciere, Ilze, Ritma Rungule, Maruta Pranka, Tana Lace, and Nora Dudwick. 2000. *Listening to the poor - a social assessment of poverty.* UNDP: Latvia/Ministry of Welfare.

UNICEF Innocenti Research Centre [UNICEF]. MONEE project. 1999. *Women in Transition.* 1999. Regional Monitoring Report, 6.

United Nations [UN]. 2003. *United Nations Beijing Declaration and Platform for Action.* [cited 05/14/03]. Available from <http://www.un.org/womenwatch/daw/ beijing/ platform/index.html>.

Vanags, Alf. 2004. *Gender mainstreaming in the public employment service. Statements and comments.* [cited 11/09/04]. Available from <http://peerreview.almp.org/pdf/denmark%2004/LV_Vanags%20-%20DK04.pdf#search='Alf%20Vanags%20gender%20ma instreaming>.

Van der Molen, Irna, and Irina Novikova. 2005. Mainstreaming gender in the EU accession process: The case of the Baltic Republics. *Journal of European Social Policy* 15:139–156.

Wennerholm, Carolina. 2002. Trafficking in women and girls and HIV prevention. Paper presented at the Conference Together Against AIDS. [cited 05/14/03]. Available from <http://search.qweb.kvinnoforum.se/sites/qweb/trafficking/ onlinearticles.html>.

Women's NGO Network in Latvia. 2005. *Alternative report on the implementation of the Beijing Platform for Action in Latvia 1995–2005. For the United Nations Commission on the Status of Women.* [cited 10/15/05]. Available from <http://www.un-instraw.org/revista/hypermail/alltickers/es/att-0094/Latvia_Beijing_10_Alternative_Report.doc>.

Zake, Ieva. 2002. Gendered political subjectivity in Post-Soviet Latvia. *Women's Studies International Forum* 25(6):631–640.

PART 2
Agency

Chapter 6

The Parameters of the Political: Does Meaning Matter for Participation in Public Life for Women in Poland and Ukraine?

Ann Graham and Joanna Regulska

Do women's non–governmental organizations and informal groups in Poland and Ukraine define their work as "political"? Despite numerous scholarly debates on the nature of the political and its meaning for women in the region of Central and Eastern Europe, the literature only rarely asks women themselves how they understand its meaning in their work and its implications for their lives as community actors. If women themselves do not define their work as political and/or question their activity and that of other women as "political," can we construct a meaning of political that explains and legitimates their public activity? Can their interests and issues be included in public policy agendas from which the distribution and redistribution of public goods are determined?

To explore these issues, we will look at the behaviors and attitudes of women in Poland and Ukraine to discover what has meaning and what works for them. To examine the words and actions of the women in Poland and Ukraine whose actions we wish to interpret, we must look not only to the meanings given to these words and actions but also to their interrelationships with the political culture and historical context in which meaning is constructed and actions occur. We must be cognizant of Scott's admonition that "experience is ... not the origin of our explanation, but that which we want to explain" (Scott 1992, 26).

This chapter will examine the political culture of Poland and Ukraine and present data on how selected women in both countries participate in the public life of their communities.[1] The data provides some answers to the following questions: 1) do women's non–governmental organizations and informal groups define their work as "political"?; 2) how does the type or purpose of their non–governmental organization [NGO] or group influences this definition?; and, finally 3) to what extent does the understanding of their purpose affect the political efficacy of women's groups? Based on surveys, observation, and discussion during training workshops held for a two–year women's leadership advocacy and lobbying project in Poland and Eastern Ukraine, the data indicates distinct differences in the ways in which women in the two countries interpret the political and how the organizations act "politically". Through analysis of the project outcomes, we begin to understand the Polish women's reluctance to identify with the "political" and the Ukrainian women's willingness to work within former President Kuchma's political system.[2]

Political Culture

Political participation is influenced by political culture. Political culture explains "how collective groups sometimes resist authority by insisting on new meanings for old practices" (Kaplan 1997, 197). Based on shared meanings and the identities formulated, political culture can vary according to gender, historical specificity, and geographical region. Thus, political participation in different environments has different meanings based on the context in which political action occurs. Different kinds of experiences mold different degrees of participation and create different understandings of the meaning of an action or actions. The understanding of political culture and how women's activism (whether defined by them as political or not) is perceived within that culture provide us with a perspective from which to frame an understanding of the "political" for women who live and work within that context. For women, political culture "depends on day–to–day habits and social norms that individuals acquire first in families and communities" (Jaquette and Wolchick 1998, 16).

In Poland and Ukraine, analysis of political, economic, and social dimensions of past and current regimes repeatedly point to an insular, patriarchal matrix of legislative, institutional, and social norms that prevent women's entries into public and political spaces. For women in Poland and Ukraine, neither the official "sameness" imposed by the communist political culture nor the "difference" engendered by differing degrees of democratization liberates women as fully participating citizens. Evident through years of totalitarianism, patriarchal political culture has not diminished during democratic transition, and its manifestations emerge in different patterns throughout each country. In both countries, women did not share political power under communism, did not exercise it during the early, euphoric years of transition, and remain marginalized even now, albeit to different degree in each location.

At the same time, the construction of political culture and the definitions of women's political activism in Poland and Ukraine occur at different sites. Although both sites of activism remain marginal, strongly influenced by the socialist past, and only slightly altered by the different "democratic" transitions in each country, the reasons for this marginality are not the same. As this chapter will demonstrate, women in both countries have not found significant opportunities to challenge the current political systems – regardless of each country's political, social, and economic environment.

In Poland and Ukraine today, the tensions produced by continuing political negotiations between the socialist past and the transition to a democratic present indicate a shifting political environment.[3] Under communism, individual differences were a matter of official political irrelevance, and the rights, privileges, and benefits awarded by the communist state were touted as equal, but in actuality were not. The rhetoric of liberal democracy by political elites in Poland now legitimizes the recognition of the individual and applauds individual difference. Individual difference, however, has not afforded political equality to women. Whereas women's interests were manipulated by the instrumental needs of the totalitarian state, they are now submerged in a new collective identity defined primarily by "democracies" comprised of male interests.

In Poland, the collective past and the more individual present is further complicated by what is called the politics of anti–politics (Linz and Stepan 1996; Ost 1990). One example is the extensive underground activism by Polish society in civic organizing and protests during the 1970s and 1980s. Protesters opposed the authoritarian regime on moral rather than political grounds, and, consequently, civic protest was stripped of the political. Dirty, immoral, and corrupt communist politics was the subject of contestation and not of democratic participation, and the opposition politics that emerged appropriated a moral rhetoric more easily defined as anti–politics. The politics of anti–politics played an instrumental role in creating a sphere of freedom, independent of the socialist state.

Despite the "dirty" perception of politics in post-1989 Poland, male representatives of the old communist regime as well as the opposition moved quickly to assume control of the political process, its institutions and agendas and initially certainly safeguarded women's exposure to its "dirty" activities. Although women have achieved visible gains in political participation, their reluctance to engage in politics, to become active party members (Fuszara 1999; Regulska 1998; Siemińska 2005), and/or to run for political office continues to return as a topic of debate (Szawarska 2005; OŚKa 2005). Yet, they increasingly believe that their representation in political life should be greater (Fuszara 1999; Graff 2005). In addition, there is also an increased interest by the media and the general public concerning the lack of women in public office that indicates a slow, but positive change in attitudes toward women's participation in public life (Fuszara 2001).[4]

Poland has one of the strongest traditions of mass protests in Central and Eastern Europe, yet women have only occasionally come together to protest about women's issues (Kubik and Ekiert 1999). The two most known examples are the continued protests against the loss of abortion rights after extreme anti–abortion measures were introduced by post–1989 parliaments and demands in the late 1990s for increased pay and improved working conditions by nurses.[5]

In Ukraine, the transition had a different starting point for women, and the negotiations between the socialist past and a more recent democratic present took an additional fifteen years to be concluded. Yet, already in 1991, during the final months of the Soviet Union, women themselves organized two mass protests to emphasize women's political demands (Bohachevsky-Chomiak 1995, 12-17). Both protests focused on the practical concerns of women as mothers: the drafting of their sons and the environmental problems related to Chernobyl, and its effect on their children. Although women began to undermine the socialist claims that women were liberated and to distance themselves from the socialist ideology of equality, their protests and newly formed women's organizations were organized to work within and influence male–dominated political structures. Initially, the organizations were also directed primarily toward reviving traditional, historical ideals of Ukrainian women (UNDP 1999). Furthermore, as in the case of the Russian women's movement, the simultaneous timing of the movement protests with periods of extreme instability in the Soviet Union ensured that women activists would "avoid forms of mobilization that could be construed as conflictual or instability–provoking" (Sperling 1999, 50). Thus, women engaged in simultaneous struggles with the Soviet ideology of the past which, although it advanced women's employment, never really questioned traditional domestic gender roles, and the unstable post–Soviet political and economic realities.

In fact, in both Poland and Ukraine, state ideology is strongly influenced by the resurgence of traditional norms of the role of women. Through this rhetoric of nationalism, new cultural and political values are constructed that profoundly affect the development of women's political identity. In both countries, "a direct connection is established between restrictions of female activity – such as holding high public office, for example, and the process of state–building" (Rubchak 1996, 318). Such restrictions include employment discrimination, prohibitions on types of jobs, and abortion rights in Poland (with the strong support of the Catholic Church). In Ukraine, its 337–year history of Russian domination and Soviet rule ensures a more difficult process of independent state building. Characterized as "a nation without a politically usable past," the traditional gender matrix as well as social stereotypes (such as the perception that it is not necessary for women to be successful professionally or that women should stay home and take care of the children) contribute to the reproduction of patriarchal models of gender relations (Prizel 1997, 331; Von Struensee 2002).

Ukraine's task of developing an independent political state is constrained not only by the political and ideological legacies, but also by its economic decline. For women, the decline bears serious implications. According to the United Nations Development Fund, women in Ukraine experienced an "accelerated decrease in income" compared to men (Buchanan 2003). Although official figures placed women's unemployment at nearly 44 percent in 1997, the unofficial figures are higher and guarantee that women's ideas and hopes for democracy are submerged by the daily struggle of finding enough for their families to eat (Buchanan 2003). In fact, "democracy and independence are becoming increasingly associated with economic decline" (Prizel 1997, 360). The data provided, in 1997, by the Institute of Sociological Research at the Academy of Sciences, Ukraine, indicated that these figures were even more dramatic for young women with over 44 percent of women under the age of 30 unemployed, and for women with a higher education for whom the unemployment rate was 70 percent. Moreover, while men left their jobs freely (56 percent), women were predominantly fired (74 percent of women were dismissed due to staff cut-downs) (Von Struensee 2002, 7). Thus as Von Struensee concludes, "at the level of mass consciousness, women are primarily seen as mothers whose place is in the family. Such stereotypes hinder real equality between women and men, and obstruct harmonization of professional and family roles for Ukrainian women" (Von Struensee 2002, 10). These marginalizations translate directly into the under–representation of women in politics and decision–making processes, and further perpetuate traditional stereotypes. It is only now, since the Orange Revolution in the fall of 2004, that the minimal requirements for democracy (open, regular elections, and basic civil liberties) are emerging for both women and men. Whether this translates into increased political representation for women is not yet known.

In both countries, however, women were limited from public participation in public life. In Poland, women participated significantly in pre-1989 underground activities, but their roles were subordinate and "invisible". Their unwillingness to see themselves as political subjects rendered them invisible (Kondratowicz 2001; Penn 2003; 2005). In Ukraine, a similar distaste for communism and its harmful effects on the health and well being of their children encouraged women to try to associate with the political process in order to focus attention on issues that were of immediate importance to women. Yet, in the case of Ukraine, two profoundly troubling ecological and military disasters (Chernobyl and Afghanistan) intervened to require their immediate attention and force them to use existing political resources to resolve them. In neither case were women in a position to claim prominent roles in the transition or a more powerful voice in the construction of public and political discourses. Women certainly understood, however, that "demonstrations were temporary measures that did not always result in lasting changes" (Bohachevsky-Chomiak 2000, 275).

In both Poland and Ukraine the post–1989 changes exposed the hidden, unequal gender equality that prevailed under socialism. Under communism, the state's higher degree of control of all aspects of public, economic, and private life skewed distinctions among the public and private spheres and rendered the state the sphere of primary importance. Although during the socialism women "participated" as elected or party officials in the communist party, the high numbers (approximately 23 percent of the total members of parliaments throughout the Central and Eastern European region in general) were imposed through false ideologies of gender equality. The drastic initial decline, after 1989 in Poland, and the continuing decline in Ukraine of elected women officials at the parliamentary level, and the simultaneous decrease in political party membership by women certainly proved the point. In Ukraine, women held 7.8 percent of seats in the *Verkhovna Rada* [Upper Parliament] in March 1998, but this number declined to 5.3 percent by 2002 (Karatnycky, Motyl, and Piano 2002, 613).[6] In Poland, 16 percent of the candidates in the 1998 parliamentary elections were women and 13 percent were elected to the *Sejm* [Lower Chamber of Parliament]. However, by 2001, 93 women were elected as deputies to the Sejm (20 percent) and women comprised 23 percent of the Senators in the *Senat* [Upper Chamber of Parliament] (a rise from the previous 12 percent) (Fuszara 2001, 6; Sroda 2005). These numbers show that despite obstacles women are slowly making gains in Poland, but not in Ukraine; although such numbers do not tell the full story.

"Political" Activity

Participation in public life is most often understood as running for elected office, or exercising power as an elected official or top government administrative employee, but, more recently, it has also begun to be understood as activism through non–governmental organizations. The number of women's NGOs has certainly increased and their membership has grown over the last ten years in both countries, yet in many ways, they can only partially offset the need for women's greater participation and representation in more formalized public and political structures.

Non–governmental organizations are new entry points into the public policy decision process that were not available in the past (Einhorn and Sever 2003; Keck and Sikkink 1998; Kuehnast and Nechemias 2004; Lang 1997, 101–20; Naples and Desai 2002). The rise of NGOs is one consequence of the search for avenues to negotiate successfully with state institutions at different scales. In countries undergoing transformation, the engagement of NGOs exemplifies the state's inability to address citizens' basic needs, and to provide services and support to groups that are marginalized socially and politically (Phillips 2000, 23–9). There is also the recognition that transnational activism (with international and regional NGOs) does offer possibilities for strengthening women's collective power and using resources that might have not been available domestically. How much impact these organizations have on influencing public policy depends on a multiplicity of factors and varies from case to case and across locations. Moreover, the ongoing scarcity of independent domestic funding, further constrains NGOs in their efforts to establish themselves as separate from state control or sponsorship. Since admission of Poland to the European Union, in 2004, the differences between women's positions in the two countries have widened. Women and feminist NGOs in Poland, at least in theory, can now access EU funding. Funding, however, is only one of the challenges faced by NGOs. Questions of who is represented, and who is not represented by NGOs remain unanswered. Furthermore, in both Poland and Ukraine, NGOs are more prevalent and powerful in larger rather than smaller cities. During the time period of this study, women's organizations in smaller cities in Ukraine and the small towns and villages in Poland rarely received Western and/or outside funding for their projects.

At the time of our research, there were approximately 200 non–governmental women's organizations in Ukraine, out of almost 5,000 registered organizations (Galbraith 1999; Phillips 2000). Of these, only 100–120 were active; the remaining existed primarily on paper. The focus of the majority of these organizations was traditional and historical, but also social and economic to assist the Ukrainian family with "urgent social problems caused by changes" after the break–up of the Soviet Union (UNDP 1999, 21). Very few classified themselves as feminist, and in comparison to Polish NGOs, NGOs in general belatedly asserted their independence as Ukrainian NGOs separate from their traditional ties to Russian women's organizations (Bohachevsky-Chomiak 2000). This may have contributed to their belief that NGOs "cannot participate in elections except indirectly, by supporting a political candidate or party." Simply put, citizens active in a "political party have more chances to strive for their goals and attain public office than those who belong to an NGO and merely perform social or advocacy work" (Kupryashkina 2000, 17). These "party" connections could partially explain the tendency of the women participants in Ukraine to marginalize the effectiveness of NGOs. NGO or group activity is subordinate to political parties and electoral activities that acquire much higher political efficacy in the eyes of Ukrainian women.

Ukrainian women's NGOs did participate in the 1995 Beijing conference and their participation led to parliamentary hearings on women's issues and the implementation of the UN convention in Ukraine (Bohachevsky-Chomiak 2000). The Ukrainian government subsequently signed the Beijing Platform for Action. That Platform, along with the ratified in 1981 Convention on the Elimination of All Forms of Discrimination Against Women [CEDAW] was integrated into national legislation. In 1996, a national women's conference "Beijing's Strategies: Program of Actions in Ukraine" led to the adaptation of changes in the Constitution and the incorporation of more gender sensitive language. The Ukrainian government also established the office of Ombudsperson in 1998. In general, however, women remained unfamiliar with national and international developments and mechanisms that could assist them in asserting their social, economic, and political rights. Moreover, numerous reports repeatedly assert that these developments are primarily on paper confirming that widespread marginalization and discrimination of women continues to exist (Buchanan 2003; Von Struensee 2002). Nevertheless, women's groups are attempting to address wide-ranging issues such as prevention of trafficking in women, domestic violence, and developed a variety of programs focusing on crises management, hotlines and legal assistance, self-help, job training, assistance to families with children of varying degrees of physical and mental abilities or AIDS (Buchanan 2003; Phillips 2000; Rudneva, et al. 2002).

In Poland, in the late 1990s, women's organizations totaled approximately 250 of the over 30,000 associations, foundations, self–help organizations, parent school committees and many other organizations that have been created since 1989.[7] Approximately 90 of them were actively pursuing their missions at the time of our research. Initially, the majority of groups emerged in Warsaw, and although Warsaw remains the center, women's NGOs became active in Poznań, Olsztyn, Wrocław, Katowice, Kraków, and Toruń and in many other larger and smaller cities. Over the years, the geographical span as well as the diversity of organizational purpose has increased. Women's right centers, professional women's associations, self–help groups, women's studies centers, and conservative and religious groups are only a few of the many categories of women's groups created. The early growth of women's NGOs in Poland (for example, Pro Femina, The Polish Feminist Association, The Federation for Women and Family Planning) was spurred by the government's attempt to eliminate women's rights to free abortion and to restrict their reproductive rights. This initial focus on a single issue translated into the growth of women's advocacy and broader agendas. Unemployment, employment discrimination, sexual harassment, political participation, violence, and general deterioration of social and economic rights became the focus of increasingly wider attempts to influence government agendas and to provide assistance to women in need (for example, the Center for Advancement of Women, Women's Rights Center, The National Women's Information Center [OŚKa]). Since the 1995 Beijing Conference (and Poland's more recent acceptance to the EU) women's lobbying and activism are not only restricted to domestic issues. Women's NGOs have become visible and active participants in the European and global movement for women's human rights, advocacy and lobbying. In the last few years, some women's organizations have joined collaborative efforts to create a more collective feminist agenda through the creation of gender studies, publications, or collective lobbying efforts.[8] These actions have ensured the rise of stronger women's networks, albeit still a fragmented one that often lacks a clear consensus on what the most pressing issues are and what are the most effective strategies for addressing these issues.

The Meaning and Practice of the "Political" for Women's Organizations

In order to explain the meaning and practice of "political" for women working in formal or informal women's organizations, in Poland and Ukraine, we must examine what constructs the activity and the ability to influence public policy decisions; the structure of the action itself must be delimited in the larger context of the parameters of the political culture. Noting that "subjects have agency ... subjects whose agency is created through situations and statuses conferred on them" through what Scott calls "definite conditions of existence" within political cultures, we cannot continue our explanation without outlining the parameters of the activity or action of that which we seek to explain (Scott 1992, 34). In this discussion, the action is the "political" or how the "political" is experienced by women in this study.

The project "Advocacy and Lobbying" engaged, through a series of five workshops in Poland and four in Ukraine, approximately 50 women (20 women from Ukraine and 30 women from Poland), representing a total of 25 NGOs in Poland and 12 in Ukraine from a total of 25 communities in both countries[9] (Figure 6.1). During the workshops women learned how to establish clear organizational missions and goals, to identify and analyze community problems, to identify options to address these problems, and to devise workable plans to solve them. The emphasis was put on the development of organizing skills, creating and sustaining coalitions, sharing resources,

Figure 6.1 Participating Communities, 1997/1998

and understanding the role of gender in public policy decision–making. Between work-shops, the participants returned to their communities and worked with the members of their organizations or with small groups to put into practice the skills and knowledge learned. As a result of their participation the women developed strategies to define com-munity needs and initiated advocacy projects such as establishing health centers and youth clubs, teaching resume–writing and job interview skills, assisting women and families in need, and encouraging and organizing women to run for public office.[10]

To explore the experience of the political for the women project participants our discussion will focus on the following questions: 1) do women's non–governmental organizations and informal groups define their work as "political"?; 2) how does the type or purpose of their non–governmental organization or group influence this definition?; and finally, 3) to what extent does the understanding of their purpose affect the political efficacy of women's groups? These questions are germane since to understand how women participate in the public life of their communities, it is important to know how they define their organizational activities.

Our methodology stressed the involvement of participants in a number of ways. First, we asked the women participants to answer pre- and post-project question-naires, participants were listened to and interviewed informally during the work-shops, and many of them wrote about their experiences for published project guide-books. Second, to gather further information, the researchers also participated as observers and trainers during the workshops. All verbal and written responses were assured confidentiality. Thus, although the names of the communities in which the women worked are presented in Figure 6.1, the organization names are not included for reasons of confidentiality.

The questionnaire posed identical questions before the project, in 1997, and after the project in 1998 and asked participants the following: 1) to discuss whether or not they considered the work of their NGO political; 2) to describe how their work is or is not political; 3) to give examples of the type of work they consider political or not political; and 4) to indicate organizational ability to influence public policy.[11] Prior to a discussion of the results, it is important to acknowledge that the results represent the voices of 50 women participants and 37 women's NGOs from Poland and Eastern Ukraine. Thus, the results are not a representative sample of all women's NGOs in either country.

Feminist scholars repeatedly emphasize certain dilemmas faced by research-ers when conducting feminist fieldwork of this kind. During this project, we were extremely cognizant of the different power relationships between the trainers/re-searchers and the women participants (Cheng 2001; Nagar 2003; Wolf 1996). The researcher's positionality is implicated in the research results. Interviewing and working with women from small towns and villages (especially in Poland) who initially felt less knowledgeable about world affairs, the training subject matter, and the significance of gender and its analytical power placed the researchers in a more powerful position. However, this "unequal" relationship diminished during the se-ries of workshops as the researchers began to know and learn from the participants and the participants began to know and learn from the researchers. Another factor also influenced the results. The training, interviews, and informal discussions were each conducted in Polish, Ukrainian, or Russian with English interpreters. Thus, language difficulties (including the quality and variation of interpretation) remained a barrier despite increased familiarity between participants and the different language abilities of the researchers.

Finally, because the researchers also participated as trainers, it is inevitable that the outcomes achieved and the knowledge learned was influenced by the training received. The project did influence participants' knowledge of political activism, their perception of this knowledge, and, thus, how they defined its meaning in the post–project surveys. On the other hand, researchers, through their participation in training workshops, became more embedded in the realities of women's struggles in Poland and in Eastern Ukraine.

Organizational Purpose

Participating organizations in both countries ranged from small, informal groups from small Polish towns to more established NGOs in larger communities in both Poland and Ukraine. The purpose of the organizations or groups varied. In Ukraine, the participating women believed strongly in the necessity to "attract the attention of public officials to the status of women" and the women in Poland focused predominantly on providing direct services and education. As a result of the workshops, however, organizational purpose was often refined or clarified. For example, at the beginning of the project, a number of organizations often stated very broad goals such as "improving the lives of women," and, as a result of the two–year series of workshops, changed their goals to provide a more specific service such as opening a food bank for women and children, employment counseling, and educational seminars concerning women's human rights, or health care.

In Ukraine, the purpose of 84 percent of the organizations was to promote issues of interest to women to local or regional government officials through close association with political parties and/or government officials and to elect women to political office. Although the purposes identified in Figure 6.2 distinguish between promoting the issues of women (50 percent) and supporting the election of women (34 percent), these activities were closely related within and among the participating organizations.[12] During early seminars, the participating organizations defined their tactics as "attracting the attention of government officials" to a particular issue (Advocacy and Lobbying 1997a). In other words, primarily through personal conversation with officials and newsletters, women "appealed" to members of legislative bodies and/or political parties to consider their cause (Pre-Project SR # 5 Ukraine 1997). For example, one participating organization "cooperated with political deputies" to reverse a decision by local authorities to close a sanitarium for children (Pre-Project SR #8 Ukraine 1997). This support was discussed by the women participants in terms of "cooperation with city legislators regarding the involvement of women leaders" in

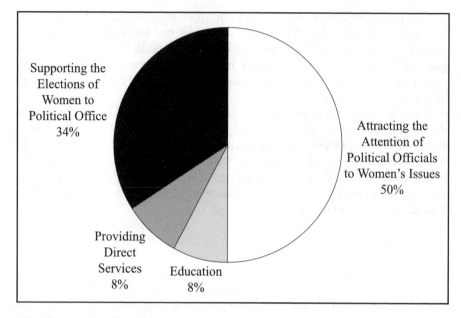

Figure 6.2   Organizational Purpose, Ukraine, 1997/1998

the political process (Advocacy and Lobbying 1997b). In Zaporozhje, Ukraine, the women's organization identified problems concerning women's health and the environment through newsletters and community meetings. In the early years of transition, support for their organization derived specifically from local council members. The defeat of these members in subsequent elections guaranteed the demise of the organization's influence and a change in its leadership.

Thirty–four percent of the Ukrainian organizations (Figure 6.2) stated their purpose as providing open support to women candidates in parliamentary, oblast, or city elections. The group, Journalists for Women's Rights, in Dnipropetrovs'k, published a newsletter featuring women candidates and encouraged women to support them in local elections. At the same time, the journalists also sponsored a local women's competition, "Women of Prydniprov'ya", that featured local women and had the explicit goal of raising the "status of women in the eyes of the mayor of the city and state officials and attracting their attention to women's problems" (Pre-Project SR #3 Ukraine 1997).

Sixteen percent of the Ukrainian organizations (Figure 6.2) existed to provide direct educational or social services to women. In Ukraine, the services organized by the participating groups included seminars on women's leadership and community awareness campaigns on selected issues. In Kharkiv, the NGO Women in Science and Technology organized a summer school in cooperation with Iowa State University for women leaders in the sciences. The Kharkiv's Women's City organization organized seminars for women about the situation of women and cooperated

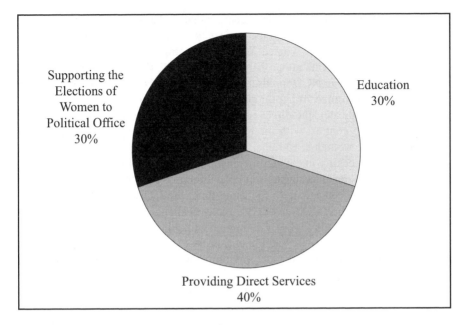

Figure 6.3   Organizational Purpose, Poland, 1997/1998

closely with La Strada–Ukraine, an organization that works to expose problems associated with the trafficking of women.

In Poland, the purpose of 70 percent of the organizations (Figure 6.3) was to offer direct educational or social services. Thirty percent of the organizations offered educational seminars on issues of importance to local women, and 40 percent of the organizations provided direct services (Figure 6.3). Women's groups taught courses on the English language, women's rights, health care, and computer skills. Services provided included: assistance to women with varying degrees of physical disabilities, and women and children in need of economic support, counseling to victims of domestic violence, resources for coping with spouses' alcoholism, and support for unemployed women. In Łęczna, the participating women's organization held seminars on women's health care issues (funded by a locally written proposal to the Polish Batory Foundation), and the women's group in Lidzbark–Warmiński taught English–language classes for women to improve employment skills. The group also created a resource center for women with family problems and conducted meetings with lawyers in order to raise awareness about domestic violence. In Przeworsk, women organized a soup kitchen for poor women and their families, and women in Miastko began to incorporate issues of gender and disability into their organization for disabled adults and children.

Thirty percent of the participating organizations in Poland identified their purpose as supporting the election of women candidates to parliament or local councils.

In Łódź, the Women's Human Rights Center organized a press conference to highlight the need for more women in the city council and national parliament and encouraged women to vote for women. Women, they emphasized, "are better qualified and tend to solve problems rather than fight for power" (Pre-Project SR #3 Poland 1997). Women Also, an NGO in Olsztyn organized several local meetings to stress the importance of women voting for qualified women candidates.

As the data indicates, the direct educational and service provision purposes of the Polish women contrast with the more decidedly electoral and political lobbying activity of the women in Ukraine. The participating women in Ukraine strongly believed in the necessity to "attract the attention of public officials to the status of women" and the women participants in Poland focused predominantly on providing direct services and education. At the same time, the lobbying or "attracting" activities of the women in Ukraine rarely directly challenged or proposed specifically feminist views to elected officials. The women worked within the established system to bring problems of primarily traditional concern to women to the attention of male officials including children's health, environmental hazards affecting families, or children's rights.

Although the clarity and specificity of organizational purpose improved immensely during the course of the two–year period of workshops, neither country's participants significantly changed their original general categorization of organizational purpose; for example, electoral or service provision. Participants in Poland, however, were initially and, throughout the project, less abstract and more concrete concerning organizational purpose and goals. During one workshop discussion in Ukraine, women hypothesized that their tendency to espouse lofty, often unrealistic goals derived from two sources: 1) a residue of socialism's lofty, unrealistic goals; and 2) an admittance that real life is difficult, and often high aspirations and much talk are regarded as substitutions for the inability to act and as a method of coping with unpleasant realities (Advocacy and Lobbying 1997b; 1998a).

Political culture and the law also influence organizational purpose. At the time of our research in Ukraine, NGO laws were (and in fact still remain) much stricter than in Poland, especially in terms of the excessive power of the state to regulate NGOs as well as the lack of clarity in regard to individual organizations' tax exempt status. The Kuchma's Ukrainian state was reluctant to develop a third sector because of its potential for accumulated subversive political power. Over 70 years of Soviet domination fostered the belief that civil society and the state are one and the same. Thus, the legal and financial situation of NGOs was unstable and contributed to an "insufficiently developed" culture of philanthropy and volunteerism (Karatnycky, Motyl, and Piano 2001, 665). In fact, at the same time that the public and local communities indicated an increasing knowledge of the role of NGOs, national polls showed a decline in the population's belief in their necessity. Such inconsistencies continued to undermine the support of NGOs by the government and the parliament which severely limited the financial independence of NGOs, and delayed and discouraged their registration (Karatnycky, Motyl and Piano 2001, 666–68). According to

Freedom House's *Nations in Transit* report, NGOs in Ukraine had very few opportunities to receive support from the government. Although some large groups received financial aid from the state budget (youth, veterans, and the disabled), the process is generally closed and there are few solicitations or grant competitions for NGOs – especially in small communities (Karatnycky, Motyl and Schnetzer 2001; Haran 2001). By 2000, only one-fifth of NGOs benefited from local donors. According to one workshop participant, a small town organization's efforts to register with the local government can be thwarted simply because the registration office's familiarity with the purpose and the number of previously registered groups gave it licence to say that a women's organization already existed, and therefore one more was unnecessary (Advocacy and Lobbying 1998b).

In Poland, NGOs had more autonomy. Much of this autonomy is directly related to the immediate establishment of local self–government and the subsequent opening of new channels of participation by citizens in governmental processes. Polish NGOs can access funds from the local and national state, as well as private donors and businesses. The Polish legal environment was, at the time of our research, "relatively positive" and contrasted significantly with the insecure situation in Ukraine (Karatnycky, Motyl, and Piano 2001, 487). Thus, NGOs in Poland, have gained acceptance, but they continue to struggle financially, especially since most of the "western" funding was terminated. This "drying up" of external sources disproportionately affected powerful women's NGOs; reflecting continued strong reluctance to acknowledge such groups as legitimate political actors.

Political Meaning

When asked if they considered the work of their organization to be "political", women in Ukraine consistently stated that they did.[13] The Ukrainian women defined the term as working through party politics to elect specified candidates, encouraging women to vote, and organizing women to strengthen their influence to draw attention to women's issues. One woman articulated the opinion of the majority of women in the seminar stating, "that to change consciousness and improve public opinion concerning the needs and situation of women, there must be a rise in political activity by women … to realize our program, we must gain power" (Post-Project SR #8 Ukraine 1998). Power, in this case, is directly translated to electing representatives to parliament, oblast, and local councils or, as she emphasized, "political" power. This belief increased during the course of the project. In 1997, 60 percent of the Ukrainian women believed their organizational work was political and, in 1998, 70 percent of the Ukrainian participants identified their work as political (Figure 6.4). The majority agreed with one of the participants who commented that, "women need to gain high levels of professional positions which will lead to the strengthening of their political influence"; this reflects that in Ukraine, professional positions often depend on political contacts (Post-Project SR #6 Ukraine 1998).

Two Ukrainian organizations were more reluctant to identify the work of their

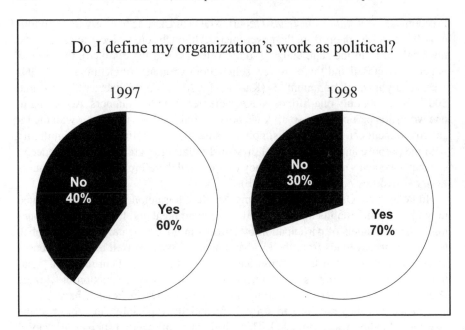

Figure 6.4   Political Meaning, Ukraine

organizations as political. Although they understood that "any NGO creates public opinion and therefore influences the political situation," one organization member stated, "to give women scientists the opportunity to find themselves in improved living conditions will not depend on politics" (Advocacy and Lobbying 1998a).

Interestingly, another organization member's insistence that she did not consider the group's work political emphasized that supporting or not supporting the authorities implies that "we involuntarily take part in political life" (Post-Project SR #2 Ukraine 1998). Thus, regardless of how narrowly the organization viewed the meaning of the term "political", the women in the group reluctantly admitted politics to be a common, inescapable reality of daily life in Ukraine. They understood that "any NGO [in order to be successful] works in cooperation with the authorities" (Post-Project SR #5 Ukraine 1998). The majority of participating women in Ukraine understood the meaning of the power of the current political system, and the necessity of their organizations to take part in its requirements to exist.

In Poland, in 1997, only 8 percent of the women believed their organizational work to be political while, in 1998, 28 percent indicated this belief (Figure 6.5). Over 70 percent of the participants in Poland continued to insist that the work of their organization was not political. In Poland, women negatively associated politics with political parties. For them, the goals of the majority of their organizations focused on improving the lives of women in "every part of their lives despite their political standing" (Advocacy and Lobbying 1998c). Furthermore, "political affilia-

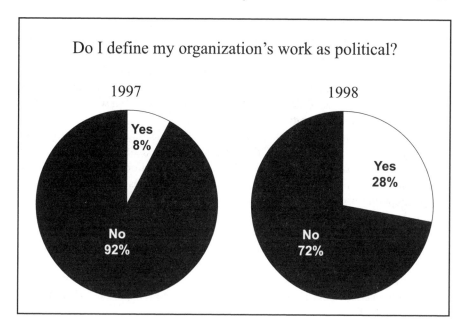

Figure 6.5 Political Meaning, Poland

tion is not important … women and their concerns are important." In Poland, politics is a man's job. The goal of women's organizations is "to solve social problems, not to participate in male, political power struggles" (Post-Project SR #3 Poland 1998). Organizational needs are "addressed to all women no matter what their political affiliation" (Post-Project SR #5 Poland 1998). To ensure their ability to work with all women, the majority of participants insisted that organizations cannot consider their work political. The activities in which they engaged (courses, workshops, and/or support services for women), should not espouse a particular political opinion. As one participant stated emphatically, "we are dealing with the community's issues and its needs" and thus, the organization could not advocate political opinions perceived to endanger resolution of what women in the community required for daily life (Post-Project SR #4 Poland 1998). Another participant declared that, "we are only helping women who need our help" (Post-Project SR #10 Poland 1998). Two organizations indicated that their work was not political precisely because their organizational purpose targeted women's unemployment and family problems. Because the state, in their view, was no longer interested in women's employment and family or social problems (as evidenced by a decrease in state subsidies and funding for jobs, childcare, and social services) the work of their organizations, therefore, required actions outside state–supported activities. Thus, in their view, these services could not be influenced by politics. In the words of one participant, "helping people with alcohol–related problems has nothing to do with politics; it is a health issue"

(Advocacy and Lobbying 1998c). For her (and many of the respondents), the state has not only abdicated its role, it has also failed to articulate an interest. Women's organizations exist "to solve problems" and these problems cannot be left to the uncertainty of slow and often unresponsive political bureaucracies. Furthermore, men are involved in politics and it is a "man's job; women take care of family–related issues" (Post-Project SR #4 Poland 1998). Politics is partisan, but women's needs as well as those of the community are not.

The few organizations in Poland that focused on electing women to local and parliamentary seats insist that, "if the organization's goal is to integrate women into the political domain, it is political" (Advocacy and Lobbying 1998c). These groups, however, are in the minority. Throughout the series of workshops, all of the participating organizations broadened, with some hesitation, their understanding, and acceptance of the political. Their definitions expanded and became not only limited to electoral activities, but also included, according to one participant from Lidzbark–Warmiński, "influencing self–government officials" which, in her opinion, was "somewhat political" (Post-Project SR #13 Poland 1998). Another participant recognized that although "we do not want to gain political power, we do need to influence the decisions that affect us. So maybe it is politics" (Post-Project SR #6 Poland 1998).

Political Efficacy or the Ability to Influence Policy–Makers

In both Poland and Ukraine, participating organizations believed strongly in their capacity to influence local officials whether they defined the activity as political or not. In both countries, this belief did not alter significantly between 1997 and 1998 (Figures 6.6 and 6.7) and remained consistently high (Poland – 60 percent in 1997, 75 percent in 1998 and in Ukraine – 72 percent asserted their political efficacy in both years). Despite the differences between the meanings of "political" in each country, the perception of their organizations' political efficacy was strong.

In Poland, particularly, the higher number of participants from small towns is an important factor in how this ability is perceived. People know one another in small towns; yet, the high percentage of the belief in their political influence versus the lower percentage of indicating their work as political, offers further explanation of Polish women's non–political stance. In 1997, 92 percent of the respondents (Figure 6.5) answered "no" to the question concerning their organization's political activity, but at the same time 60 percent responded positively and offered evidence of their ability to work with local officials (Figure 6.6). In 1998, 72 percent responded "no" to considering their organization's work as political (Figure 6.5), but insisted even more strongly (75 percent) in their political efficacy (Figure 6.6). Regardless of their more affirmative belief in their ability to influence local officials, they consistently insisted that their work was not political. Their examples, however, are extremely "political" to the Western observer. One group created a local coalition of NGOs that asked and received financial backing for projects in their community; a group

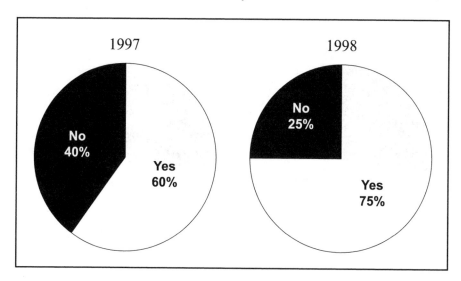

Figure 6.6   Political Efficacy, Poland

of unemployed women met with local parliamentary deputies and lobbied for more equitable distribution of unemployment funds; and a newly formed organization was allocated funding from the *gmina* [municipality] budget for health care seminars. Groups that did receive governmental allocations of funds or that affected change in government policy insisted that the benefits would benefit the entire community, not only the women, and therefore, they were not political. Women do not believe their issues are political in part because NGOs are not perceived by the general population or by party officials as political organizations and also because the NGOs are working primarily with socio–economic issues. The "political" for women's organizations in Poland was understood primarily as political rights and not the electoral politics of primary concern to the Polish women participants. Again, despite their belief in their organizational political efficacy, the definition of the "political" and what can be achieved through political access is narrowed by its perceived negativity.

While the women tackled a wider variety of issues in Poland, their reluctance to categorize the organizational problems as issues that require resolution through political systems may have limited their ability to resolve many of them successfully. Participating women described constant frustrations as they attempted to approach local officials to request funding, space in which to offer services or cook and serve food to needy families, or merely to ask for verbal support for community ideas.

The consistently high belief in their political efficacy by the Ukrainian women (72 percent) in both years does not tell a complete story (Figure 6.7). The evidence indicates that, in order to achieve their goals, women's NGOs cooperated with or assisted local government in the performance of their pre–determined duties. One organization "cooperated with local authorities to identify needy families who re-

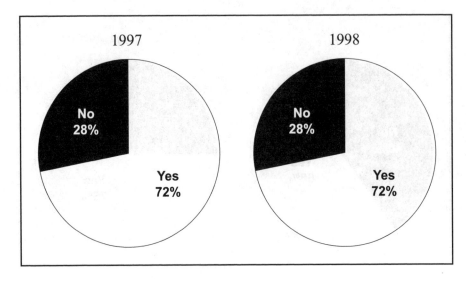

Figure 6.7   Political Efficacy, Ukraine

quired assistance" (Post-Project SR #8 Ukraine 1998). Another group "attracted attention to the status of women in the eyes of the Mayor and the local council" (Post-Project SR #3 Ukraine 1998). In most cases, cooperation and attracting attention did not result in increased funding or policy revisions. One group, however, did lobby the local government to overturn a decision to close a sanitarium for children. Interestingly, this group was one of the few in Ukraine that did not want to regard its actions as political. In fact, the group characterized their cooperation with authorities as "involuntary". This response, while isolated, does indicate a striking similarity to the responses of the Polish women who believed that because they worked on social issues they did not consider their work as "political".

Although, in the end, the women in Ukraine believed consistently and strongly in their political efficacy, the results of such convictions were negligible. Their belief in their efficacy derived from their continued association with political party and/or government officials and the need to do so regardless of policy outcome. The association is what counts, and NGOs, in and of themselves, were subordinate to the power of political parties and electoral activities.

Discussion of Results

The results of the two–year project indicate that women in Poland and Ukraine slightly broadened their understanding of the political to include the capacity of NGOs and the socio–economic issues these organizations embrace as players in the distribution of public resources in the political environment of their countries. While, their behaviors and actions did redistribute local resources in Poland and in Ukraine, women increasingly drew attention to requests that their interests be included in local and national policy agendas, although NGOs are not necessarily regarded as major political actors. Most significantly, the organization members dramatically improved their ability to understand and clearly articulate the purpose of their organization or why it existed. Clear articulation of their mission and goals or knowing what it is they want to accomplish will result, in the long term, in more measurable outcomes that are not visible at the present time. Most recently, the political changes in both countries did provide opportunities for greater visibility of women's NGOs. In Poland over the last few years, and primarily because of the high level of activism related to the EU accession process, women's and feminist NGOs did indeed gain greater visibility and a more positive social perception. In Ukraine, their active participation in the international arena (for example, their preparation of the shadow report for the UN Committee on the Status of Women) and more recently during the Orange Revolution may have enhanced their visibility in numbers, but not in actual decision-making.

The question remains: does the definition of "political" matter to women who participate in political activity? Can such a definition emerge when the political is often dismissed as inapplicable or invisible in Poland and as the only means available in Ukraine? Although Kaplan insists that women worldwide are now creating their own political cultures based on their own understanding of rights, customs, and history, and the more recent context of the international feminist movement; our contention is that women in this project have neither made that connection or acknowledged the potential existence of what Regulska calls after Fraser a "subaltern counter publics" (Kaplan 1997; Regulska 1998, 311). Such alternative spaces of participation certainly exist, but are not comprehended fully as political spaces that matter in Ukraine or as political spaces that should be utilized in Poland by the women who construct them (Graham and Regulska 1997). Thus, can we call it political in Poland if women do not acknowledge it as politics? Can we also call it political in Ukraine if the women readily subordinate their own political spaces?

Yet, this "visible" picture may not tell the entire story. Women in both countries are working within very different political cultures that also affect the ways in which they construct their political space. In Ukraine, the space only recently has gained more legitimacy, and, in Poland, the legitimacy that allows NGOs to operate with fewer constraints is still marginalized by the larger political environment. Thus, can political work be done without naming it "political"? Can one be gender–conscious, and deny at the same time the existence of that consciousness? Is it possible that in fact women's political activity is emerging because they have a need for action, but have no need for a "political" name? Can it successfully influence the redistribution of public resources without the "political" label? Can a women's movement emerge in Ukraine if it is too strongly tied to male party politics?

What the above struggles signal are not only the continuity of the anti–politics model for NGOs (especially in smaller communities in Poland), but also a new simultaneous construction of public and private spheres with interrelated, permeable boundaries. The first public is visible, acknowledged and a site of continuous contestation among political elites and constructed predominantly by men encompassing formal political institutions and agendas that control the distribution of resources. The second is often invisible and powerless in the view of the traditional political system. Yet, it is meaningful for the women involved as it is the site where women attempt to alter the distribution of resources and where they try to fill the void left by the state. It is also the result of some Polish women's acceptance of their position as non–political subjects in the traditional sense, and women's frustration at their failure to be accepted as political actors in Ukraine.

Notes

[1]   The project "Advocacy and Lobbying: Women's Strategies for Empowerment in Central and Eastern Europe" was developed and implemented throughout 1997–1998 by the Center for Russian, Central and East European Studies [CRCEES], at Rutgers, The State University of New Jersey, through its Local Democracy Partnership Program, in cooperation with the National Information Center on Women's Organizations and Initiatives [OŚKa] in Warsaw, Poland and the Kharkiv Centre for Women's Studies in Kharkiv, Ukraine. It was funded by the United States Agency for the International Development [USAID] through the Promoting Women in Development [PROWID] program administered by the Centre for Population and Development Activities [CEDPA] for Poland and Ukraine and the Open Society Institute's Institute for Local Government and Public Service in Budapest, Hungary for Poland. We are very grateful for Polish and Ukrainian women's interest in this project and for their agreement to acknowledge their voices in this chapter.

[2]   Since the completion of this project, Ukrainians overturned the regime-controlled election results, and a new president was elected in the fall of 2004.

[3]   While Poland's transition, given the more than fifteen years of its duration, can be defined as more consolidated than in Ukraine, whose real reforms began only in the fall of 2004, tensions were created in both countries by new meanings associated with the individual and a continuing dialectic between individualism and collectivism.

[4]   While, in 1995, only 40 percent of respondents believed that more women should hold appointed posts in government, by 2000 50 percent believed so. Similar trends can be observed regarding public administration (28 percent vs. 44 percent); political parties (26 percent vs. 44 percent); and judiciary positions (25 percent vs. 39 percent).

[5]   More recently, women began to seize new opportunities offered by the EU eastern enlargement in order to protest the continually restrictive anti–abortion law (for example see, The Open Letter to the European Commission, 2002).

[6]   On the other hand, in 2002, 42 percent of women were council members of the local *rada*. However, these high numbers reflect the lack of decentralization reforms at the local level, rather than an establishment of new local democratic practices.

[7] Kurczewski (2003) pointed to a rapid increase of such organizations in Poland, citing anywhere between 50,000 and 100,000, including 36,000 associations and 5,000 foundations. Karatnycky, Motyl, and Piano (2001) pointed also to over 50,000 civil society organizations.

[8] For example see *Katedra* [cited 6/28/05]. Available from *http://katalog.czasopism.pl/pismo.php?id_pisma=705; Zadra [Splinter]*[cited 6/28/05], available from http://katalog.czasopism.pl/pismo.php?id_pisma=621; or the recently created Polish Women's Lobby, 2005 [cited 5/16/05]. Available from http://OSKa.org.pl/infopage.phpid=34.

[9] In Poland participants were drawn from two larger cities (Olsztyn and Katowice) and from many smaller communities. In Ukraine participants primarily came from larger cities located in the eastern part of the country (Kharkiv, Dniepropetrosk, Donetsk). (See Figure 6.1). The organizations were selected based on the following criteria: 1) interest in women's issues and willingness to advocate on their behalf in their communities; 2) potential organizational capacity; and 3) their commitment to attend all training workshops. The number of project participants and participating NGOs is larger in Poland than in Ukraine. As there was no statistically significant difference in the results, the results of the two Polish projects are combined.

[10] The results of the projects were published in three volumes written in Polish and Ukrainian, and included case studies authored by some of the participants who discussed the lessons learned during the project for their organizations and their applicability to other organizations (Zakrzewska, Graham, Regulska 1998, 1999; Rudneva 1998).

[11] Respondents participating in the pre-project survey are identified in the text as Pre-Project SR and post-project survey respondents as Post-Project SR.

[12] More than one person from an NGO attended the workshops. Thus, the organizational purpose figures represent the total number of organizational responses and the primary stated purpose of the organization. There were no changes in the broad categories of organizational purpose during the project. The percentages and numbers of the organizations or respondents do not always equal one another due to more than one person from an organization answering the same questionnaire.

[13] The political percentages and the following political efficacy percentages represent the total number of individual women who worked for the participating organizations.

References

Advocacy and Lobbying. 1997a. "Advocacy and Lobbying: Women's Strategies for Empowerment in Central and Eastern Europe." Workshop #1. Kharkiv, Ukraine.

Advocacy and Lobbying. 1997b. "Advocacy and Lobbying: Women's Strategies for Empowerment in Central and Eastern Europe." Workshop #2. Kharkiv, Ukraine.

Advocacy and Lobbying. 1998a. "Advocacy and Lobbying: Women's Strategies for Empowerment in Central and Eastern Europe." Workshop #1. Kharkiv, Ukraine.

Advocacy and Lobbying. 1998b. "Advocacy and Lobbying: Women's Strategies for Empowerment in Central and Eastern Europe." Workshop #3. Kharkiv,Ukraine.

Advocacy and Lobbying. 1998c. "Advocacy and Lobbying: Women's Strategies for Empowerment in Central and Eastern Europe." Workshop #4. Warsaw, Poland.

Bohachevsky-Chomiak, Martha. 1995. Practical concerns and political protest in post-Soviet Ukraine. *Transition* 1 (16):12–17.

Bohachevsky-Chomiak, Martha. 2000. Women's organizations in independent Ukraine, 1990–1998. In *Ukraine: The search for a national identity*, edited by Sharon L. Wolchick and Volodymyr Zviglyanich. New York: Rowman and Littlefield Publishers.

Buchanan, Jane. 2003. Women's work: Discrimination against women in the Ukrainian labor force. *Human Rights Watch* 15 (5).

Cheng, Shu-Ju Ada. 2001. Weaving intimacy and reflexivity: The locational politics of power, knowledge and identities. In *Feminist (re)visions of the subject: Landscapes, ethnoscapes and theoryscapes*, edited by Gail Currie and Cella Rothenberg. Lanham, MD: Lexington Books.

Einhorn, Barbara, and Charlotte Sever. 2003. Gender and civil society in east central Europe. *International Feminist Journal of Politics* 5 (2):163–90.

Fuszara, Małgorzata. 1999. Puch ciągle marny. [Fluff still weak]. *Gazeta Wyborcza*, July 21, 1999, 11–13.

Fuszara, Małgorzata. 2001. Bilans na koniec wieku. [The balance at the end of the century]. *Katedra*, 1 (April 15):4–25.

Galbraith, Cara 1999. West NIS Project Coordinator for the NIS-US Women's Consortium, personal interview. Washington, DC.

Graff, Agnieszka. 2005. Człowiek, mężczyzna po prostu – i inne istoty obdarzone płcią. [*Human being, meaning men-and others with sex identity*] [cited 5/20/05]. Available from http://www.OSKa.org.pl/articles.php?id=11.

Graham, Ann, and Joanna Regulska. 1997. Expanding political space for women in Poland: An analysis of three communities. *Communist and Post-Communist Studies* 30 (1):65–82.

Haran, Olexy. 2001. Director of Freedom House, personal correspondence with authors. Kyiv, Ukraine.

Jaquette, Jane S., and Sharon Wolchick. 1998. Introduction. In *Women and democracy: Latin America and Central and East Europe*, edited by Jane S. Jaquette and Sharon L. Wolchick. Baltimore: The Johns Hopkins University Press.

Kaplan, Temma. 1997. *Crazy for democracy*. New York: Routledge.

Karatnycky, Adrian, Alexander J. Motyl, and Aili Piano. 2001. *Nations in transit, 1999–2000: Civil society, democracy, and markets in East Central Europe and the Newly Independent States*. New Brunswick, NJ: Transaction Publishers.

Karatnycky, Adrian, Alexander J. Motyl, Amanda Schnetzer, and Freedom House (US). 2001. *Nations in transit, 2001: Civil society, democracy, and markets in east central Europe and the newly independent states*. New Brunswick, NJ: Transaction Publishers.

Karatnycky, Adrian, Alexander J. Motyl, Amanda Schnetzer, and Freedom House (US). 2002. *Nations in transit, 2002: Civil society, democracy, and markets in east central Europe and the newly independent states*. New Brunswick, NJ: Transaction Publishers.

Katedra. 2005. [cited 6/28/05]. Available from *http://katalog.czasopism.pl/pismo.php?id_pisma=705*

Keck, Margaret, and Kathryn Sikkink. 1998. *Activists beyond borders: advocacy networks in international politics*. Ithaca, New York: Cornell University Press.

Kondratowicz, Ewa. 2001. Szminka na sztandarze: Kobiety Solidarności 1980-1989. [*Lipstick on the banner: Solidarity women 1980–1989*]. Warsaw: Wydawnictwo Sic!.

Kubik, Jan, and Grzegorz Ekiert. 1999. *Rebellious civil society: Popular protest and democratic consolidation in Poland, 1989–1993*. Ann Arbor: The University of Michigan Press.

Kuehnast, Kathleen, and Carol Nechemias, eds. 2004. *Post Soviet women encountering transition: Nation building, economic survival, and civic activism.* Washington, DC: Woodrow Wilson Center Press.

Kupryashkina, Svetlana. 2000. Ukraine: End of the "NGO Dream". *Give and Take: Journal of the Initiative for Social Action and Renewal in Eurasia* 3 (3):16–17.

Kurczewski, Jacek. 2003. Civil society as the third sector in Poland today. In *Civil Society in Poland,* edited by Jacek Kurczewski. Warsaw: Institute of Applied Social Sciences, Warsaw University, Center for Social Research.

Lang, Sabine. 1997. The NGOization of feminism. In *Transitions, environments, translations: Feminists in international politics,* edited by Joan W. Scott, Cora Kaplan, and Debra Kates. New York: Routledge.

Linz, Juan, and Alfred Stepan. 1996. *Problems of democratic transition and consolidation: Southern Europe, South America and post-communist Europe.* Baltimore: Johns Hopkins University Press.

Nagar, Richa. 2003. Collaboration across borders: Moving beyond positionality. *Journal of Tropical Geography* 24(3):356–72.

Naples, Nancy A., and Manisha Desai, eds. 2002. *Women's activism and globalization: Linking local struggles and transnational politics.* London: Routledge.

OŚKa Foundation. 2005. *Kongres kultury: Kobiety w polityce. [Congress of culture: women in politics]* [cited 5/20/05]. Available from http://www.OSKa.org.pl/news.php?id=1118.

Ost, David. 1990. *Solidarity and the politics of anti-politics: opposition and reform in Poland since 1968.* Philadelphia, PA: Temple University Press.

Penn, Shena. 2003. *Podziemie Kobiet. [Women's Underground].* Warsaw: Wydawnictwo Rosner and Wspólnicy.

Penn, Shena. 2005. *Solidarity's secret: The women who defeated communism in Poland.* Ann Arbor: University of Michigan Press.

Phillips, Sarah D. 2000. NGOs in Ukraine: The makings of a women's space? *The Anthropology of East Europe Review* 18(2): 23–9.

Polish Women's Lobby. 2005. [cited 5/16/05]. Available from http://OSKa.org.pl/infopage.php?id=34.

Prizel, Ilya. 1997. Ukraine between proto-democracy and "soft" authoritarianism. In *Democratic Changes and Authoritarian Reactions in Russia, Ukraine, Belarus, and Moldova,* edited by Karen Dawisha and Bruce Parrott. Cambridge: Cambridge University Press.

Regulska, Joanna. 1998. The political and its meaning for women's transitional politics in Poland. In *Theorizing Transition: The political economy of change in central and eastern Europe,* edited by John Pickles and Adrian Smith. London: Routledge.

Rubchak, Marian J. 1996. Christian virgin or pagan goddess: Feminism versus the eternally feminine in Ukraine. In *Women in Russia and Ukraine,* edited by Rosalind Marsh. Cambridge: Cambridge University Press.

Rudneva, Oleksandra. 1998. *Women's advocacy and lobbying: Strategies for women's empowerment in Ukraine.* Kharkiv: Kharkov Center for Women's Studies.

Rudneva, Oleksandra, Ganna Khrystova, Inga Kononenko, Natalya Orlova, and Olena Kochemyrovska. 2002. *Alternative report to the U.N. Committee for the Elimination of all Forms of Discrimination against Women [CEDAW].* Kharkiv: CEDAW.

Scott, Joan W. 1992. Experience. In *Feminists theorize the political,* edited by Judith Butler and Joan W. Scott. New York: Routledge.

Siemieńska, Renata, ed. 2005. Płeć, wybory, władza. [Gender, elections, power]. Warsaw: Wydawnictwo Naukowe "Scholar" and Fundacja im. Friedricha Eberta.

Sperling, Valerie. 1999. *Organizing women in contemporary Russia: Engendering transition.* Cambridge: Cambridge University Press.

Środa, Magda. 2005. Balanced participation of women and men in Poland. Paper read at The 10-year Review and Appraisal of the Implementation of the Beijing Platform for Action, the 49th Session of the Commission on the Status of Women, at The United Nations, New York.

Szawarska, Elżbieta. 2005. *Elementarz wyborczy dla kobiet.* [*Electoral ABCs for women*] [cited 5/20/05]. Available from http://www.OSKa.org.pl/articles.php?id=16.

United Nations Development Program. 1999. *Gender analysis of Ukrainian society.* Kyiv: UNDP.

Wolf, Dianna L., ed. 1996. *Feminist dilemmas in fieldwork.* Boulder, CO: Westview Press.

Von Struensee, Vanessa. 2002. *Gender equality: Legal and institutional framework on women's rights Ukraine* [cited 1/15/02]. Available from http://www.pili.org/cgi-bin/a2j?_show.name=resourceand_show.file=resources/30.xml.

Zadra. [Splinter]. 2005. [cited 6/28/05]. Available from http://katalog.czasopism.pl/pismo.php?id_pisma=621

Zakrzewska, Agata, Ann Graham, and Joanna Regulska. 1998. *Being active in public life.* Warsaw: Wydawnictwo OŚKa.

Zakrzewska, Agata, Ann Graham, and Joanna Regulska. 1999. *Being effective in public life.* Warsaw: Wydawnictwo OŚKa.

Chapter 7

Belgrade's Protests 1996/1997: From Women in the Movement to Women's Movement?

Marina Blagojević

Introduction

The purpose of this chapter is to shed light on one specific aspect of the Belgrade Protests of 1996/1997, namely, their gender dimension or their "genderness." "Genderness" here is used both as an assumption and as a theoretical concept. It is a theoretical concept in the sense that in a patriarchal society everything is coded and "pervaded" by gender; the more a society is patriarchal, the more "genderness" is pronounced, which can be, as an assumption, operationalized and empirically tested in different social domains: culture, politics, economics. The level and type of "patriarchalism" shapes the level and type of "genderness" of certain social phenomena. In that sense, there is nothing in patriarchal society that is "gender neutral." Even when women were included in the protests on an equal basis, when there is "quantitative equality," their participation is still "gendered," expressing "qualitative inequality." Whether this is an issue of legitimate gender differences or patriarchal mechanisms of exclusion is the object of the following analysis.

I will examine the "genderness" of the protests on two levels: firstly on the empirical, factual, level of participation, behavior, attitudes, and political representation; and secondly on the level of cultural/symbolic representation. In the last part of the chapter, I will relate the protests, as societal movements, to the feminist movement to examine their mutual influences and dependence in constructing civil society. The assumption here is that each of these movements was helping the other to "open up" society in a process of establishing democratic order.

Background to the Protests of 1996/1997

The history of the last decade of political life in Serbia can be traced as a history of protests.[1] The Belgrade Protests of 1996/1997 were, from the perspective of 2005, an important and necessary step in the long lasting process of building a democratic society, which has not been unilateral or simple in any way (Motyl and Schnetzer 2004; Mundiju–Pipidi and Krastev 2004).[2] Belgrade's Protests had two major "branches": the Citizens' Protest of 1996/1997 and the Students' Protests of 1996/1997, both took place from November 1996 until March 1997.[3] They were wide, intense, and largely spontaneous reactions to the annulment of local elections in a number of cities in Serbia, including Belgrade.[4] The ruling "left coalition", composed of the Serbian Socialist Party (headed by Slobodan Milošević), the Yugoslav Left (headed by Milošević's wife, Dr. Mira Marković), and a small party called "New Democracy," at first publicly recognized the victory of the Coalition "Together," which took place in most of the Serbian cities, including Belgrade The citizens of Belgrade were preparing to celebrate this victory by gathering spontaneously in the center of the city, but suddenly, overnight, the "left" coalition decided to alter the results, claiming that there were "irregularities" in many of the instances where the Coalition "Together" had won the vote. Thus, the gathering intended to celebrate the victory turned into one of protest. The open, unashamed, and cynical theft of citizens' votes by power holders directly provoked spontaneous mass revolts throughout Serbia. For the first time since Slobodan Milošević came to power in Serbia (in 1987), his authority was questioned by a deception that was obvious to the voters.

In Belgrade two Protests took place simultaneously: the Citizens' Protest [CP], initiated by the Coalition "Together," and the Students' Protest [SP], initiated by students who claimed to be independent from the Coalition "Together." In some instances, protests in Belgrade and other cities throughout Serbia attracted up to 500,000 people. Demonstrations were peaceful, with a very definite and decisively non–violent orientation, which was especially pronounced after the first several weeks of the protests. The most important societal characteristics of both protests were that they mainly involved the urban middle class, and that both parents and children were protesting together.

From 1991 to 1996, there had been a number of similar anti–regime oriented protests in Belgrade. In 1992, there had also been two simultaneous protests: one from the students of Belgrade University and the other, *Vidovdanski sabor* [The Assembly of Vidovdan], which was organized by the opposition. Some of the similarities between the 1992 and the 1996/1997 protests are striking, especially when comparing the students' protests.[5] As one of the scientists/participants stated, especially at the beginning of the 1996/1997 Students' Protest, it seemed as if it were a continuation of the same protest rather than a different one. Most people had a feeling of "*deja vu*." This made everybody, including scholars and even opposition leaders, somehow better prepared.[6] The experience of the previous protests had helped guide the articulation and organization of the new ones. One of the "secrets" of their success and their duration was precisely in this process of learning civil resistance, which took time, but which unmistakably produced a different political culture.

Although it is extremely hard to summarize the political situation that produced the protests, or to "catch" the essence of the protests, it is necessary to make several points, with the risk that they still may not be transparent to outsiders. Firstly, the most important characteristic of Serbian society in the 1990s was a high level of chaos and anomie, a high level of institutional disintegration, co–occurring with processes of state centralization, which concentrated power into the hands of the President of the Republic, Slobodan Milošević. The dismantling of the previous system was a much faster process than the construction of a new one (Lazić, 1995). Serbia had therefore found itself very much "dragged" into a vicious spiral of bad political decisions and even worse consequences. However, a great part of the population, having been "brain–washed" by the media and having no democratic tradition to rely on, developed neither the critical attitude nor the behavior necessary for preventing such phenomena. Pushed into the corners of their private lives, striving for survival, too often many people could not find enough knowledge, strength, courage, or moral integrity to loudly speak out about the real causes of their disastrous situation.

The second important point is that the protests of 1996/1997 were centered on the problems of chaos, the lack of rules, the non–existence of the rule of law, and, accordingly, the high level of political voluntarism. To illustrate, the official slogan of the Students' Protests of 1996/1997 was "*pravo*," which in Serbian has multiple meanings: straight, direction, justice, law, the legal system, and righteousness. The graphic presentation of this slogan was an arrow that pointed neither to the left nor to the right but, instead, pointed forward. This slogan captured the essence of the protests of 1996/1997 – a demand for the establishment of "game rules." This was the smallest common denominator that gathered so many different people under the same, very basic demand. On the other hand, the slogan of the Students' Protests in 1992 was "*dosta*," simply meaning "enough!" This slogan, at the beginning of the period of the violent destruction of ex–Yugoslavia, revealed all the despair and powerlessness of young people at that time, as well as their readiness to plead with power–holders for a change in a direction away from their disastrous politics. Compared to this, the 1996/1997 slogan "*pravo*" [straight], reveals quite a different spirit and tactic.

Students in 1992 closed themselves in at the University, the protest lasted for several weeks, and then it simply imploded, with the help of outside (pro–regime) political elements. The Students' and Citizens' Protests of 1996/1997, on the contrary, took to the streets, thereby becoming highly visible. They did not implode, but, on the contrary, they exploded. The energy and willingness to change away from the downward direction of Serbian politics with its devastating effects simply flooded the streets of Belgrade and other cities throughout Serbia. The sophistication of the Student Protest of 1992, which turned into an exciting cultural event, and its failure to ensure wider acceptance within the population, formed a good basis for the development of a different collective wisdom in the protests of 1996/1997.[7]

The 1996/1997 Protests involved a new strategy and organizational approach. This surprised not only the power–holders, but also the actors themselves. The slogan "*pravo*" meant, for the first time, that there was a strong political will, articulated well enough to follow its own direction. Students and citizens were going for "a walk" for days, although weather conditions were bad, although "the walks" were forbidden, although strong police forces were threatening the streets ready to provoke conflict. Therefore, the essence of the protests of 1996/1997 was exactly the clear demand for "*pravo.*" The strength of the revolt corresponded to the clarity of the aims and strategies. On another level, the protests encouraged specific sociability. In the three months of the protests, people were finding old friends and making new ones, they were meeting acquaintances and neighbors. The protesters' particular sociability was closely connected to an overwhelming feeling of catharsis and the "discovery" of similar "others". Since the war started the people of Serbia endured long years of both collective (UN sanctions) and individual isolation and suffering. They simply stopped believing that there could be others who might feel the same way. Protests brought this joy of mutual recognition, of belonging to some other Serbia, a Serbia that exists and that will exist, as part of the rest of the world.[8]

Although very successful, judging by the length and scope, these protests failed to achieve concrete political victory. Six months after the protests, many of the "walkers" were quite ambivalent and confused about what really had happened and what had produced the failure. Six months after the process the Coalition "Together" ceased to exist. Part of the Coalition had accepted running for elections under obviously unfair conditions, while the other part had decided to boycott them. At first sight, it seemed that all the energy expressed during the protests had "gone with the wind." But deeper political and sociological analysis could reveal that what had happened immediately after the protests was simply the result of pre–existing structural factors which could not have been changed overnight. Chaos, anomie, Mafia infiltration of the state, and Mafia–like privatization processes could not have been annulled by simple street demonstrations, no matter how persistent and charming they might be. The chaotic societal context, the weakness of institutions, and the lack of rules affected the opposition, as it affected everybody else, especially those who were powerless. The failure of the protests showed that the strategy had to be changed. The chaos of the regime could be attacked only by a similar "chaoticness" from the resistance. This finally happened with the "Resistance," the national resistance movement, which was highly decentralized, widely spread, and carried out many simultaneous and unpredictable actions, which finally resulted in the great victory against Milošević's regime in October 2000.

Gender Perspectives of the Protests

Although not the main issue of the protests, which emphasized the defense of basic citizenship rights (for example, the right to vote), a gender perspective is necessary to understand both the depth and the complexity of the social transformation towards civil society, which often contained paradoxical or contradictory elements. Resistance does not happen in a vacuum, and is largely shaped by the existing patriarchal structures of society. And although this "patriarchalism" of resistance movements has been extensively documented in feminist historical research, and the case of Serbia is not very special and extraordinary, it is still worth exploring for a number of reasons. Particularly, it is because this type of research is something rather new for the post–socialist world; because "patriarchalism" of the resistance is a good indicator of the future direction of the transformation process; and because subtle analysis reveals the complex legacies of socialism in relation to gender relations.

To explore the "genderness" of the protests I will combine an insider's (activist) position with an outsider's (researcher) position. I believe that this kind of approach is useful for the revelation of the basic characteristics of a movement. An insider's engaged view is highly relevant for understanding and even predicting future societal development. To explain my epistemological starting point even further, I will list the multiplicity of roles I have "naturally" found myself in during the protests. As a university professor, I took an active part in the protests, as most other professors did. As a feminist activist, I also took part in a number of different feminist actions aimed at expressing support for both the Citizens' and Students' Protest. As a sociologist, I was analyzing survey results during the protests. Further, I was not only a participant in the protests, but, as most of other social scientists, I was also a participant–observer. And finally, throughout the three months of the protests, I was a passionate believer (that things will change), a "graduated noise–maker" during the Radio–Television Serbia News Two, as well as one of the hundreds of thousands of people who really enjoyed the protests, their humor, playfulness, and energy.[9]

An academic could pose the question: am I qualified to give an "objective" picture, a serious "scientific" analysis, and a dispassionate view on the protests? The point I want to make here is that I do not intend to be an "objective" scientist. "Objective" science with "scientific" methods was quite incapable of predicting the protests; moreover, there was not a single "scientific" social indicator before 17 November 1996 that any sound would break the silence at the dawn of the protests. But, nevertheless, the miracle happened! Miracles like this one can neither be predicted nor fully explained by an academic sociological knowledge that ignores activist perspectives. Within the very essence of predictability in social science lies the power to be active in that reality. More power brings better predictions. The strength of the agency that produces the change is closely connected with the reliability of predictions. Activism gives power, and it enables more sensitivity to future events and more power to actually create them. While academic sociological knowledge has a basically static, structural, generalizing view, even of the dynamics of such a social movement, the activist approach understands and provokes social change by analyzing the steady, small, multiple, step–by–step efforts taken to create social change. Analyzing and memorizing these efforts is the basis for predictions related to future movements, because movements do not come into existence only as reaction to structural needs for change, but also through their own self–articulation, in which self–understanding, memorizing, obtaining skills, and learning techniques become equally important. Therefore, it is impossible for me, with this particular topic, to separate activism from knowledge (Blagojević 2004). Not only did I use my knowledge for activism for defining the protest's strategy and influencing concrete actions, but I was also learning from my own activism. Activism sensitized me to "social facts," which would otherwise have remained invisible. It also helped me to contextualize these "social facts," thus strengthening my power to predict and to envision, when the protests failed and general despair prevailed.

Although it is hard to prove through regular "scientific" methods, Serbia became a different country after the protests of 1996/1997. Although six months later the protest Coalition "Together" had split up, although part of it was going to the new elections, while the other was advocating a boycott, although it seemed that the existing power structure had largely consolidated itself after the failure of the Protests, Serbia had still become a different country. This difference was only materialized in October 2000. However, retrospective analysis convincingly shows that the great victory of the October Revolution in 2000, a victory that was even greater because there were only a few victims, simply would not have been possible without all the previous protests or their failures.

Participation, Attitudes, Behavior Along Gender Lines: Women's "Share" of the Protests

The surveys made during the protests provide a unique opportunity to get a precise picture on women's participation.[10] Data from the surveys on the SP and CP of 1996/1997 showed that women were included in both protests almost on an equal basis. In the CP of 1996/1997, women were protesters in 44.9 percent of cases. In the organization of the SP of 1996/1997 (press, information, public relations, program organizing, security), 20.7 percent of male respondents and 17.8 percent of female respondents were involved. This data reveals that the SP of 1996/1997 had a widely branched–out organizational structure, based almost equally on both men and women.

Female and male students also had had experience from previous protests, with 40 percent of men and 35.2 percent of women from the SP of 1996/1997 taking part in the SP of 1991/1991. Altogether, 77.1 percent of male students and 61.6 percent of female students had some previous protest experiences. Women included in the CP of 1996/1997 claimed more often than men that they had some previous protesting experience. This proves that one of the keys for successful protesting, in fact for the creation of a democratic society is the cumulating experience of protesting, both on an individual as well as on a collective level.

Who Were the Women Protesters?

Women students came, as men did, from an urban middle class background. Half of them lived with their parents, meaning that they had an urban origin. Their fathers (as were the fathers of male students) had university degrees in 65 percent of the cases. The style of the SP, with its obvious lack of kitsch, had a lot to do with the mainly urban background of the protestors. The SP of 1996/1997, as well as the SP of 1992, were remarkable cultural events with sophisticated and humorous political messages.

The average age of women participating in CP 1996/1997 was 41.3 years, while the average age of men was lower (38.5 years). The generational differences between men and women who participated in the CP were very interesting: men were over–represented in all age groups from 19 to 39, and from 60 years onwards, while women were over–represented in the of group of 40–59. This age difference, in fact, reveals gendered patterns of pre–protest social inclusions and exclusions. While male protesters were mostly younger men, who were largely unemployed, in fact not socially integrated, women protesters were middle–aged, employed and educated, but usually not supporters of the previous communist regime, and certainly not supporters of Milošević's regime.[11] One could go even further and assume that younger men were protesting for themselves, while middle–aged women were on the streets to protect the rights of their children. Having in mind the severe brain–drain which Serbia experienced in the 1990s, and the strong family ties in Serbian society, it seems that women's protesting could be seen as a strategy to protect their families and slow down the dissolution of their families, which was occurring as a result of emigration.

Differences in education between men and women in the CP of 1996/1997 were much smaller; 49.4 percent of women and 47.7 percent of men completed secondary level education, while 46.5 percent of women and 45.1 percent of men had obtained college and university degrees. It is, again, obvious that a well–educated population was over–represented in comparison to Belgrade, or Serbia as a whole. Accordingly, the occupational structure of the protesters showed that most of them were professionals, semi–professionals, or retired professionals.

Age differences connected with differences in public/private sector employment actually show that there were some important differences between the men and women who participated in the protests. Namely, the women who participated in the protests were those who, although well educated, stayed on the margins of the public sector for most of their careers and who most probably were not included in the political life of the previous regime. They were protesting most probably not only for fostering a better position for themselves, but also for the improvement of living conditions for their children, and their families in general. Younger men, often from the private sector, were actually protecting their own right to better living conditions.

As could be expected, male students were more often members of political parties (12 percent) than female students (4.6 percent), although irrespective of sex, a great majority of the students were not party members. Consequently, male students more often took part in citizens' protests that were organized by political parties. It was 75 percent of male students who attended the citizens protests, compared to 57.7 percent of female students. But still, many believed that their protest should be "political, but not party–spirited" (76.3 percent of male students to 78.9 percent of female students). This indicates an emergence of civil political engagement outside of a "polluted" political scene, which was at that time highly disorganized, chaotic, manipulative and manipulated, as well as highly corrupt. Data showed that these non–partisan politics were less gendered within younger than within older generations. Similar to the SP, women in the CP of 1996/1997 were party members in 11 percent of the cases, while men were party members in 19.2 percent of the cases. But basically a great majority, 50 percent of both men and women, were neither members nor supporters of any political party. These facts prove not only that women were reluctant to take part in institutional politics (and they still are), but also that the CP of 1996/1997 was largely a citizen protest, rather than a protest of the Coalition "Together." So, in hindsight, with the non–existence of the Coalition "Together," this resistance to party affiliation seems wise. This skeptical attitude towards partisan politics also provided an important framework for the later Resistance movement.

What Did Women Want?

On a very basic level, women included in both protests fought for their own civil rights – the right to vote, which was severely curtailed by the public abrogation of the elections. In that sense, their basic demand was not gendered. But what were the more specific demands of women protesters, and were there any relevant differences between men and women relative to the more concrete aims, motives, and expectations of the protests?

The empirical data from the surveys showed that both men and women had very similar demands. However, male students have shown a somewhat clearer and more precise set of demands. Another interesting difference is that although most of the male and female students in the SP of 1996/1997 advocated an "opening up" of the protest and bringing it out into the streets of Belgrade, transforming it into ritual "walks," instead of "closing it up" within faculty buildings, women were slightly more in favor of the "closing up" of the protests than was the case in 1992. As this other strategy proved to be unsuccessful, it is good that the "street strategy" prevailed, giving strength, public support, and vitality to the SP in 1996/1997, which were previously absent in the protests of 1992. Obviously, women's choices were based on a fear of violence.[12] During the protests these fears were well grounded when police attacked peaceful citizens, without making any distinction between men and women.

What Did Women Think?

It comes as no surprise that the protesters showed an extremely low level of trust in the key social and political institutions of Serbia, similar to other countries in transition (Heinrich 1999; Harrison and Huntington 2000). In fact, educated as they were, protesters were very much capable of identifying rather precisely the institutional collapse that was/is happening with the dissolution of ex–Yugoslavia, demagogically labeled by the regime as the process of "democratization" and "transition."

Within generally high distrust, some relevant differences between men and women still existed in relation to legislature, church, and academic institutions. While male students believed more in the "classical authorities," such as the legislature and the church, female students rated "academia" the highest. In the context of the university, this appreciation of science makes sense. However, as the church proved to be extremely traditional and conservative, especially concerning abortion, female students showed much greater skepticism towards it than males.

Students in the SP of 1996/1997 were very skeptical towards opposition leaders as well even during the protests. Half of the female students did not consider any opposition leaders qualified enough. In general, opposition leaders got a better rating from male students. This is closely connected to another fact revealed by the survey: in the SP women, more often than male protesters, wanted to be independent from the citizens' protest. Although a great majority of both men and women agreed on this issue, this fact is another indication of a somewhat different understanding of "politics" that women have relative to men. Similarly, women did not want any workers' or union organizations to be involved in the SP of 1996/1997, but preferred that each stay independent, in fact they wanted it to be isolated. Male students had different strategic ideas about the protest, in a sense that they wanted to see it spreading, "contaminating" other social groups as well. This difference, again, reveals much deeper differences in women's and men's understanding of political action. Women protesters were more inclined to fight for "idealistic" goals, while leaving "political arenas" to men. It is obvious that this relation to politics has many different layers, one of which is that women are not, due to prevailing socialization patterns, prepared to compete with men in politics, nor to take leadership responsibilities.

One of the most important characteristics of both protests is that the people engaged were not very optimistic regarding the final outcome of the protests; but they were nevertheless very determined to go on until "the end." This unique combination of high commitment together with low expectations, in fact, reveals that the fear of failure was lower then the cost of not even trying. Later events, including the NATO war against Yugoslavia, retrospectively make sense of this complicated cost–benefit analysis on an individual and collective level. On the basis of this rather low level of optimism, a scrupulous social scientist would have predicted that the protest would not have lasted long; but they did, and s/he would have been wrong. What this scientist would have missed is an understanding of how activism generates itself, out of "nowhere".

Women in the Protests' Hierarchies[13]

Although women played a very important part in all organizational activities of the SP (press, information, public relations, program organizing, security, and so forth), making up at least 50 percent of those engaged, and in some competencies even more. At the same time they were heavily marginalized from the higher levels of the SP hierarchy, from the public representation of the SP, and from higher–level decision–making (about the strategy, official aims, length of the SP, coalitions, and so forth.) Namely, the Initiative Committee was at the top of the SP, and amounted to 11 members and one chairperson. Only one of those members was a woman. In the Main Board, consisting of representatives of different Belgrade University departments, women accounted for about 30 percent of the total. Bearing in mind that the Initiative Committee was the very body that actually made decisions, it is clear that the role of women at the highest level of decision–making was symbolic.[14] Of greatest importance is the fact that out of the three spokespersons of the SP of 1996/1997, two were men and one a woman. However, since only men were vociferous in their public appearances, the student's protest became symbolized in the public by its leader, Dušan Vasiljević, more than was the case with the CP of 1996/1997, where an almost ritually equal participation of its leaders, two men and one woman (Zoran Đinđić, Vuk Drašković, and Vesna Pešić), was manifested. Contrary to the facts, the media representation of the student protests was that men led the protests, with women playing the role of "adornments." The case of the citizens' protests was very different, with the strong and pronounced role of Vesna Pešić. In that sense this was yet another turning point for women in the political life of Serbia. Namely, Pešić became a promoter of a new role model for women in politics, by denoting an independent women's political engagement, highly sensitized for feminism, outside of marriage or family ties, in contrast to other cases of influential women in politics who were recruited in their role as "the wives."

Gendered Humor and/or Sexism in the Protests?

Genderness was even more pronounced in the realm of cultural/symbolic representation. An important source for this investigation is the set of artifacts made for the protests. As in the SP of 1992, when a mainly political protest turned into an exciting cultural event, in which "imagination was in power," the SP of 1996/1997 re–affirmed its cultural identity by offering a great number of artifacts (slogans, transparent banners, writings, comments, and songs) and by organizing many different actions with symbolic content, as well as creating a festive and sub–cultural atmosphere in the streets.

I will give an example of an effective public gender twist. Beauty contests for women students, judged by photographs, were organized by the opposition newspaper *Demokratija* [*Democracy*] and were completed on 22 January 1997. The most beautiful female student was announced in the "Discotheque Blue Cordon" which was in the open air, in the very center of Belgrade, where an action called "cordon against the cordon" had been pursued for days.[15] Accompanied by the runners–up, Miss SP 1996/1997 strolled along the police cordon. "The beauties" kissed "the boys in blue," and a police officer inquired about Miss SP's phone number telling a "colleague" from the students' security: "Give me the number, I won't harm her, I am a man just as you are ..." (Demokratija 1997). The front page of that day's edition carried the headlines: "Beauty against the Truncheon." Two large photos showed the Miss Students' Protest and a young woman looking a "tame" police officer straight in the eye, holding his face in her hands. Another competition, "Mister Policemen", organized by students among the ranks of those who stood in the cordon facing them, also successfully utilized the strategy of humor and irony elicited by fear and authoritarianism.

Yet are women in the protests merely an "adornment"? Does this and similar "witticisms" intensify or erase their otherness? Do women overcome their otherness or their marginality by participating in the protests, or is it merely that they once again fit into a world designed according to the standards of men? When female students and police officers are placed into the same objectified position by selecting the prettiest among them it becomes quite clear that patriarchal values coexisted with the pro–democratic orientation of the protests.

The dimension of male–female relations was markedly present in the 1996/1997 protests and was even more pronounced in the Students' Protests than in the Citizens' Protest. One might say that the "undermining" of the firmness of the police developed in two directions: by invoking awareness, on the one hand, and by invoking beauty, on the other. Unfortunately, women were offered as a kind of peaceful pledge, as sacrificial lovers. Naturally, the humor, exceptional in originality, charm, and irony, which "covered" all of this, served to tone down the sad picture.

Patriarchalism is so deeply embedded that the journalist of *Vreme* was unfortunately right when he said, during a moment in the protest when tensions between police and citizens was somewhat relaxed, that:

> The female citizens of Belgrade in no small numbers, displaying enthusiasm excessive for the circumstances, as if in a subconscious twitch of slave mentality, started to smack kisses on uniforms who were paid to beat them if ordered, and who would have probably done just that, regardless of their figures or the color of their hair, had things taken a different course and had they received a different order (Milošević 1997, 5).

And in reality, two weeks later, when police brutally beat citizens in the streets of Belgrade, it turned out that gender or the color of one's hair were equally unimportant. This need to communicate with police officers and to try to "soften" them by using traditional female seductive strategies could be understood as a kind of historical atavism, or historical reflex, but also as a learned and accepted female role easily activated in moments of crisis.

It is quite clear that both protests were largely based on an element of playfulness, on carnival, irony, and sarcasm. Yet different metaphors used in the protests were not always devoid of pejorative gender characteristics. As the protests themselves changed over time from being more conflict–oriented with police to being more civil, peaceful, and self–controlled, so did the symbols. The starting symbol – the eggs, derived from the idea that "they" (regime representatives) were actually "egg thieves" (because they stole citizens' votes), in other words, that they lacked "eggs" or "balls" – was relatively quickly substituted with a more neutral symbol, a whistle. "Walks" and "whistling" became the major ways of expressing the resistance. Protesters identified each other on the streets of Belgrade even outside the "walks" by carrying the whistles around their necks and responding with smiles. The extremely male meaning of the first symbol of resistance, the eggs, was highly concordant with the rather aggressive start of the movement. The more the protests, especially the CP, became peaceful, the fewer "eggs" were used, both as ammunition and as a symbol.[16] Therefore, it seems rather obvious that the tendency towards non–violent methods of resistance correlated highly with the abandonment of male symbols.

Just how clear the "male" symbols were, was evident from a series of protest paraphernalia (slogans, posters) that used the male sexual organ or its symbol (the middle finger). The first issue of a humorist paper *Krmača* [*Pig*], which was published especially for the protests (it appeared on 5 December 1996), carried a picture of a truncheon over broken eggs on its front page. The symbolism is patently clear: the force is without the courage. But both the symbols of force and courage were used to celebrate male virtues. Thus "the war" between courage and force seems altogether to be a male war. This was not empirically true (having in mind the reality of women's inclusion), but symbolically, culturally, most probably, it was.

Conclusion: From Resistance to Cooperation

Insistence on the existence of sexism is not intended to reduce the importance and to diminish the role of the above–mentioned protests in any way. Quite the contrary, the main idea is to demonstrate how much the protests themselves were part of a wider, patriarchal, context. For the very same reason, the creation and reinforcement of democratic institutions does not suffice to resolve the problem of transforming patriarchal legacies (Gal and Kligman 2000).

The survey findings indicated that women were as equally involved as men in the protests and that they also had experiences from previous protests. This means that the ongoing protests were largely the result of previous ones, that is, that the creation of a civil society and civil resistance should be viewed as a continuity. The protests in 1996/1997 were themselves part of a process, prepared through all the previous protests, actions, and resistance to the anti–democratic, aggressive, and militant policies of the previous ruling elite. Similarly, they prepared and made possible the last step in that process, the October Revolution in 2000. Women's organizations and actions were an important part of that process.[17] The high inclusion of women in both the students' and citizens' protests convincingly showed that the social change was created with equal engagement of both men and women. The very same high inclusion was present later in the Resistance movement. Additionally, in 2000, women in Serbia organized five independent campaigns, which prepared the ground for the electoral victory of Koštunica.

The women's movement in Serbia in the 1990s was at the very core of the peace movement (Blagojević 1998). Within the women's movement, the resistance to war and to the manipulation of national interests was learned over time. It was learned primarily through different autonomous and/or more or less related initiatives, reactions, appeals to the public, and symbolic actions (for example, dumping war toys into garbage containers), and through the forming of new groups active in resisting the war or assisting war victims. Resistance to the war gradually gave rise to a civil society and the spreading of civil initiatives. Civil resistance was taught, developed, and disseminated through the protests, first in 1991, then in 1992, and finally in 1996/1997. There was a diffusion of methods, communication models, and actions from one protest to the next. One could even say that the methods, techniques, and organizational "know–how" used in various other groups, initiatives, protests, and demonstrations, were quite successfully transported and extended to similar, but new political movements. This is, for instance, apparent in the use of bells and noise, the idea of "awakening," which was launched by the Center for Anti–War Action at the beginning of the war, and then used in the protests of 1996/1997. The Resistance movement also, at the level of techniques and events, created actions and symbols, showing a quite clear connection with the previous anti–regime demonstrations.

On a more concrete level, women in Serbia actively participated in conceiving and implementing various peace movement actions ("Yellow–Band," the Bell, "Black–band," etc.), either as individual actors through the Center for Anti–War Action (Dr. Vesna Pešić, Biljana Jovanović, and the author), or as collective participants in demonstrations and events. They organized the first peace demonstrations in Belgrade in front of the Serbian Parliament in 1991 with the leading slogan: "Nobody has the right to decide about the war, everybody has the right to decide about the peace." In all of the civic protests a feminist presence was clear and strong. In the protests of 1996/1997, in their public appearances, proclamations, leaflets, and articles, feminists reminded the public of the continuity of their resistance to war and violence. At the same time they "welcomed all forms of self–organized civil, non–violent protests against the violating principles of a legal state," supporting the "incorporation of women's human rights into all institutions of civil society" and emphasizing that the "whistling" was not only a form of organized civil disobedience, but also a proven method of women's self–protection against violence.[18]

One may conclude that the continuity of women's activism is beyond doubt, whether manifested as a peace movement, which has primarily been represented by women, as a mass protest of mothers, or as participation in populist gatherings, student, or civil protests. Regardless of what use was made of populist rallies during Milošević's regime, or precisely because they were used for that purpose, they themselves, paradoxically, represented an awakening of civil consciousness through their resistance to an institutional blockade. It is on this continuity of resistance to institutions that the political self–awareness of women has been strengthened, along with that of civil society. But the activism of the 1990s was largely extra–institutional, reactive, and protective. Namely, it appeared in reaction to a denial of a civil right (to vote) or out of the need to protect a specifically endangered group of women (for example, refugees or victims of violence). However, in Serbia after 2000 this has largely changed (Milić 2001). Communication between NGOs and the state is becoming easier and state institutions often consider NGOs to be partners in the hard and painful process of the reconstruction of society. Feminists regularly appear in the media and their previous efforts have largely been recognized. Yet, institutional rewards are still lacking and there are still only a small number of women involved in institutional politics.

Serbia, in comparison to other post–socialist societies, is no exception to the general rule of the transformation process. The rule is simply that women were engaged equally with men in establishing democratic order. But, once they were established, women are almost excluded from these new "democratic" institutions (Blagojević 2003). The question: "to collaborate with the institutions or to stay out," which was an open question during the decade of Milošević's regime, is not an issue any more. The institutions, no matter how undeveloped, burdened with problems, or slow their transformation, have become "our" institutions. The choice between institutional or non–institutional politics is not a political, or even an ethical issue, as it used to be during Milošević, but an issue of personal preferences and choices.

Although women are still less inclined to participate in institutional political life or join political parties, this does not mean that they are apolitical. This is where a parallel between the students' protests and women's participation in the protests can be drawn. In 1992 and 1996/1997 students tried to remain detached from the parties, thus affirming a new form of political action: a non–party, supra–party, or extra–institutional political action, a new approach to politics, close to the idea of civil society. The political objectives of both the students' protests and the women's movement in Serbia were basically related to the problems of daily life, the concern for the individual, and his or her quality of life. In that sense women's politics could be understood as a specific kind of "universal" but also as "concrete" politics, based on the feminist axiom that the "personal is political." With the change of politics, the very meaning of "political" changed, thus turning the major dilemmas of the women's movement in the nineties " political or not political," "with institutions or outside institutions" – into false dilemmas. Institutional, or non–institutional, women's public presence in today's Serbia is very strong.

New times ask for new strategies. It is very clear that the present political elite in Serbia, in its effort to accept European norms, will introduce all legal mechanisms necessary for the equal participation of women. However, society, patriarchal as it is, will resist many of these changes. Feminist strategies, it seems, need to be turned in the direction of sensitizing women and men for new values related to human rights, tolerance and solidarity.

Notes

1   During the "communist past" there were student protests in 1954, 1966, 1968–71, 1989, and 1991–92.

2   However, what is a clear and simple statement now has a prehistory, from 1996 to 2005, of changes of my own political and epistemic positioning and accordingly changes of my interpretation of the research findings. This text has been written and re–written in four very different historical and political time–segments and has been greatly expanded. The major part of the text's body had been written during the Protests with one single motivation, to help the Protests' articulation and efficiency by enhancing general self–understanding. My major concern at that moment was an in–depth analysis that could help the empowerment of the resistance to the regime of Slobodan Milošević. My political aims were completely interwoven with my intellectual endeavor. Then, the text was re–made a year after the Protests failed and the prevailing social climate was one of deep despair and depression. I was facing a challenge not only to realistically evaluate the process of "building up civil society," but also to evaluate women's role in that very process. Intellectually and emotionally, I distanced myself from the prevailing despair and tried to understand the failure of the Protests, as yet another step in the complicated, painful, and very specific road of Serbia towards democracy. At that particular moment I felt that I had a responsibility, as a social scientist, someone who enjoys trust and holds a position of social authority, to help re–establish hope by choosing this long–term approach for providing a deeper understanding of how difficult it is for social and political change to take place if society is in chaos and social institutions are destroyed. In other words, instead of a simple interpretation of the weakness of the opposition, I was defining a broader approach by insisting on the importance of the specific, in the case of Serbia, chaotic social context, which by itself sets up limits to any social action. The third revision of this text was made while the "master of chaos," Slobodan Milošević, the one most responsible for the Serbian and ex–Yugoslav destruction, was already in the Hague, in jail (28 June 2001) and when the societal reality began to disclose many potential conflicts, previously invisible. Finally, this text underwent its fourth revision in 2005, while Serbia was still being shaken by many contradictions and political tensions. Serbian Prime Minister Zoran Đinđić, who was one of the major figures of the Protests 1996/1997, was assassinated in 2003. Serbia has since slowed down the reform process, while on the other hand anti–reformists and the remnants of the old regime are growing stronger.

3   From an outsider's perspective, one could even say that there was only one Protest, instead of two. On the other hand, from an insider's perspective the two protests defined themselves as two different protests. It seems that the leaders of both protests were much more eager on delineating differences. However, for the purpose of this chapter, the difference between the two is relevant because the demographic characteristics of the participants were different. (Henceforth the Student's Protest of 1996/1997 will be abbreviated as the SP of 1996/1997, while the Citizen's Protest will be the CP of 1996/1997).

4   Unfortunately, the international public was not informed about the events, because Serbia at that time was under UN sanctions and foreign journalists were mostly absent.

5   Vidovdan is a religious holiday in Serbian Orthodox tradition.

6   A number of people who were previously engaged in analyzing the Protests of 1992 repeated their investigations, while a number of young sociologists reacted efficiently in collecting data in two different studies, which will be analyzed in this chapter.

7   The imagination that "was in power," during the students' protest in 1992, was so seduc-
    tive that one could even say that the cultural elements "swallowed" the political ones. The
    protest became self–sufficient and self–appeasing.

8   One of the leading students' buzzwords at the protests was "Belgrade is the world," which
    meant that Belgrade belonged to the world, and that students felt part of the world, not of
    a ghetto called "Serbia."

9   One of the popular actions during the Protests was to make noise in the streets, or in apart-
    ment buildings, during the News on the first TV channel, which was/is state controlled.
    This was a reaction not only to the general editorial policy of this channel, but also to the
    very concrete manipulations of information about the protests.

10 For the analysis I use databases from the following three surveys: 1) research on students
    (second week of the Students' Protest, sample) from Popadić, *Studentski protest*, with 383
    respondents; 2) research on students (second week of the Students' Protest, sample) from
    Lilijana Čičkarić and Mihajlo Jojić. 1997. Ulična nastava – Studenstki protest, 1996/1997.
    In *Ajmo, 'ajde, svi u setnju!* [*Let's go for a walk!*], with 585 respondents; and 3) research
    on citizens (fourth and fifth week of the Protest, sample) from *Ajmo, 'ajde, svi u setnju!*
    [*Let's go for a walk!*], with 483 respondents. I thank the above mentioned authors for their
    readiness and willingness to let me use their empirical evidence.

11 Serbia has had an extremely intensive brain–drain since the beginning of the 1990s. Some
    estimates are that as many as 500,000 young, educated people have left, especially from
    Belgrade. One could easily suppose that those people would have been on the streets of
    Belgrade, and other cities, if they had not left the country. The actual regime in Serbia has
    been very tolerant and in many ways supportive of this emigration, thus "exporting" the
    critical mass of people who could produce the social change, or at least provoke it. One
    of the failures of the protests of 1991/1992 was the actual intensification of emigration.
    Young people were leaving the country without hope that anything could be changed. On
    the other hand, according to the vicious political arithmetic of power–holders, those who
    were the most faithful supporters of the regime and President Milošević were old pension-
    ers, who could not leave the country.

12 As Belgrade and other cities changed tremendously in the 1990s, becoming increasingly
    dangerous due to the Mafia infiltration of the state and society, police attitudes towards
    safety also changed. So women's reluctance to "go out" could be at least partially under-
    stood from this perspective. One survey recently made in Serbia reveals that 50 percent
    of women are afraid of being attacked in the streets. See Marina Blagojević. 1997. Jaja i
    zviždaljke – šetnja u rodnoj perspektivi. [Eggs and whistles: Walking in gender perspec-
    tive]. In *'Ajmo, 'ajde, svi u šetnju!* [*Let's all go for a walk!*]. Belgrade: Media centre and
    ISIFF.

13 Relevant data about women's inclusion in the hierarchy of the SP of 1996/1997 was given
    to me by the organizers. Data was collected at the Press Centre of the Students' Protest.

14 On the basis of my own interviews with student protesters, I got the impression that within
    the SP 1996/1997 there was a "spontaneous" gender division of labor. Women were not
    "making coffee," but were very much engaged in both the organizational and creative ac-
    tivities within the SP of 1996/1997. On the other hand, men were more active in defining
    "pure" political strategies.

15 Since police officers were unjustifiably making their presence felt by blocking the "walks,"
    students decided to make an action called "the cordon against the cordon," which many
    citizens joined.

[16] The idea for this symbol came out of one of the first speeches of one of the male leaders of Coalition "Together," who claimed that the regime representatives do not have "the balls" (in Serbian, "the eggs").

[17] The Women's Study Centre of Belgrade, (Marina Blagojević, project director) has conducted a project entitled The Women's Movement in Belgrade 1989–1997, in which 20 of Belgrade's activists contributed documentary and analytical texts about different women's groups and different feminist activities (studies, publications, art projects, etc.). The results were published in: Marina Blagojević, ed. 1998. *Towards a visible women's history: The women's movement in Belgrade in the 90s*. Belgrade: Women's Study Center. During the war, women organized a whole series of autonomous women's groups (the SOS phone line, Women in Black, the Center for Women's Studies, the Women's Lobby, the Women's Parliament, the Autonomous Women's Center for the Struggle against Sexual Violence, the Women's Safe Houses, women's autonomous "flea market" actions, the Incest Trauma Center, the SARA Center for the Young, the Group for the Support of Disabled Women, the women's Legal Group, and lesbian organizations such as "Arkadija" and "Labris," among many others). Six years of resistance to the war, violence, ethnocentrism, and "unbridled" patriarchy resulted in the creation of 14 autonomous women's groups in Belgrade.

[18] Belgrade Women's Lobby leaflet printed and disseminated during the protests (Women's Lobby against Violence. 1997. Belgrade: Women's Lobby).

References

Blagojević, Marina. 1997. Jaja i zviždaljke – šetnja u rodnoj perspektivi. [Eggs and whistles: walks in gender perspective]. In *Ajmo, 'Ajde, Svi u Šetnju!* [Let's all go for a walk!]. Belgrade: Media Centre and ISIFF.

Blagojević, Marina, ed. 1998. *Ka vidljivoj ženskoj istoriji: ženski pokret u Beogradu 90-ih.* [*Towards a visible women's history: The women's movement in Belgrade in the 90s*]. Belgrade: Women's Study Center.

Blagojević, Marina, ed. 2000; 2004. *Mapiranje mizoginije u Srbiji: diskursi i prakse*. [*Mapping misogyny in Serbia: Discourses and practices*], vol. I and II. Belgrade: AŽIN.

Blagojević, Marina. 2002. Žene i muškarci u Srbiji: Urodnjavanje haosa. [Women and men in Serbia 1990–2000: Engendering chaos]. In *Srbija krajem milenijuma, razaranje društva, promene i svakodnevni život.* [*Serbia at the end of Millennium. Societal destruction and everyday life*], edited by Ađelka Milić and Silvano Bolčić. Belgrade: ISIFF.

Blagojević, Marina. 2003. *Women's situation in the Balkan countries*. Report for the EU Parliament (No. IV/2002/16/03). Paper read at the EU Parliament, Committee on Women's Rights and Equal Opportunities, Brussels.

Blagojević, Marina. 2004. Creators, transmitters, and users: Women's scientific excellence at the semi–periphery of Europe. In *Gender and excellence in the making*. Luxemburg: European Commission, Directorate–General for Research.

Čičkarić, Lilijana, and Mihajlo Jojić. 1997. Ulična nastava – Studenstki protest, 1996/1997. [Street School – Students' Protest 1996/1997]. In *Ajmo, 'ajde, svi u šetnju!* [*Let's all go for a walk!*]. Belgrade: Media Centre and ISIFF.

Demokratija [*Democracy*]. 22 January 1997.

Gal, Susan, and Gail Kligman, eds. 2000. *Reproducing gender: Politics, publics, and every-day life after Socialism.* Princeton, New Jersey: Princeton University Press.

Harrison, E. Lawrence, and Samuel P. Huntington. 2000. *Culture matters: How values shape human progress.* NY: Basic Books.

Heinrich, Georg Hans, ed. 1999. *Institution building in the new democracies: Studies in post–post–Communism.* Budapest: Collegium Budapest. Krmača (Belgrade), 1997, 1.

Lazić, Mladen. 1995. Osobenosti globalne društvene transformacije Srbije. [Characteristics of the global societal transformation in Serbia]. In Društvene Promene i svakodnevni život, Srbija početkom 90–ih, [*Societal changes and everyday life; Serbia in the 90s*], edited by Silvano Bolčić. Belgrade: ISIFF.

Milić, Anđelka. 2002. *Ženski pokret na raskrsnici milenijuma.* [*Women's movement at the millennium crossroad*]. Belgrade: ISIFF.

Milošević, Milan. 1997. Belgrade's protests, Belgrade: *Vreme,* 11 December 1996.

Mundiju – Pipidi, Alina, and Ivan Krastev, eds. 2004. *Nacionalizam posle komunizma:* naučene lekcije. [*Nationalism after communism: Lessons learned*]. Belgrade: Beogradski fond za političku izuzetnost.

Popadić, Dragan. 1997. Studentski protesti: uporedna analiza studentskih protesta 1992 i 1996/1997. [Students protests: comparative analysis]. In *Ajmo, 'ajde, svi u šetnju!* [*Let's all go for a walk!*]. Belgrade: Media Centre and ISIFF.

Women's Lobby against Violence (leaflet). 1997. Belgrade: Women's Lobby.

Chapter 8

"A Right and a Great Need":[1] Food Rights and Praxis in Silesia, Poland

Anne C. Bellows

The following case study is set in Poland. I introduce work conducted mostly by women, but also by men, who are engaged in the non–governmental organization, the Gliwice Chapter of the Polish Ecological Club in the Upper Silesian region of southwest Poland. Their activities connect the interrelated fields of food security, environmental management, and political engagement. The chapter considers how the activists' own interpretation of rights and their strategies of resistance have developed the spaces of their political work across political and economic transition. I claim that the majority of women in the case study group is not coincidental, but based on their traditional roles forged out of claims for food, to feed, and to be fed as well as their networks of (mostly) women who work together and help each other in multiple spaces from kitchens to research laboratories (Bellows 1996; 1999; 2001; Van Esterik 1999). The chapter therefore does not claim that political labor on behalf of food and environmental rights is women's labor. Rather, it asserts that the fact that there is a majority of women active in such social movements is not surprising, and even more importantly, that their presence substantively impacts the priorities and strategies for political activism. Because, however, these women work with men and because their own and their groups' primary goals lie in broad community welfare, I argue that the gendered uniqueness of their political labors is neglected by women's groups, environmental groups, food and agricultural research groups, and reigning political elites (women and men alike). The oversight of these characteristics results in the reification of social assumptions about a male gendered "nature" of political work and rights that are transacted in public. The multiple locations of the largely female activists' work are not understood and are trivialized. The gendered and co-operative aspect of their social contributions remains invisible, rendering vulnerable the women's own ability to claim access to political office and influence policy. An impractical outcome is that the neglect of gendered political work limits the possibility to replicate positive achievements in other communities. The discussion in this chapter attempts to identify some of the multiple spaces and mobile actors in this work in order to identify them in terms of gendered enactments of claims to rights and political labor.

It seems to me, writing from the West, that East European activism on food issues has a regional particularity because of different historical relationships to rights and expectations of what one can expect from a government. It also seems unique because of well–documented differences in the way East and West societies (women and men) mystify or horrify feminism as a form of political intervention (see, Snitow 1993; Havelkova 1997a). Finally, the fundamental changes and experience with state and economic uncertainties is not unique to post–Soviet countries. It is, however, more dramatic, more sudden, and has impacted the broad population instead of marginalized minorities as is more often the case with instability in the political economies of the West. In the US, for example, recent changes in welfare laws (impacting, among other things, food stamp access) did not happen "overnight." Policy changes since the 1980s have re–concentrated poverty consistently among racial minorities and in the growing national proportion of the poor. Further, it has done so in ways that our historical legacy of racism and liberal individualism encourages us invariably to discount as a social pattern. Unlike in the East, the entire population has not been required to find work and daily consumables in a radically changed ideological environment.

Rights Claims and Political Labor

> People living in a polluted environment such as Upper Silesia, Poland, have a right and great need for access to uncontaminated and nutritious food. Uncontaminated nutritious food is an essential preventative health measure to fight against increased risks of illness stemming from biologically unfavorable environments (Kacprzak et al. 1996).

The moral basis for the Soviet communist system was grounded in "the holy trinity of labor, bread, and housing" (Merkel 1994, 57). This promise defined the citizenship rights that distinguished communist populations from those in Western liberal democracies. In Poland in the 1980s, the struggle to produce those rights foundered against the realities of heavy international debt, distributional inefficiency and inequity, growing alarm over increasing environmental and public health concerns, and a repressive dictatorship nervously submissive to the Kremlin. The combination produced a synergistic outpouring of public opposition, commonly called "popular," as though the resistance was homogenous or seamless. In reality, it was an intoxicating mixture of different groups with different objectives for citizenship identity and rights. Within the narrow parameters of political space available to those in opposition, diverse groups were ready to collaborate against a common enemy. In the unfolding of the post–1989 new political economy, the differences have reasserted themselves. The ideal of broad access to political and economic space has been checked by new forms of discrimination, market competition, and a loss of the moral basis – although perhaps not its memory – of the former communist system.

Gendering the Human Right to Food[2]

When Jasia traveled from Gliwice to nearby Opole to give a presentation on the Tested and Organic Food for Silesia Program at the first Women and Environment Conference organized in 1996 in Poland, she stopped at a local church, as she always does, and brought me along to see the chapel dedicated to the Polish military officers, her father–in–law among them, murdered in the forests of Katyn. That chapel, established years before the historic 1989 Round Table talks, existed as a hushed but stark site of resistance. This whispered dissent resonated in the underground work of environmentalists trying to publicize the full danger of environmental pollution on human health in Silesia, and in the public prosaic labors of standing in endless lines – mostly but not only by women – waiting to exchange ration cards for butter and meat. Jasia is a retired chemical engineer who spent much of her career testing the integrity of agricultural products grown in Upper Silesia for toxics like heavy metal concentrations. At the conference in Opole, she talked about the impact of industrial and transportation contaminants in food on the public's and especially on children's health. She also spoke about the dangerous occupational conditions of her profession – unprotected contact with toxic laboratory chemicals – and suggested that it was not surprising that women, and not men, obtained these jobs. A result of this discriminatory labor practice has been that women also had the first contact with data that was then buried for so many years, and to some degree, continues to be obscured today. Activism to reveal data means not only making it public, but turning it into the various forms that different community members will come into contact with and absorb. Jasia, a co–founder of the Gliwice City Chapter of the Polish Ecological Club [PEC–Gliwice] has pulled together friends in her home to discuss and develop strategies for these challenges since long before the formal founding of the group in 1992. As in so many households, her home became an intimate centrifuge for reconceptualizing the "naturalness" and inevitability of life around them. Friends read, wrote, copied, and filed their reports in washbaskets. They exchanged information about the welfare and health of their colleagues and families, debating over interminable cups of tea and good things to eat. Jasia's husband, a wonderful cook himself, socializes a bit and then retreats to the kitchen during the meetings. An architect, he is supportive but doesn't seem to feel part of the group. Perhaps it is the activists' friendships; perhaps it is the different career foci. Over time, changes, good and bad, seem to spread from and return to the physical perimeter of Jasia's home. She is so proud of the small eco–shop that opened in 1993 near her block apartment building. The young owners carry organic and tested vegetables that she and the Club members were instrumental in developing the wholesale distribution for. What a change from the pre–1989 queuing for whatever the state might hand out.

And yet, by 1995 and 1996, Jasia found children from her part of town at her door and watched them move from one neighbor to the next begging for food. "Is the Club dedicated first to food or to the environment?" she asks rhetorically and answers for herself, "both, of course it's dedicated to both in order to protect human health and human environments."

The human right to food is listed in the 1948 International Declaration on Human Rights (Article 25) and is expanded in the 1966 International Covenant on Economic, Social, and Cultural Rights [ICESCR] (Article 11). While the former shows intent, the latter connotes international treaty law. As with all United Nations doctrines, the ICESCR actually "comes into force" only after a predominance of UN member countries ratify it on a country–by–country basis by a national parliament. Poland signed in 1977; the United States, among a few others, never has. State level implementation requires state laws to be written in concert with international covenant language. Under the reigning cold war ideologies of the era, the ICESCR represented the communist sphere guarantees to its citizenry. It was countered by the 1966 International Covenant on Political and Civil Rights [ICPCR], which championed the individualist rights of Western market economies and liberal democracy (Eide et al. 1985; 1986; Buckingham 1998; Bellows 2003; Bellows and Hamm 2003a). Both came into force in 1976. Thus communist Poland contributed to a history of legal and rhetorical–based rights to food (and other economic rights) that influences the way rights are understood in the post–Soviet era.

This chapter makes the claim that women as a group, with all the differences among them, react politically to infringements on the right to food more often than do men. Women traditionally accept and/or demand the right to protect (for example, the civil and political right of organizing) their children and households (Scheppele 1994). As the traditional providers of domestic nutrition and health care labor, this includes the right to food (Wells 1998; Schneider 1991; Charlesworth 1995; Howard 1995; Youssef 1995). In other words, women work politically on food more often than men because, first of all, they conduct most food work, and secondly, because they are most exposed to, and knowledgeable about, the violences associated with a lack of food security and rights. Because the right to food can be understood to include the right for food, to feed others, and to be fed (for example, in destitute conditions or incarceration, see Van Esterik 1999), women are the ones most likely to protest a loss of a complex bundle of food rights (Thompson 1966; 1971; Kaplan 1982; Walton and Seddon 1994; Bellows 2001; 2003).

Activism for the right to food involves, not individualist expectations, but group claims on society. There are at least two ways that the group right to food has been conceptualized. First, a group right can be identified in terms of the collective body, in other words, a right to which everyone is entitled (Scheppele 1994). The ICESCR largely promotes group rights. Food, housing, and employment, for example, are collective rights for everyone. The experience of people in Eastern Europe includes a familiarity with and the expectation for collective rights. Second, group rights can be identified for a group that is an identifiable part of the whole collective, of the "everyone." Groups obtaining specific sets of international rights have included children, prisoners of war, women, economically underdeveloped peoples, indigenous groups, among others (Scheppele 1994).

Cold war ideologies generated different outcomes for women's exclusion in the East and the West. In the West, the right to organize was confounded by liberal individualism that considered group economic claims counterproductive to a liberal democracy and market economy. In the East, group economic rights were defined by the state and not subject to a political and civil right of critique. In the East and in the West, women have organized in groups (employing civil and political rights) for food or child welfare (defined as group economic and social rights). In other words, they have asserted both civil/political and economic/social sets of rights under diverse political economies that have selectively devalued the legitimacy of one or other of the sets of rights. In the process, however, they have experienced that their identity as a group of women is deleted or harassed and their political capacity as a group is trivialized – even to themselves. I argue that this dismissal of women's political power and their equal entitlement to basic human rights reflects the radical edge of their political activism for economic rights on behalf of the entire population. Small wonder that, in both the East and West, feminism as an action–based theory that legitimized women organizing would be considered threatening to state apparati. Perhaps this repression has been more severe in the East, where political organizing was *de facto* and *de jure* restricted, even when the objective of the activism – a right to food – received greater respect than in the West.

Spaces of Rights Activism

Kasia left Warsaw as a young woman to take a financial scholarship at the Technical University in Gliwice and study chemical engineering. Her family thought she was crazy, leaving the bright capital for a provincial outpost known for its industrial concentration and a Silesian miner population that the cosmopolitan center felt superior to. Kasia found only great freedom, she relayed, in the independence the scholarship afforded her, allowing her to be herself outside the patronizing constraints she felt in her first home. Studying in the late 1950s and early 1960s, she remembers all–night boating parties floating lazily down the Klodnica River, and waking at dawn at points near Opole. She remembers the river turning dirtier and smellier throughout the 1960s, and knew that her subsequent labors in a major manufacturing center contributed to the pollution. Everyone knew it, but all were caught in a machine of production and censored silences that seemed inevitable, even natural. In the early 1990s, she abruptly found herself in a suddenly changed environment. She was retired, pensioned at wages that did not reflect the inflation rates, widowed, and her children were grown, married, and moved out. As we drank tea and she packed me a bag with jars of her gooseberry preserves and pickles, she said that she needed and wanted to stay involved and active. So she bought a small public allotment garden adjacent to her apartment block in a garden complex (ogrod) that was originally dedicated to military workers. With her beloved Dalmatian dog, she worked there regularly, learning from her neighbors how to prune fruit trees and when to thin strawberries. Kasia met with old friends and colleagues in their PEC–Gliwice Club and began to organize against pollution and poor health perhaps as much out of participation in good company as in dedication to environmental change. She volunteered to teach in local primary schools about food, nutrition, pollution, health, and minimizing risk. She spoke with others in her own tract of public allotment gardeners about the risks of food production in Upper Silesia and helped the Club organize workshops for gardeners. Part of the motivation for these activities, Kasia confided, was to atone in a new way for her participation in the pollution history, production, and problems, as well as in the former silences. And, she repeated, she needed to remain connected to neighbors, friends, and young people.

Elsewhere, I have defined *food praxis* as the politicized quotidian labor of food work (cooking, shopping, monitoring family health, and so on) that integrates economic rights to food security and political rights to articulate those needs (Bellows 2001). Food praxis is influenced both by the location and spatial conditions of food work (kitchens, markets, workplaces, and so on). This food work creates new spaces, for example, spaces that are safe from the violences of hunger, malnutrition, and poisoning caused by unsafe foods, especially for the household and community. The diverse locations, mobile actions, and interactions with others that result from food work produce a politicized reflection on personal experience as mediated by and upon the physical space through which we pass and in which we live and work (Anderson 1983; Appadurai 1993). Politicized reflection on personal experience signifies understanding a group's condition based on individual circumstances ("thoughtful experience", per Lefebvre 1991) and considering possibilities for social change ("social imaginaries"; per Appadurai 1993). Agency, the power and conviction of effecting social change, arises as a product of migration, mobility, action, and transmutations of learned knowledges into strategies for change. Food praxis as a form and potential of political agency theoretically can be engaged in by anyone, in any place. However, the gendered social conditions of food work, such as, who does the work, where it is done, in whose company it is practised, and so on, implicate women as the chief – though not the sole – arbiters of food praxis.

The diverse and mobile locations of food praxis and the associated social relationships of practitioners who perform it situate "political activity" beyond the more limited activities, spaces, and memberships recognized in classic public space theory (for example see, Habermas 1989). Why is the socially determined leadership role in creating public policy around food rights and needs not as female–gendered as the socially determined labor that delivers those rights and needs? Along with misogyny generally, and implicated therein, is the argument that public political and private (non–political) household lives are separately functioning spheres of life. Recognizing food work as praxis (that is the political agency and potential in routine daily work that occurs outside what is traditionally called public political life) is a leverage point of addressing the detachment of the labor of food work from formal public representation in legislative and policy development.

Rights Activism in Poland

Zefiryna's kitchen looked somewhere between a medieval woodcut of an herbalist's apothecary and a contemporary home catering operation. Her huge shepherd dog walked confidently through the old but beautiful apartment, fit, well mannered, and well loved. Zefiryna taught sports and gymnastics in the lyceum all her life. She is beautiful, powerful, and moves with athletic self–confidence. Further, she aspires to help others find these qualities in themselves. Retired and widowed now, Zefiryna had in earlier years encouraged the former PEC–Gliwice president, Maria, in sports. Maria was no athlete, yet Zefiryna had recognized her as a natural leader and turned her into the volleyball team captain, though never its best player. Huge trays hang in her kitchen sprouting pulses. She used a greater variety of beans than I had ever been able to find in Poland. Maria recruited her to produce fabulous repasts for breaks during the PEC–Gliwice Club's training programs. To highlight the availability and usefulness of tested and organic fruits and vegetables grown according to the Club's program, Zefiryna would prepare dishes with whatever was in season and being distributed through the Club's wholesaler. Her dishes would enliven audiences, lure their imaginations with her herb garlic butters, vegetarian bigos, and multi–grain sprouted–seed breads beyond anyone's experience. Such a bigos! If the traditional mixed meat and sauerkraut stew could be made without meat and taste like that, then perhaps the world was indeed changeable! In her apartment we tried the salads she was experimenting with for the next Club workshops. Her skin always shone, packed into winter layers of wool or framed by summer cottons. Zefiryna wanted to start a restaurant or even a catering business and was always nurturing future clientele and thinking about possible capital start–up ideas. Her daughter dropped by to visit with her boyfriend. She glowed like her mother, as though she'd just hiked down off of a glacier. Soon we were all testing the salads, feeling warm and alive to the bone. Zefiryna sent us all away with wrapped food, passing on her gifts at home and in public, as much an act of her career and life as any other – leading children and adults to physical health and self–confidence.

In Poland before 1989 and to a greater extent than after 1989, household relations were usually structured in direct and immediate opposition to the power of the state. Havelkova defines the sanctuary–like characteristic of household space before 1989 in terms of this resistance to state power. It was a resistance wherein women and men cooperated closely against the real threat of state violence (Havelkova 1997b; Snitow 1997). Drakulić stresses that the family is not a public institution, but it is political (1991). The paradox is that whether or not household political agency achieves public acknowledgement depends upon the degree to which men have worked there (Gal 1997, 37). Women as part of a household's agential potential remain invisible.

This invisibility is part of a larger veil over the situation of women's lives in household space. Veneration of these more private domestic spaces, whether for political underground movements or romanticized families supporting the nation, collapses the full complexity of life there. The simplification obscures not only the political activism of women, but some of the household's best kept secrets of violences: those of hunger, malnutrition, and poisoning which can affect all household members, especially those in low income homes; and those against women (Benet 1951; Fuszara 1994; Corrin 1996; Bellows 2003).

Many have written of the rise of a "male democracy" and the loss of economic and political opportunities for women in Poland and across the post–Soviet domain (Fuszara 1991; 1993; Graham and Regulska 1997; Regulska 1992; 1998; Verdery 1996; Watson 1993; 1997). The civic/political/agential work in private household spaces, such as protecting household food security, receives small account although it precedes and endures after the short term "political undergrounds" of the 1980s. Forgotten is the political and gendered aspect of food riots and the smoldering anger against needing to queue for limited food stocks that played a major role in bringing down the totalitarian Polish state (Szymanski 1982; Touraine et al. 1983, 162; Ash 1984; Lepak 1988; Fuszara 1993; Kurczewski 1993; Walton et al. 1994; Verdery 1996). Invisible remains the gendered and political work to address post–1989 falling living standards, including increasing or consistent food insecurity for a marginalized portion of the population (Drakulić 1991, 17; Beskid et al. 1992; Michna 1992; Sufin 1994, 69; Beskid et al. 1995; Titkow and Domanski, eds. 1995; Centrum Badania Opinii Społecznej [CBOS] 1996, 20; Snitow 1996, 176). Contemporary shortages, poverty, or environmental contamination may be acknowledged today. The characteristics of activism behind those issues – gendered, daily, repetitive, group–based, mobile, spatially networked, socially expected, and alternative political labor – are ignored.

How do women organizing around food and environmental issues move through local and non–local communities, identifying themselves, forming friendly alliances, and presenting themselves to hostile audiences? Food and environmental organizing necessarily begins from a "radical," that is, non–mainstream position. Altering public opinion and policy entails a process of education and changed public understanding such that "radical" knowledge becomes "normal" or "mainstream" knowledge. The process is embedded in social and politicized prescriptions of who has "credible" knowledge and who "should" and "should not" be a political and public person. The spaces of food praxis and political organizing are not only located along a "more private" (for example, households) to "more public" (for example, public office) continuum. The work of broadening network alliances also expands the geographic circle of alliances in terms of scale, that is, to non–local and even international levels. Non–local connections are important in establishing the important resource of credibility in local political spaces. However, if the connections are "sensitive" (such as, from a hostile or meddling country) or "suspicious" (such as from feminists generally or industrial polluters–turned–environmental funders) they can also undermine local credibility. Local organizers publicize their network alliances to augment their position, for example, pointing out that people elsewhere recognize their work enough to support them financially. Activists might not want to broadcast that a group of international feminists have called them a model of "women's and environmental organizing." To extend such a scenario, should the international group insist on a highly public profile of their assistance and feminist identity, local activist women may resent or shun their help. The outcome might be the submergence, locally and non–locally, and by women as well as men, of gendered aspects to the food and environmental political work.

A central difference between citizenship claims in the East and West is the recent memory of state level promises of group rights to food, housing, and jobs in the East. Certainly this does not mean that these economic needs were fully met before 1989. The often dire straits of post–communist populations prove starkly that there is no legacy of assurance. Nevertheless, the pronouncement of "a right and a great need" in the tract by the Polish Ecological Club of Gliwice reflects a demand that is understood in the East through the historical experience of a citizen's right to expect economic support. The PEC–Gliwice presses this memory to a similarly receptive public in the post–1989 period by engaging the newly available civil and political rights to organize politically and to promote independent businesses. Critically, it is not the entire populace advocating for universal access to safe and nutritious food. A small geographically situated subset has studied the specific environmental and health problems, defined the claims, and taken the political risks to pursue change. The identity of the agitators and the spaces where they accumulated the experiences that form the group's passions and goals remain indistinct. Only in naming them can we understand the political work that created dynamic and volatile social change. In naming them, perhaps we can better understand why the changes are vulnerable and how to reinforce them.

Activists: Identities and Spaces

Consistent, safe, and affordable access to food serves as an indicator of public health, economic security, and the fulfillment of a basic human right to food (Bellows and Hamm 2003a; 2003b; Lang 1996; FAO 1996). In Upper Silesia, home of the Gliwice municipal chapter of the Polish Ecological Club most of Poland's wealth, energy power, *and* environmental pollution is produced. Gliwice lies within the two percent of Poland that comprises Upper Silesia (as defined by the pre–1998 voivodship boundary of Katowice, the main city of Upper Silesia). The region contains 3000 factories of which 300 are considered environmental hazards, as well as 30 percent of the national dust emissions, 40 percent of national non–dust air pollution; and 60 percent of the total national waste disposal. Nevertheless, up to 50 percent of the land is used for agriculture and urban garden allotments and 40 percent of all locally consumed fruits and vegetables are grown in these soils despite warnings of health risks (Peterson 1993; Potrykowska 1993, 255–56; Ragland and Kukula 1994; Kacprzak et al. 1996). The most severe threat to health from soil pollution in the Upper Silesian region is from food contaminated with lead and cadmium, and excessive concentrations of nitrogen compounds. Literature from the World Health Organization and Polish research demonstrate that 60–80 percent of all heavy metal toxins enter the human body through ingestion, and that intake by breathing polluted air is of relatively lesser importance (Kacprzak et al. 1996).

Why do urban and peri–urban food producers in Upper Silesia grow food under conditions of known environmental health complications? Research shows that gardeners and farmers balance diverse risks against the pleasures and traditions of food production (Bellows 2000). On the broad scale, these risks include war, regime change, political instability, and economic uncertainty (Bellows 2004). More specifically in Silesia, the population has faced health risks associated with the ingestion of locally–grown foods grown in an environmentally distressed region, compounded by a market supply that carries no guarantee of safer food. Against these risks, cultivation for domestic consumption historically augments food security. Additionally, it creates biodiverse landscapes around cities, provides traditional pastoral pleasures, and introduces relief from the hard urban design and monotony of much industrial–based paid work (Moszkowski 1995; Bellows 1996; 1999; 2000; 2004).

When I walked from the Club's offices on Kaszubska Street to Maria's house, I passed through the center of Gliwice and then, directly adjacent, past the still operating First of May factory. This belching establishment was built in the 1790s. It houses the first coke oven in Europe which, according to Club members, has similarly antiquated (i.e., no) environmental safeguards. With the factory on one side and soot–covered pre–Soviet era workers' apartment buildings on the other, I swooped as quickly as possible through an exhaust–filled passage under the railroad line that links Berlin and Krakow. My eyes always hurt that winter and spring of 1996 and my skin broke out in unusual ways. Maria, who sold cosmetics to bolster her infrequent reimbursement from the Club as president and trainer, always tried to introduce me to new astringents and soaps, suggesting that I did not know how to defend myself in Upper Silesia. After the bridge, I would head uphill to her home at the outskirts of town. Her neighborhood was considered a fortunate district to live in. Its distance from the factories and the prevailing wind that passes through a small neighboring forest reward it with relatively cleaner air. Maria's youngest child was two and already suffered from respiratory complications. It is a condition that, she said and I heard oft repeated, was appearing with increasing frequency in Upper Silesia. Two hundred years of factory conditions, which have only intensified with time, produce a hypnotic sense of normalcy about early death. Like the German industrialists before them, the communists tried to lure and stabilize the labor with relatively high wages. Now, local and national governments have less money and less authority to pay higher wages to encourage labor to accept the environmental risks. Yet just having a job is enough during the post–1989 condition of unemployment to attract labor in dangerous fields. Where does the idea to protest come from? Like her mother and friends, Maria too is a chemical engineer and also knows the data that connects local heavy metal concentrations in the soils and farm produce with health risks and actual local health statistics. During her studies in the 1970s and early 1980s, Maria's mother expected her to attend Solidarity labor union meetings and read the underground press as much as she expected good grades from her daughter. There was a kind of fashion and flair, indeed a lifestyle around protest that linked Maria's friends, her work, and her knowledges. With inflation after 1989, state wages could not support her and her family and she left her engineering job to sell cosmetics. Perhaps activism is like a habit. As we folded clothes off of the line, we talked about the environmental and labor politics of General Motors trying to buy degraded industrial land to build a new factory in Gliwice. The fate of a sympathetic mayor in nearby Tarnowskie Gory, whose support for Club projects produced election time jeers of "he cares for nothing other than carrots," was debated as one child was chased after running into the street and another came home with a skinned knee and a broken bicycle. Two years later I saw Maria in the U.S. She was still based at PEC–Gliwice but her focus had turned toward moving agricultural practice toward sustainable and organic operations throughout the Baltic six–country region. Maria had come to believe that having local governments change policy and support radical projects like "Tested and Organic Food" was a short–term goal with short–term successes that were vulnerable to cycles of municipal fiscal health and fickle voters. Sitting in New Jersey, we argued strategy and talked about our families. As often as finances permitted, she called home to counsel her children on homework and encourage her nervous and unwell father to eat the warmed leftovers. He was thinking about his grapes swelling on the terraces built around their house. I was remembering his homemade wine.

In Gliwice, a town with a population of about 215,000, the PEC–Gliwice members know each other from school, the university, their workplaces, their neighborhoods, and from a common participation in the pre–1989 underground. The parents of many of the members migrated from Lwow, in what is today western Ukraine. They came to Silesia after World War II as part of the Eastern Polish population herded into today's Polish borders even as the resident Germans were driven out. Some of the original Club organizers had parents who were part of the disbanded Polish–ethnic faculty, staff, and students of the chemical engineering department at the University in Lwow. The uprooted academics re–organized within the Technical University of Gliwice to form a new powerhouse of industrial capacity in Poland, expanding the institution's primary research base in mining. Perhaps something in the forced dislocation of habitat and occupation makes one feel that the human and physical environment of home are not inevitabilities. Confidence that "nothing can change" is lost to those whose lives are destabilized and unalterably changed. Revolutionary ideas unfold: dictatorship is not natural; conditions of pollution and poor health can be alleviated; friends can and should unite to resist what they see in their daily lives as wrong. The first generation of post–World War II Silesian–born children of the expatriated academic elite – and significantly the young women among them – formed an important part of the core resistance to endemic pollution in Silesia. Their parents brought the technical capacity to articulate it.

The Polish Ecological Club of Gliwice formally began its "Tested Food for Silesia" program with a grant from the local City Council in 1992 (Gliwice Municipal Act, #214 June 1992; Bellows 1996). Although the national–level Polish Ecological Club [PEC] had achieved official recognition in 1980, the official toler-ance for the PEC's actions to educate the public and lobby for change ranged from minimal to non–existent. After 1989 many of the male opposition activists were voted into local governments. Many of the women activists moved into NGOs. The PEC–Gliwice members note that the early grant to start the "Tested Food" program was connected to relationships that developed in the pre–1989 opposition. By gen-erating a dialogue with the newly autonomous and increasingly male local govern-ments, the mostly female PEC–Gliwice integrated the advantages of a privatizing economy into a new wholesale and retail distribution system of agricultural goods. They formed an active NGO to enter the new political spaces of private, non–profit civic life. Just as they had used all available spaces to resist state policy under com-munist rule, the PEC–Gliwice used the private non–profit world to challenge the new market state.

As its primary objective, the PEC–Gliwice claims the right to identify and sup-plant hazardous locally grown foods with safe alternatives. Their goal is to mini-mize risks where local production continues. The Club argues that contaminated foods effect a violence on the human immune system and they target populations most vulnerable to the absorption of toxics: the youngest of children, pregnant and lactating women, and persons with already impaired health, especially the elderly (Kacprzak et al. 1996). The program promotes organic farmers whose produce can also pass chemical testing for heavy metals and nitrates. These chemical tests exam-ine produce beyond traditional certified organic growing standards. Through its test-ing, distribution, and labeling programs, the PEC–Gliwice supports (and regularly inspects) retail food shops that agree to carry the organic and tested foods as well as schools and hospitals that will supply their populations with the produce. Related community education programs reach the schools (teachers, administrators, parents, and children), other environmental NGOs, local government administrators (includ-ing City Council members, and environment, agriculture, and health officers), farm and allotment gardener food producers, and the media. The Club's secondary objec-tives embrace more systemic, expensive, and/or slowly achievable horizons. They organize against polluters to reduce and eliminate source contamination and intro-duce the remediation of regional soils. Instead of trying to close down gardens and farms, they fight to save urban green spaces from being converted out of food pro-duction purposes. Cultivators are recognized for their environmental contributions. They receive training on minimizing risk, not condemnation for a situation outside their control. To achieve these diverse goals, the PEC–Gliwice cooperates with other organizations to leverage support.

The first time I visited the Polish Ecological Club in Gliwice in 1993, I arrived after a two–hour train ride during which I became suddenly, violently, and ironically ill with food poisoning. The tour and extraordinary dinner awaiting us represented the gastronomic specialties of the Club leaders. Much to my dismay, I spent the time in bed while women came in and out urging me alternately to sleep and to drink tea and an herbal liqueur, krupnik. I especially remember Halina who was, I thought, a medical doctor and later learned was the Chief of Research at the Polish Regional Agricultural and Chemical Research Testing Station in Gliwice. Her hands soothing my face had qualities of both exact precision and great warmth. Over the years I often saw this balance in her that fused a professional competence and neutrality with profound care. In later years, she invited me to her research station and listened with interest to my understanding of "Silesian" food contamination before pointing out, always supportively but uncompromisingly, how I had collapsed vast differences among "Silesians" and how the level of food contamination is variable across the Silesian landscape. Indeed, she said, Silesian–grown food is often safer than imports like some of the nitrate–loaded Dutch hydroponic tomatoes that she tested. Her thoughtfulness and diplomacy has well served the Club that, of course, needs such presence when internal tensions over underpaid work and passions about organizational priorities conflict. Local governments, businesses, and residents need these qualities as they vacillate between acceptance and suspicion of the Club's unexpected knowledge and authority in the community. In June 1995, I participated in a Club–organized training program for Upper Silesian local government officials. Toward the end of the two–day workshop, a male participant commented, "It is very good that women start projects like the 'Tested Food for Silesia'; they do it very well. However, once established, it should be turned over to the work of men." The audience collectively gasped. The PEC–Gliwice had never presented itself as a women's organization. The local officials present were divided fairly equally between women and men. Halina, who was presiding over that part of the program, responded in a nonplussed way, "all people are necessary to address pollution problems" and continued without further ado.

In challenging the political and economic systems behind local practices of pollution, PEC–Gliwice members ironically confront the skeletal patriarchal framework of those systems. The members are "allowed" women's social role of "clean up", in this case a contaminated community or regional environment instead of a household living space. They are "granted" this unpaid work in the same breath that denies them the associated political power because the group is perceived (correctly) as (largely) female. Members re–establish authority by self–dismissing their gendered identity.

The Gliwice Chapter of the Polish Ecological Club provides a lens with which to look at how gendered social activisms adapt their social critique across regime change according to the changing conditions of a centralized socialist state to a more decentralized market economy. As the Polish government was de–emphasizing economic rights after 1989, the Club steered away from competing cold war ideologies and clearly articulated their political *and* economic demands in terms of locally–defined needs for and rights to safe food and environmental health. The Club used gendered strategies for local food security that arose from diverse and routine food labors dispersed throughout the community.

As the PEC–Gliwice's work becomes better known and more institutionalized with time, the question arises, how it will be passed on and replicated elsewhere? The radical edge of the once subversive knowledges of contamination was built on experience gained largely by women at home and at work. The fact that these activisms were unpaid meant few men participated, further concentrating the connection between household food labor and organizing strategies. This raises the question of whether the Club's success can be replicated. In the post–1989 market–based world, it is less possible to volunteer or work for low pay, especially if one is not on a pension or eligible for other support. As its work becomes mainstreamed and paid, the PEC–Gliwice attracts more young people and more men, in general. Who will receive this paid work? In a male democracy that prioritizes paid work opportunity for men, what happens to the linkages between food knowledges, activisms, and creative program development? How will the linkages that sustain and inform social critique – and that are crafted across household, community, and professional spaces, be replicated elsewhere?

Conclusion

Basia and Marek are civil engineers and both have been retired for some time. In 1992, Basia was among those who challenged the new city government officials to recognize publicly the severity of industrial pollution and to dedicate funds to address the problems. She ran for public office in the early 1990s on a defiantly anti–pollution platform, lost, and threw her energy and passion into defining the environmental non–profit sector at its inception. Quiet, steady, and indomitable, Basia serves on the governing counsel and manages the office. Since its inception, Marek has helped the Club with English translations. His multiple language capacity is partly self–taught, reflecting a need, almost unknown and vastly underappreciated in North America, of communicating across nationalities, even – or especially – when forbidden to do so by his own former totalitarian government. Basia and Marek's son stops by the Club office sometimes to help with computer problems. He is recruited, like many children of Club members to help out at the office or take on more responsibilities at home while their parents stay late or struggle with new technologies and no budgets for technical training. Only retirees can afford to work for the Club, says Basia, because they at least have a regular if completely inadequate pension income. How can they recruit young people if they have no budget to pay them, she laments. Dinner at Basia and Marek's combines Marek's zurek soup (for which he begins the essential first stage of souring the barley flour himself), Basia's salads, and so much more. After dinner, we stroll through the allotment garden tract adjacent to their apartment block. The July flowering paths and trees laden with fruit belie possible contamination from an adjacent new petrol station that has leaked oil into the ground water. We talk about the environmental investigation underway, the garden harvests hoped for, and strategies to assure both.

Women members form the core of the PEC–Gliwice, but are not its only members. The predominance of women developed a specificity of voice, I argue, that provides valuable and different contributions to strategies for social and environmental change. The activists organize on behalf of the whole population, not just women. They also try to organize the whole population, not just other women. PEC–Gliwice members balance their accomplishments against a community that remains tenuous about the power of women. As a result they downplay their gendered identity in the hopes of uniting the community in action and not dividing it. However from this identity comes the experience and capacity of their gendered food praxis. There can be neither a true replication of the PEC–Gliwice activists' claims for a right and great need for safe food nor their model for organic and chemically tested foods without an appreciation for the women, their lives, and the gendered world around them.

Notes

[1] Generous funding for my field research (1993–2000) was received from the International Research and Exchanges Board (IREX), the Woodrow Wilson International Center for Scholars, the American Council of Learned Societies, the Kosciuszko Foundation, the Polish Ministry of National Education, the Society for Women in Geography, the Institute for International Education, The New School for Social Research, and Rutgers University.

[2] The biographical sections of this chapter reflect interviews and participatory research conducted in 1993, 1996, and 2000 in the City of Gliwice, Poland and in 1998 in the U.S.

References

Anderson, Benedict. 1983. *Imagined communities: Reflections on the origin and spread of nationalism*. London: Verso.

Appadurai, Arjun. 1993. Disjuncture and difference in the global cultural economy. In *The phantom public sphere*, edited by Bruce Robbins. Minneapolis and London: University of Minnesota Press.

Ash, Timothy Garton. 1984. *The Polish revolution: Solidarity*. New York: Charles Scribner's Sons.

Bellows, Anne C. 1996. Where kitchen and laboratory meet: The "Tested Food for Silesia" program. In *Feminist Political Ecology: Global Perspectives and Local Insights*, edited by Dianne Rocheleau, Barbara Thomas–Slater, and Esther Wangari. London and New York: Routledge.

Bellows, Anne C. 1999. Urban food, health, and the environments: The case of Upper Sile-
sia, Poland. In *For hunger-proof cities: Sustainable urban food systems,* edited by
Mustafa Koc, Rod MacRae, Luc J.A. Mougeot, Jennifer Welsh. Toronto: International
Development Research Centre [IDRC] and The Centre for Studies in Food Security,
Ryerson Polytechnic University.

Bellows, Anne C. 2000. Balancing diverse needs: risks and pleasures of urban agriculture
in Silesia, Poland. *Trialog: Zeitschrift fuer das Planen und Bauen in der Dritten Welt* 2
[Trialog: Journal for Planning and Architecture in the Third World] (Special issue, Urban
Agriculture):24–27.

Bellows, Anne C. 2001. The praxis of food work. In *Feminist locations: Global/local theory
practice in the twenty-first century,* edited by Marianne DeKoven. New Brunswick, NJ:
Rutgers University Press.

Bellows, Anne C. 2003. Exposing violences: Using women's human rights theory to reconceptualize food rights. *Journal of Agricultural and Environmental Ethics* 16 (3): 249–79.

Bellows, Anne C. 2004. One hundred years of allotment gardening in Poland. *Food and
Foodways.* 12 (4):247–76.

Bellows, Anne C., and Michael W. Hamm. 2003a. International origins of community food
security policies and practices in the U.S. *Critical Public Health* 13 (2):107–23.

Bellows, Anne C., and Michael W. Hamm. 2003b. U.S.–based community food security: Influences, practice, debate. *Journal of the Association for the Study of Food and Society.* 6
(1):31–44. Also available from, <http://food–culture.org/Bellows–Hamm.pdf>.

Benet, Sula. 1951. *Song, dance, and customs of peasant Poland.* New York: Roy Publishers.

Beskid, Lidia, Malgorzata Misiuna, Roza Milic–Czerniak, Joanna Sikorska, Antonina Ostrow-
ska, and Zbigniew Sufin. 1992. *Warunki życia i kondycja Polaków na początku zmian sys-
temowych.* [*Living standards and conditions of Poles at the beginning of system change*].
Warsaw: Polish Academy of Science, Institute of Philosophy and Sociology.

Beskid, Lidia, Roza Milic–Czerniak, and Zbigniew Sufin. 1995. *Polacy a nowa rzeczywistść
ekonomiczna.* [*The Poles and the new economic reality*]. Warsaw: Polish Academy of
Science, Institute of Philosophy and Sociology.

Buckingham, Donald E. 1998. Food rights and food fights: A preliminary legal analysis of the
results of the World Food Summit. *Canadian Journal of Development Studies*, vol. XIX
(Special Issue: The Quest for Food Security in the 21st Century):209–237.

Centrum Badania Opinii Społecznej [CBOS]. 1996. *Materialny poziom życia gospodarstw
domowych.* [*Households' material level of life*]. Warsaw: CBOS.

Charlesworth, Hilary. 1995. Human rights as men's rights. In *Women's rights human rights:
International feminist perspectives,* edited by Julie Peters and Andrea Wolper. New York
and London: Routledge.

Corrin, Chris, ed. 1996. *Women in a violent world: Feminist analyses and resistance across
"Europe."* Edinburgh: Edinburgh University Press.

Drakulić, Slavenka. 1991. *How we survived communism and even laughed.* New York: Harper
Perennial.

Eide, W. B., Holmboe–Ottesen, G., Oshaug, A., Perera, D. Tilakaratna, S. and Wandel, M.A.
1985. Theoretical contribution, from the series, *Introducing Nutritional Considerations
into Rural Development Programs with Focus on Agriculture.* Oslo: Institute for Nutrition
Research, University of Oslo.

Eide, W. B., Holmboe–Ottesen, G., Oshaug, A., Perera, D. Tilakaratna, S. and Wandel, M.A.
1986. Towards practice, from the series, *Introducing Nutritional Considerations into*

Rural Development Programs with Focus on Agriculture. Oslo: Institute for Nutrition Research, University of Oslo.

Food and Agriculture Organization of the United Nations. 1996. Food and international trade. World Food Summit 96/TECH/8 (April) Rome.

Fuszara, Malgorzata. 1991. Gender equality in the process of transformation. Unpublished paper. September, 1991.

Fuszara, Malgorzata. 1993. Abortion and the formation of the public sphere in Poland. In *Gender politics and post–communism: Reflections from Eastern Europe and the former Soviet Union*, edited by Nanette Funk and Magda Mueller. New York and London: Routledge.

Fuszara, Malgorzata. 1994. Market economy and consumer rights: the impact on women's everyday lives and employment. *Economic and Industrial Democracy* 15:75–87.

Gal, Susan. 1997. Feminism and civil society. In *Transitions, environments, translations: Feminisms in international politics*, edited by Joan W. Scott, Cara Kaplan, and Debra Keates. New York and London: Routledge.

Graham, Ann, and Joanna Regulska. 1997. Expanding political space for women in Poland. *Communist and Post–Communist Studies* 30 (1):65–82.

Habermas, Juergen. 1989. *The structural transformation of the public sphere: An inquiry into a category of bourgeois society*. Translated by Thomas Burger with the assistance of Federick Lawrence. Cambridge (USA): The MIT Press.

Havelkova, Hana. 1997a. Transitory and persistent differences: feminism East and West, in *Transitions, environments, translations: Feminisms in international politics*, edited by Joan W. Scott, Cora Kaplan, and Debra Keates. New York and London: Routledge.

Havelkova, Hana. 1997b. Where political meets women: creating local space in Poland. *The Anthropology of East Europe Review* 15 (1):4–12.

Howard, Rhoda. 1995. Women's rights and the right to development. In *Women's rights human rights: International feminist perspectives*, edited by Julie Peters and Andrea Wolper. New York and London: Routledge.

Kacprzak, Halina, Janina Sokolowska, Maria Staniszewska, Jan Sliwka, and Barbara Migurska. 1996. Tested and organic food for residents of densely industrialized urban areas. Report. Gliwice, Poland: Gliwice Chapter, Polish Ecological Club.

Kaplan, Temma. 1982. Female consciousness and collective action: the case of Barcelona, 1910–1918. *Signs* 7 (3):545–566.

Kurczewski, Jacek. 1993. *The resurrection of rights in Poland*. New York: Oxford University Press.

Lang, Tim. 1996. Food security: does it conflict with globalization? *Development* 4:46–50.

Lefebvre, Henri. 1991. *The production of space*. Translated by Donald Nicholson–Smith. First Published in 1974, Editions Anthropos. Oxford and Cambridge: Blackwell Publishers.

Lepak, Keith John. 1988. *Prelude to solidarity: Poland and the politics of the Gierek Regime*. New York: Columbia University Press.

Merkel, Ina. 1994. From a socialist society of labor into a consumer society? The transformation of East German identities and systems. In *Envisioning Eastern Europe: Postcommunist Cultural Studies,* edited by Michael Kennedy. Ann Arbor, MI: The University of Michigan Press.

Michna, Waldemar. 1992. *Poland's food security and agricultural policy at the turn of the 20th and 21st Centuries*. Warsaw: The Friedrich Ebert Foundation.

Moszkowski, Janusz. 1995. Ogród działkowy wczoraj, dziś, jutro. [Garden allotments yesterday, today, and tomorrow]. In *Nowoczesny Ogród Działkowy Elementem Ekosystemu*

Miasta. Wroclaw: Wojewódzki Zarząd Polskiego Związku Dzialkowców we Wrocławiu, Regionalne Samorządowe Centrum Edukacji Ekologicznej przy Sejmiku Samorządowym we Wrocławiu [Contemporary Allotment Gardens as Elements of City Eco-systems. Wroclaw: The Voivod-regional Administration of the Polish Association of Gardeners and the Wroclaw-regional Central Office of Environmental Education].

Pakszys, Elzbieta, and Dorota Mazurczak. 1994. From totalitarianism to democracy in Poland: Women's issues in the sociopolitical transition of 1989–1993. *Journal of Women's History* 5 (3):144–50.

Peterson, D.J. 1993. *Troubled lands: The legacy of Soviet environmental destruction.* Boulder, CO: Westview Press.

Potrykowska, A. 1993. Mortality and environmental pollution in Poland. *Research and Exploration* 9 (2):255–56.

Ragland, J., and S. Kukula. 1995. Balancing agriculture with physical and economic environment in Eastern and Central Europe with special reference to Poland. In *Agriculture and environment: Bridging food production and environmental protection in developing countries,* edited by Anthony S.R. Juo and Russell D. Freed. ASA Special publication, 60. Madison, WI: American Society of Agronomy.

Regulska, Joanna. 1992. Women and power in Poland. In *Women transforming politics, worldwide strategies for empowerment,* edited by Jill M. Bystydzienski. Bloomington and Indianapolis: Indiana University Press.

Regulska, Joanna. 1998. Local government reform. In *Transition to democracy in Poland,* edited by Richard F. Starr. New York: St. Martin's Press.

Scheppele, Kim Lane. 1994. Rethinking group rights. Unpublished manuscript. University of Michigan.

Schneider, Elizabeth M. 1991. The dialectic of rights and politics: Perspectives from the women's movements. In *Feminist legal theory: Readings in law and gender,* edited by Katharine T. Bartlett and Rosanne Kennedy. Boulder, CO: Westview Press.

Snitow, Ann. 1993. Feminist futures in the former East Bloc. *Peace and Democracy News* 7 (1):40–44.

Snitow, Ann. 1997. Response. In *Transitions, environments, translations: Feminisms in international politics,* edited by Joan W. Scott, Cora Kaplan, and Debra Keates. New York and London: Routledge.

Sufin, Zbigniew. 1994. Households at the beginning of economic and social transformation. *Polish Sociological Review* 1 (105):69.

Szymanski, Leszek. 1982. *Candle for Poland: 469 days of solidarity.* San Bernardino, CA: The Borgo Press.

Thompson, E.P. 1971. The moral economy of the English crowd in the 18th century. *Past and Present* 50:76–136.

Thompson, E. P. 1996. *The making of the English working class.* New York: Vintage Books.

Titkow, Anna, and Henryk Domanski, eds. 1995. *Co to znaczy byc kobieta w Polsce. [What it means to be a Woman in Poland].* Warsaw: The Polish Academy of Science, Institute of Philosophy and Sociology.

Touraine, Alain, Francoise Dubet, Michel Wieviorka, and Jan Stzelecki. 1983. *Solidarity: The analysis of a social movement: Poland 1980–1981.* Cambridge: Cambridge University Press, Written in collaboration with Grażyna Gęsicka, Anna Matuchniak, Tadeusz Chabiera, Małgorzata Melchior, Anna Kruczkowska, Krzysztof Nowak, Ireneusz Krzemiński, Włodzimierz Pankow, Paweł Kuczynski, and Dorota Reczek. Translated by David Denby.

Originally published in 1982 by Paris: Librairie Artheme Fayard, 1983.

Van Esterik, Penny. 1999. Right to food; right to feed; right to be fed. The intersection of women's rights and the right to food. *Agriculture and Human Values* 16 (2):225–32.

Verdery, Katherine. 1996. *What was socialism, and what comes next?* Princeton, NJ: Princeton University Press.

Walton, John, and David Seddon. 1994. *Free markets and food riots: The politics of global adjustment.* Cambridge and Oxford: Blackwell Publishers.

Watson, Peggy. 1993. The rise of masculinism in Eastern Europe. *New Left Review*, 198.

Watson, Peggy. 1997. Civil society and the politics of difference in eastern Europe. In *Transitions, environments, translations: Feminisms in international politics*, edited by Joan W. Scott, Cora Kaplan, and Debra Keates. New York and London: Routledge.

Wells, Betty. 1998. Creating a public space for women in U.S. agriculture: Empowerment, organization, and social change. *European Society for Rural Sociology* 38 (3):371–90.

Youssef, Nadia H. 1995. Women's access to productive resources: The need for legal instruments to protect women's development rights. In *Women's rights human rights: International feminist perspectives*, edited by Julie Peters and Andrea Wolper. New York and London: Routledge.

Chapter 9

Disabled Women's Everyday Citizenship Rights in East Europe: Examples from Slovenia

Darja Zaviršek

Introduction

In post-socialist societies, political subjecthood has been increased for some people but not all; many people are still subjected to the traditional understanding of citizenship, that is, they are denied full participation in economic, social, and political life. Women and men with disabilities are among those for whom this is true. After 1991, socialist ideology was replaced with an economic ideology and the dictates of free market. Many people internalized the neo-liberal belief, that the "happy hours" of history, when everyone had the right to a flat and paid work, were over, and now "real life began." Neo-liberalism exploited the idea that there was no alternative to the economic organization of the new world order. One consequence of this has been that after 1991, in Slovenia many women and men with disabilities lost paid employment. In 1999, the Employment Service of Slovenia registered 14,787 disabled job seekers and in the year 2000, the number increased to 16,141 (Slovenia has a population of 2 million). Currently, out of all people who are registered as unemployed, about 10 percent are people with various disabilities.[1] Additionally, people labeled as moderately, severely, and profoundly intellectually disabled (the exception are those that are labeled as borderline or mild), are still, according to an old communist law from 1983, completely excluded from paid employment, because this law defined them as being "unemployable" and "incapable for independent living."[2] Regardless of the fact that Slovenia, in its accession into the European Union in May 2004, adopted several new laws that promoted inclusion and equal treatment, there are still many burning issues which could at least be partly resolved with some formal guidelines for change. However, neither the EU social policy officers nor the national politicians seem to have any interest to promote such guidelines.[3] A limited concept of citizenship, which in the socialist period included able–bodied proletariat and privileged disabled war veterans (predominantly men), has today been replaced with another type of exclusionary version of citizenship, which only includes those people who can respond to the demands of the new neo-liberal market. For many minorities (especially people with intellectual disabilities and ethnic and sex minorities) the end of the communist regime did not bring the basic everyday citizenship rights and in some cases did not even bring them formal rights.[4]

Disabled people in the post-socialist countries of Eastern Europe are still called *invalids* (based on the Latin word, *invalidus* which means weak; powerless). In Slovenia, a disabled woman is called an *invalidka*.[5] To categorize someone by such a name produces a certain response from the person who is objectified with the injurious name and fashions a power relationship between the agent who calls and the one who is interpellated. The act of naming, calling someone an injurious name (*invalid*), is rationalized as "caring for the other", and hides the fact that it assures a long–term subordinate place for the person being defined as invalid. Even more, it seeks to assign a social site or locus to the one who labels, who has the power of naming.

Since women with disabilities have historically been silenced and have remained invisible even within the core feminist writing in both the West as well as the East, this article brings forward not only a gender aspect of disabled people's rights, but also women's personal testimonies and narratives. These narratives and testimonies will demonstrate that public care is also a form of the violation of citizenship rights because it continues the physical segregation of disabled women as well as their experiences of sexual violence, which not only happen at home but also in public care. In both cases women experience the abuse of their citizenship rights. The following ethnographic data is derived from a study that was carried out between 2001 and 2002, and was focused on different aspects of exclusion against disabled people, particularly on violence against disabled women in Slovenia. The study consists of twenty-five narratives of women living either at home or in public care. The bulk of each interview was devoted to the re-collection of both violence against self-determination as well as sexual violence. This ethnographic research aimed to de-individualize the debate about sexual violence against disabled women and to show its contexts, which is very often the context of living a segregated life instead of one of independent community living. The research collected individual women's narratives as given by the women themselves, rather than being based on the censored, non-disruptive professional stories, which patronize and do not re-call their personal experiences. During the socialist government, professionals and institutions controlled public knowledge and decided which stories were allowed to become a part of the public memory. When disabled women talk about their experiences, which previously did not have the right to be heard, or to exist, the personal testimonies of women with disabilities also have a political connotation and form some parts of their citizenship status. This article focuses on women with physical and sensory impairments, intellectual disabilities, and mental health problems who have spent most of their lives in a variety of institutional settings. As the deinstitutionalization processes in central and east Europe have only hardly begun, most of the women who were interviewed still have not entered everyday civic life and still live in public care (Pečarič 2001; Iarskaia–Smirnova 2005).

State Care Institutions: Inclusion as a Form of Exclusion

Personal testimonies of people with disabilities who lived in public care (asylums, boarding schools, and nursing homes) in the former communist countries are almost nonexistent (McCagg and Siegelbaum 1989; Buda and Gondos 1998; Zaviršek 2000). An extended comparative research about the enforcement of rights in psychiatry in Eastern European countries showed that those who used psychiatric services had no rights to provide informed consent, received no personal respect, experienced no regard for their personal safety, had no privacy, and no advocacy support system (Buda and Gondos 1998). People with disabilities who have lived in public care institutions have often been treated as if they did not share the same humanity and personhood as their guards and professional staff did.

State care institutions symbolized the "good father" who cares for his children and can always take the place of other people close to the person. The remains of this welfare regime still can be found in the legislation that continues to exist across Eastern Europe. In Slovenia, the court can make the decision to restrict or remove an individual's civil capacity, and appoint a guardian for a person with disabilities. The guardianship can be carried out by parents or, if the parents cannot or will not be legal guardians, by a social worker from the local center for social work. In the latter cases, since the removal of full capacity (plenary guardianship) means that the obligation of the guardian are the same as in the case of a juvenile under the age of 18 years old, the institution replaces the will of the person and therefore represents the person under the law, and makes decisions for them in regards to finance as well as in all other issues. In 2002, there were 4,837 adults under guardianship, however no gender–specific statistics are available (*Rights of People with Intellectual Disabilities Slovenia* 2005, 34). In Bulgaria, the dominant status of state care institutions is even more obvious, since the staff member from an institution where the person is placed can be the guardian for the disabled person. One of the local reports even states that "the director or a staff member was appointed as a guardian to 41 per cent of the residents in all homes for adults with intellectual disabilities" (*Rights of People with Intellectual Disabilities Bulgaria* 2005, 32). Here the paternalistic nature of a public care institution is obvious; the guardian is responsible for the person's life, health, property, and financial interests, or as one of the early state socialist documents from Slovenia pointed out, "from conception till the grave" (Zaviršek 2005, 251). When a director of an institution is appointed as a guardian, the actual and invisible dependency becomes legitimized. The person cannot leave the institution if the director does not agree to it, and has no independent person outside of the institutional system who can speak for his or her rights in cases of abuse or maltreatment. The social care institution not only symbolically but also legally becomes a family type placement where the director as a "good father" can allow or forbid the requests of the disabled "resident children."

A Slovene woman in her early forties, who was born with a muscle dystrophy and has had to use a wheelchair since childhood, described how the communist regime subjugated her to a normative identity, which is, at the same time, an oppressed identity. From an early age she was told that she was a "child of the state," which meant that she lived on state money while being sent to different state institutions for disabled children and youth. When she was 19 years old, she was sent to an old people's home in the capital, Ljubljana, where she lived until her death in 2004. Her memories about the past showed that the internalized identity of a "child of the state" prevented her from complaining, she felt guilty and thankful. She was infantilized and patronized through this system of care, within which she was like a child who never was seen as a political subject. The state defined her personhood through physical segregation and personal silence.

These examples represent many people who are excluded from everyday life through the exclusionary system of public care and who are at the same time included as welfare subjects through the same system that provides them with some social benefits and everyday needs. The dynamic between exclusion and inclusion had been metaphorically described by many authors through the use of the famous "Central European" Franz Kafka story, *Vor dem Gesetz* [*Before the Law*]. This story can also be used for analyzing the social limbo experienced by people with disabilities in central and east Europe today. Kafka's story describes a man from the country who goes to an open door of the Law in order to enter, but *der Tuerhueter* [the doorkeeper] will not allow him to enter. The man from the country does not give up, he waits there for years, observing and talking to the doorkeeper in order to understand the logic of entering the Law. Time passes, he becomes very old, and before he dies asks the doorkeeper: *"If everybody wants to enter the Law why has nobody entered through this door?"* The doorkeeper responds with the words that mark the end of the story: *"No one else could enter here, since this door was destined for you alone. Now I will go and shut it"* (Kafka 2003, 162–63).

The symbolic understanding of Kafka's story with regard to disabled people shows again the dialectic of inclusion and exclusion. The open door, destined only for the man from the country, includes him as a citizen who spends his life waiting to be allowed to enter the door (living in a public care institution and being a recipient of care), at the same time that it excludes him by preventing him from entering the Law (to become an equal citizen). Most of the consumers of social care services encounter the same paradox of the Law, when they are included in the form of an exception (they are called "the different", in Slovenian, *drugačni*), as it was pointed out by Giorgio Agamben, *"The exception is what cannot be included in the whole of which it is a member and can not be a member of the whole in which it is always already included"* (1998, 25). The woman living in an asylum is included through exclusion and is therefore, symbolically speaking, "matter out of place" (Douglas 1994). She is included through her "invalid" category but her inclusion is, at the same time, an exclusion from full citizenship rights as she is spatially, politically, economically, and socially excluded. The concept of citizenship rights remains in this way a flexible category, because the state arbitrarily affords or withdraws citizen rights to different groups and in such a way constructs their identity. This compli- cated dynamic shows that the rights to different social benefits turns people with disabilities into welfare consumers, and at the same time prevents them from having such basic citizenship rights as the right to vote, work, or make financial decisions, among other things. Further in line with Kafka, the question arises, why didn't the man from the country break the law and enter the door, anyway? Internalized op- pression is one of the constructions of identity created by welfare regimes. When the welfare regime positions people with disabilities as being passive welfare subjects, this in turn can become their "true identity". This also contains the fear that more active citizen rights might put their current welfare benefits in danger.

According to Michel Foucault, a society's "threshold of biological modernity" is situated at the point where bodies become politicized bodies, constructed by state power. The woman who was called a "child of the state" was not only seen through her impaired body, but her body became politicized through the state apparatuses of care (1981; 1990). Exactly like Kafka's man from the country, the person who is called a "child of the state" is neither free nor un-free, since her identity, as a "child of the state" is an inclusive as well as an exclusive one. Even after the decade of political changes following the change of the regime, the woman who lived in an old people's home remained spatially segregated and still without the right of self- determination. For her, the new democracy, and the new welfare interventions (for example: "inclusion," "independent living," and "empowerment") did not bring any changes. She remained in the past, from which she carried her frozen citizenship identity until she died.

This example shows that political changes do not automatically change the social welfare order or the cultural images attached to stigmatized groups seen as "inva- lids." Under communism, according to the idea of universal needs and rights, the extensive building of the large institutions during the 1960s and 1970s, were seen as a form of modernization and progress. Educational training taught the professionals that the invalids are "those who had to be cared for in a socialist society." The cul- tural images of a woman with disabilities who can be an active citizen, make deci- sions, and participate in biological and social reproduction, still seems to threaten the knowledge of professionals who were taught that "invalids" should only be treated with respect as welfare subjects, not as equal citizens.

In comparison to the above, some earlier ethnographic research from the Soviet Union showed that during the communist regime people with disabilities were seen not only as dependent but also as powerful and dangerous. Dunn and Dunn col- lected examples of the everyday life of physically impaired persons in the Soviet Union, who were either abandoned, such as one women who lived isolated in a flat for years, despite the fact that she was not able to move and was only brought food once a day; or those who were punished when they demanded rights (1989). An example of this was an almost non-existent civil initiative undertaken by a group of disabled activists who called themselves the "Action Group." During the 1980s its members soon became demonized, institutionalized by force, and criminalized. Genady Gus'kow, a member of the Action group, and physically impaired himself, became an innovator and entrepreneur, "traveling around on a primitive cart" (Dunn and Dunn 1989). When he became economically successful (he was making and selling prostheses), the local government started to construct him as a "dangerous problem" for the local politicians and the community. His life contrasted with the belief that a person with disabilities cannot remain mobile and active. He disturbed the historically constructed image of the dependent cripple, subjected to the institutional order. On the contrary, he earned his own money, was able to travel, and was quite innovative. Eventually, the local authorities forcibly removed him to an old people's home that was far away from the community where he was living (Dunn and Dunn 1989). Here the phenomenon called the "hierarchical turn," when greater power is ascribed to people with less social, symbolic, and economic power, can be observed. The omnipotent communist state ascribed great power to a small group of disabled, disempowered, poor, and often symbolically polluted citizens. These individuals were active and resisted being isolated by a closed state institution, they were well organized, and took social action against the "powerless" state.

In an analysis about mothering children with disabilities in today's Russia, Iarskaia–Smirnova showed how placing children with disabilities in a large institution was a common practice supported and expected by the medical professionals of the time: "Today's struggle faced primarily by women choosing to raise children with disabilities at home must be understood within the context of decades of professional medical advice to parents that they place their children in state institutional care and 'try again' for a child without 'defects'" (1999, 69). A female social worker in her seventies from Slovenia recalled something very similar when she talked about her work during the communist era: "I worked very hard to persuade parents to put a child into public care. I said to them, 'Don't revolt, this will be good for you and for your child!'" (Zaviršek 2005, 211).

Spatial segregation itself contains several elements of violence that were analyzed and identified by Erving Goffman almost fifty years ago (although in a gender–neutral manner). The gender aspect of the oppressive caring practices show that, as an environment for "the outcasts", boarding schools and other public care institutions are places of all sorts of abusive practices, such as violence, sexual abuse, and psychological abandonment. This becomes visible through women's personal testimonies.

Gendered Discrimination

It took a long time for feminists to recognize that the structure of discrimination and violence experienced by disabled women was similar to that experienced by non-disabled women. Feminist researchers have only recently recognized that disabled women, even more than non-disabled women, are vulnerable to different forms of physical and sexual violence. Here I will claim that feminist writing has inherited the same historically constructed stereotypes towards disabled women as can be found within other non-feminist writing. While over-looking and minimizing violence, feminists have reproduced the avoidance, discrimination, and hierarchization of disabled women; and have not challenged the exclusionary welfare regime to any degree in this area. Slovenia for instance, has eight safe houses for women and children who flee domestic violence, but none of them are accessible to women in wheel–chairs. According to some of the feminist social workers in those safe houses, women with disabilities are seen as "difficult clients" (especially those with mental health problems), and are often advised to find some other social service to help them. These attitudes show that even professionals who see themselves as feminists, some of whom initiated the first safe houses themselves, have gradually become medically oriented and dominated by managerial logic (dividing women either as "easy" or "difficult" clients).

When critical writers eventually did use a gender perspective to understand the everyday life of disabled women, it was best done by disabled and non-disabled feminists themselves because they were the first to find the existence of a long historical memory of discrimination towards disabled women (Morris 1992; Rommelspacher 1995; Wendell 1996; Linton 1998; Fawcett 2000). Many feminist disability activists have shown that disability itself reinforces discrimination against women at the structural level as well as on the everyday interpersonal level. Disabled women challenge the idea of a perfect body as part of a constructed women's identity. Those disabled women who decide to have a child also challenge the naturalized heterosexual matrix, which connects femaleness, heterosexuality, reproduction, and motherhood into a natural, undivided bond (as many women with disabilities can only get pregnant with the assistance of new reproductive technologies). Since ideas about sexuality are strongly connected with reproduction, the prevention of sexual activities also means the protection of a non-disabled world from the "danger" of unwanted pregnancies. Women with impairments might even be seen as productive (when they suffer from physically or sensory impairments, but not with intellectual impairments), but they are not allowed to reproduce. Even if a woman becomes disabled during her lifetime, most professionals in central and east Europe advise her not to have intimate relations or children (Iarskaia–Smirnova 2005). In 2000, the Slovene parliament passed a law which forbade the use of any kind of new reproductive technology by single women, based on the belief that assisted reproduction might expand the rights of single women, including disabled women, to have children without necessarily having a partner. Some women with disabilities protested against this decision, claiming that in the times of "perfect bodies" there is almost no chance for them to get married, but rather than being heard they were ridiculed and patronized.

Within the state–funded organizations for invalids, established during the social-ist era as the privileged sphere of social protection, no awareness of gender can be found. In the majority of post socialist invalid organizations, most of the money to-day is still spent on sports activities, where men dominate in high numbers. Most of the invalid organizations which grew up on the image of the male "heroic invalid", have been led by men while the experiences of women are only recognized when Western foundations give money explicitly for "disabled women's activities." In some Central and East European countries, women were able to form women-only groups or in some cases were only able to become members of disability groups because some foreign funder demanded their participation.[6]

Gender discrimination also remains obvious within the education system. Young people in Slovenia who are categorized as having mild intellectual disabilities and have finished either six years of mainstream elementary school (instead of nine years) or completed a special school (which are mostly spatially segregated and highly stigmatized institutions) are only allowed to continue their education within various lower vocational programs (which consists of two and a half years of educa-tion). Slovenia has, at present, fifteen different lower vocational programs, out of which only one program is explicitly offered for girls (assistant housewife), while the rest of the programs are almost explicitly designed for boys, such as metal or wood worker, assistant glazier, assistant electrician, baker, butcher, pastry cook, amongst others (Urh 2005).

During the inter-war period of the 20th century, an early Slovenian anthropolo-gist named Božo Škerlj reported a similar gender gap. He himself was a controversial scientist, fascinated with the eugenic movement of the 1920s and 1930s. In his study about the "less-valued children" in Ljubljana auxiliary schools, conducted in 1933, he discovered that parents of disabled boys made more effort to make their sons in-dependent and to teach them special skills then they did for their disabled daughters. He found that most of the parents preferred to send disabled girls to special institu-tions for disabled youth while preferring to keep their disabled sons at home:

> It is not uncommon that parents, in hope of having some use of the child, decide first to give an auxiliary school the care of a girl. The number of differences between the sexes is so great that it cannot be merely coincidental … It is necessary to prepare a son for independent work, this does not seem for many parents to be so important for a girl and therefore perhaps they leave them to repeat a class two or three times (Škerlj 1933).

His report also showed that the common knowledge from that period viewed public care institutions as places that did not increase the social and vocational skills of the children who were sent to them. In order to strengthen those skills, the parents were more interested in keeping the child outside of closed and segregated places. In the post-war period, this knowledge was replaced with another welfare ideology. The institutionalization of children and young people with disabilities was seen as a form of modernization of state social protection. It was also seen as a form of completing the socialist vision of the just society in which the state cares for the "needy" (Haney 2002, Zaviršek 2005). In the same study Škerlj drew attention to another type of gender difference that was obvious in the different levels of material care for male and female children: "In relation to being well-nourished, girls provide a much worse picture than boys, since at least 75% of them are below normal" (Škerlj 1933).

In recent times, sheltered workplaces have been developed for people with moderate intellectual disabilities and even for some with milder disabilities. Most of people labeled with mild intellectual disabilities could easily work in paid employment if they would get additional support and assistance. Here, another form of gender discrimination can be interpreted from the number of women and men who work in sheltered workplaces across Slovenia, since most of them are men aged between 26 and 36 years (*Rights of People with Intellectual Disabilities Slovenia* 2005, 103). The numbers show that men more often than women have the chance to spend half a day in sheltered workplaces, while women usually stay at home and help with the family's household. Regardless of the fact that the labor in sheltered workplaces does not bring the workers any economic independence, it does offer friendships, exchange, symbolic payment, and, for some people, an important sphere of personal freedom, which can increase their self-respect and personal dignity.[7] Once again, however, women with disabilities have fewer possibilities for activities and networking outside of the private household domain than men do.

All of these examples show that women with disabilities have even fewer citizenship rights than men, are more dependent on the existing system of care, and as will be shown below, experience different types of violence. Being disabled reinforces the discrimination against women from an early age.

Safety from Abuse as an Element of Citizenship Rights

The comparative research, as well as the testimonies of women living in public care in Slovenia, has shown that experiences of neglect and abuse are, for many of these women, a central part of everyday life. These experiences influence their everyday citizenship rights. Many of them are not able to live in a space of safety and respect. Therefore, the issues of abuse and violence also have to be part of the citizenship debates, especially because women with disabilities do not have the same rights to share their sexual desires with other people as non-disabled people do. The same is true about the disclosure of their personal stories of abuse. Both double standards regarding the right to sexuality and the public silence about the abuse do not give disabled people the symbolic permission to recall and voice their personal stories. There are no public spaces where the stories could be easily told without a running risk that nobody would want to bear witness. Not having an outside witness, as Dori Laub has pointed out, prevents the victim from bearing witness for oneself. Thus, personal memories remain silent (1992).

It is not only women with disabilities, but also female children with disabilities who are more often objects of sexual abuse and neglect than non-disabled children (Pugh 1997). Several studies show that among disabled people there are more girls who are abused than boys, and when they disclose abuse girls are less often believed than boys (Brown and Craft 1989; Sinason 1992; Sobsey 1994; Pugh 1997; Cross 1998; Brown 2001; Zaviršek 2000). In a study conducted in 2000 by Michelle McCarthy, 32 percent of the cases of the abuse of women with intellectual disabilities were not even taken seriously enough to be reported to service managers, whereas this was only the case for 7 percent of men who reported abuse. McCarthy speaks about the "different thresholds of belief and intervention" connected to the pre-conceptions of a gendered hierarchy (it is not unusual that a Slovene teacher reacts to sexual harassment of a girl with the words: "Don't make a fuss out of that, these are boys!").

There are four major reasons why neither feminist social workers nor professionals dealing with different types of violence against women have been able to recognize the vulnerability of disabled women to sexual violence. All four reasons are linked with the explanatory systems used for understanding interpersonal violence and with the long historical legacy of prejudices against disabled persons. These reasons include:

The Sexualization of Abuse

The debate about sexual violence remained for a long time an explanation system that was framed by a naturalized gender code. It was believed that violence was caused by the strong sexual drive of men. Sexual violence was therefore explained either as the result of female sexual resistance, or as the social incapacity of lonely male persons to find a sexual partner. In juxtaposition to those opinions stood the belief that disabled people and especially disabled women did not have any sexual drive and no sexual life. Since disabled persons were not seen as sexual beings, it was widely believed that sexual violence could not happen to them. The more they were perceived as children or as child-like adults, the more it was believed that disability itself prevented them from becoming objects of sexual abuse.

In cases of reversed stereotypes, as in the case of disabled persons who have over-sexualized behavior, the victims were seen as the initiators or as triggers of sexual abuse. Similarly, Merry Cross states: "Already we have touched on the classic stereotype of people with physical and sensory impairments as asexual, and people with learning difficulties as sex-mad monsters" (Cross 1998, 81). In this case, disability does not prevent the person from abuse but, on the contrary, causes the abuse. The medical label covers abuse in the language of disease and pathology.

The De-sexualization of Abuse

After the broader influence of feminist explanatory models, the debate about sexual abuse moved towards the idea that sexual violence was simply another form of violence, most commonly used by men to control women. Juxtaposed to this idea, common attitudes towards disabled people were dominated by the notion that they were powerless, "innocent cripples" towards whom nobody would react violently. In this view, again, disability itself was believed to protect disabled persons against sexual violence. The substantial vulnerability of disabled children to be sexually abused was turned around and reinterpreted as the protection of disabled children and adults against violence.

Abuse as a Shared Activity

Another common idea regarding sexual abuse was that abuse always involves "two sides" where every side "plays" a specific part in the drama of sexual violence. This view assumes two equally powerful and active agents who share the responsibility for the sexual violence acted upon them. In juxtaposition to this view is the belief that disabled persons are passive human beings without personal autonomy who are not able to enter the "violent drama." If disabled persons do not have their own sexuality and agency, or even any knowledge about sex, they are not able, it was believed, to share the responsibility for sexual violence. Their not knowing prevents them from becoming actively involved in an activity that demands two "actors." For most professional helpers in Slovenia sexual abuse is still an individual matter, connected to the deviance and illness of the perpetrator as well as, to a "certain degree," to the deviance and illness of a passive victim. The models of "shared responsibility" and a "pathological family" (that sexual abuse demonstrates a pathology of all family members) prevails.

The Romantization of Sexuality

Another view, which obscured the high rate of sexual abuse against disabled people, was the common belief that sexuality and sexual abuse do not have anything in common. Sexuality was connected to love, innocence, and beauty, whereas abuse was dirty, immoral, and removed from everyday life. In opposition to this view, many researchers have shown that violence and sexuality are not at all *a priori* distinct from each other, they are very strongly connected.[8]

In public care, the romanticization of sexuality manifests itself in cases where the institutional relationships start to be seen as personal relationships (between the inmates and the paid caregivers), which in turn justify the sexual acts. This erases the aspects of coercion and intimidation involved in the sexual act and hides the fact that sexuality accumulates a great deal of power. Sexual acts in public care as well as in the domestic sphere cannot be distinct from the question of control: the person who controls the space (the house, the rooms of the disabled persons, the keys from the bathrooms) also controls the everyday life of a disabled person (the food, timetable, other contacts etc.). Consequently, those who care and protect the person also control the bodily space of the disabled individual under their care. Because of the strong romantization of sexuality, sexual relationships, which are in fact an institutional relationship of dominance and control, fail to be recognized as an instrument of the administrative apparatuses of closed or semi-closed institutions.

Personal Memory

Women with physical disabilities, such as impairments of hearing and vision, have fewer chances to avoid abuse because they cannot see or hear the perpetrator, and therefore cannot scream or run away. Some people with intellectual disabilities might not be aware of what is going on. In addition, in most cases, relatives and other unpaid caregivers as well as professionals, as was already discussed, do not believe the children or adults when they report abuse or pay attention when they show signs of "unusual" behavior, which is often a symptom of the abuse. Most often, they individualize the personal stories (a disabled person is "unstable," she made up "the story" because she desires intimate contact etc.), pathologizes them (she or he needs more drugs), or educates them (with punishment, more control, or physically moving them to another peer group or another building). Most people are convinced that in hospitals, schools, residential homes, and boarding schools abuse happens only among peers.

Much of the research conducted so far has shown that the perpetrator enjoys having the feeling of power and control over someone who is weak and prefers people who cannot defend themselves. Therefore, it is not surprising that people with more severe mental disabilities are more often sexually abused than those with milder impairments (Sobsey 1994). The wider and more disparate the social status between the able and the impaired, the more likely the disabled persons will be subjugated to abuse and victimization. This gap in the social status between two individuals will assure that the abuse and victimization will have less social consequences and condemnation for the abuser.

Many people with physical, sensory, and intellectual impairments in Slovenia spend most of their childhood in various institutions (hospitals, rehabilitation centers, special institutions, boarding, or special schools) where they internalize the message that they are not the same as "normal children;" even more so, that they are of a lesser value because they are "invalids." They are reduced to a disabled body that is controlled by others. Some of them experience different types of institutional violence, which make them more vulnerable to other types of abuse. Veronika, a woman in her late twenties with a physical disability testified about her sexual abuse at rehabilitation centers and physiotherapy:

> I had very bad experience with the staff at the health spa. The first year after my attack of sclerosis multiplex I had massages and physiotherapy by male staff. I hated verbal contacts with them because they use such expressions that they abuse you just by talking to you. They often said, "You will never have a boyfriend because you are different, you should use what you have here, now, because you will never have a chance for anything else!" I tolerated that and decided to go to someone else next year. Then came the following year, and then another year and I found out that it would be the same also the fourth year. So I decided not to go to the spa again although I have everything paid for [silence]. They wanted me to sleep with them. It was terrible to come to the spa because I am a local

girl and I knew they were talking about me outside of the rehabilitation center. I isolated myself from local people, I was ashamed [silence].

Her experiences of continuous hate speech and verbal abuse were followed by sexual abuse:

> At first, it was verbal. Since I was able to move around, I was having the massage done at the hotel. Because I am communicative and I was talking with them, they thought that they could do whatever they wanted with me. I can tolerate one wrong move on my body, but then they start touching you, and I made quite a fuss about it. At first, they massaged me in a normal way. I know well that my prescribed massage includes legs, arms, and back. But then they came to my breasts. Although I did not want that, which I told them clearly, it was getting worse and worse. I don't know what would have been the reaction of the manager if I had told him, I didn't know how to tell. It was the same with physiotherapy. In Ljubljana, at physiotherapy they treat every group of muscles: arms, legs, and then they slowly came to the parts where I felt that it was not what it was supposed to be. I told them that I did not want that. But the reaction was the same: "You will always be like that, who would take responsibility for you, who would want you for a girlfriend?"

A disabled body is an imaginary locus of sexual activities, which does not necessarily include any kind of emotional relationship or consent from the disabled person. There are "other" rules connected to the relationship with a disabled person, than with a non-disabled person. The totality of the disabled body deprives the person of the right to an ordinary intimate relationship (*"You will never have a boyfriend, use the opportunity which you have now, you will not have another one"*).

Hate speech not only affected the interpersonal relationship between Veronika and the staff, but it also affected her social network and her social well being in a close community. Her first reaction to the hate speech and sexual harassment was silence, adopted in the hope and as part of a strategy that would make the event disappear. The repetition of abuse increased her terror and powerlessness, which not only silenced her but also caused her withdrawal from the therapy that she had the right to receive. The public silence made her more powerless and less capable of disclosing the events. Since there was nobody who would bear witness, she was not able to bear witness on behalf of herself, therefore her personal memory did not become part of the public knowledge.

In Veronika's testimony, the abuser presented himself as "her opportunity," as someone who was giving her a chance, which she would otherwise not get. Here the manipulative element of an abusive situation can be observed: an abuser presents himself as someone who is doing something for the benefit of the disabled person. Sexual abuse becomes therapeutic and is normalized by being medicalized.

Traumatic events thus not only produce thick silence as a form of narrating what should not be disclosed and re-called, but these events can also be a reason why disabled people often talk about their wish for their bodies to physically disappear. Miriam, a 37-year-old woman diagnosed as mentally disabled, who has experienced recurrent sexual abuse, spoke about her wish to disappear from the world:

> You know, when it happened to me I was in the special primary school. And he said to me: "Oh, you damn bitch, why can't you give it to me, tell me, why can't you give it to me? Come on!" And I said: "Here I am so take me," you know. He was persuading me that much, so I said: "Here I am so take me!" He persuaded me … I thought about suicide, it was so hard for me. I wanted to cut my veins, but so nobody would know, my mother mustn't know, and father mustn't know, nobody at home must know, and none of the teachers. All the time I had in my mind that I should kill myself, how do I kill myself, how do I do it so that no one would know. How, how am I to "vanish," how do I get out of this world, how to pack myself out of it?

This testimony shows a specific dynamic of abuse where Miriam unwillingly consented after verbal victimization *("damn bitch, why can't you give it to me, tell me, why can't you give it to me? Come on!")*. In traditional conceptions of sexual violence, dominant in post-communist countries, similar events are not defined as sexual violence. The consequences are that most victims of rape report sexual violence only when they can prove the "unproblematic dynamic" of an assault in which they had physically defended themselves. Women's consent for sexual activity is also linked with the socially constructed images of a woman and female sexuality, where girls and women often consent because they were told that this is the way to be accepted and loved. McCarthy showed that within public care women sometimes consent in order to get some rare privileges within the closed institution or in order not to lose these privileges (2000).

Miriam's wish to "pack herself out of the world" could also be understood in connection with her unwilling consent. She was not able to protect herself, but she also did not expect protection from outside. Many researches show that, often, women who have already been victims of sexual or physical abuse are less able to protect themselves from new abusive situations. In this respect, her unwilling consent could be interpreted also as a part of learned behavior. Her powerlessness to protect herself and her experiences of how other people did not protect her, led to her wish to "pack out of the world" in which she is not safe. The idea could be understood also as a desire for her physical body, upon which so much pain was inflicted, to disappear. At the same time, her wish to disappear physically is a metaphor for overcoming the traumatic memory of the event. Her hope that nobody would know about her suicidal thoughts can be understood as an actual fear that somebody would discover her plan and punish her, or interpret her suicidal fantasies as a symptom of mental disability or mental health problems. She was afraid of more pathologization since people might make her responsible for the abuse. Miriam's fear that somebody should find out about her plans could be understood as a metaphor of shame and guilt for what happened to her. Her hope that nobody would find out that she wanted to hurt herself was also the hope that nobody would know that others had hurt her. This story has also shown that the everyday life of disabled people is a space without privacy, controlled by institutional staff or parents. It is a life of taboos concerning the body and sexuality, which is one of the reasons why disabled peoples are so often sexually abused.

Human Agency: Remembering for Oneself and for the Others

As has been shown, the right to share personal memories in the public sphere is an important segment of active citizenship rights. Telling what was impossible even to think of shows that the person who tells carries a certain degree of human agency and power. This is especially important because many people with disabilities, especially those diagnosed with moderate, severe, and profound intellectual disabilities, or those who have an "invalid status" under the already mentioned Social Care Act from 1983, are declared completely or partially incapacitated by the courts and placed under guardianship as described earlier. They do not enjoy the rights of an adult and are dependent on their guardian (they have no right to vote, marry, be a witness in a criminal court procedure, or work). The grounds for an order that would in turn restrict or remove an individual's civil capacity were that the individual was deemed "incapable of taking care of himself or his interests" due to "mental illness, intellectual disabilities, addiction to alcohol or illegal drugs, or for other reasons influencing his/her physical or psychological state."[9]

Maja is an adult women diagnosed with an intellectual disability who lives with her parents. In the following paragraph she recalls the traumatic memory of a group rape that she experienced:

> I have such a hard life, I had bad luck, I know how it is when you are seventeen, I was young, not even of age. I have this feeling, you know. I'd rather be safe or with some friend so that I feel safe. I know how hard it is to live like that, that you go out and somebody grabs you and takes you somewhere … [tears], I know, I had such life, I'm telling you, if anybody knew how a woman like me suffered, with tied hands and tied legs, that two men took me to a flat, that it was dark in there, and they lubricated my lips when I came there, when we came there. I didn't know what it was, I couldn't speak, you know [silence], and then they told me what it was, [silence] they caught one of them but they didn't catch the other. But then the worse thing was, I tell you [silence], I cannot go alone, I like to have someone to go with me, I can't go by myself, I had a hard life, I tell you, my life sucks. I know how it is when some man grabs you, and drags you to some place where they touched me, they pulled my shirt off [silence], That's why my parents don't let me go out, or I'm happy just to go to the castle, they let me go there and I'm pleased. Only for me, it is so difficult that it will never be the same again and that's why I have this feeling that [silence], you have to trust someone, you must trust, don't you? Only I am more quiet you know, and no one has ever felt what I felt, you know [silence]. Yes, and that's why I'm so quiet, but it is all right to tell, isn't it.

Maja speaks about rape as a sudden, unexpected event, a shock, which became a traumatic experience. She tells about her fear, which is a continuous response to the trauma and marks her attitude towards the world (*"only for me it is so difficult that it will never be the same again"*). The world will never be the same as it was before the traumatic experience. What she went through gives her a special knowledge (*"I know how it is ..."*), which produces her exceptionality (*"no one has ever felt what I felt"*). However, the knowledge also deepens her loneliness: if there is nobody who experienced what she did, then she cannot share her entire story with anybody (she herself states that she is more "silent"). No one can be her "witness from the inside." During the process of testifying Maja encouraged herself with normative messages (*"you have to trust someone, don't you"; "that's why I'm so quiet, but it's alright to tell, isn't it?"*). She looked for a confirmation from the outside that it is right to talk about the event (*"it's alright to tell, isn't it?"*). She spoke about her own silence, which formed her narrative (*"only I'm more quiet"*). Her narration, which touched a "deep memory" (a term used by Holocaust memory researcher L. Langer (1991)), has been from time to time switched into the normative knowledge, that it is "alright, to tell." She needed support that she could testify and touch her "deep memory."

Because of the rape, she is even more dependent on her parents who "do not let her go out." The event of rape affected not only her personal attitude towards the world, but also affected her limited social network. Loneliness is the price that Maja has to pay in order to feel protected from the dangers of the outside world. During the interview, she expanded her individualized memories to the outer world which was the moment at which her memory became a testimony, a political act of her awareness that she had to tell the story not only to recall her personal memory, but also to remember it for other people. Maja has told the story also "for others to know," as a warning, when she said: *"Sex with someone that you don't like disgusts you and you are afraid of it. I just wish it wouldn't happen to anyone. I want the others to know."* Her wounded memory becomes a point of individual action; a means for building a positive identity since her "knowledge" can help others (*"I want the others to know"*). Finally she can do something for others. She took the opportunity to recollect her memories and reciprocate them to someone, a human right that was taken away from her by the institutionalization of her disability: since she was labeled as intellectually impaired, she was seen as "stupid" and unworthy to enter reciprocal relationships. She took the opportunity to share her personal, "special knowledge" to protect others from the same violent event.

Maja did not only remember the event, but she also spoke about the continuing traumatic responses and about the bodily memory that render her unable to differentiate between "sex" and "rape." On a rational level, she defines "sex" and "rape" as two separate things, but on the emotional level, they merge into feelings of "disgust." Her bodily memory is not only present in the case of sexuality but also continuously in the public space, which is for her not a safe space; instead it is a place where she can become a victim again. Public space reactivates the feeling of fear, which she herself experiences as a re-emergence of trauma, which lives as a bodily memory. This became obvious when she talked about her boyfriend, who she sees as a protection against violence:

That's why I like to see him, that he is there if I go somewhere, I have the feeling that I'm more safe because when I go somewhere I have the feeling that someone will grab me all the time [silence]. Because it happened, when I was walking, I have the feeling that those two men grab me, that's why I don't like to walk in the darkness alone.

Maja's memory has continued throughout her life. Instead of having a chance to be protected from abuse, having the right to start a legal court procedure, or to be heard and believed, her traumatic memory became her life itself.

Conclusion

From the perspective of gender, it is not only the right to education, paid employment, independent living, and public access that are important for women with disabilities in order to gain more active citizenship rights, it is also the right to make reproductive decisions (with the help of reproductive technologies and supportive professional network); the right to be safe (from violence and abuse); to be protected (while still living in public care); and for what they have experienced and lived through to be heard. In Slovenia, the liberalization of the market and political access to the EU has yet to bring everyday citizenship rights to the most vulnerable people, particularly those who were, during the socialist regime, seen only as passive welfare recipients. Soon, the power of the old images has to be confronted with updated legislative reflections and actual inclusionary practices of all those spheres that create an important part of everybody's everyday life in today's societies.

Notes

[1]   Employment Service of the Republic of Slovenia, 2005.

[2]   The Act Concerning the Social Care of Mentally and Physically Handicapped Persons, passed in 1983, *Official Gazette of the Republic of Slovenia*, 41/1983.

[3]   One of the newest laws on the employment of people with disabilities is called the "Vocational Rehabilitation and Employment of Disabled People Act" (adopted in May 2004) which surprisingly includes a variety of employment support schemes and creative, individual–based possibilities to enter the employment market. Although, it is said to open the opportunity for all people with disabilities, it entirely excludes people with intellectual disabilities who are still supposed to be treated according to an old communist law from 1983 that was mentioned above.

[4]   The distinction between "passive" and "active" rights, which was the division that created the traditional concept of citizenship, is still very obvious. Passive rights (or natural civil rights) were defined as those "for whose preservation the society is formed," and were given to everyone, while the active rights were denied for women, children, foreigners, and those "who would not at all contribute to the public establishment" (meaning disabled persons and those condemned to a punishment). Since the end of the 18th century the public realm and civil society were the spheres where only "the rational ones" and "men of

best quality" were exclusively defined as political subjects. One politician expressed this very clearly: "The people who own the country ought to govern it," (in Noam Chomsky. 1999. *Profit over People. Neoliberalism and Global Order*. New York: Seven Stories Press). The Marxist concept of civil society included only the male proletariat who were seen as having political subjectivity, as being the privileged subjects of history and thus laying claim to all citizen rights. The post WW2 conceptions of citizenship, which were implemented in communism, was essentialist and overlooked the gender, class, and eth-nicity–biased concepts of citizenship. In 1999, Plugh and Thompson pointed out, it was based on the idea of universal and undifferentiated citizenship, which *presumed that "all people have the same needs."*

5   This is an example of a very gendered naming, as the suffix *-ka- (invalid-ka)* marks the female gender. In spite of the political demands of the disability rights activists to change the oppressive terminology, the new laws adopted in the last few years have not changed the old terminology. Women invalids are, in the current laws, even subsumed under the male grammatical form "invalid."

6   In Slovenia such an example was the first disability-led activist organization YHD-Association for the Theory and Culture of Handicap, founded and led by a woman, Ele-na Pečarič since the mid–1990s. The members started a personal assistance scheme for individual persons with disabilities who wanted to live in their homes and was entirely supported through the help of Western foundations such as Soros (USA) and Matra (The Netherlands). This example shows, as Nanette Funk emphasizes in this volume, that the western foundations that funded eastern NGOs did not only import Western ideology, but also contributed to democratic changes and the support of several left and critical–ori-ented not-for-profit organizations in Eastern Europe.

7   People who work in sheltered workplaces receive only monthly awards and not salaries. In 2005 the awards are between 5 USD and 180 USD, but on average between 20 USD and 80 USD per month (*Rights of People with Disabilities Slovenia* 2005, 102).

8   A large art history exhibition, *Sexual Strategies in the Art of the West*, which was dis-played in the Louvre in 1999, showed a close connection between violence and Western sexual politics. In the words of curator Regis Michel, the director of the Louvre exhi-bition, "the art of the West knows sex only through a single word, violence, better to say, rape" (Nochlin and Solomon-Godeau 2000, 93). Visual art demonstrates that sexual drives and desires most often manifest themselves through the symptoms of castration, fe-tishism, disturbances, and violence. Looking from a gender perspective this is even more true in women's lives and was most wonderfully shown in the exhibition of surrealist art in the Tate Modern in 2001, where "unbound desires" were manifested in the fragmented, violated, and toy-made female bodies. See also Henrietta Moore 1994.

9   Non-litigious Civil Procedure Act of the Republic of Slovenia, art. 44.

References

Agamben, Giorgio. 1998. *Homo Sacer. Sovereign power and bare life*. Stanford: Stanford Univ. Press.

Brown, Hilary. 2001. *Committee on the rehabilitation and integration of people with disabili-ties, safeguarding adults and children with disabilities against abuse.* Council of Europe.

Brown, Hilary, and Ann Craft. 1989. *Thinking the unthinkable. Papers on sexual abuse and people with learning difficulties.* London: FPA Education Unit.

Buda, Bela, and Anna Gondos, eds. 1998. *Costs of rights in psychiatry.* Budapest: Constitutional and Legislative Policy Institute (COLPI).

Chomsky, Noam. 1999. *Profit over people. Neoliberalism and global order.* New York: Seven Stories Press.

Cross, Mary. 1998. *Proud child, safer child. A handbook for parents and careers of disabled children.* London: The Women's Press.

Douglas, Mary. 1994. *Risk and blame. Essays in cultural theory.* London: Routledge.

Dunn, Stephen, and Ethel Dunn. 1989. Everyday life of the disabled in the USSR. In *The disabled in the Soviet Union. Past and present, theory and practice,* edited by William O. McCagg, and Lewis H. Siegelbaum. Pittsburgh: University of Pittsburgh Press.

Fawcett, Barbara. 2000. *Feminist perspectives on disability.* Harlow: Prentice Hall.

Foucault, Michel. 1981. *Power/Knowledge: Selected interviews & other writings 1972–1977,* edited by Colin Gordon. New York: Pantheon Books.

Foucault, Michel. 1990. *History of sexuality, vol. 1.* London: Penguin Books, [orig. 1976].

Goffman, Erving. 1957. Characteristics of total institutions. In Symposium on preventative and social psychiatry, Sponsored by the Walter Reed Army Institute of Research, the Walter Reed Army Medical Centre, and the National Research Council. Washington: Government Printing Office.

Haney, Lynne. 2002. *Inventing the needy. Gender and the politics of welfare in Hungary.* Berkeley, Los Angeles, London: University of California Press.

Iarskaia-Smirnova, Elena. 1999. "What the future will bring I do not know": Mothering children with disabilities in Russia and the politics of exclusion. *Frontiers. A Journal of Women Studies* 20 (2):68–86.

Iarskaia-Smirnova, Elena. 2005. Once upon a time there was a girl who liked to dance … Life experiences of Russian women with motoric disabilities. *Journal of Social Work. Special Edition: "What a nice woman but an invalid",* edited by Darja Zaviršek. 44 (1–2):29–38.

Kafka, Franz. 2003. *Die Erzählungen.* Frankfurt a. Main: Fischer.

Langer, Lawrence L. 1991. *Holocaust testimonies: The ruins of memory.* New Haven: Yale University Press.

Laub, Dori. 1992. An event without a witness: Truth, testimony, and survival. In *Testimony,* edited by S. Felman and D. Laub. New York: Routledge.

Linton, Simi. 1998. *Claiming disability, knowledge, and identity.* New York: New York University Press.

McCagg, William O., and Lewis H. Siegelbaum, eds. 1989. *The disabled in the Soviet Union. Past and present theory and practice.* Pittsburgh: University of Pittsburgh Press.

McCarthy, Michelle. 2000. Consent, abuse and choices: Women with intellectual disabilities and sexuality. In *Women with intellectual disabilities. Finding a place in the world,* edited by R. Traustadóttir and K. Johnson. London, Philadelphia: Jessica Kingsley Publishers.

Morris, Jenny. 1991. *Pride against prejudice. Transforming attitudes to disability.* Philadelphia: New Society Publication.

Morris, Jenny. 1992. *Disabled lives: Many voices, one message.* London: BBC Education.

Moore, Henrietta. 1994. The problem of explaining violence in the social sciences. In *Sex and violence,* edited by P. Harvey and P. Gow. London: Routledge.

Nochlin, Linda, and Abigail Solomon-Godeau. 2000. Sins of the fathers. *Art in America* December: 92–102.

Pečarič, Elena. 2001. Hendikepirano telo in nadzorovanje spola. [The disabled body and the gender control]. *Delta. Journal for Women Studies and Feminist Theory* 7 (1-2):89–105.

Pugh, Richard. 1997. Considering social difference. In *Protecting children: Challenges and change*, edited by J. Bates, R. Pugh, and N. Thompson. Aldershot: Arena.

Pugh, Richard, and Neil Thompson. 1999. Social work, citizenship, and constitutional change in the UK. *International Perspectives in Social Work and the State (special edition)*. Brighton: Pavilion.

Rights of people with intellectual disabilities. Access to education and employment, Slovenia. 2005. Open Society Institute/EU Monitoring and Advocacy Program. Budapest and New York: Open Society Institute.

Rights of people with intellectual disabilities. Access to education and employment, Bulgaria. 2005. Open Society Institute/EU Monitoring and Advocacy Program. Budapest and New York: Open Society Institute.

Rommelspacher, Birgit. 1995. *Dominanzkultur. Texte zur fremdheit und macht.* [The Dominant culture. Texts on strangeness and power]. Berlin: Orlanda.

Sinason, Valeri. 1992. *Mental handicap and the human condition. New approaches from the Tavistock.* London: Free Association Books.

Škerlj, Božidar. 1933. Social-anthropological study upon the questions of the undervalued child. [Orig.: Socialno-antropološka študija k vprašanju manjvrednega otroka]. *Pedagogical textbook of the Slovene School Association* [orig.: Pedagoski zbornik Slovenske solske matice]. Slovenia: Slovene School Association.

Sobsey, Dick. 1994. *Violence and abuse in the lives of people with disabilities, the end of silent acceptance?* Baltimore: Paul H. Brookes.

Urh, Špela. 2005. Položaj oseb z oznako duševne prizadetosti s posebnim poudarkom na izključenosti intelektualno oviranih žensk. [The status of people with the label mental retardation with a special emphasis on women with intellectual disabilities]. *Socialno delo* [Journal of Social Work] 44 (1-2): 93-100.

Wendell, Susan. 1996. *Rejected body. Feminist philosophical reflections on disability.* London: Routledge.

Zaviršek, Darja. 1998. Disability as gendered taboo. In *Women participating in global change*, edited by E. Fernandez, K. Heycox, L. Hughes, and M. Wilkinson. Australia: University of New South Wales.

Zaviršek, Darja. 2000. *Hendikep kot kulturna travma.* [*Disability as a cultural trauma*]. Ljubljana: cf*.

Zaviršek, Darja. 2004. Surviving ethnicity and disability. Minority children in public care. *The Journal of Social Policy Studies.* Russian Sociological Society. Center for Social Policy and Gender Studies 2 (2): 189–202.

Zaviršek, Darja. 2005. "You will teach them some, socialism will do the rest!" History of social work education in Slovenia during the period 1940-1960. In *Need and care. Glimpses into the beginnings of Eastern Europe's professional welfare,* edited by K. Schilde and D. Schulte. Opladen & Bloomfield Hills: Barbara Budrich Publisher.

Chapter 10

The Making of Political Responsibility: Hannah Arendt and/in the Case of Serbia*

Daša Duhaček

The small Bosnian town of Srebrenica has become a metaphor for the atrocities committed during the wars in the Balkans that took place from 1991–1999. However, ten years after the events in Srebrenica for which the Hague Tribunal has ruled (genocide) in Serbia, the public discourse is still far away from unequivocally condemning war crimes committed by the Milošević regime as ones committed in the name of Serbia. The argument of this text is that ultimately the citizens of Serbia are politically responsible for these events. In June 2005, immediately after being presented at the Hague Tribunal, a short documentary was shown, first on the B92 TV station, a Serbian channel, and then, in part, on most of the other TV stations; it depicted the Serbian military forces shooting six young Moslems. Although the documentary did shake up the public in Serbia, and the government efficiently apprehended the perpetrators, subsequent surveys concluded that the public was still in a systemic denial and were not able to consider the possibility that they were responsible for any of the events of the Milošević regime (SMMRI 2005).[1] According to the surveys, 74 percent of Serbian citizens believe that the Serbs committed the least number of war crimes (with the exception of Slovenians) and 81 percent believe that Serbs were the greatest victims of these wars! Although the majority of the population does think that it is important to face the truth about these events, almost half (47 percent) think that this truth is important because it will prove that the Serbs were not responsible for the war crimes ascribed to them.

The surveys in question were conducted by a reputable agency, the Strategic Marketing and Media Research Institute [SMMRI], which has for some time been analyzing public opinion in Serbia as to its sensitivity concerning the issues in dealing with its recent past. One of these was conducted in April 2001, with the aim of answering how people in Serbia perceive the events of the Milošević era; more specifically it focused on their information and knowledge about the events as well

---

* This text is dedicated to the memory of Žarana Papić.

as the degree of truth to these events. The survey was especially designed to analyze the respondents' perceptions of responsibility for the crimes and tragedies that took place during the Milošević regime.[2] Some of the statistical data presented thereby deserves to be highlighted: for example, answers to the questions that juxtaposed factors as to their responsibility were as follows: Slovenians are more to blame than the Serbs (45.3 vs. 10.8); or, the international community bears more responsibility than all the peoples of former Yugoslavia (44.8 vs. 20.5); or, the US is more to blame than Europe (54.5 vs. 7). Therefore, in Serbia, the responses to this series of questions which asked "Who bears more responsibility and/or guilt for the disasters that happened?" were in the survey correctly summarized as follows: *greater responsibility lies more with the others than with ourselves* (Logar and Bogosavljević 2001). What is noteworthy is that each answer in reference to a particular choice as a rule pointed to a factor *further* from the persons giving the answer as the one(s) who should be held responsible. It is never about a "we," or any collective that is inclusive of the one "I" belong(s) to.[3]

However, responses to the statement: "Milošević is more to blame than the people who elected him" (42 vs. 17.6) merit special consideration within the framework of this text. It is the articulation of this response that is especially important since it leads to the conclusion that the citizens of Serbia perceive that that they have little or no responsibility for their own political choices.

This text will lay out the problem of civic responsibility in the specific context of the tragic events that occurred during the last decade in Serbia and, as a point of departure, this text will first claim that Hannah Arendt's political theory can serve well in the analysis of the case of Serbia. Arendt's political theory was built primarily as a reflection on the history of Nazism and is based on the experiences of those events. I argue that, differences notwithstanding, for the citizens of Serbia there is a lesson to be learnt from the history of Germany, during the period of 1933–1945. The objective of this work is to answer how Arendt's theory can be used for the analysis of what has happened in the Balkans.

At this point in time, I believe that the focus should be directed toward a process of *self–reflection within Serbia*. If Serbia is to grow as a civil society, then all those who aspire to constitute its citizenship have to face the truth about the deeds committed *in their name* and they should recognize that this implied, at the very least, their tacit consent (assuming, of course, that the active participants in these deeds will be dealt with in criminal procedures with the utmost efficiency). Moreover, it is my contention that what construes complicity follows directly from the status of citizenship. Namely, the political maturity of citizenship can only be attained and consequently recognized by way of civic responsibility and accountability.

An Arendtian theoretical format will also benefit from an analysis that does not lose sight of a gendered political perspective; given the fact that Hannah Arendt is by no means a feminist theorist, this may be perceived as a problem; however, aside from the obvious – that is that a non-gendered (pre)text may be ground for a gendered analysis – Hannah Arendt's political theory does share some concerns with contemporary feminist theory.

Finally, the text will return to the case of Serbia. Taking into account that Serbia has been, and still is, a political space of extremes covering a full spectrum in between, the text will primarily mark the position of women within its political space. The text will specifically focus on those women who are publicly present, organized, and occupy the end of the spectrum of political choices that have been issuing a public call for responsibility, such as the group that is known as Women in Black.[4]

Theoretical Framework: Arendt on Political Responsibility

Regardless of the overwhelming reality, theory has yet to adequately address responsibility as a *political* category. Responsibility has so far either been discussed as an ethical category; or, if appearing within political theory has only laid dormant and been used to underlie the political analysis of evil and thereby, for the most part, it has bypassed the central issue of responsibility; and, regarding the present state of our world, neither approach will suffice.

Although Hannah Arendt has not articulated a theory of political responsibility, or even developed a corresponding category (as she did with the categories of action, the political, totalitarianism, and so on) she has been able to establish parameters for such a theory. It is the perceptive claim of Arendt's interpreters that the pivotal point in her analysis, and what singles her out from entire Western political thought, is her identification of some manifestations of evil as *political* (Kateb 1992; Villa 1999). Moreover, facing the totalitarianism of the 20th century, she formulates the parameters by which we can define *"evil as a policy"* (Villa 1999, 23). Therefore, although Arendt does not have a theory of responsibility she does have a highly developed political analysis of evil within which – in keeping with her own methodological requirements – "crystallizing" elements for the category of political responsibility can be distinguished.

Full appreciation of Arendt's contribution to the issue calls for the introduction of Karl Jaspers' work, *Schuldfrage,* as well as the documented exchanges between Jaspers and Arendt on this subject (Jaspers 1947; Kohler and Sener 1992). Communication between Jaspers and Arendt after World War II [WWII] was an extension of a prewar teacher student relationship, which resulted in their shared affiliation for philosophy, a language, and a culture; perhaps that was the reason why their exchanges on their points of disagreements were not only possible, but also open and nuanced. Consequently, for us, these exchanges are theoretically provocative and all the more valuable.[5]

Karl Jaspers' *Schuldfrage* was a pioneering work on the subject of guilt and responsibility; here the discussion of *political* guilt, as one of the key issues, sets a framework comparable to Serbia after the wars from 1991–1999.[6]

Arendt's biographer, Elizabeth Young–Bruehl, testifies to the disagreements that Hannah Arendt and her husband, Heinrich Blücher, both expressed in reference to

Jaspers' *Schuldfrage* (Young-Bruehl 1982, 215–216). In correspondences between Blücher and Arendt these disagreements are most sharply stated by Blücher, both in respect to the level of disagreement but also in terms of the clarity of Blücher's position; in that "Germany finally had the opportunity to make clear the *fronts of the real civil war of our times, republicans against the Cossacks, in other words the battle of the Citoyen against the Barbarian ...*" (Kohler 2000, 84–5).[7] Blücher's comments speak to many of the conflicts of our contemporary world, and could very well refer to the diagnosis of the recent ones in the Balkans.

It appears that Blücher has reached the core of the matter: responsibility needs to be materialized as an issue of citizenship, whereas Jaspers is making a continuous effort to define "what we are and should be – what is *really* German?" thereby keeping open a Pandora's box of nationalism (Jaspers 1947, 85–6).[8]

The parameters for establishing the format for responsibility are here graphically formulated by Blücher, as they are present throughout Arendt's theory: significantly, they are designated as the urgency to recognize the option of "Citoyen."

Hannah Arendt addressed the issue of responsibility in a series of texts after WWII, leading to her text, *The Origins of Totalitarianism*, which was her first book in the "new world" and grew "out of shock and horror and out of an even deeper grief" (Arendt 1972a, 313).[9] In order to attempt to answer her own burning question of how such horrors were possible, Arendt used her own lens and reconfigured the world that she was trying to understand; and through this lens she saw the bourgeoisie, the mob, the masses, the leaders, and the elites.

The people who played a part in building the Nazi empire and committed the crimes against humanity that it was built on, were, "because of the sheer numbers," what Arendt called the masses. These masses constituted the first support system for Nazism. Arendt perceptively claimed that (even) in a democracy it was an illusion that the majority took an active part in the government, or exercised its presence in the public life; however, it turned out "that a *citizen's duties and responsibilities* could only be felt to be a needless drain on his limited time and energy" (Arendt 1972, 313).[10] It was this state of affairs that rendered the hitherto un–political, inactive majority, which was under extreme economic pressure, and had all social and psychological safety nets withdrawn, easy prey to totalitarian ideology. Citizens, in great numbers, responded unconditionally to the claims on their individual political choices and never pledged "total unrestricted loyalty," never demanded concrete political programs, or any aspect of accountability on the part of their leaders. In fact, they tacitly complied and succumbed to the total domination on the part of the apparatus that built its whole system of control not so much on violence as the "total domination from within." This is the key analysis that should be applied to issues of responsibility, but not as a series of extenuating circumstances; quite the contrary: because, in effect, the majority gave their tacit, if not express *consent to the policy of evil*.

Though they will prove to be comparable only consequently, the cases of Germany, from 1933–1945, and Serbia from 1991–1999 do diverge in their initial set up. Namely, in Serbia, before the 1990s, democracy did not exist even as "an illusion" and therefore there is no framework upon which to state that the "majority took an active part in the government." However, that is precisely the point, because the masses also constituted the support system of the Milošević regime and, consequently, in every other respect Arendt's analysis is applicable to Serbia.

The fact that the elites and the leaders, in comparison to the majority of the population, are those who are responsible *and guilty* is obviously not to be questioned; and, for the most part, it is an issue of criminal proceedings. My point, relevant to the case of Serbia, is that *politically* it is the majority that should be held responsible or, better said, politicized in regards to their civic responsibility. Moreover, their responsibility lies in holding the elites and the leaders answerable – held in an obligation to answer to and respond to – the population they are assumed to represent. This has been from inception and still is precisely the direction of all those that ask for responsibility in Serbia, such as the group, Women in Black.

However, it appears that Hannah Arendt's initial construct, in a somewhat desperate attempt to understand, revolved around the concepts of absolute or radical evil. The point here, in relation to the issue of responsibility, is that Arendt, overwhelmed by the scope of horror, is turning to the concept of evil, at the expense of assessing responsibility. The concept of evil in itself does retain the question of responsibility, but only as an underlying issue that then needs to be recovered. The problem is that the concept of evil is not conducive to a secular, and consequently a political understanding of responsibility. Increasingly, becoming aware of this problem Arendt later asks: "How can we approach the problem of evil in *an entirely secular* setting?" (Kohn 1997, 155).[11] With this rephrasing, Arendt is once more moving along a clearly politically defined trajectory.

The issue of evil reappeared forcefully in Arendt's texts more than a decade later; and only then could the issue of responsibility actually be fully placed on the agenda.

Hannah Arendt's text (on the trial of) *Eichmann in Jerusalem* generated a heated polemic. One of the reasons for this was that her phrase, "the banality of evil", overtook the space that hitherto in her work had belonged to the concept of radical evil. In her correspondence with Karl Jaspers concerning the evil of totalitarian regime(s), Jaspers cautioned her not to ascribe to a war criminal any attribute of greatness, be that in evil, or in any other respect when Arendt's perspective threatened to attribute magnitude to the appearance of evil because, as he stated, "[b]acteria can cause epidemics that wipe out nations, but they remain merely bacteria" (Kohler 2000, 62).

Arendt's shift from radical evil to the banality of evil had serious political consequences: evil was of our own doing and was to be looked for in the actions of an(y) individual. She was most clearly *faced* with the issue of personal responsibility at the trial of Adolf Eichmann (Levinas 1997). While reporting directly from where the trial took place she confronted an embodiment of evil in, what she later came to judge as, all its banality. The controversy raised speaks to the complexity of the issue of responsibility within which Arendt clarified a pivotal point: " ... in a courtroom there is no system on trial, no history or historical trend, no 'ism', anti–semitism for instance, but a person ... an individual, with a name, date and place of birth, identifiable and therefore not expendable ..." (Arendt 1964, 1). The designation of a "courtroom" translated as a spatial metaphor, and understood as a metaphorical placement of any process of judgment, underscores that it is always already about the individual.

The individual, the personal, is to be used as a point of departure and from it all other distinctions follow. Whenever responsibility is under scrutiny, it is primarily about the individual; furthermore, responsibility of a plurality of individuals would always already necessitate that it be grounded in the individual. Therefore, following any events which constitute manifestations of the policy of evil, regardless of whether we attempt to assess responsibility or guilt, regardless if the concern is moral, metaphysical, political, or just criminal it is always already about the individual and only subsequently can it concern a collective.

Two forms of basically one argument, both attempting to shake off personal responsibility came alive during the Eichmann trial: one, the "cog theory" and the other, a claim that participation in the policy of evil was just a consequence of following and obeying orders.[12] "We heard the protestations of the defense that Eichmann was after all only a 'tiny cog' in the machinery of the Final Solution" (Arendt 1965, 289). Careful to maintain her position of assigning individual responsibility – which is the kernel of assessing the issue of responsibility – Hannah Arendt, not without irony, said: "It is the grandeur of the Court proceedings that even a cog can become a person again" (Arendt 1987, 44). Although where Serbia is concerned, this line of argument could not have been – nor was it – taken up during the Milošević trial at The Hague Tribunal, it could be relevant in other cases tried there.

Despite the distinction between the elites as the centers of political power ('leaders' in Arendt's terminology) and those that are not members of any elite, her counter– argument analyzes obedience and translates it into what this particular choice of active participation in effect was: *support*. "What is wrong here is the word 'obedience'. A child obeys; if an adult 'obeys' he actually supports ... it would make much more sense to look upon the functioning of the 'cogs' and wheels in terms of overall support for a common enterprise ..." (Arendt 1964, 6). It is in this sense that the Belgrade Women in Black have unambiguously and publicly declared their disloyalty to the governing structure of their state (Zajović 1994). No leader, no hierarchical structure can stand without the support of a plurality of individuals, and each one of the individuals makes a personal choice to extend or withdraw that support. It was therefore and will remain an individual's choice for which s/he should – as a rule – be held responsible.

Having established that (it is initially about the individual choice), let us now move forward by emphasizing the *plurality* of individuals, an emphasis that leads to the issue of collective responsibility. Hannah Arendt unambiguously stated that such a responsibility exists. She introduced it by way of another important conceptual distinction, namely the one between guilt and responsibility.[13]

My agreement [with Mr. Feinberg's paper] concerns his firm distinction between guilt and responsibility. 'Collective responsibility,' he says, 'is a special case of vicarious responsibility; and there can be no thing such as vicarious guilt.' In other words, there is such a thing as *responsibility for things one has not done*; one can be held liable for them. But there is no such thing as being or feeling guilty for things that happened without one actively participating in them (Arendt 1987, 43).[14]

The criterion for this distinction was the im/possibility of vicariousness: whereas in responsibility lies the possibility of vicariousness, guilt is direct and could never be transferable or distributive. Namely, "responsibility exists for things one has not done ..." (Arendt 1987, 43). Whereas with guilt, the case is precisely the opposite, it is meaningless in the absence of a particular act one is being accused of. Arendt makes the claim – that one can be held *responsible without acting in person* – which is significant for the issue of collective responsibility. Discussing collective responsibility requires assessing a complex issue – what constitutes a collective that can be held responsible, that is liable? When and in which way can I talk as a "we"? It is my argument that politically, the relevant collective is citizenship.

Although Arendt had, on many occasions, expressed decisive impatience with what she referred to as "misplaced feelings of guilt", from everything stated it follows that this Arendtian dictum "where all are guilty, nobody is" does *not* mean that the issue of collective responsibility is dismissed from her analysis.[15] On the contrary, in Arendt's texts, the collective, analyzed as a political concept, is also under scrutiny specifically for its *political* responsibility; and it is for the most part in her text considered in reference to a concrete collective; which in the case of Arendt's analysis are German citizens. "It is, rather, the product of that vast machine of administrative mass murder in whose service not only thousands of persons, not even scores of thousands of selected murderers, but *a whole people could be and was employed*" (Arendt 1994, 126).[16] The point made here concerns a multitude that went about their business while employed in mass extinction.

Arendt also emphasizes the threat of recurring evil as a policy; and that is, among others. Sadly, after the assassination of Zoran Đinđić, the first Prime Minister after the fall of Milošević, this scenario is now in its many modifications applicable in Serbia.

Unfolding the content of political responsibility as a response to a policy of evil, Hannah Arendt articulates an ethical demand issued to each individual: a request of non–participation (Arendt 1964, 205).[17] The criterion of Arendt's briefly presented ethical demand of non–participation in dictatorships and totalitarian systems is based on making a conscious decision of non–participation in public life – as opposed to an unreflective position of "participation, which meant complicity with crimes" (Arendt 1987, 48).[18]

In itself, the decision for non–participation is an individual, moral decision that appears to have no substantial political consequence. The step of making a decision not to participate – to which Hannah Arendt prescribes critical value – cannot, in itself, amount to "preventing wrong," which is actually her true ethical–political expectation, nor can it constitute resistance. However, if following Arendt we take into account the plurality of human beings, transformed into a multitude who are making a similar, or even the same decision, especially as a concerted effort, then it may well constitute a form of resistance, rare as it may be. This is what has been known to happen and it is in fact precisely what did happen in Serbia. Moreover, in Serbia, the events that constitute such a form of resistance took place twice, the first time – unsuccessfully, in terms of the outcome – in the mass protests of 1996–1997; and for the second time in the Fall of 2000 which culminated in the undisputable downfall of the Milošević regime on 5 October 2000.

Therefore, there are corresponding realities of introducing the critical step from the decision of non–participation made by many to the coordination of those decisions; this step undoubtedly constitutes political action. The substance of this action amidst the policy of evil is non–activity only in its initial stage. Whereas, fundamentally it is not only a public announcement – made oftentimes by demonstrating it – but also a public outcry that denies any consent to the policy of evil and ultimately takes away the legitimacy of a government or of a leader; in the end, they lose the right to represent its citizenship in every way. Importantly, non–participation is always already primarily an individual act.

However, it is significant to note that responsibility appears twice, and is hence a two–fold problem: it is a presence in reference to a current event, an event of the present, but it also comes alive *post factum*, after the event; raising this issue is still a revived source of heated debates in Serbia, especially recently. The matter becomes even more complex since responsibility is a question asked not only with a view to the political community internally, but is even more relevant while looking at the policy of evil when inflicted upon *other* political communities. The process of clarifying these issues and raising this self–awareness is always painful, as post WWII Germany testifies, and as is evident in Serbia today.

Along those lines, I would like to propose a parameter concerning the issue of responsibility. Since this is a *post factum* claim there is a pivotal concern here: when pronouncing *now* who is responsible for *the past*, claims should be grounded in answer to the following question: what collective do we want to build in this process, or better said, how can we contribute to building the *future, by assessing the past?* By stating who should be held responsible and by proclaiming the liability of the people who, although confused between severe distortions about ethnic loyalties and religious commitments, vague political ideas, and clearly substantial social needs, need to become citizens. Only by proclaiming them responsible can we contribute to building a citizenship that is based on civic responsibility for their political space. Perhaps in that way the past can be carried into the future, but as a burden that is consciously carried.

Resistance to the Policy of Evil in Serbia

In a theoretical framework, it should also be noted that feminist theory unfolds as one of the rare processes of reflection that oftentimes includes what it has even named as *mea culpa* statement(s) (Barrett and McIntosh 1985, 24). Moreover, theoretical accounts that have appeared within feminist theory followed from processes of self–reflection that, with utmost scrutiny, examined "how 'I' becomes a 'we'" and looked into all the aspects of belonging to a "we" while constantly raising the issue of accountability (Rich 1986).

It happens that, in Serbia, this task is persistently pursued by some women.

The following anecdotal material presents two instances of women's choices in reference to the issue of responsibility in Serbia that simultaneously attest to the fact that Serbia is a space of extremes and that political choices have full, albeit uneven, representation from any part of the political spectrum. The first scene illustrates the position of most women and supports the findings of the Strategic Marketing agency, whereas the second opens up other political options for the future. Both, however, testify to the role of women within the context of Serbia.

Scene One: Portrait on the Wall

It is the tradition of the Serbian rural and even a would–be urban population to decorate the furniture with embroidery. In some parts of the country, there is a tradition of weaving portraits as small tapestries; they follow blueprints that circulate among women. It is a well–known fact that these take considerable time to be completed and thus present a task not to be taken up lightly. The portraits on the wall were at one time, of a king; then in the decades after WWII one could find portraits of President Tito thus weaved and embroidered. After his death, in the late 1980s, in many houses women had taken to weaving portraits of Slobodan Milošević. These were to hang next to the patron saint of each home.

Beneath those portraits, during the 1990s, on the eve, or in the wake of any of the numerous elections, one could oftentimes find the "man of the house", the only one who would be called upon in any "political" discussion. Indubitably thoroughly dissatisfied by the state of affairs in his country – where he was cheated out of his crop which almost had no market value, and where his son and heir was on some battleground – he would be asking the question, if not Milošević, *who* then?

The concept of a country without a strong personified leadership, without a portrait on the wall was, and, in many homes still is, beyond comprehension. In that context most women still serve, recycle, and even decorate the patriarchy that rules.

Scene Two: Women in Black

Once a week, every week since October 1991, and for many (war) years to come a group of women dressed in black stood in silence in the center of Belgrade. They displayed anti militarist, pacifist, and anti nationalist political messages while wearing black as a sign of mourning, unambiguously stating that they mourned all the war victims; hence the name of the group, Žene u Crnom, ŽuC [Women in Black].[19] Their silent protest spoke loudly to the Serbian regime about its responsibility for the wars that were raging throughout the Balkans in the 1990s, but even more so to the people, raising people's awareness of the responsibility that we all had. They were perceived as traitors to the national cause.

Only well after the signing of the Dayton Peace Agreement in 1995 did these protests space out but they also spread out; namely, to this day Women in Black are not only on the streets of Belgrade but are also on the streets of other Serbian cities, and presently form a wide network of women's political activism.

This activism, based on anti–militarism and non–violence, supports women by raising their self–awareness, and strengthens them to make their own political choices. The politics of Women in Black goes far beyond the tolerance of ethnic and other differences – it aims for a solidarity with the different. Their activism is not only confined to the public bodily expression of their political statements, but also takes the form of organizing workshops for groups throughout Serbia, participation in public debates, public announcements, producing written work, as well as carefully documenting, publishing, and publicizing their work. Much of this documentation testifies to the fact that Women in Black are a case in point to the process of raising the issue of responsibility in Serbia. In one of the texts that are characteristic of their statements, entitled, "We resist," Staša Zajović, one of the founders of Women in Black, writes:

> We *Women in Black Against the War* decided to transfer our anger and helplessness into action, therefore:
> –Our women's resistance against the war is visible,
> –Our resistance is not a part of our 'natural' role of women, but our conscious political choice,
> –Our visible permanent, non–violent protest is a message to the regime: 'We are not a Serbian collectivity, *don't speak in our name*, we speak for ourselves …' (Zajović 1998, 180)

Although their primary activity was public protest against the wars, over the years they also gave shelter to, and advocated for, all those who refused to fight in any of those wars. They have campaigned for a civil service in the army and the recognition of conscientious objection. They have also been present in all the refugee camps, bringing food, clothing, and support in every possible way.

All of these activities have been met with numerous difficulties from both within and without, such as: public accusations and attacks, the questioning of one's own identities, pain, fear, and sometimes even despair. All of this caught up with them more often when they met with friends and activists from places that were attacked by troops coming from Serbia; rather than when they were publicly abused while standing in the center of Belgrade carrying slogans for peace and solidarity with Croatian, Bosnian, and Albanian women; or, when threatened by extremists. On the other hand, it was rewarding to see people publicly express solidarity, though sometimes too timidly and all too often in small numbers.

During the last decade, Women in Black have become an international movement within which women primarily protest their own respective government's policies. As a result, they are building a model of citizenship that is based on responsibility *for the political unit* they belong to.

Women in Black have consistently proclaimed disloyalty to the state; but by the very act of asking for the accountability of their government, they have demonstrated their citizenship. By raising awareness as to the suffering of other political communities and all victims of war, they have pointed to the fact that it was caused by their own government and by assuming political responsibility, they could not but speak *as citizens* of their own state. Although, their slogans and texts did speak – and still do – *to* the governing structures, *and to* citizens of Serbia, significantly they also spoke *as* citizens of Serbia.

Without generalizing, or even at this stage attempting to interpret, let me simply state a fact: today in Serbia there are many *women,* who as individuals and/or activists within a group, raise and confront the public with issues of responsibility, for what was done *in our name*; they do this as citizens of the state of Serbia. Women in Black being such a group constituted themselves from women's activist groups; consequently, they have a strong self–awareness of themselves as women; and, for the most part, they are feminists.[20]

Among other women in Serbia there are also some peace–activists who probably do not think of themselves as feminists; moreover, they have never publicly represented themselves *as women*. However, the self–perception of being *a woman* was arrived at as a result of a secondary, albeit continuous, process of denigration and sometimes even public humiliation that was grounded in, among other things, the fact that they were women.[21] And to paraphrase Hannah Arendt (who said that when attacked as a Jew she will defend herself as a Jew), when attacked as women, they did perceive of themselves as women; one of them underlines: " … it is not unimportant that a few *women* in Serbia are endlessly exposed to insults, threats and degradation precisely because they are trying to open up the process of reconciliation by way of establishing the truth and taking on responsibility" (Kandić, 2002, 62). This passage refers to Nataša Kandić – the author of these words – and the Director and founder of the Humanitarian Law Fund; but also to Staša Zajović, feminist peace activist, co–founder of the Women in Black; Sonja Biserko, the Director of the Helsinki Committee in Belgrade; Biljana Kovačević–Vučo, founder and Director of Yugoslav Lawyers Committee for Human Rights [YUCOM]; and Borka Pavićević, who has created and sustained an alternative space in the "Center for Cultural Decontamination."[22] The list of women active on the public scene could of course be extended, while still not generalizing or falling into the trap of essentializing (Duhaček 2002). Thus, another example: Drinka Gojković, a translator, and a writer, who has started a Center for the Documentation of the Wars of 1991–1999. In what is recognized as an alternative space of Rex Cinema in Belgrade, Drinka Gojković has tirelessly organized panel discussions between adversarial positions, organized exhibitions that stirred emotions, and has introduced controversial guest speakers and their texts – all on the issues of truth and responsibility during the wars that have been waged from 1991 until 1999 in this region. She has often been faced with violent words, threats, and on every occasion she has been faced with the pain of the realization of the denial on the part of her fellow citizens, of what happened during those years. Yet, every time, there may have been a step forward. She herself demonstrates that every step of the way there is no other way, which is why this process "requires a special kind and a special level of social and personal energy ..." (Gojković 2000, 33).

These women have all, each within some non-governmental organization, relentlessly pursued every instance of Serbian nationalist policy or propaganda.[23] For this they have often been attacked as "traitors to the national cause" and not only by and during the Milošević regime, but also after Milošević as well as by some members of the opposition to that regime, which reveals that this opposition still remains to stand the difficult test of raising the issues of responsibility. However, my main point is that the political culture in Serbia has at least two problems relevant to our topic. First, it harbors a suspicion as to the presence of women on the public scene; and, second, it publicly displays a deep conviction that, as a political collective, it can do no wrong. If these two problems collapse into one frontal attack, designations are easily used interchangeably; so, peace activists are attacked as women ("ugly", "frustrated", and the like). Again, to fall back on Arendt – as she was named "a self–hating Jew" – these women are branded as "having problems with their gender and/or ethnic identities" (Kandić, 2002).

Conclusion

There are two critical elements for constructing a theory of political responsibility. The first one is that only by, with, and through the secularization of political space can the issues of responsibility be raised with theoretical seriousness and practical political effectiveness, thereby distancing them from sin and guilt; and, that only by relying on a secular grounded judgment can *we* be the ones who judge at all.[24] This point and Arendt's positioning within the analysis of evil is that "she showed herself ready to dispense with the Devil, ready to face the problem of evil in entirely secular terms," which is precisely why she is relevant for the issues of political responsibility (Villa 1999, 58).

Even more importantly, for our immediate concern, is the second element, citizenship, since it provides the only format for political responsibility. Responsibility is initially individual, because the individual is always already the one who judges – a collective can only "judge" metaphorically, or construct procedures for a series of individual judgments that can be perceived as collective ones. Namely, as hard as it most certainly is, every individual is answerable for herself, regardless of the collective she or he belongs to.

Having noted the initiating power of individual responsibility, let me emphasize that the policy of evil in our times cannot come about without a support of a multitude of individuals, a *collective* support (of the masses); ultimately, it is oftentimes the case of collective responsibility that needs to be assessed. One of the important questions is: what is the collective? In order to be *politically* answerable we need to be fully aware of the complex ways through which we reach our decisions. Therefore, we need to be aware of when, and by which of the many mechanisms it is that, politically, an "I" becomes a "we." In the contemporary world, for lack of a format more easily identifiable, those that form a collective that is structurally identifiable and politically relevant, and therefore the only one that can and should be held collectively responsible, are those that apply to the citizenship of a designated political unit, a state.

The question that is almost forced upon us, especially in the case of Serbia is: why do we not place the burden of responsibility on a collective that is most often targeted as the apparent projected "beneficiary" of some of the most atrocious policies of evil, namely an ethnicity or a nation?[25] There are at least two reasons, one from the past, and the other pointing to the future: first, ethnicities and nations do function as *imagined* communities and therefore lack the formal format necessary for assigning and distributing *political* responsibility (Anderson 1991). However, much more importantly, placing the burden of responsibility even *post factum* can work towards the future, since it can be a significant – even if it is a painful – part of building the status and the institution of citizenship; it can greatly contribute to the maturation required – in fact it can install it.

Consequently, there is an absolute urgency to place a greater burden than has ever before been placed on the shoulders of citizenry for what has been done *in their name*; because unless that burden sobers up the mankind, *the policy of evil will be implemented again and again*. The only way to minimize this probability is to alert the citizens not to serve as a support system for a totalitarian policy of evil, not to allow them to be molded into an obedient mass.[26] The contribution of women was summarized by Vesna Krmpotić, a poet; she concluded in a text "dedicated to Natašas, Sonjas, and all Biljanas" that: " ... all of the this I had to say, so that I could in the end, succinctly state: a society that has Natašas and Sonjas, that society has honor and hope" (Krmpotić 2002).

Undoubtedly, many questions remain. Given the fact that citizenship is a varied collective especially in its role in the creation of a policy, is there a way to differentiate between the ones who resisted the policy of evil, the ones who were indifferent, and finally between the ones who supported the system? The question can be taken to its painfully extreme formulation when the citizenship of a polity includes the truly innocent ones, such as the children who constitute the future generations and who will necessarily share the consequences of any policy.

Regretfully this cannot be avoided, but it can be somewhat reduced and perhaps softened but only by accelerating the process by which the generation of the present takes on its political burden of responsibility and does not leave this burden to be a heavy legacy to the future generations. This holds a promise of starting anew; for Arendt, this promise of starting anew was what she did hold on to – it was a promise that in the dark times when the whole world falls apart, not all is lost and the only way out depends solely on us.

Notes

1   This survey was conducted by the Strategic Marketing and Media Research Institute [SMMRI] from April–June, 2005 for the Belgrade Center for Human Rights (see also the web site, <www.bgcentar.org.yu>) and the Serbian Ministry of Human and Minority Rights; it was also presented at the seminar on *Transitional Justice* at the Center for Cultural Decontamination in June 2005.

2   The results of the survey were presented at a conference: "In Search of Truth and Responsibility: Toward a Democratic Future", organized by Radio B92 in May 2001; they were published later in an article (Logar and Bogosavljević 2001). Regretfully, subsequent analyses in Serbia did not produce substantially different results of public opinion regarding the crimes committed during the wars 1991–1999; although there is some recognition of the necessity for cooperation with the Hague Tribunal. See, for example, Zagorka Golubović, Ivana Spasić and Đorđe Pavićević, eds. 2003. *Politika i svakodnevni zivot.* [*Politics and everyday life*]. Beograd; or the more recent results of the Strategic Marketing and Media Research Institute, available from, <www.bgcentar.org.yu>.

3   This naïve, pre–political reasoning: "*they* are to blame ..." should of course be differentiated from comprehensive assessments that attempt to include all the many factors which were complicit, but are inclusive of a "we."

4   *Women in Black* is a feminist pacifist group active in Serbia from 1991 until today.

5   At this point in time, neither of them dwelt particularly on the key concepts they used when explicating or debating the issue; Arendt used both terms, responsibility and guilt, but later almost dropped the term guilt, whereas Jaspers primarily adhered to the term *Schuld* [guilt, debt] and only occasionally used co-responsibility and liability (Jaspers 1947, 28).

6   Karl Jaspers distinguishes between criminal, moral, political, and metaphysical guilt. These distinctions create two rubrics, one of publicly relevant guilt, that being criminal and political guilt, and, the second of privately considered guilt, which can be moral and metaphysical, both of which remain open to further issues. The presupposition of metaphysical guilt may lead to a conceptual confusion: God, as the jurisdictional instance here points to impending inevitable guilt, or perhaps more precisely sin and consequently precludes the issue of responsibility. This renders the whole aspect of metaphysical guilt as non-political. The point here is that any reference to the political necessitates an unequivocally secular framework.

7   Emphasis added.

8   Emphasis added.

9   Emphasis added.

10   Emphasis added.

11   Emphasis added.

12   Politically speaking, in the Eichmann trial and many similar cases a strange and ugly process of reversal took place: when the expected victory turned into absolute defeat, those who hitherto had considered themselves as key political actors started posing as mere "cogs" thereby dissociating themselves from any decision-making process within the policy of evil. This was attempted repeatedly, by making the claim of an individual's minor or practically non-existing role.

[13] A distinction between guilt and responsibility was made by Feinberg, to whose paper Hannah Arendt responded with the text, "Collective Responsibility."

[14] Emphasis added.

[15] Arendt claims that the existence of "political responsibility which every government assumes for the deeds and misdeeds of its predecessor and every nation for the deeds and misdeeds of the past;" and she adds: "When Napoleon Bonaparte became the ruler of France he said: I assume responsibility for everything France has done from the times of Charlemagne to the terror of Robespierre." The closest to articulating the *political* criteria here is that "we are always held responsible for the sins of our fathers as we reap the rewards of their merits" (Arendt 1987a, 45). The only ones, reminds Arendt, who are exempt from this responsibility are the ones who have been denied the opportunity to "reap the rewards" – the refugees and the stateless. The price of being displaced and losing a space of belonging is much higher than the burden of collective responsibility

[16] Emphasis added.

[17] This request is in its basic form, albeit in a different context and content discussed in Arendt's well-known text, "Civil Disobedience," in *Crises of the republic.*

[18] Arendt also reminds us of an additional parameter in the case of members of any elite, where non–participation does suffice and, does not apply: Arendt. 1987b.

[19] I address the resistances to war and nationalism in former Yugoslavia, resistances of women in particular in more detail in Duhaček 2002.

[20] Some men joined particular peace manifestations and were accepted as members of the group, especially since this group organized many activities against drafting.

[21] Slobodan Antonić, a local political analyst, has also named a group of contemporary historians in Serbia the "Female School of History"; they perceive themselves as professionals with integrity who happen to be women.

[22] Staša Zajović and Sonja Biserko are among the women who were nominated in June 2005 for the Nobel Prize for Peace.

[23] The work of these NGOs as well as the work of Nataša Kandić and Sonja Biserko requires much more attention than can be set aside here.

[24] It is in this sense that the words of Goetz in Sartre's play *The Devil and the Good Lord* should be understood: "You see this emptiness over our heads? That is God ... Silence is God. Absence is God. God is the loneliness of man. *There was no one but myself. I alone decided on the Evil; and I alone invented Good*" (Sartre 1960, 141). Emphasis added.

[25] See Dimitrijević 2001. Also Dimitrijević 2000.

[26] "[R]esponsibility does not belong only to the intellectuals. *It is even more important that each citizen is aware of his or her own responsibility* ... He or she must feel particularly responsible for the constitutive horizontal bond of the will to live together. In short, he or she must ascribe public safety to the vitality of the associate life which regenerates the will to live together" (Ricoeur 1996, 21) [Emphasis added]. See also Balibar 1991.

References

Anderson, Benedict. 1991. *Imagined communities: Reflection on the origins and the spread of Nationalism*. London & New York: Verso.

Arendt, Hannah. 1972a. *The origins of totalitarianism*. New York: World Publishing.

Arendt, Hannah. 1972b. Civil Disobedience. In *Crises of the republic*. New York: Harcourt Brace Jovanovich.

Arendt, Hannah. 1987a. Collective responsibility. In *Amor Mundi. Explorations in the faith and thought of Hannah Arendt*, edited by James W. Bernauer, S.J. Boston, Dordrecht, Lancaster: Martinus Nijhoff Publisher.

Arendt, Hannah. 1987b. The deputy: Guilt by silence. In *Amor mundi. Explorations in the faith and thought of Hannah Arendt*, edited by James W. Bernauer. Boston, Dordrecht, Lancaster: Martinus Nijhoff Publishers.

Arendt, Hannah. 1994a. *Eichmann in Jerusalem: A report on the banality of evil*. Harmondsworth: Penguin Books.

Arendt, Hannah. 1994b. Organized guilt and universal responsibility. In *Essays in understanding*, edited by Jerome Kohn. New York: Harcourt Brace & Company.

Arendt, Hannah. 2003. Personal responsibility under dictatorship. *Responsibility and judgment*, edited by Jerome Kohn. New York: Schocken Books.

Balibar, Etienne. 1991. Citizen subject. In *Who comes after the subject*, edited by Jean- Luc Nancy and Eduard Cadava. New York: Routledge.

Barrett, Michelle, and Mary McIntosh. 1985. Ethnocentrism and socialist feminist theory. *Feminist Review* 20.

Dimitrijević, Nenad. 2000. The past, responsibility, and the future. In *Truths, responsibilities, and reconciliations: The example of Serbia*, edited by Dejan Ilić and Veran Matić. Beograd: Samizdat B92.

Dimitrijević, Nenad. 2001. Slučaj Jugoslavija. [*The Case of Yugoslavia*]. Beograd: Reč.

Duhaček, Daša. 2002. Gender perspectives on political identities. In *From gender to nation*, edited by Rada Iveković and Julie Mostov. Ravena: Longo Editore.

Gojković, Drinka. 2000. What do we do now? In *Truths, responsibilities, reconciliations: The example of Serbia*, edited by Dejan Ilić and Veran Matić. Belgrade: Samizdat Free B92.

Jaspers, Karl. 1947. *Question of German guilt*. New York: The Dial Press.

Kandić, Nataša. 2002. Neprijatelj u Srbiji: Otvorenost, snaga i integritet nekoliko žena. [Enemy in Serbia: Openness, strength and integrity of a few women]. *Vreme*, [*Time*], no 607. 22 August 2002.

Kateb, George. 1983. *Hannah Arendt. Politics, conscience, evil*. Totowa, New Jersey: Rowman and Allanheld Publishers.

Kateb, George. 1992. On political evil. In *The inner ocean*. Ithaca: Cornell University Press.

Kohler, Lotte. 2000. *Within four walls. The correspondence between Hannah Arendt and Heinrich Blücher 1936–1968*. New York, San Diego, London: Harcourt, Inc.

Kohler, Lotte and Hans Sener, eds. 1992. *Hannah Arendt Karl Jaspers correspondence 1926– 1969*. New York, San Diego, London: Harcourt Brace Jovanovich, Publishers.

Kohn, Jerome. 1997. Evil and plurality. In *Hannah Arendt. Twenty years later*, edited by Larry May and Jerome Kohn. Cambridge, Massachusetts, London: The MIT Press.

Krmpotić, Vesna. 2002. Zid za mitološku fresku. [A wall for a mythological fresco painting]. *Danas*, 8 March 2002.

Levinas, Emmanuel. 1997. *Ethics and infinity. Conversations with Philippe Nemo*. Pittsburgh: Duquesne University Press.

Logar, Svetlana, and Srđan Bogosavljević. 2001. Vidjenje istine u Srbiji. [The perception of truth in Serbia]. Reč (*Word*) 62.

Popov, Nebojša, ed. 1996. *Srpska strana rata. [Serbia in War]*. Belgrade and Zrenjanin: Gradjanska čitaonica.

Rich, Adrienne. 1986. Notes toward a politics of location (1984). In *Blood, bread, and poetry*. New York and London: W.W. Norton and Co.

Ricoeur, Paul. 1996. *The hermeneutics of action*, edited by Richard Kearney. London, Thousand Oaks, New Delhi: Sage Publications.

Sartre, Jean-Paul. 1960. *The devil and the good Lord*. New York: Alfred A. Knopf.

SMMRI (Strategic Marketing and Media Research Initiative) 2005.

Villa, Dana. 1999. *Philosophy, Politics, and Terror*. Princeton: Princeton University Press.

Young-Bruehl, Elizabeth. 1982. *Hannah Arendt. For the love of the world*. New Haven and London: Yale University Press.

Zajović, Staša. 1994. I am disloyal. In *What Can We Do For Ourselves?* Proceedings of the East European Feminist Conference. Belgrade: Center for Women's Studies.

Zajović, Staša. 1998. Abuse of women on a nationalist and militarist basis. In *Women For Peace*. Beograd. Women in Black.

PART 3
Transnational Dialogues

Chapter 11

Poetics, Politics and Gender

Jasmina Lukić

[I]f you wish to uphold basic human justice you must do so for everyone, not selectively for the people that your side, your culture, your nation designates as okay (Said 1994, 69).

I am no one. And everyone. In Croatia I shall be a Serb, in Serbia, I shall be a Croat, in Bulgaria a Turk, in Turkey, a Greek, in Greece a Macedonian, in Macedonia a Bulgarian... Being an ethnic "bastard" or "schizophrenic" is my natural choice, I even consider it a sign of mental and moral health. And I know that I am not alone (Ugrešić 1988, 269-70).

Excessive social situations, like the political crisis and war in the former Yugoslavia, produce important test cases for the study of the gendered aspects of citizenship rights. In this chapter, such a case will be studied from an intersectional point of view, taking into consideration issues of citizenship, gender, nationality, and moral responsibility as they are reflected in the works and personal experiences of contemporary woman writer Dubravka Ugrešić.[1]

Dubravka Ugrešić was one of the earliest and most highly articulated critics of the new nationalist and repressive political practices that were part of the creation of the new nation-states in the region of the former Yugoslavia. Having lived in Croatia, she draws upon this context within her critiques of nationalism, and soon became a target of attacks herself. After an orchestrated media lynching in 1992, she left Croatia and moved to the Netherlands where she has continued her writing. The analysis that follows takes into account both sides of her case, including her own personal experiences and her critical writings.

Dubravka Ugrešić's works reflect upon the political crisis and wars in the former Yugoslavia, and point out the hegemonic character of nationalist ideology. In her work, she demonstrates how structural violence operates on different levels, from the most immediate and clearly visible forms, to those that are more subtle and hidden, yet still highly destructive. As a response to the structural violence of the state, she calls upon intellectuals to perform their moral obligation and reject the "culture of lies" produced by the nationalist regimes. In terms of citizenship rights, her call translates into a claim for equal participation, that is, for the contested right to active participation in the public sphere for those individuals who are socially ostracized on ideological grounds within the new states that were created by the dismemberment of the former Yugoslavia.

The following analysis intends to show that the violent nature of the public reactions to her criticism in Croatia, were not only generated by the arguments and examples she was using in her articles, but also by a high level of gender prejudice, which was supported, and partly induced, by the new nationalist state ideology. Because of the nature of some of the criticism lodged against her, her case is also indicative of the gendered relationship between citizens and the state.

Being the Other: Women and the State

In understanding the current relevance of the Balkan conflicts of the early 1990s, I am very much in agreement with Étienne Balibar, as he argues, "in reality, Yugoslavia's situation is not atypical but rather constitutes a *local projection* of forms of confrontation and conflicts characteristic of all Europe", and that in that sense, "the fate of European identity as a whole is being played out in Yugoslavia and more generally in the Balkans" (2004, 5–6). Rejecting exclusionary views that locate the conflicts in the Balkans outside its imaginary European borders, Balibar emphasizes the centrality of the problem of nationalism behind the events in the former Yugoslavia.

Balibar sees nationalism as:

> ...the organic ideology that corresponds to the national institution and this institution rests upon the formulation of a *rule of exclusion, of visible or invisible 'borders'*, materialized in laws and practices. Exclusion – or at least unequal ('preferential') access to particular goods and rights depending on whether one is a national or a foreigner, or belongs to the community or not – is thus the very essence of the nation-form (Balibar 2004, 22).

In his view, nationalism is necessarily an exclusionary, hegemonic ideology, a secondary identity that tends to "win over" all other identities and "arrive at a point where national belonging intersects with and integrates all other forms of belonging" (2004, 23). Moreover, nationalist ideology is articulated by "a *structural violence*, both institutional and spontaneous," which makes the question of the differentiation between "good" and "bad" nationalism pointless.

> The difficulty does not reside in the good or bad, advanced or backward character of nationalism, but in the combined economy of identities and structural violence, in the subtle differences between the forms of violence combined with beliefs, ideals, and institutional norms, and in the ways those norms crystallize on the mass scale (2004, 24-5).

Agreeing with Balibar on these points, I also want to note here that in his analysis of the complex relationships between nationalism and citizenship, he does not take into account gender, which is an important dimension of this intersection. In speaking about "sexual citizenship", Terrell Carver defines gender as the "ways in which sex and sexuality become political", which include both the processes of obscuring gender issues as much as openly dealing with them (Carver and Mottier 1998, 19). When we speak about the influence of nationalist ideology in the Balkans, it is important to keep in mind that these practices were deeply gendered. One of the most visible outcomes of the crisis was an obvious, induced tendency towards the re-patriarchalization of the new nation-states that emerged out of the former Yugoslavia. This re-patriarchalization was partly related to the rise of the war-culture, but it was also deeply embedded in the dominating narratives of the new nationalist ideologies, which promoted highly traditionalist images of national identity. In that sense, narratives related to the building of the new states tended to be deeply patriarchal, and therefore, gender-blind. This was visible in many areas of public life, where national identity as a *secondary identity* (Balibar 2004, 25–30) managed to impose itself as the dominating one, suppressing all the other identities as less important and marginal, as was the case in both Serbia and Croatia during the 1990s.

The (re)construction of new nation-states coincided with the (re)construction of new cultural identities, which were, strangely enough, seen to be both the ultimate source and the ultimate confirmation of national identities. Being exclusive and strongly ideologically driven, these processes were also marked by the same patterns of structural violence that permeated other spheres of social life. Promoting narratives of unity, "[n]ationalist ideologies and movements reject the constitutive 'otherness' at the source of all culture; more often then not, they seek to 'purge' the culture of its impure or foreign elements and thus render it whole again" (Benhabib 2002, 8).

In the case of Dubravka Ugrešić, this "work" of nationalist ideology in the sphere of culture is exemplified as a case of "otherness" that needs to be purged. It clearly demonstrates the ways in which structural violence operates, and how, at certain moments, it becomes a "normalized" element of public life. It is exactly these processes of the social "normalization" of structural violence that Dubravka Ugrešić attempts to unmask in her writings. In that respect, the present study attempts to employ a double perspective. It discusses the case of Dubravka Ugrešić as the ostracized Other, while also drawing upon her own critical analyses of the situations in the former Yugoslavia that allowed the practices of ostracism to once again not only be possible, but also socially acceptable.

The core of the problem, in Dubravka Ugrešić's view, is state-promoted violent behavior; therefore, the relationship between the citizens and the state proves to be of particular importance within her work. As soon as Dubravka Ugrešić started experiencing ostracism, she took a rebellious position, claimed her agency, and her citizenship right to think differently. This is clearly visible in many of her public statements. The following excerpt, from one of the interviews that she gave before she decided to leave Croatia in voluntary exile, is a characteristic example of this:

> In one way, my media executors are right. I am, in a way, a "traitor of the state". As we know from history, writers and states have never been, and never should have been, in

love. Totalitarian states and post-totalitarian states, particularly the small ones, loudly and hysterically repeat their claim to be loved. For some unknown reason, they ask to be loved especially by writers. They go so far as to put their state face under the face of the homeland, which, as we all know, does not ask for love for it already has it in some way. Hence, as long as this state will be as it is now, as long as it asks me to love it without any reserve, I will be its "dissident". When it becomes, if it becomes, decent and civilized, when it starts respecting all my civil and human rights, only then can it evoke my respect (Ugrešić 1993, 15, authors' translation).

When accused of being a "traitor of the homeland" (an accusation which implies an immediate, total condemnation without any rational analysis of the assumed guilt), Ugrešić responded by turning the table, and unmasking the manipulative gesture of a state that equated itself to a *nation*, and equated nationalism to patriotism within public life. This is then taken by the state as sufficient grounds for it to demand un-critical love from its citizens, which in fact is nothing else but a (state-controlled) form of obedience. Such an attitude excludes any critical debate of state policy, and of the state-promoted concept of the *nation*. In practice, it becomes a very useful basis for the promotion of new "strategies of representation" where "*the people* is constituted as one" (Benhabib 2002, 9).[2]

In the case of Dubravka Ugrešić, the general accusations of "treason," and the emotional "blackmail" behind it, are reinforced by the fact that the traitor was a woman. The various texts published in 1992 and 1993, which were part of an in-tense media campaign lodged against Ugrešić by the Croatian media, provide many examples that confirm this view. The attacks on Ugrešić began when she started to publish critical essays on the situation in Croatia and the region of the former Yugoslavia. In these essays, she was openly critical towards the new nationalisms in the region. In 1991 and 1992, these texts were primarily published in the foreign press, which, in Croatia, served to further reinforce the accusations.[3] The attacks significantly increased after the public scandal that involved five Croatian female intellectuals, who were together exposed to a media lynching because of their criti-cal comments on the situation in the country. Labeled the "Croatian witches" these women included: feminist philosopher, Rada Iveković; feminist journalist, Vesna Kesić; feminist journalist and writer, Slavenka Drakulić; journalist, Jelena Lovrić; and Dubravka Ugrešić.

The best evidence of the gendered character of these assaults can be found in an article published in December 1992, with the indicative title "Croatian Feminists Are Raping Croatia." The article, in a significantly depersonalized way, was signed by the "Investigating Team" (Investigacioni tim 1992). Within an extremely gen-dered framework, the article denounced the five women as "national traitors." As much as it was offensive on the surface, the title within itself carried an additional web of interrelated, implicit allegations. It accused them of nothing less than "rape," a crime that was very present and spoken of in the ongoing wars that were occur-ring at the time. Through these accusations, the women, recognized as metaphorical "rapists," were equated with the enemy solders, that is, they were masculinized and represented as an actual threat to the homeland. This masculinization had a very definite purpose, it justified in advance any form of assault on the women, for an enemy solder has to be "neutralized" in whatever means necessary. On the other hand, being labeled as feminists, the five women were presented as traitors not only of their homeland, but also of their femininity – in the given context, when taking into account the public attitude towards feminism, it also meant they were not "real women." Thus, feminism is included in the article as both an accusation, and a proof of guilt.

The article did not analyze any of the critical statements the accused women had made, it presupposed that the allegations were well founded, assumed their guilt, and "exposed" them to the public.[4] The article listed personal information about them, including the year of their birth, the nationalities of their parents, the addresses of their homes and work, whether or not they were married, who they were married to, and if they had any children. The article was obviously framed as a call for a general assault on the "culprits," and it very consciously manipulated the data and the way the women were presented.

Again, the gender dimension proves to be highly important here. It is obvious that the article relies on the simple fact that the publication of very personal information is somehow more "acceptable" in the case of women, who are supposedly located in the sphere of domesticity. By pointing out the nationality of their parents, the article intended to prove that the named women were "nationally unsuitable." This again marked them as suspected traitors, and disqualified their criticisms as irrelevant. The article also claimed that these women were socially privileged, which was again aimed at taking away the weight of their criticisms, and gaining widespread support for an attack on them by the journal's readers, most of whom were impoverished by the deep social crisis and war. The data given about where the five attacked women lived did not list their exact addresses, but gave information about the size of their apartments and the parts of the city that they lived in. At a time when many people had lost their homes in the war, this was supposed to further evoke the negative emotions of the readers. Similarly, information about their places of employment was given at a moment when many people were without jobs and the proper means for living. Furthermore, it should be remembered that, according to the basic logic of patriarchal culture, women could hardly earn respect through their own knowledge and professional merits. So the very fact that all of the women were working, and were working in prestigious positions, was supposed to prove the high level of benevolence granted by the same state that they attacked in their writings. Added to this were comments on their marital status, and the identity of their husbands. It was clearly indicated that some of them were not married, and that some of them did not have children or "suitable" husbands. Again, the patriarchal system of values is brought to mind (and through this, is also legitimized), particularly the notion that a woman's identity is determined through the men that she is related to. Unmarried women and women without children are considered to be an anomaly, while women who have "unsuitable" parents or husbands (and we speak here both of national and ideological "unsuitability") should be seen as "unsuitable" themselves; because it is their fathers and husbands who, according to the logic of patriarchal culture, give them their primary identity.

Of course, I do not want to claim here that the media attacks on the "Croatian witches," as well as the media campaign against Ugrešić that lasted for almost two years, can be fully explained through these gendered arguments. The most important element of the whole affair was the low level of social tolerance towards any kind of dissonant, critical voices, which was influenced by the ongoing war in Croatia. Nevertheless, the gender dimension ultimately framed their cases in a very specific way.

Poetics and Politics: The Writer and the State

Before we go on with a more detailed analysis of the works of Dubravka Ugrešić, it will be useful to address an important literary question, that of the autonomy of literature. This question underlies both the analysis of Ugrešić's work, as well as the debate over the role of literature in the Balkan wars.

Introduced by the Russian formalists, and strongly promoted by other formalist approaches to literary studies, the idea of the autonomy of literature was embraced rather early on in the socialist Yugoslavia as a tool to protect the sphere of literature from ideological intrusions. On the other hand, the recent cultural history of the region of the former Yugoslavia, and particularly the case of Ugrešić, are good illustrations of how the concept of literary autonomy was itself both contextualized and "contextualizable." From a contemporary perspective, it can be seen as a significant indicator of the relationship between poetics and politics, as well as of the relations between writers and the state in a specific moment in time.

In all the books that Ugrešić wrote, both before the beginning of the crisis in the former Yugoslavia and after it actually broke out, one poetical assumption proves to be of particular importance, her deep belief that literature should not be functionally related to any tangible reality as its primary referent, nor should it aim to "reflect" it in any immediate way. This authorial stance also meant, quite consequently, that Ugrešić rejected a traditionalist concept of literature and writing. According to this tradition, literature was given a certain recognizable social function, and a writer was supposed to be promoter of state or national ideology.

Ugrešić's poetical views, as they were framed early in her career, must be contextualized within the wider framework of the dominating literary and critical practice in Yugoslavia during the 1970s and 1980s, which was unique in comparison with other socialist countries of the time. A rather high level of freedom in the domain of culture was considered an important aspect of the so-called "softness" of the former Yugoslav socialist system. Hence, Ugrešić's acceptance of the idea of the autonomy of literature was both in accordance with the mainstream tendencies in literary studies (knowledge which was accessible to literary scholars in Yugoslavia), and the orientation of a particularly younger generation of Yugoslav writers and critics. It is worth noting here that when it comes to the cultural life of former Yugoslavia, formalist approaches were introduced rather early, during the late 1950s and 1960s, through stylistic criticism, Russian formalism, and New Criticism. In the late 1960s and 1970s, French structuralism also gained numerous followers in Yugoslavia, which added to the variety of interpretative models that were based upon the assumption that a literary text has to be seen as an entity in and of itself, autonomous from its immediate social context.

The openness of the Yugoslav literary scene to the formalist approach must also be socially contextualized. To a certain extent, this openness was related to the strong tendency of the state authorities to prove their democratic qualities after Yugoslavia's break with the Soviet Union, and its turn towards "socialism with a human face." This confirmed Yugoslavia's difference from other communist regimes. For various reasons, the sphere of culture, and in particular the sphere of literature, was considered appropriate for such a purpose. Understanding that literature can have a significant representational role in a society, the state authorities did not oppose its liberation even though some other highly sensitive social domains remained under the very strict control of the centers of power.[5]

The state also had a certain interest in making intellectuals, in particular writers, its allies, with the hope of receiving a confirmation of the legitimacy of its political project. A rise in the level of freedom in the sphere of culture was seen as a significant element in the building of this alliance, an important symbolic "currency," as Stephen Greenblatt put it in his description of the relationship between art and the state.[6] A result of the "exchange" between writers and the state was the authority's consent to open the sphere of culture to ideas that were considered incompatible with the communist ideology of other countries. It also allowed for a rather high level of freedom for artists. Of course, the sphere of culture was never fully liberated from the control of the official ideology, and the level of this control depended on the specificities of the given moment, as well as on the sensitivity of the given topic. Still, at least from the 1960s onwards, the state was more inclined to leave a certain space free in the domain of literature, which also meant that formalist approaches in literary studies were welcomed in academia, as well as in critical practice.

The acceptance of formalist approaches, with their insistence on literary autonomy, was one of the elements of literary life that contributed to the significant liberation of the space of culture from the immediate control of the ideological apparatus. Belonging to the fictional reality of literary texts, literary characters were protected by a shared assumption that literature (the arts) is autonomous: therefore, they were given the possibility to speak more freely about actual social problems, and even to oppose the state ideology to a certain extent. While in the 1960s, the state apparatus was still not able to accept and tolerate "the black wave" in film with its strong element of social criticism, in the 1970s and 1980s social criticism became one of the more or less tacitly recognized criteria for the evaluation of literature (and of film) at that time.[7] An interesting situation was therefore created; literary criticism strongly promoted the idea of the autonomy of literature, while literary practice proved that the literature of the time was silently given a very special role as a privileged public space where it became possible to articulate various political standpoints (an option that was otherwise excluded from the official political arena).

While many writers (and artists) extensively used this possibility to "politicize" their writings in an obvious way, among the generation of writers who entered the literary scene during the 1970s, and later in the 1980s, there were also authors who wanted to use their freedom of speech differently. Dubravka Ugrešić was one of them.[8] From the beginning, her writing was founded upon the acceptance of the idea that literature had to be autonomous. This was an idea she initially adapted from the Russian formalists and avant-garde artists whose work was the object of her scholarly studies: later on, she was also influenced by post-structuralist theories on the text and postmodernist poetics. In other words, from the beginning her works were founded on the assumption that immediate reality should not be considered as a primary referent in literary texts, but as one possible world of equal standing with the other possible worlds of literary texts. It is a poetical model in which the privileged status of immediate reality, traditionally assumed unquestionable, becomes contested. For Ugrešić, as for many other postmodern writers, the world is understood as a text, and a text is understood as a world in itself (McHale 1987; Ronen 1994). This also means that the primary relationships between various texts/worlds are not mimetic ones, rather ones of mutual correspondence and citation.

With these poetic assumptions in mind, it is not difficult to understand why an author such as Dubravka Ugrešić, whose work was based on such premises, could not accept the claims of any collectivist ideology. In the times of socialism, she was one of the most well known representatives of postmodern literature in Yugoslavia. In the Yugoslav cultural scene of that time, such a poetical position also connoted a clear distance from not only the state ideology of socialism, but also from the unofficial but clearly present ideology of new (old) nationalisms in the domains of literature and culture.

In Yugoslavia, the propagation of nationalist ideas in literature was enabled by the same policy that liberalized the sphere of culture and opened a space for the inclusion of other political ideas and alternative cultural concepts. Their undeniable presence and influence was already clearly visible during the 1980s, before various forms of nationalism had become legitimized in the domain of public political discourses.[9] This went along with the re-enforcement of the deeply traditionalist, patriarchal attitude towards society as a whole, which occurred during the late 1980s and 1990s and also influenced the domain of literature. According to these traditionalist views, literature should primarily be seen as an expression of "national being", therefore a writer should perform the role of a so called "national bard", in order to keep national traditions throughout his writings, help educate his people, and show them the proper ways of the future. This was a concept of literature that was inherited from the 19th-century formation of the European nation-states. As the developments in 1990s have clearly shown, this concept of literature was never really abandoned in Yugoslavia, although it was less influential during the times of the liberalization of the political system. Thus, after a period of relative freedom in the 1970s and 1980s, literature was once again given an ideological task, this time to promote the "interests of the nation." Before the dismemberment of the common country, it was not an official task issued by the state; rather it was a visible manifestation of an already present rise of nationalist ideology. Once new states had been created in the region of the former Yugoslavia, an induced feeling of pride for doing something for one's "homeland" and the "nation" became an element of the symbolic "exchange" between writers and the new states. In both cases, the writers were positioning themselves as national bards in the traditional sense of the term.

However, the role of a national bard is highly gendered, and as a rule, it is performed primarily, if not exclusively, by men. The concept itself was a product of an overtly patriarchal tradition, which enclosed women in the sphere of domesticity and excluded them from the public domain. Generally speaking, within such a system of values a woman can symbolically represent the "nation" (like the image of the "motherland," for example), but she cannot *speak* in its name, because she is *a priori* seen as the Other, a deviation from the norm.

That is why Dubravka Ugrešić's critical position against nationalism was especially seen as troublesome. She was a *female* voice that was articulating political and moral opinions that were different from the ones that were being promoted by the majority, this added to her subversive potential. A *woman* who is expressing radical social criticism as a *writer* subverts the traditional role of a "national bard," that is, the logic of the traditionalist patriarchal society, and stands in a place that is reserved for men. As the case of the five Croatian "witches" clearly demonstrated, the critical statements by women who act as socially responsible intellectuals are much more likely to produce a higher level of negative reactions than similar statements issued by men under the same circumstances. In other words, the criticism of the new nationalist regimes in the region of the former Yugoslavia, which Dubravka Ugrešić articulated so strongly, was received with additional hostility because it was voiced by a woman; that is, by someone who is deprived of subjectivity by the very logic of nationalist ideology.

Antipolitics as a Politics of Writing: The Role of the Intellectual

The essays of Dubravka Ugrešić that provoked a strong media campaign against her in 1992 and 1993, as well as her other texts that dealt with the situation in the region and with her own experiences, were later collected in a book entitled, *The Culture of Lies*, significantly subtitled, "Antipolitical Essays." This expression was drawn from the work of Hungarian writer, György Konrad, and a quotation from his book *The Antipolitics of a Novelist* is given as an explanatory motto at the beginning of *The Culture of Lies*.[10] Using Konrad's terms, it can be said that in this book Ugrešić defends "her language and her philosophy" from the totalizing forces of nationalism.

As indicated by the title, Ugrešić's book deals with the creation of a particular type of social situation, termed the "culture of lies." Under the circumstances of this social situation, people accept being manipulated by the dominating ideology, and/or overlook the structural violence that this ideology brings upon society. The book uncompromisingly points to some characteristic cases and situations that demonstrate how widely the new "culture of lies" was accepted, and how deeply it penetrated all the strata of social life. Ugrešić speaks of the various forms of discriminatory practices of the new regional states, and points to the responsibility that their citizens had by uncritically accepting them. She reflects on the various strategies of mimicking that people used in order to make themselves socially invisible. In her view, the "silent majority" gave the most significant contribution to the social "normalization" of exclusionary practices as well as the violence related to those practices.

On the other hand, it is clear that Ugrešić does not find everybody to be equally responsible for the promotion of structural violence and the creation of the "culture of lies." In her book, she is particularly interested in the role of intellectuals, in particular, writers as those who are supposed to be "anti-political" (in Konrád's sense of the term). By calling upon intellectuals, especially writers, to act as morally responsible critical agents in the given social situation, Ugrešić is also in accordance with the views of Edward Said. The task of an intellectual, Said claims, is to keep a critical distance in all circumstances, and to be able to deal with eventual problems even in those projects whose aims he may himself support. In particular, an intellectual has to be critical towards his own tradition and his own society:

> The fundamental problem is therefore how to reconcile one's identity and the actualities of one's own culture, society and history to the reality of other identities, cultures, peoples. This can never be done simply by asserting one's preference for what is already one's own: tub-thumping about the glories of 'our' culture or the triumphs of 'our' history is not worthy of the intellectual's energy, especially not today when so many societies are comprised of different races and backgrounds as to resist any reductive formulas…No one can speak up all the time on all the issues. However, I believe, there is a special duty to address the constituted and authorized powers of one's own society, which are accountable to its citizenry, particularly when those powers are exercised in a manifestly disproportionate and immoral war, or in deliberate programs of discrimination, repression, and collective cruelty (Said 1994, 69–72).

The dismemberment of the former Yugoslavia, and the political crisis and wars related to it, produced highly complex and socially sensitive situations, in which injustices of various forms easily occurred. It was also a time in which there was a definite call for the active involvement of the region's intellectuals. While there is no doubt that many writers and other public figures did take a public stand in the events, what Dubravka Ugrešić emphasized in her book was that too many of them failed to recognize the need for a critical distance against the authorized powers within their own societies. Given that the dismemberment of the common country was related to the creation of new ones, it also, in turn, was related to the promotion of new national ideologies and strategies of identification. In such a situation, too many public figures of the time thought that "tub-thumping" about the glories of "our" culture or the triumphs of "our" history was precisely their task. Of course, there were also individuals who acted like critical intellectuals (in Said's sense of the term); however, particularly in the first years of the conflict, they were much fewer in number.

The Culture of Lies confronts the various strategies that produce Otherness, and create both new lines of social divisions as well as social homogenization within society. Being a skilled fiction writer, in this text Dubravka Ugrešić uses a specific narrative strategy, which intentionally produces the strong effect of defamiliarization. This gives her essays a distinct literary quality. She narrates from a marginal and highly personalized position, which in this case proves to be a point of clear vision: "My texts do not speak of the war itself, rather they are concerned with life on its edge, a life in which little is left for the majority of people" (Ugrešić 1998, 78–9).

Speaking from the margin, Ugrešić recalls the side of the war that usually remains less visible. As a rule, situations that are charged with high social tensions - like wars, deep political crises, or radical changes – tend to be interpreted along the main lines of events, too often translated into rather general statements that primarily concern public events and political decisions. Ugrešić wants to go beyond that; she is interested in the ways in which declared policies affect the real lives of people in whose name all the changes are being made; who, at the same time, are not seen as genuine agents of the events in question. In that sense, Dubravka Ugrešić's position is close to that of a micro-historian who opposes the institutionally legitimized interpretation of history.

The Culture of Lies unmasks strategies used by the new nationalistic oligarchies in the Balkans, to create and impose a particular interpretation of the current events. According to this interpretation, the new nationalist oligarchies were to be seen as a positive, indispensable outcome of historical processes, which ended up being their almost teleologically inevitable result. In constructing such images, they used mechanisms that were very much alike to those that were used during the times of the one-party system of power, based upon a similar systemic dichotomy of inclusion/exclusion. Previously, "sameness" was considered one's affiliation to the state ideology of communism; however in the new nationalist ideologies it is based upon one's ethnic origin, which is translated as the basic constituent of one's national identity. However, in both cases, significant energy was invested in marking out the bodies of the Others who were seen as socially unacceptable. Similar to the way that the communist regimes re-wrote history in order to promote their ideological project, the new nationalist regimes in the Balkans reconstructed the past in accordance with their own projects. When it came to the most immediate past, all the positive experiences from actual life in those times tended to be obscured, and any serious debate about alternative ways to introduce changes and re-frame the space of the previously common country were excluded.[11] Thus, Ugrešić speaks about the "terror by forgetting," which is present in most of the new countries:

It seems that it is not only fear, that aroused national (and nationalist) emotions, hatred of the enemy, vulnerability, the establishment of an autocratic system, media propaganda, and war that have reinforced the culture of lies. One of the strategies with which the culture of lies is established is terror by forgetting (they force you to forget what you remember!) and terror by remembering (they force you to remember what you do not remember) (Ugrešić 1998, 78–9).

Stereotyping was one of the main strategies that was used in the production of new past/present/future images. Since every stereotype is based on the acceptance of a certain level of homogenization, it strongly reduces the space for critical thinking.[12] Ugrešić reveals the practice of stereotyping used by institutions of power to create an illusion of order in times of social turbulences. However, this was a false order that enhanced differences and fixed hierarchies. Thus, the processes of stereotyping in this case have to be analyzed in close relation with the processes of the Othering, which are, as we have already seen, highly gendered.

The Culture of Lies demonstrated how stereotyping, which deprived people from authentic emotions and the experience of their actual meaning, was strategically utilized by the new ideology of nationalism, and thus became a dangerous weapon in the ongoing power-struggle. Stereotyping produced a simplified image of the world in which the loss of individuals' rights and the possibility for them to make their own choices were disregarded in the name of a new, collective identity. Again, the nationalist ideology seemed to have learned well from the logic of hard-core communism. Since an individual is considered less important in the face of the collectivity, actual human hardships, and even sufferings tend to be obscured by stereotyped images in the media and public discourses. The same logic was used to differentiate between "our" and "their" people in death, as well as in life. The sufferings of "ours" were represented as sacred sacrifices for the homeland; the sufferings of the Others were minimized or negated by the very fact that they were recognized as "enemies."

It seems that the large amount of human misery that was produced by the wars in the Balkans also supported an intense production of a new, "national" kitsch, which was given an important role within the field of culture.[13] Explaining the concept of kitsch, Ugrešić draws upon the work of Nabokov, and his interpretation of the Russian word *poshlost'*. She emphasizes that it could be "because of its wealth of meanings, that Nabokov prefers it to its English equivalents such as *cheap, inferior, sorry, trashy, scurvy, tawdry*, and the like" (Ugrešić 1998, 49). While some of the simple forms of the word *poshlost'* can bring about just a smile, other uses of it can be very disturbing, particularly when they are not obvious, and pretend to belong to the highest reaches of art and thought. The dominating forms of kitsch and stereotypes she pointed to were either taken from the repertoire of the 19th-century nationalist legacies, or produced during the early 1990s. In both cases, they strongly relied upon the "eternal values" and "unquestionable ideals" of national myths. In this way, they fixed their meanings in a realm out of the reach of rational criticism, actual history, or any of the concrete parameters of critical evaluation. *The Culture of Lies* demystifies these processes, making them visible, and unmasks the strategies behind them; in my view, this is one of the main reasons why the essays from this book were recognized as a threat by the new nationalists.[14]

Gender, Identity, and Citizenship

The case of Dubravka Ugrešić and her "anti-political essays" demonstrates yet another important point, the impact of both gender and citizenship on the perception of people's identities within other spheres of life. If the reception of Ugrešić's essays in Croatia were strongly framed by the low level of social tolerance produced by the social crisis and the war in the early 1990s, their readings abroad would assumingly be devoid from the personalized, emotional involvements of her Croatian critics. Nevertheless, the same kind of personalized national sensitivity, intersected with gender prejudices, proved to be present in cases where Ugrešić extended her sharp wit beyond the borders of her own country and the borders of what was assumed to be her, "local competence." An indicative example is her collection of essays *Have a Nice Day: From the Balkan Wars to the American Dream*, written during the early 1990s, at the very beginning of the war in Croatia. In a highly witty and amusing, but very insightful way, Ugrešić contrasts the typical American way of life, and the specificities of its everyday culture, with some of the specific features of daily life in the early transitional years of Eastern Europe and the horrors of the Balkan wars, which were, at that time, still in their early phases (see Lukić 2002). *Have a Nice Day* is written from the position of an exile, whose homeland is descending to war and whose present retreat (America) literally looks to her like a New World, in which she is in the position of a distant observer.

It is insightful to see that Ugrešić's extremely witty but also sharp critical comments on the American way of life were primarily seen as problematic by her male critics – strangely enough, not because these comments were wrong, but because of the identity of the person who made them. It was if, being a stranger, an exile, Ugrešić was not qualified to be critical of the American way of life. Thus, Paul Goldberg, in a paternalistic way, reproached her by saying that she was watching too much television, instead of making friends (Goldberg 1995). Robert Kaplan, on the other hand, acknowledged that Ugrešić's observations were well founded, but reproved the reasons that he felt were behind her criticisms of American culture:

> *Have a Nice Day: From the Balkan Wars to the American Dream* is a cynical and ironic description of the USA, written from a perspective of a foreigner whose society the United States did not manage to protect (Kaplan 1995).

His assertions about her text, do not in any way exist within Ugrešić's text, hence this comment speaks more of Kaplan's own deeply patriarchal and colonial position, reflected here in his obvious assumption that the US is some kind of global "father" or "policeman", who is expected to solve all the problems that others have to struggle with.[15]

Of course, not all the male critics of *Have a Nice Day* reacted in the same way. For this analysis, it is particularly interesting to consider the statement of another male writer and critic, Josef Brodsky, who quoted on the American edition of the book, "It takes a stranger to see how dark the world is. Dubravka Ugrešić is that stranger" (Ugrešić 1995). Brodski values here exactly what Kaplan does not recognize as a quality, the detachment of the narrator produced by her exile. In the narrative text, this detachment produces the effect of defamiliarization, which makes us see what would have otherwise remained unnoticed. This, according to the Russian formalists, is exactly the specific quality of literature.

It should not be forgotten here that Brodski is himself an exile, which obviously makes him more sensitive towards the strong feeling of otherness that permeate throughout Ugrešić's writing. Similar to Brodski, female critics of the book have found the feeling of detachment to be a productive literary element. "She defines herself as exile, without a center, without a home. Yet, she is still the citizen of the human race, we are all exiles in some way," writes Janet St. John (1995). Pamela Daubenspeck claims that Ugrešić's "wry observations on Western culture...reveal as much about this particular exile's internal life as they do about American society's shallow obsessions" (1995). However, how can these differences and similarities be interpreted without essentializing them? In my view, they clearly point to the intersection of gender and ethnicity in the formation of identity. They also offer a strong ground upon which to further investigate the gendered aspects of identity construction, which follows the lines indicated by feminist theory and assumes that women, because they themselves are socially marginalized, tend to be more open to various manifestations of otherness.

Instead of a Conclusion: A Few Remarks on Cultural Citizenship

A number of questions referring to gender and the ethnic aspects of citizenship can be raised in relation to the case of Dubravka Ugrešić. To complicate the picture further, I would like to add some elements from a contemporary perspective. After having been a voluntary exile for years, Dubravka Ugrešić is now a Dutch citizen. Would Kaplan and Goldberg have read her book *Have a Nice Day* differently if they perceived it as being written by a Dutch instead of a Croatian writer? Moreover, what exactly does a new passport mean for the perception of a writer who comes from a peripheral country, and still writes in her native Croatian language, but whose works have been translated into numerous languages, including English, and has been awarded a number of international literary prizes? Beginning with the replacement of the old country, former Yugoslavia, with the new one, Croatia, Dubravka Ugrešić describes this very particular situation as follows:

With my Croatian passport, I abandoned my newly acquired homeland; and set off into the world. Out there, with the gaiety of the Eurovision Song Contest, I was immediately identified as a Croatian writer. I became the literary representative of a milieu which did not want me any more, and which I did not want any more either. But still, the label "Croatian writer" remained with me, like a permanent tattoo.

At this moment I posses a passport with a red cover again, Dutch. I continue to wear the label of a literary representative of a country to which I am not connected to, even by a passport. Will my new passport make me a Dutch writer? I doubt it...

And why am I so sensitive to labels? Because in practice it turns out that identifying baggage weighs down a literary text...Because I come from the periphery (Ugrešić 2003, 468).

It is obvious that writers like Dubravka Ugrešić challenge the concept of national literature as they "trespass" both the actual and symbolic borders in their lives. Can a simple change of framework solve anything? Would labeling her as a "European writer" put an end to the problem, or would it just perpetuate it on another level, which again asks the simple question of who "qualifies" as a European writer today? To these last questions, Dubravka Ugrešić answers in her typical way. She claims that her "hero" among her fellow writers, and the most European occurrence in European literature is one Joydeep Roy Bhattacharaya, an Indian who lives in New York and writes about Central Europe. Bhattacharaya refuses to follow the pattern set to him by the usual practices that propose that he embrace India as his primary subject (Ugrešić 2003, 468).

Dubravka Ugrešić is speaking here for many other contemporary writers who live and write across different kinds of borders – of states, languages, and cultures – and who experienced similar problems. In discussing citizenship and identity, Isin and Wood have stated that, "Cultural citizenship is not only about the rights to produce and consume symbolic goods and services but also an intervention in this identity work. It is not only about redistributive justice concerning cultural capital but also about the recognition and valorization of the plurality of meanings and representations" (Isin and Wood 1999, 192). If cultural citizenship is to secure these rights, it cannot be tied to the concept of the nation-state. However difficult it may be to detach certain forms of culture from the concepts of the nation and national identity, it is equally important to keep in mind how reductive and context dependent these notions are. In light of what has been discussed here, it seems that a conception of cultural citizenship that takes into account one's right to produce, as well as exchange and consume cultural goods, in an unobtrusive way – beyond and across various kinds of borders – can become one of those areas of our common experience where the actual level of social liberty can be measured.

Notes

[1] Dubravka Ugrešić is a freelance writer living in Amsterdam. She is the author of the novels *Fording the Stream of Consciousness, The Museum of Unconditional Surrender*, and *The Ministry of Pain*; a collection of short stories titled *In the Jaws of Life* and several collections of essays including, *Have a Nice Day, The Culture of Lies*, and *Thank You for Not Reading*. Ugrešić's books are translated into all major European languages and have been awarded several literary prizes, including The Charles Veillon European Essay Prize, The Dutch Versetprijs, the Austrian State Prize for European Literature, and the Heinrich Mann Prize. Dubravka Ugrešić also occasionally teaches in American universities.

[2] Similar strategies of emotional blackmailing were used by the socialist states to support more formalized systems of control over their citizens.

[3] The same logic operated equally as strong in Serbia at the time. For example, Ivan Đurić, a noted historian and a strong political opponent of Slobodan Milošević, was also strongly attacked in Serbia for his criticism of the Serbian regime, and particularly for his statements given abroad, which were generally taken to be an unacceptable "crime" by a very wide audience.

[4] The scandal broke out when criticism, concerning the media situation and freedom of the press in Tuđman's Croatia, started to be voiced in international circles. One occasion, out of many, where this criticism was raised was at the 58 Congress of PEN centers in Rio de Janeiro, in December 1992. Reporting from the congress, the president of Croatian Pen Center at the time, pointed his finger at women intellectuals who were critical against the regime of Franjo Tuđman, and blamed them for putting the world congress of PEN centers, which was to be held in Duborvnik in 1993, in jeopardy. As the organization of the congress in Dubrovnik was taken as a matter of the utmost importance for the confirmation of the new Croatian state, and a confirmation of the importance of national culture in the international scene, the five women mentioned in this report then became the victims of a series of very strong media assaults.

[5] Here, I mean that, in the first place, the political system itself and the one-party system of government remained an untouchable issue, which actually meant that all the power was concentrated in the hands of the privileged political elite. This, in the end, proved to be one of the strongest barriers to the more comprehensive processes of transition to a market economy, which at that time had already started in some areas of social life.

[6] "[T]he work of art is the product of a negotiation between a creator or a class of creators, equipped with a complex, communally shared repertoire of conventions, and the institutions and practices of society. In order to achieve the negotiation, artists need to create a currency that is valid for a meaningful, mutually profitable exchange. It is important to emphasize that the process involves not simply appropriation but exchange, since the existence of art always implies a return, a return normally measured in pleasure and interest. I should add that the society's dominant currencies, money and prestige, are invariably involved, but I am here using the term 'currency' metaphorically to designate systemic adjustments, symbolizations and lines of credit necessary to enable an exchange to take place" (Greenblatt 1989, p. 12).

[7] And while in the case of some important authors like Borislav Pekić or Bora Ćosić, this kind of critical political engagement was included in their texts as an "added value," there were also cases when direct social criticism was used as a tool to get literary attention, which would not have been deserved otherwise. It is important to note here that the ac-

quired space for critical thinking was characterized by a rather simple division between those who were "in power" and those who were in the "opposition," with an assumption that all the "opposition" was generally democratic and progressive. This attitude turned out to be a delusion with the beginning of the political crisis and the war in the region of the former Yugoslavia, when a rather large, heterogeneous, group of critics of the communist regime became more stratified. While some of them continued to argue for actual social changes and democracy, many previous "oppositionists" became promoters of the new nationalist regimes. The case of Gojko Đogo is highly indicative here. See Gojković 2000 for more about this case.

8   Some other names to be mentioned here are Pavao Pavličić and Goran Tribuson, her generational colleagues from Zagreb, as well as David Albahari, a fiction writer from Belgrade, now living in Canada, whose poetical standings concerning the role of writing seems to be closest to those of Dubravke Ugrešić.

9   Renewed interest in the historical novel, as a genre that supports an intensified discussion on national issues, can be found in most of South Slavic literature, and it is clear today that those narratives can be seen both as indicators, and as generators of an intense growth of nationalist feelings, later to be used so efficiently by local nationalist political elites. (See Lukić, 2004.)

10 "Anti-politics is being surprised. A person finds things unusual, grotesque, and more: meaningless. He realizes that he is a victim, and he does not want to be. He does not like his life and death to depend on other people. He does not entrust his life to politicians, he demands that they give him back his language and his philosophy. A Novelist does not need a minister of foreign affairs: if he is not prevented from expressing himself, he is capable of doing so. He does not need an army either; he has been occupied for as long as he can remember. The legitimization of anti-politics is not more or less than the legitimization of writing. That is not the discourse of a politician, not a political scientist, not a technician, but the opposite: of a cynical and dilettante utopian. He does not act in the name of any mass or collective. He does not need to have behind him any party, state, nation, class, corporation, academic council. Everything he does, he does of his own accord, alone, in the milieu, which he himself has chosen. He does not need to account to anyone; his is a personal undertaking, self-defense" (quoted from Ugrešić, *The Culture of Lies*, from the motto of the book).

11 The creation of the new nation-states in the region of the former Yugoslavia could have happened without war and destruction on such a large scale. However, to find alternative ways out of the political crisis also meant to get involved in more intense negotiations, which would have jeopardized the privileged position that new nationalist oligarchies took for themselves at the beginning of the crisis. In other words, prolonged and more transparent strategies of negotiation would probably have undermined the position of authority that nationalist oligarchies managed to obtain by playing upon, as well as contributing to the heated social tensions between the former Yugoslav nations.

12 Michael Pickering explains this in the following way: "For those who use a particular stereotype, this may create an element of order by seeming to lock a category irrevocably in its place, in an apparently settled hierarchy of relations. The feeling of security or superiority resulting from this may help to explain why such imprecise referencing of other people or other cultures spreads rapidly and is taken up uncritically on a widespread basis. The imprecise representations involved in this process of social dissemination create the illusion of precision, of order, of the ways things should be. This is convenient

for existing relations of power because it lends to them a sense of certainty, regularity, and continuity…Stereotyping imparts a sense of fixedness to the homogenized images of disseminates. It attempts to establish an attributed characteristic as natural and given in ways inseparable from the relations of power and domination through which it operates" (Pickering 2001, 4–5).

[13] In Serbia, media close to Slobodan Milošević strategically promoted certain forms of populism. This phenomenon was analyzed in detail in Čolović 2002 and Gordy 1996.

[14] Some of these essays were widely discussed in Croatian papers, while the media campaign against Dubravka Ugrešić was going on in 1992; however the actual articles written by Ugrešić that were discussed in the campaign were not translated and therefore not accessible to the Croatian public until the first edition of the book, in 1995. In one of her interviews, answering to a strong article against her writings published by her university colleague Prof. Viktor Žmegač, Dubravka Ugrešić raises the same issue: "Finally, we have to ask a question which is much more interesting than writing opened personal letters and closed truths. Namely, how come a country which is attacked by a much stronger enemy, with a third of its territory occupied, in a country which every day counts its dead and where hundreds and hundreds of destroyed homes are all around, which moans under the burden of exiles, which suffers endlessly – as the respected Germanist also states – how come, then, that in such a country the whole cultural, media and political public in such a unison way, so unanimously, so collectively, so devotedly, got together to react to some articles of some writer. My sins, namely, do not go beyond twenty written pages." (Nedjeljna Dalmacija, 16 June 1993).

[15] It is also indicative to look at Kaplan's book on the Balkans (1993), which is founded upon revolting stereotypes of the Balkans. Kaplan represents the Balkans as a place where savage tribes live, waiting for nothing else, but a possibility to start Dawson, Jane I. killing each other. If Kaplan sees the Balkans in such a way, then it seems logical that, while reading Ugrešić's book, he cannot take seriously any criticism of America which comes from a person (shall we say, a woman) who is coming from such an "inferior" place, unless a personal reaction, a narrator's undeclared but understood disappointment in an expected paternal protection, is not inscribed in it.

References

Balibar, Étienne. 2004. *We, the people of Europe?* Translated by James Swenson. Princeton and Oxford: Princeton University Press.

Benhabib, Shyla. 2002. *The claims of culture: Equality and diversity in the global era.* Princeton and Oxford: Princeton University Press.

Carver, Terrel and Véronique Mottier, eds. 1998. *Politics of sexuality.* London and New York: Routledge.

Čolović, Ivan. 2002. *Politics of identity in Serbia.* New York: New York University Press.

Daubenspeck, Pamela R. 1995. Review of D. Ugrešić, *Have a Nice Day. Library Journal* 3 January 1995.

Gojković, Drinka. 2000. The birth of nationalism from the spirit of democracy. In *The road to war in Serbia: Trauma and catharsis,* edited by Nebojša Popov. Translated by Central European University Press. Budapest: CEU Press.

Goldberg, Paul. 1995. Phone Calls to Zagreb. *New York Times Book Review*, 25 June 1995, p. 14.

Gordy, Eric D. 1996. *The culture of power in Serbia: Nationalism and the destruction of alternatives*. University Park, Pennsylvania: The Pennsylvania State University Press.

Greenblatt, Stephen. 1989. Towards poetics of culture. In *The new historicism*, edited by H. Aram Veeser. New York and London: Routledge.

Investigacioni tim. [Investigation Team]. 1992. Hrvatske feministice siluju Hrvatsku! [Croatian Feminists Rape Croatia!]. *Globus*, 12 December 1992, 41.

Isin, Engin F., and Patricia K. Wood, eds. 1999. *Citizenship and identity*. London: Sage Publications.

Kaplan, Robert D. 1993. *Balkan ghosts: Journey through history*. London: Macmillan.

Kaplan, Robert D. 1995. Inside the Balkan Nightmare. *Washington Post*, 3 May 1995.

Lukić, Jasmina. 2000. Witches fly high, the sweeping broom of Dubravka Ugrešić. *European Journal of Women's Studies* 7 (3):375–383.

Lukić, Jasmina. 2002. Pisanje kao Antipolitika. [Writing as Antipolitics]. *Reč, časopis za književnost i kulturu, i društvena pitanja* 66:73–102.

Lukić, Jasmina. 2004. Recent historical novels and historical metafiction in the Balkans. In *History of the literary cultures of East-Central Europe: Junctures and disjunctures of the 19th and 20th Century*, edited by Marcel Cornis-Pope and John Newbauer. Amsterdam and Philadelphia: John Benjamins Publishing Company.

McHale, Brian. 1987. *Postmodernist fiction*. New York and London: Methuen.

Pickering, Michael. 2001. *Stereotyping, the politics of representation*. Basingstoke and London: Palgrave.

Popov, Nebojša, ed. 2000. *The road to war in Serbia: Trauma and catharsis*. Translated by the Central European University Press. Budapest: CEU Press.

Ronen, Ruth. 1994. *Possible worlds in literary theory*. Cambridge: Cambridge University Press.

Said, Edward W. 1994. *Representations of the intellectual: the 1993 Reith Lectures*. London: Vintage books. [orig. pub. c.1988].

St. John, Janet. 1995. Review of D. Ugrešić, *Have a Nice Day. Booklist* March 3, 1995.

Ugrešić, Dubravka. 1993. Da, ja sam izdajica države. [Yes, I am a traitor of the state]. An interview. *Feral Tribune*, 13 November 1993, 14–15.

Ugrešić, Dubravka. 1995. *Have A Nice Day, From the Balkan War to the American Dream*. Translated by Celia Hawkesworth. New York: Viking Penguin.

Ugrešić, Dubravka. 1998. *The Culture of lies*. Translated by Celia Hawkesworth. London: Phoenix House. Originally published as *Kultura laži*. 1995. Zagreb: Arkzin.

Ugrešić, Dubravka. 2003. *Thank you for not reading*. Translated by Celia Hawkesworth. Dalkey Archive Press.

Ugrešić, Dubravka. 2002. What is European in European culture? *European Journal of Women's Studies* 10 (4):465–471.

Chapter 12

Looking at Western Feminisms through the Double Lens of Eastern Europe and the Third World

Kornelia Slavova

The past fifteen years of post–communist transition have been full of painful ne-
gations and paradoxes, some of which are visible in the situation of women: the
standard complaint is that "women are the losers of the democratic changes", yet
there is still a resistance to Western feminist ideas and practices, and few signs of
feminist movements in the region. Following the debates surrounding the differences between feminisms in the West and those in Eastern Europe (at conferences,
in publications, and unofficial discourses) I was surprised to see similarities amongst
the critiques of Western feminist theories expressed by women from regions as diverse as the Third World and Eastern Europe. Surprising as they are, I believe that
such similarities need exploration.

In what follows I will analyze two questions. First, by questioning a number of
assumptions about the universality of feminist goals across cultures, to what extent
can emerging East European feminisms and Third World feminist critiques serve as
case studies for global feminism? Second, what can East European feminists gain
from the accumulated knowledge of Western feminisms? Before turning to these
questions I need to make a provisional remark about the terms I am using, which
sound quite totalizing. I am aware that the label "East European" reduces the experiences of women in the 29 countries in Central and Eastern Europe, as well as the
former Soviet Union, to a singularity, ignoring their varied historical, cultural, and
religious backgrounds (which are further diversified as the respective countries go
through transition to a market–oriented economy).[1] However, in order to develop my
argument that in this region feminism embodies yet one other difference (that of the
political system of communism); I need such an embracing entity. I feel the same un-
easiness about the unified labels "Western feminisms" and "Third World feminisms"
– even vaguer terms, both politically and historically loaded. I am using "Western
Feminisms" as a broad concept to incorporate major ideas from feminist practices
and theories in North America and Western Europe. The term "Third World" is also
used in a broad sense, as defined by Cheryl Johnson Odim, "to refer to underdevel-

oped/overexploited geopolitical entities, that is, countries, regions, even continents; and to refer to members of oppressed nationalities from these world areas who are now residents in developed First World countries" (1991, 314). Despite the pitfalls behind such grouping, I believe that focusing on differences *between* rather than *within* these groups will be helpful for the analysis of some overarching feminist ideas, as well as the degrees of convergence and divergence in feminist thought across cultures.

Why is it necessary to study common themes in women's issues and the variations of these common themes between radically different geographical and socio-political regions? Looking at Western feminisms through the eyes of East European and Third World women provides a double lens – a very provocative view, yet also an endeavor that attempts to widen the scope of the lens and provide a more in-clusive (though at times refracted) vision of Western feminisms. Moreover, such a cross–cultural comparison is especially significant in light of the current globaliza-tion processes which necessitate the approaching of feminist issues both situationally and relationally. Additionally, there are certain, more general, similarities in the situ-ation of post–communist countries, sometimes categorized as the "Second World", and those of the "Third World". In terms of technology, infrastructure, economy, and finances, both regions are clearly subordinated to the Western World (for example, through the structures of the International Monetary Fund, The World Bank, and other Western–centered institutions), even though the degree of subordination may vary. There are also some common features in these countries that are related to the transition to democracy and a free market such as: the economy, fluctuating class stratification, poverty, and family issues. Finally, East European and Third World women both have a similarly ambiguous attitude of both acceptance and rejection in regards to Western feminist theories and practices. For example, in the past decade and a half, East European women have demonstrated a growing engagement with feminist theories and practices (such as: women's NGO activism, the opening of women's studies centers and gender programs, an increasing amount of research on women's issues, changes in legislation, and women's protests against poverty or the war in ex–Yugoslavia, amongst others).[2] However, for the majority, the discourses of resistance to feminism, including the label "feminism" itself, prevail. In a similar manner, many women activists in Latin America and Africa, as well as Black women in the United States, have become far more mobilized in their struggles against sex-ism and sexual oppression, especially when analyzed against the background of the backlash against feminism that spread within the United States, Canada, and Great Britain during the 1980s (in the wake of Reagan, Bush, Mulroney, and Thatcher politics). However, even these women have expressed their suspicion and criticisms of Western feminist theory.[3]

By drawing such brave parallels of "diverse similitude", I am far from suggesting that the experiences of Third World women are identical to those of East European women. However, I believe that their visions and revisions of Western feminist theory (perhaps because of their "belated" entrance into the second wave of feminism) pose similar questions about the validity of certain assumptions and theories that attempt to embrace "global" feminist developments, such as: the universality of feminist goals and methods, "the equality of rights" agenda, the role of patriarchy, and the easy alliance between feminism and Marxism.

Questioning the Universality of Feminist Goals and Methods

Since the 1980s, many feminist scholars have illuminated the social and cultural context in which "female" identity is located by writing about the limits of universalism. For example, in her theories, Judith Butler cautions against the politics of universality by proposing that women are constructed as subjects of sex, gender, and desire:

> The political assumption that there must be a universal basis for feminism, one which must be found in an identity assumed to exist cross–culturally often accompanies the notion that the oppression of women has some singular form, discernible in the universal or hegemonic structure of patriarchy or masculine domination (1990, 3).

Even earlier, Third World feminists also called attention to the fallacies of essentialism present in any claims of a homogeneous "womanhood", "woman's culture," or "patriarchal oppression of women."[4] They claimed that race plays the role of a metalanguage by calling attention to its powerful, embracing effect on the construction and representation of other social and power relations, namely gender, class, and sexuality. Black women historians have largely refrained from an analysis of gender based only along the lines of the female/male dichotomy and, at the threshold of the twenty–first century, they continue to emphasize "the inseparable unity of race and gender," because the separation of the two would "bifurcate the identity of Black women (and indeed, of all women) into discrete categories" (Higginbotham 1996, 18).

At the beginning of her article, "Under Western Eyes: Feminist Scholarship and Colonial Discourses," Chandra Mohanty describes the orientation of Third World feminists to the politics of Western feminism in the following way: "Any discussion of the intellectual and political construction of "third world feminism" must address itself to two simultaneous projects: an internal critique of hegemonic "Western" feminisms and the formulation of autonomous, geographically, historically, and culturally grounded feminist concerns and strategies" (1991, 51). Here Mohanty delineates two seemingly oppositional projects: one which is focused on "deconstructing and dismantling" and the second which is focused on "building and constructing." Emerging East European feminisms are engaged in a similar double–sided project: on the one hand, they are critically appropriating and subverting established Western feminist models, while on the other hand, they are striving to construct their own feminist identity and politics. Mohanty analyzes the Western discursive forms of appropriation and codification of scholarship and knowledge in their writings on Third

World women. She argues that Western writing functions as a colonizing act by producing ethnocentric universalism (which implies that sources of oppression and identification are the same everywhere). She claims that, by employing particular analytic categories, some Western feminists are constructing a simplistic and incorrect image of the average "monolithic third world woman" as "sexually constrained, ignorant, poor, uneducated, tradition–bound, domestic, family oriented, [and] victimized" versus the implicit self–presentation of Western women as "educated, modern women who have control over their bodies and sexualities, and the freedom to make their own decisions" (Mohanty 1991, 56).

Some East European feminists have voiced similar objections to the same Western analytic, methodological, and political principles discussed by Mohanty. For example, Hana Havelkova claims that "the tensions in the dialogue between Western and East European women are rooted in the direct application of Western feminist theory to post–communist reality," which leads to the false assumption that, "East–European women are second–class citizens, and that they are conservative" (1996, 243). Other scholars have commented on how East European women refuse to see themselves as "backward, apolitical, full of apathy," and in return, call Western feminists "an international messianic brigade, banging the drums of feminism, implicitly universalizing and brainwashing, and thus imperialistic" (Busheikin 1997, 141). In addition, East European feminists point to other dangers of positing feminist knowledge as Western-centered. Marina Blagojević claims that the "strong and indisputable imposition of Western theories" places feminists in the region in an asymmetrical position to Western feminists because they become "transmitters of Western knowledge but not creators" (2003, 145). Ralitsa Muharska explains how the gaps in the communication between the feminist communities of the East and West have created "silences, distortions, and parodic effects" in feminist discourses that are the result of the unequal positioning of power resources in the marginal East and the dominant West (2005, 93).[5] Most of these apprehensions and critiques are related to the strategy of "universalizing," that is, believing that the category of "women" is an already constituted group with identical interests, goals, and priorities regardless of their locations (hence, the false analytical assumptions about certain universal gender and sexual difference across cultures, as well as the political prescriptions derived from these analytic strategies).

One such example of failing to transmit Western feminist knowledge across cultures is Betty Friedan's feminist agenda in her work, *The Feminine Mystique*, which has been heralded as having paved the way for the contemporary feminist movement. When I teach the book, my Bulgarian students complain that the concerns of middle–class suburban housewives, that are articulated in the outcry "I want something more than my husband and my children and my home," in other words, "I want a career," sound outdated and irrelevant (1963, 29). Of course, Friedan's conclusion that being a housewife creates a "sense of emptiness and non–existence" is important in historical terms, but, from the perspective of women in Eastern Europe, it provides thin ground for them to identify with. The major reason behind this divergence in responses to Friedan is the fact that in the West during the 1960s (and to a great extent the present day), a middle–class woman's identity was shaped by her role as a wife, her duty to attend to the needs of her children and husband, and the lifestyle related to this role; whereas, under communism, the majority of East European women were overworked and simultaneously performing the triple role of "mother", "working class hero", and "socialist citizen." We should also keep in mind that what Friedan calls an "occupational housewife" was a phenomenon that did not exist under communism and is only now emerging during Eastern Europe's transition to capitalism. Thus, we as East European women have had a different sense of women's identity, as relatively financially independent of the husband figure but closely related to the communist state. We have not yet experienced the Western's "cult of domesticity", "beauty myths", and consumerism. Instead, we have internalized the socialist myth of "the superwoman" – combining domestic and social obligations, often at the cost of sacrifice, self–effacement, and self–negation. Therefore, we may sympathize with the plight of educated middle–class housewives but cannot accept these tenets as a manifesto of a feminist movement in our post–communist condition. In a similar manner, bell hooks rejects Friedan's one–dimensional perspective of women's reality, claiming that "it is a case study of narcissism, insensitivity, sentimentality and self–indulgence," because it ignores "the needs of women without men, without children, without homes, that is, the masses of American women" (1984, 3).

The early feminist belief that it is women's position as "second–class citizens", with unequal opportunities, who suffer oppression and exploitation at the hands of men, is yet another universalist claim that does not communicate in the same way across cultures and, in the case of East European women, has failed to communicate at all. This position of being "worse" and "powerless" is taken for granted, and women's status as victims is often seen as the common denominator of women's issues. There are two very dangerous implications at work in this presupposition. First, female bonding as "victims" devalues women's sense of achievements; it is self–defeating, depriving them of strength, and a sense of responsibility. Such an ideology cannot work among East European women because most of them consider themselves self–sufficient, educated, emancipated, and have an occupation. I have heard so many East European women state: "Why should I be a feminist? I don't feel inferior to men!" Of course, we should keep in mind that the myths of gender–equality have so deeply entered mass consciousness that still there is very little sensitivity and awareness of real gender dynamics, and this is further coupled with ignorance and negative stereotypes of what feminism stands for. Victimization as a unifying basis for feminism, has also been rejected by Black feminists such as bell hooks who states that: "Rather than repudiating this equation (which mystifies female experience – in their daily lives most women are not continually passive, helpless or powerless 'victims'), women's liberationists embraced it, making shared victimization the basis for woman bonding" (1984, 45).

The other dangerous implication behind the common denominator of women's "worse position" is that it simultaneously springs from and produces the supposedly accepted notion of the "universality of women's oppression." While I do not intend to enter a discussion of the various types of oppression and their rankings because it is both counter productive and can obscure the roots of women's oppression; what I do find most dangerous in relation to this discussion is the implication that there is one single type of oppression (in this case, sexist oppression) because this belief automatically precludes the discussion of other forms of oppression, and deprives feminism of a more inclusive framework. In connection to this, Mohanty argues that Third World women's victimization is not only the result of men, but also of colonial processes, economic development processes, the Arab familial system, and the Islamic code, among other things. In a similar way, Johnson–Odim concludes, "gender discrimination is neither the sole nor perhaps the primary locus of women's oppression" (1991, 320). From her comparative view–point, First World women's oppression is linked to gender and class relations, whereas, for Third World, there are two added dimensions: race and imperialism. These are some of the reasons why Third World feminists have continued to address the problem of a feminism that is too narrowly defined.[6] Some have gone even further: for example, Alice Walker rejects the term "feminism" because it does not take into account the problems of Black women and she instead proposes an agenda of "womanism" or "feminism of color."

> A womanist," she says, "is a Black feminist, a woman who loves other women, sexually and/or nonsexually, appreciates women's culture, women's emotional flexibility and strength, is committed to survival and wholeness of entire people, male *and* female … Loves music. Loves dance. Loves the Spirit. Loves love. Loves struggle … Loves herself. *Regardless* (1983, xi).

As we can see from this poetic definition, Walker's understanding of a political identity incorporates many other important issues. The inclusive aspects of Walker's "womanism" in many ways anticipated today's idea of "nomadic feminism" – which analyzes gender at the intersection of race, region, ethnicity, class, age, nationality, sexual orientation, as well as other individual differences, and seeks new interrelations that are non–phallocentric and non–ethnocentric.[7]

In my view, East European feminists have added another two, culturally specific dimensions to the feminist agenda: the role of the communist state or, in more general terms, the "political system" as well as the consequences of women's pseudo–emancipation. The communist legacy in relation to the so-called "woman's question" is a very complicated and double–edged issue. On the one hand, we cannot ignore the fact that during the 45 years of communism two generations of women were educated and entered the work force. On the other hand, however, we have to take into consideration how these achievements operated within the system of a state–managed economy and communist collectivist ideology. We cannot stay blind to the real motivation behind women's right to work: it was not designed as a sheer liberation project to empower women, instead it was grounded in the necessity to have a workforce that was doubled, therefore cheaper, in order to materialize the grand projects of the communist state. Exploited as they were, most women in Eastern Europe believed (and still believe) that under communism they had the same rights as men as far as: access to work, education, professional qualification, and political affiliation. "The myth about women's equality in the Soviet Union was never actually questioned – even today," says Olga Voronina (1994, 34). The communist rhetoric of duplicity did manage to convince women that they enjoyed special privileges as mothers and workers. I am not trying to diminish the significance of the latter, but we should keep in mind that some of these options were small or non–existent privileges. For example, it would not have been possible for women to work on construction sites, in factories and offices, and simultaneously give birth and raise children, if they did not have access to childcare facilities and longer maternity leave. Presently, the obvious regression in women's status and the restrictions of some rights have evoked nostalgic feelings about socialism.[8] Yet, it is very difficult to make women realize that we were complicit in our own over–exploitation, that we were given some rights, but at the expense of being deprived of other important human rights – such as the right to freedom, self–expression, individual choice, and mobility.

Questioning the Narrowness of "the Equality of Rights Agenda"

The controversial communist legacy of women in Eastern Europe raises some questions about the liberal feminist agenda of "equality of rights," that is, securing women's social, political, and economic parity with men. Feminism begins with a keen awareness of exclusion from the male-dominated social and political order. If East European women did not have a feeling of exclusion from male social, political, sexual, cultural and intellectual power (as illusionary as this feeling is), what else could they want? Liberal feminist theory cannot explain this gender trap. By working within existing social and political structures, liberal feminism's framework proves to be too narrow to explain the ambiguous situatedness of socialist women who are simultaneously located *inside* and *outside* power relations. This is because liberal feminism fails to address the conditions that produce gender inequality masked as gender–neutrality. It also does not challenge the power mechanisms of the state, the place from which women's illusions and problems stem. The fact that the majority of women worked outside their homes may seem an impressive achievement, but when we look at this "right" as a compulsory service to the state and the family, as a continual struggle to fulfill the dual demands of performance and efficiency both inside and outside the home, work is no longer a self–fulfilling activity, it becomes a double or triple burden.

Many women in Eastern Europe have complained that they feel like "the working mule of the world" – which echoes the statements of many Black American writers (for example, Zora Neal Hurston, Lorraine Hansberry, Alice Walker, and Toni Morrison). Quandra Prettyman argues that Black women have had a natural relationship with feminism because of their quest for economic security or personal fulfill-ment, but some Black women turned away from the women's movement because it seemed to offer nothing new. "For some of us," she says, "rights were already burdens" (1996, 17). How can "rights" be burdens? It is evident especially now, in the new realities when the overall and repeated crises in practically all spheres of life (economy, society, morality, and so on) have predominantly burdened the female part of the population. Michaela Miroiu calls the transitional situation of post-com-munist women a transformation from "pseudo–power to lack of power," and sum-marizes the disparity between women's situation in Eastern Europe and in the West with the following contrast: "While women in the West were fighting for emancipa-tion, East European women were struggling for the survival of their families in harsh conditions" (1994, 108). The changing social conditions in the last decade and a half also demand a serious investigation of the intersection of gender with social posi-tion, and the category of class during the current restratification of post- communist societies. It is only now that we are discovering all the dynamic differences created by the intersection of class, nation, ethnicity, religion, gender, and sexual orientation that had been suppressed and masked before as "sameness" and "equality," and have now exploded (or imploded rather).[9]

The liberal feminist agenda of the "equality of rights" has already been criticized by radical cultural and materialist feminist theorists in the West. In my view, the ex-periences of women from Eastern Europe and the Third World again show that this agenda is both limited and limiting because it does not meet the different priorities and goals of women who confront other sources of oppression – be it imperialism or totalitarianism, overexploitation, poverty, crime, democracy, or economic transition – which therefore points to the need to challenge all systems of oppression in order to envision greater social transformations through feminist practices.

Redefining the System of Patriarchy

From a feminist point of view, patriarchy is usually defined as a subcategory of male dominance. According to Heidi Hartmann it is: "a set of social relations which has a material base and in which there are hierarchical relations between men, and solidarity among them, which enable them to control women. Patriarchy is thus the system of male oppression of women" (1983, 194). There are many variations of the feminist definition of patriarchy (for example, Gayle Rubin argues that we should instead use the term "sex/ gender system" to refer to the realm outside the economic system where gender stratification based on sex differences is produced and repro-duced), but they all boil down to the status of women defined primarily as wards of their husbands, fathers and brothers, that is, at the household level.[10] So far there have been numerous studies of the link between the gender and generational aspects of patriarchal structures, of how fatherhood (family headship) is a source of power over both women and children through its control over the labor of family members, marriage and property, or of how the development of capitalism has transformed patriarchal institutions and so on.

However, little research has been done on the intersection of patriarchy with the communist system. The communist state, the so called "Father–state," that operated in the Soviet block countries, used similar structures of control, combining the idea of fathering and masculinity. In fact, the very existence of the so called "woman's question," (which sounds like women posing a problem) and the way it was handled, is a conspicuous form of patronizing attitude. Some Western feminist scholars, for example Nanette Funk, have wondered whether the conservative tendencies with regard to women in the current East European transitional context are "an expression of a cultural system that pre–dated communism (that is, patriarchy) but had been held in check by the Marxist system, or whether they are a result of the Marxist system itself" (1993, 8). I believe that the relationship between patriarchy and communism in Eastern Europe was not one of rupture *or* continuity but rather of overlap and contemporaneity, where the two systems mutually reinforced each other – that is, patriarchy indoctrinated women on the family level that sexist oppression and women's sacrifice were "natural," while the state expanded the content of the sacrificial contract with women, and inculcated values supportive of hierarchical gendered control and coercive authority on a more general level.[11]

In what sense was the communist state another agent of patriarchy for women? With its constant practices of panopticism and surveillance, it acted as a paternalistic agent prescribing women to work both inside and outside the family, interfering into the private sphere, and even controlling women's bodies. For example, the legal right to abortion was recognized in Bulgaria in 1957, but it was restricted in 1968 and in the 1980s due to pro–natalist state policy.[12] In addition, the communist patriarchal state took care of political decision making, it policed individual desires and goals, prescribing norms of femininity and masculinity, speaking for (or rather against) the individual self, limiting social interaction, imposing censorship on the media, art, and education – through diverse strategies of muting individual forms of expression through a collective political voice. Thus, women's subordination in Eastern Europe was a result of the combination of both *collective male power* and *individual male power*, exercised in a very manipulative manner, coated in the hypocritical rhetoric of "paternalistic" care for the well being and security of all socialist citizens, especially women and children. Unlike in the West, women's oppression was carried out through a very different structuring of women's lives: for example, through the decrees of the Communist party, directives at the work place, and promotion policy. For that reason, East European gender analysts diagnosed, and still diagnose, the sources of their oppression differently from Western feminists. The best case in point is the so–called "German" example. After the fall of the Berlin Wall, women from East Germany and West Germany diverged when it came to identifying women's problems. Susan Gal sums up the controversial role of the socialist state institutions as follows:

East German women's already deep involvement in the labor force prevented them from seeing wage work as the solution of gender inequality that it was taken to be in the West. Rather, they analyzed their problem as the extensive intrusion of the state into their lives and bodies, and as usurpation by the state of men's role in families. The paternalist social-ist state provided benefits such as generous maternity leaves for women, but also infan-tilized the entire population, taking over the "paternal role" of men directly through sup-port of children and the socialization of some household functions. In contrast, the gender regimes of parliamentary welfare states more standardly work by delegating power over women to individual men in the families. These states support the relative power of men by indirect involvement in families through tax law, property and family law, and in al-lowing or encouraging the different bargaining power of men and women in labor markets among other means (1996, 77).

Regardless of the manner of state intervention – direct or indirect – both men and women in the Soviet block countries identified the "system" as the major source of oppression: women thought it usurped men's role in the family or provided in-sufficient help; whereas men considered themselves emasculated by the totalitarian structures, which deprived them of freedom, personal dignity, and economic power. The example of East German women also demonstrates how patriarchal structures functioned beyond the family level, which necessitates a revision and expansion of the understanding of patriarchy beyond the level of the family. In a similar vein of thought, Myra Ferree claims that, for East Germans, the conventional woman was not at the disposal of an individual man, but was "instrumentalized by the state as pa-triarch" (2000, 513). From a comparative East to West perspective she distinguishes between two types of patriarchal state systems: that of East Germany (the German Democratic Republic [GDR]) which reflected the system of "public patriarchy," and that of West Germany (the Federal Republic of Germany [FRG]) – which reflected the system of "private patriarchy":

> In the ex–GDR, state policy tended to diminish the dependence of women on individual husbands and fathers, but it enhanced the dependence of women as mothers on the state, whereas in the FRG, the nature of the state's role in private patriarchy was to encourage wives' dependence on husbands and children's on parents (Ferree 2000, 512).

In simpler terms, it can be said that in "public patriarchy" the state provides support for "its" mothers, whereas in "private patriarchy" husbands support their wives.

I have some reservations about the terms "private" and "public patriarchies" both because of their different functioning in history, and also because I see the two types of power over women as overlapping rather than divided.[13] However, I do find the so-called "German example" a very revealing explanation of the different feminist visions of the East and West, as well as the double–bind of East European women's simultaneous dependence on the father–state and their relative financial indepen-dence from marital structures. Yet, this cannot necessarily be called "emancipation". Perhaps that is why we often ironically called the patriarchal state a "step–mother," that is, seemingly but not genuinely caring. Another aspect of the patriarchal state policy was the distribution of labor along gender lines: in the "house" of the communist state, most women were working in the low-paid ranks of the state industry or service sector, metaphorically speaking, "doing the chores", while men held the top posts in the administrative, political, and industrial structures.

Third World women have expressed similar reactions to oppressive forces outside the family enclosure – in terms of colonizing or imperialist forces. They speak of justice not only at the household level but also within the local, national, and world economic order.

"Feminism should be a philosophy and a movement for social justice: addressing issues of racism, economic exploitation (that is, problems of nutrition, infant mortality, illiteracy, health–care, and skill training), and imperialism," says Johnson Odim (1991, 321). In the United States, Black feminists have already demanded a better welfare system, more access to health insurance, and decent housing and education for their children. In broader terms, Third World feminists' demands – for better childcare and literacy, the eradication of poverty, economic opportunities, anti–discrimination laws, and representation in state and national politics – are not foreign to East European women. I am far from suggesting that Third World women's experiences with a racist and/or imperialist state are identical to East European women's experiences with the communist state, but I believe that in their critiques of the narrow feminist agenda and definitions both pose serious questions to the project of a global feminism.

If we extend the analysis of oppressive patriarchal structures to those operating beyond the family level, additional parallels can be drawn between Third World women and East European women. Both have a more flexible dynamic for coalitions with men. Both see men more as "comrades in struggle" than Western feminists. This is because of their respective histories; both groups of women have often formed joint alliances with men against things such as imperialistic policy or apartheid, as well as against the communist regime.[14] Some Black women stress the fact that Black men often felt emasculated by the imperialist, colonialist, or racist regimes and states, which is reminiscent of the feelings of emasculation imposed on men of the former Soviet block countries by the communist totalitarian practices. Gloria Joseph notes that because of the legacy of slavery, "Black women have as much in common, in terms of their oppression, with Black men as they do with White women" (1981, 96). It is on this ground that Third World women are still more likely to welcome coalitions with men than Western feminists despite possible tensions and co–optation strategies.

East European women have voiced a similar appeal in their attempts to bring men into a more central role within the family and involve them in social transformation activities, such as: education, fighting pornography, drug abuse, and the trafficking of women. This is primarily based on their previous positive experiences of joint resistance with men in their fights against the communist regime as well as their joint experience of relying on the family for survival during the communist regime.[15] In times of crisis the family often functions as a support system in opposition to the culture at large. In the communist years the family was one of the few zones where both men and women felt relatively free from the surveillance of the state, and could resist the collectivist pressure. Despite the practices of male oppression in the family, the family often created a powerful foundation for strategies of everyday resistance as well.[16] Withdrawal into the family space as a form of privacy from state coercion is another common theme that is featured in Black feminist thought. Hooks summarizes Black women's traditionally strong attachment to family structures, as follows:

> While there are White women activists who may experience family primarily as an oppressive institution, many Black women find the family the least oppressive institution. Despite sexism, in the context of the family, we may experience dignity, self–worth, and a humanization that is not experienced in the outside world wherein we confront all forms of oppression (1984, 37).

Black women note that the Black church and the Black family, both woman–centered and Afrocentric institutions, have given them enormous support and useful knowledge throughout history. Similarly, the strong attachment to the family has been listed by some East European scholars as one of the factors behind the anti–feminist tendencies in post–communist countries.[17] However, such statements are very often accompanied by the false assumption that feminism wants to destroy "the sacred" family – as if echoing the loud cry for "family values" by the conservative right in North America and their charges against feminists.

Questioning the Automatic Alliance between Feminism and Marxism

As I have already mentioned Marxist ideological discourses, intertwined with the official Communist Party politics, asserted the homogenization of gender relations under communism. In theory, Marxist ideology aspired to erase social inequality, to break down the "petty bourgeois" social and sexual contracts, and to achieve a radical transformation of the patriarchal family. However, in practice Marxist ideology did not legitimize women's status, on the contrary, it constantly obscured it. Despite the promises of socialism to alter women's role at the level of production, women's status never became equal to that of men. In practice, the marriage of feminism and Marxism did not happen in the communist bloc.[18] The few women's organizations that existed before 1945 were suspended when the communist regime was established. For example, The Bulgarian Association of University Women (established in 1924 under the auspices of the International Federation of University Women), was banned by the communist state in 1947, its property was confiscated, and its archives were destroyed, under the pretext that, from that moment on, the Communist Party was to take care of Bulgarian women as well as their international contacts. The history of the Neofeminist Movement in Yugoslavia that emerged during the

1970s is another example of how the Marxist state displaced women's structures and concerns. Rada Iveković discusses the attacks on the movement in 1978, when it was accused of "six mortal sins," such as "preaching imported capitalist ideology, the love for power, elitism, uninstitutional activities, and apoliticilization," but mostly because of its "severing [of] the relation of class with the woman's question" (Iveković and Drakulić 1984, 736). These accusations are doubly ironic: first, because the movement was grounded in Marxist philosophy, and second, because the "woman's question" did not exist in Eastern Europe – it was always postponed or put aside in order to address other more important questions such as production efficiency, the building of canals and roads, the cold war threat, and so on. Anastasia Posadskaya tells a similar story about Russia, where the "woman's question" was quickly placed within other categories of social transformation: "Soon after the Revolution, the Bolsheviks acted swiftly to merge the "woman question" into their overall social transformation" (1994, 8). In addition to these more obvious practices of suppressing feminist ideas, there were many other invisible walls erected between women's desires and Marxist dogmas. For example, sexuality issues were constantly toned down, defined as "unhealthy," and if they were analyzed at all, it was only done in gender–neutral terms, which created a feeling that citizens were uniform and sexless creatures, simply a caste of workers. Thus, as women, we were invisible – except in our capacity as "workers" and "mothers."

Many theorists have discussed the uneasy alliance between Marxism and Western feminism, the phenomenon of "socialist feminism," as well as the curious courtship of women's liberation and socialism.[19] Catherine MacKinnon claims that the synthesis between Marxism and feminism is impossible because of the antagonism between the two in terms of methodology:

> Feminism stands in relation to Marxism as Marxism does to classical political economy: its final conclusion and ultimate critique. Compared with Marxism, the place of thought and things in method and reality are reversed in a seizure of power that penetrates subject with object and theory with practice. In a dual motion, feminism turns Marxism inside out and on its head (1983, 256).

MacKinnon's analysis of the construction of feminist knowledge as having no single "author" or "authority figure" and that it is a form of "collective authorship" is extremely pertinent from the perspective of East European women. Our experience with the Marxist state, where women's personal lives did not matter, where the private, emotional, and intimate stories were erased by the single narrative of "class consciousness," proves MacKinnon's point of the uneasy alliance between feminism and Marxism in many ways. If feminism is the "theory of women's point of view" as she says, springing from "the sphere that has been socially lived as the personal," it simply could not have taken place in the traumatic communist space (1983, 247).

"The Personal is Political" – what does this feminist slogan mean? We, as East European women, still cannot grasp its meaning. Many other liberal concepts such as "equality," "emancipation," and "the woman's question," are seen as empty and corrupted slogans and because of the Marxist legacy they continue to cynically reverberate throughout Eastern Europe today. Thus, the situation of feminism in the region is quite ironic: in communist years, it was considered redundant because it was associated with bourgeois ideology and dividing the proletariat; now, after the changes, it is still a dirty word – this time, because it is associated with leftist collectivist ideology, the smacking of Leninism, Bolshevism and Marxism. Thus, feminism has always been the odd one out.

From the perspective of some Third World scholars, the relationship among feminism, Marxism, and race also forms an "incompatible ménage a trois," as Gloria Joseph calls it, because race has been left out of the triangle of power dynamics. (1981, 104) Despite the possibilities offered by Marxist philosophy to explore material social conditions and the vision of subordinated oppressed groups, the major objections posed by Third World feminists against Marxist social theory derive from the fact that it is still an analysis of social structure that is rooted in the Western dichotomous thinking of either/or and it ignores the personal experiences of Black women.

I believe that the feminist validation of personal knowledge – no matter whether it comes from the West or the Third World, could be extremely empowering for East European women in the current context. After decades of living "from the point of view" of Lenin, Marx, and Krupskaya we now have the unique chance to live and know from a woman's "first person singular/ plural point of view." [20]

Conclusion

From the discussion so far it is clear that emerging East European feminism(s) are located in a different spatio–temporality and, as a result of this, produce a disrupting effect on some grand narratives – including that of Feminism (when approached as a unified master–discourse), of Eurocentricism (that is, the idea that Western Europe is the hegemonic center and progenitor of theories which are universally applicable), and of Marxism (having failed to materialize the promise of women's equality). In the current situation of transition, these disruptions are sometimes expressed in a series of paradoxical social paradigms: for example, building a civil society but not making any room for feminist movements in it, liberal democracy's displacement of women, the rise of postmodern culture, accompanied by pre–modern processes of the re–traditionalization of women's roles, and the dismantling of the communist legacy simultaneously accompanied by a nostalgia for it. As a result of this, many Western scholars are confused when they confront the current, controversial, East European scene: "The notions of democracy, human rights, feminism, etc. so central to Western theory suddenly lost their established meanings when communism collapsed ... All these supposedly universal notions became incorporated into new political discourses in surprising and sometimes disturbing ways" (Salecl 1994, 1).

In my opinion, the recent developments and experiences of women in Eastern Europe serve both as a confirmation and as a challenge to the question of the universal phases and understanding of women's emancipation. The lived experience of women from Eastern Europe and the Third World includes both degrees of autonomy and degrees of incorporation of Western feminist knowledge and practices, as well as struggles between the two tendencies. East European feminism's double–sided project of deconstruction and construction implies both the need to de–mask the false mythology of gender–neutrality, sameness, women's rights, and "privileges" (innocently internalized under communism) as well as the need to question gender dichotomy as the single platform on which feminism can rest. Like Third World women, East European women see gender as a useful analytical category that has to be pieced together with all other social, cultural, and political categories such as race, social position, nation, ethnicity, religion, regional specifics, democracy, and political system – thus they envision greater social transformations through feminist practices. Therefore, these local inflections of feminism insist on a more comprehensive feminist framework that incorporates, yet transcends gender–specificity, enabling it to be capable of responding to current global rearrangements.

Notes

[1] For more differentiated and precise data on women's social and economic rights in the 29 countries in the region of Eastern Europe, see *Women 2000. 2000. An Investigation into the Status of Women's Rights in Central and South-Eastern Europe and the Newly Independent States*. Vienna: International Helsinki Federation for Human Rights.

[2] Women's engagement in feminist theory and practices varies drastically across the region in view of the different priorities in each country as well as their feminist history or pre-history. For example, theorists from Croatia and Serbia have made significant contributions in terms of analyzing women's victimization during war, the intersection of gender with ethnicity, nation, and nationalism issues. Polish feminists have also been more active in the region because of their longer tradition (going back to the 1980s), as well as their activism against legal restrictions on abortion in Poland in the 1990s.

[3] Women's activism in Africa, Latin America, Asia, and other regions has been discussed in detail in Amrita Basu ed. 1995. *The challenge of local feminism: women's movements in a global perspective*. London: Westview Press.

[4] For critiques of false universalism in feminist theory, see Gloria T. Hull and Patricia Scott, eds. 1982. *But some of us are brave* . NY: Feminist Press.; Barbara Smith, ed. 1983. *Home girls - A black feminist anthology*. NY: Women of Color Press.; Bonnie Dill. 1983. Race, class, and gender: Prospects for an all-inclusive Sisterhood. *Feminist Studies* 9:131–50.

[5] For more on feminist divergences East/West see: Jana Hradlikova Smejkalova and J. Siklova 1994. *Bodies of bread and butter: Reconfiguring women's lives in the Czech Republic*. Prague: Prague Gender Studies Centre; Hana Havelkova. 1993. A few prefeminst thoughts. In *Gender Politics and Postcommunism*, edited by N. Funk and M. Mueller. New York: Routledge; as well as the cluster of articles devoted to feminism in Hungary,

Romania and the Czech Republic in *Replika: Colonization or Partnership? Eastern Europe and Western Social Sciences*. Budapest: University of Economic Sciences.

6   See bell hooks. 1984. *Feminist theory*. Boston: South End Press.; Cherre Moraga and Gloria Anzaldua, eds. 1981. *This bridge called my back: Writings by radical women of color*. Watertown, MA: Persephone Press.; Barbara Smith, ed. 1983. *Home girls: A black feminist anthology*. NY: Women of Color Press.; Alil Mari Tripp. 2000. Rethinking difference: Comparative Perspectives from Africa. *Signs* 25 (3):649–675.

7   I am referring to Rosi Braidotti's idea of feminist nomadic thinking, in which she analyzes sexual difference at the intersection of differences between men and women, differences among women, and differences within each woman (Braidotti, 1994).

8   Statistics from the European Union show that, in 2002, women from Central and East European countries were paid 30 percent less than men; their participation in politics has drastically decreased (e.g. 6 percent women MPs in the Romanian Parliament, 10 percent in the Bulgarian National Assembly, 11.1 percent in the Czech Senate); and they have been affected by unemployment to a greater extent. The economic changes have also affected women in their capacity of major caregivers because kindergarten services, medical care and higher education are no longer free of charge in many countries in the region (see "European Integration in Numbers," *AnA Magazine,* 2002, vol. 12). In addition, women's freedom to abortion has become worse. For example, in 1997 the Polish Parliament delegalized and restricted earlier abortion laws; in 1995 the German Parliament passed a modified law, which did not legalize abortion but merely decriminalized it, strengthening the state's ability to exert moral pressure on abortion providers and women seeking abortions. The only dramatic exception is Romania, where in December 1989, immediately after Ceausescu regime was overthrown, the earlier repressive abortion legislation was repealed (see S. Gal and G. Kligman, eds.. 2000. *Reproducing Gender.* Princeton: Princeton University Press).

9   Some of these relatively new intersections of gender with other social categories have become extremely poignant issues, for example the war in ex-Yugoslavia has highlighted the importance of gender in national and ethnic conflicts – see Rada Iveković. 2002. Women, nationalism, and war. In *Selected papers: Anniversary issue of the Belgrade Women's Studies Center*. Belgrade; Marina Blagojević. 2000. Misogyny: Invisible causes, painful consequences. In *Mapiranje Mizoginije U Srbji: Discursi I Prakse.* Beograd: Cicero. The different social position of women in unified Germany has made more visible the connection between gender and class (see Irene Dolling. 1994. Women's experiences "above" and "below": How East German women experience and interpret their situation after the unification of the two German states. *The European Journal of Women's Studies* 1:29–42.)

10 Kate Millet claims that "patriarchy's chief institution is the family" in Kate Millet. 1969. *Sexual Politics*. Ballantine Books, 31. For more diverse feminist interpretations on patriarchy, see Gayle Rubin. 1975. The Traffic in Women. In *toward an anthropology of women*, edited by R. Reiter. Monthly Review Press.

11 Olga Voronina's article Soviet patriarchy: Past and present. *Hypatia* 8(4) provides useful insights into this non-traditional approach to patriarchy.

12 The pro-natalist policies in Bulgaria in the 1980s were carried out in two directions: first, restrictions on abortion (especially for married women who had only one or two children) and second, incentives for giving birth (such as two-year paid maternity leave, advantages for student-mothers, monthly bonuses for each child, state funding of day-care centers and

kindergartens, and others). The Bulgarian Parliament adopted a liberalized abortion law in 1990.

[13] Susan Gal and Gail Kligman have pointed out that the private/public dichotomy works like a fractal distinction because the two are constantly subject to reframing and subdivisions in which some parts of the public are redefined as private and vice versa. See Susan Gal and Gail Kligman. 2000. *The politics of gender after Socialism.* Princeton: Princeton University Press, 37–62.

[14] Patricia Collins explains that on certain dimensions, Black women may more closely resemble Black men, on others, white women, and on still other issues Black women may stand apart from both groups. She calls this more flexible position "a both/or orientation, the act of simultaneously being a member of a group, and yet standing apart from it" (Collins 1989, 746).

[15] See Myra Ferree's discussion of the tendency for feminists in East Germany to talk more positively about the family, and especially men's relationship to children (Ferree 2000, 515). See also Hana Havelkova's analysis of the greater supportive role and significance of the family in the Czech Republic (Havelkova 1996, 244).

[16] I have explored in greater detail the ambiguous place of the family unit under communism in Kornelia Slavova 1995. The family enclosure in the Bulgarian context. *The European Journal of Women's Studies* 2:21–32.

[17] For example, Jirina Siklova and Jana Hradlikova. 1997. Women and violence, In *Ana's Land. Sisterhood in Eastern Europe,* ed. by T. Renne. Westview Press, 82–87). Most of the articles about the women's situation in Poland, the Czech Republic, Hungary, and Romania in that book mention the special role of the family as a survival mechanism under communism.

[18] Some studies from China and Cuba show that work relations were changed, but sex relations were not overturned. See, for example, Julia Kristeva. 1977. *About Chinese Women.* Urizen Books.; Margaret Randall. 1974. *Cuban women now.* Women's Press.

[19] See Amy Bridges. The unhappy marriage of Marxism and feminism: Towards a new union. (Quoted in Hartmann 1983. Capitalism, Patriarchy and Job Segregation, 234).; Batya Weinbaum. 1978. *The Curious Courtship of Women's Liberation and Socialism.* Boston: South End Press.; Ann Foreman. 1977. *Femininity as alienation: Women and the family in Marxism and psychoanalysis.* London: Pluto Press.

[20] Nadezhda Krupskaya was a Russian revolutionary and wife of Vladimir Lenin.

References

Basu, Amrita, ed. 1995. *The challenge of local feminism. Women's movements in a global perspective.* Boulder: Westview Press.

Blagojević, Marina. 2003. Creators, transmittors, and users: Women's scientific excellence at the periphery of Europe. In *Gender and excellence in the making.* Brussels: European Commission Research Publications.

Braidotti, Rosi. 1994. *Nomadic subjects: Embodiment and sexual difference in contemporary feminist thought.* New York: Columbia University Press.

Busheikin, Laura. 1997. Is Sisterhood Global? In *Ana's land: Sisterhood in Eastern Europe,* edited by T. Renne. Boulder: Westview Press.

Butler, Judith. 1990. *Gender trouble. Feminism and the subversion of identity.* New York: Routledge.

Collins, Patricia Hills. 1989. The social construction of Black feminist thought. *Signs: Journal of Women in Culture and Society* 4:745–773.

Dill, Bonnie. 1983. Race, class and gender: Prospects for an all–inclusive sisterhood. *Feminist Studies* 9:31–50.

Dolling, Irene. 1994. Women's experiences "above" and "below": How East German women experience and interpret their situation after the unification of the two German states. *The European Journal of Women's Studies* 1:29–42.

Ferree, Myra Marx. 2000. Patriarchies and feminisms: The two women's movements of post–unification Germany. In *Feminist Frontiers,* edited by L. Richardson and V. Taylor. New York: McGraw Hill.

Friedan, Betty. 1963. *The Feminine Mystique.* London: Penguin Books.

Funk, Nanette. 1993. Introduction. Feminism from Eastern and Central Europe. *Hypatia* 4:1–14.

Gal, Susan. 1996. Feminism and civil society. *Replika. Hungarian Social Science Quarterly* 1:75–83.

Gal, Susan, and Gail Kligman. 2000a. *The politics of gender after Socialism.* New Jersey: Princeton University Press.

Gal, Susan, and Gail Kligman. 2000b. *Reproducing gender. Politics, publics, and everyday life after Socialism.* New Jersey: Princeton University Press.

Hartmann, Heidi. 1983. Capitalism, patriarchy, and job segregation by sex, in *The Signs reader: Women, gender, and scholarship*, edited by E. Abel. Chicago: The University of Chicago University Press.

Havelkova, Hana. 1996. Abstract citizenship? Women and power in the Czech Republic. *Social Politics* 5:243–260.

Higginbotham, Evelyn Brooks. 1996. African–American women's history and the metalanguage of race. In *Feminism Today,* edited by Joan Scott. Oxford: Oxford University Press.

hooks, bell. 1984. *Feminist theory: from margin to center.* Boston, MA: South End Press.

Hull, Gloria, and Patricia Scott, eds. 1982. *But some of us are brave.* Old Westbury, NY: Feminist Press.

Iveković, Rada. 2002. Women, nationalism and war: 'Make Love, Not War.' In *Selected papers: Anniversary issue of the Belgrade Women's Studies Center*, edited by J. Blagojević and D. Mileusnić. Belgrade: Women's Studies Center.

Iveković, Rada, and Slavenka Drakulić. 1984. Yugoslavia: Neofeminism and its mortal sins. In *Sisterhood is Global. The International Women's Movement Anthology*, edited by Robyn Morgan. Anchor Press, New York: Doubleday.

Johnson Odim, Cheryl. 1991. Common themes, different contexts. In *Third World women and the politics of feminism*, edited by C. Mohanty and A. Russo. Bloomington: Indiana University Press.

Joseph, Gloria. 1981. The incompatible ménage a trois: Marxism, feminism, and racism. In *Women and Revolution,* edited by L. Sargent. Boston: South End Press.

Kristeva, Julia. 1977. *About Chinese women.* New York: Urizen Books.

MacKinnon, Catherine. 1983. Feminism, Marxism, method, and the state: An agenda for theory. In *The Signs reader: Women, gender, and scholarship*, edited by E. Abel. Chicago: The University of Chicago University Press.

Millet, Kate. 1969. *Sexual Politics.* New York: Ballantine Books.

Miroiu, Michaela. 1994. Open space: From pseudo–power to lack of power. *The European Journal of Women's Studies* 1:106–112.

Mohanty, Chandra. 1991. Under Western eyes: Feminist scholarship and colonial discourses. In *Third World women and the politics of feminism*, edited by C. Mohanty and A. Rosso. Bloomington: Indiana University Press.

Moraga, Cherre, and Gloria Anzaldua, eds. 1981. *This bridge called my back: Writings by radical women of color.* Watertown, MA: Persephone Press.

Muharska, Ralitsa. 2005. Silences and parodies in the East/West feminist dialogue. *Lhomme.* Boehalu, Vienna–Koeln–Viemar 1(16):26.

Posadskaya, Anastasia, ed. 1994. *Women in Russia. A new era in Russian feminism.* London and New York: Verso.

Prettyman, Quandra. 1996. Visibility and difference: Black women in history and literature. In *The future of difference,* edited by H. Eisenstein and A. Jardine. New Brunswick, NJ: Rutgers University Press.

Rubin, Gayle. 1975. The traffic in women. In *Toward an anthropology of women,* edited by R. Reiter. New York: Monthly Review Press.

Salecl, Renata. 1994. *Victims and other enemies: The spoils of freedom, psychoanalysis, and feminism after the fall of Socialism.* London and New York: Routledge.

Scott, Hilda. 1974. *Does Socialism liberate women? Experiences from Eastern Europe.* Cambridge, Mass: Beacon Press.

Slavova–Merdjanska, Kornelia. 1995. The family enclosure in the Bulgarian context. *The European Journal of Women's Studies* 2:21–32.

Smejkalova, Jana, and Jirine Siklova. 1994. *Bodies of bread and butter: Reconfiguring women's lives in the Czech Republic.* Prague: Prague Gender Studies Centre.

Smith, Barbara, ed. 1983. *Home girls – A black feminist anthology.* NY: Kitchen Table: Women of Color Press.

Tripp, Alil Mari. 2000. Rethinking difference: Comparative perspectives from Africa. *Signs: Journal of Women in Culture and Society* 23:649–675.

Voronina, Olga. 1994. The mythology of women's emancipation in the USSR as the foundation for a policy of discrimination. In *Women in Russia: A new era in Russian feminism*, edited by A. Posadskaya. New York: Verso.

Walker, Alice. 1983. In *Search of our mother's gardens.* New York: Harcourt, Brace Jovanovich.

Women 2000. An Investigation into the Status of Women's Rights in Central and South–Eastern Europe and the Newly Independent States, International Helsinki Federation for Human Rights (IHF), Agens–Werk, Vienna.

*A version of this chapter was delivered as a public lecture at the Central European University, Budapest, in 2001. I would like to thank the HESP program for providing me with the opportunity to be a visiting scholar at CEU, as well as the colleagues and students who made valuable comments and suggestions in the discussion following the lecture.

Chapter 13

Women's NGOs in Central and Eastern Europe and the Former Soviet Union: The Imperialist Criticism[1]

Nanette Funk

In the 1970s and 1980s, development programs in Africa, Latin America, and Asia began to focus on non–governmental organizations [NGOs] as agents of political, economic, and social change. In the 1990s in postsocialist Central and East Europe and the former Soviet Union, an interest in the creation of a non–state sphere of civil society with active NGOs was high on the agenda of many international organizations, Western states, and funders, both state and private. Publicly, it was argued that increased citizen political participation was necessary for democracy and NGOs were an important vehicle for such participation.

Women's and feminist NGOs in the region came to be included in these strategies, albeit only a very small percentage of funding went to them. The United States' [US] Agency for International Development [USAID] funded US NGOs working in the region, including feminist NGOs, as well as women's and feminist NGOs in the region. The European Union [EU], through programs such as the Poland and Hungary Aid for Restructuring the Economy [PHARE] program and the Link Inter–European NGOs program [LIEN], and major foundations such as the Soros, MacArthur, and Ford Foundations, also funded women's and feminist NGOs working in the region.

At first sight, it would appear to be an unalloyed positive step to include women as agents of transformation of the state, institutions, and social policy and in the expansion of democracy. However, as Western support for NGOs has grown so has the criticism of them. In this paper I consider one set of criticisms as they bear on women's and feminist NGOs working in and for the region of and Central Europe and the former Soviet Union. I henceforth refer to any women's and feminist NGO in the region as a "local NGO" whether it is in a particular city or district, national, or regional so long as it is not a "Western" NGO. I examine different forms of what I refer to as the Imperialist Criticism, and what is right and wrong in them. I introduce a typology for categorizing forms of this argument, contrasting them with my own position, which I identify as a Compatibilist position. By the latter I mean that NGO support of some imperial aims can, in certain cases, be compatible with both the political justification of such NGOs and the demands of justice.

In contrast to the Imperialist Criticism, there are also Pragmatic Criticisms concerning the inefficiencies, ineffectiveness, and injustices of NGOs, including those of Anthony Bebbington and Roger Riddell, Gerard Clarke, David Hulme and Michael Edwards, Patrice C. McMahon, Sarah Mendelson, James Richter, Paul Stubbs, and Janine Wedel. These criticisms will not be discussed here. Pragmatic Critics generally accept what they consider to be the goals of NGOs, while the Imperialist Critics do not. Secondly, whereas Pragmatic Critics propose changes to improve local NGOs, Imperialist Critics often strongly reject NGO activity. Like all categorization, when it comes to individual critics the picture is more complex, with any individual critic fitting into more than one category.

I argue that although there is certainly much truth to some forms of the Imperialist Criticism, both feminist and non–feminist, some common forms of this argument are unjustified. I focus on the Imperialist Criticisms because they constitute the strongest and most principled criticisms of NGOs and are frequently espoused. I give examples of the kinds of activities local women's and feminist NGOs in the region have engaged in and their bearing on the Imperialist Criticisms.

The Imperialist Criticism suggests that local women's and feminist NGOs and their Western supporters do not promote gender, class, or transnational justice but foster an imperial agenda or Western interests. What the critics mean by an "imperial agenda" or "Western interests" differs but in the 1990s in Central and East Europe and the former Soviet Union one central meaning was the building of a neoliberal capitalist economic system and a political order that would support it in the region, to the advantage of Western capitalism but to the disadvantage of those in the region.

There are both non–feminist and feminist Imperialist Criticisms of both Western feminist NGOs working in the region and of local women's and feminist NGOs active in the region. The non–feminist Imperialist Criticism characterizes an institution as imperialist either if those acting on behalf of that institution intend to foster neoliberalism in the region or the institution has that function, or if its consequences are the fostering of neoliberalism. Both Western governments, Western NGOs that support local NGOs in the region, and local NGOs active in the region are all criticized as imperialist.

The feminist Imperialism Criticism condemns both Western feminist NGOs and local women's and feminist NGOs in the region as imperialist if: 1) it is a Western feminist NGO that promotes "Western" feminism in the region and/or the Western NGO's own interests; 2) it is a local women's NGO in the region that adopts Western feminism or promotes its own interests through cooperation with a Western NGO; and 3) (1) or (2) succeeds at the cost of causing harm or not being beneficial or as beneficial as it might otherwise be to local woman's NGO interests and/or the interests of women in the region. In what follows I examine both the nature and adequacy of these arguments, focusing particularly on the non–feminist Imperialist Criticism and what moral and political criticisms of NGOs and women's and feminist NGOs follow from it.

Non–feminist Imperialist Critics

The non–feminist Imperialist Critics include Michael Hardt and Antonio Negri, James Petras, and Henry Veltmeyer, as well as David Rieff (Hardt and Negri 2000; Petras and Veltmeyer 2001; Rieff 2002). Rieff refers to Western NGOs in general and primarily international humanitarian NGOs. He speaks of the history of humanitarian action "as a helper and partner of imperialism" and of the

> ... similarity in the way the invocation of a higher moral norm led, in practice, to an alliance between activists intent on relieving suffering and great power in the era of late 19th century imperialism, and to 20th century humanitarian interventionism (Rieff 2002, 60–1).

Hardt and Negri call transnational humanitarian NGOs "the most important" instruments and "frontline force[s] of imperial intervention," and that they employ moral categories such as "universal needs" and "universal rights" (Hardt and Negri 2000, 36). They state that

> ... These NGOs are completely immersed in the biopolitical context of the constitution of Empire; they anticipate the power of its pacifying and productive intervention of justice (Hardt and Negri 2000, 36).

James Petras and Henry Veltmeyer attacked women's and feminist NGOs in general, claiming that they replace class politics with a "heavily ... essentialist identity politics", which "focuses on the private sphere and personal politics" and are "a gross disservice to working women" (Petras and Veltmeyer 2001, 134). Petras and Veltmeyer claim that NGOs in general demobilize popular movements, promote non–confrontational politics, obscure the creation of classes through the use of the category of civil society, collaborate "with capitalists who finance their institutes and ... orient their projects and followers into subordinate relations with the big business interests that direct the neoliberal economies", as well as coopt former oppositional leaders and "popular women's organizations". Moreover, they claim that NGOs "create a new class ... supported by imperial funding to control significant popular groups" and that NGO directors are "ensuring conformity with the goals, values, and ideology of the donors" (Petras and Veltmeyer 2001, 133). Speaking generally of NGOs supported by the US, David Rieff claims that the US "generally expects" them to "broadly" support US policy.

Susan Woodward, in discussing postwar countries, offers an oft–stated argument on the role of the World Bank, International Monetary Fund [IMF], and the UN in setting policy for postwar countries. Speaking more loosely of promoting "Western interests," rather than imperialism, she says:

> A postwar country cannot participate in the international economy, including access to capital, until it comes to an agreement with the International Monetary Fund on its debt

arrears. The terms of that agreement then create a specific culture of conditionality for the country within which all other donors work ... Data bases to establish needs, track progress, and govern aid are created by outsiders according to highly standardized forms and dominant economic philosophy. And to institutionalize restraints on the power of the central government that this growth strategy requires, the World Bank and USAID, in particular, emphasize programs of community development (alternative sources of local power to local government as well). Most major donors, similarly, give priority for the same reasons to civil society, decentralization, and (programmed) participation (Woodward 2004).

Kristen Ghodsee mixes feminist and non–feminist Imperialist Criticisms, echoing Petras and Veltmeyer's Imperialist Criticism. She claims that women's NGOs in Bulgaria "may be unwittingly complicit with the proponents of neoliberalism" and "shift from a class-based analysis of oppression to a gender–based analysis of oppression" (Ghodsee 2004, 728; 742). She further claims that:

> ... women's NGOs in Eastern Europe do, in some ways, directly undermine the possibility of a united proletariat by narrowly focusing on projects for women and discursively constructing women as somehow less suited to capitalism (Ghodsee 2004, 742).

Like Petras and Veltmeyer, Ghodsee accuses NGO directors of "ensuring conformity with the goals, values and ideology of the donors," of not "challenging the social or economic relations within which patriarchy thrives" and that they work "well within the neoliberal ideological constraints" (Ghodsee 2004, 728; Petras and Veltmeyer 2001, 133). She claims that their activity "deflects attention away from the structural adjustment policies of the World Bank and the stabilization programs of the International Monetary Fund [IMF]," "coopts educated middle-class women" who could have organized "a solid class-based opposition," and "may actually weaken grassroots opposition to neoliberalism" (Ghodsee 2004).

Feminist Imperialism Criticisms

However, Ghodsee also raised a feminist Imperialism Criticism in her claim that Western feminists came to the region on "a tidal wave of grants" from the West without understanding the history and politics of the West. She also asserts that they imposed a "feminism–by–design": an essentialist "cultural feminism" that "may have done women [in the region] more harm than good," because it created "new stereotypes that women are less adaptable to the market economy" and "construct[ed] women as disadvantaged [which made] women feel they can't make it" (Ghodsee 2004, 731; 733–4; 736).

In a more nuanced way, Frances Olsen, among many others, also raised the feminist Imperialist Criticism, writing that:

Small armies of feminists are marching into central and east Europe ... The same kinds of problems of exclusion and domination, misunderstanding and "essentialism" that have marked relations between African–American women and European–American women within the United States reappear in the international context, with economic domination and cultural imperialism taking the place of racism ... These analytic categories are generally defined by feminist interests as articulated by Western women ... Yet there is reason to believe that the 'stars' America recognizes or produces [in the region] will be women most likely to benefit other women in their own countries ... There is also a risk that a kind of new colonialism will filter into the efforts of American women, preventing them from working effectively in central and east Europe. Perhaps the most obvious danger is simply the privileging of gender over all other categories, despite massive differences in national wealth...

...The American feminist emphasis on gender is sometimes said to deemphasize or even deny the importance of imperialism. By focusing attention on the conflict between the sexes, American feminists divert attention away from the conflict between wealthier countries and poor countries ... (Olsen 1997, 2223–26).

Forms of the Imperialist Criticism

Some forms of the Imperialist Criticism are functionalist arguments (Woodward), others are based on the purported intentions of funders (Petras and Veltmeyer, Rieff, Woodward), and yet others are based on the consequences of NGO activity (Petras and Veltmeyer, Ghodsee, Rieff, Olsen), although these arguments are often not distinguished.

1. Functionalist Arguments

The functionalist version of the Imperialist Criticism claims that the function of civil society and NGOs in Central and East Europe and the former Soviet Union is to replace local state socialist elites in and out of government by new elites, to shrink social benefits by privatizing former state functions, and to create stark class distinctions in the transformation of previous state socialist regimes into neoliberal capitalist states. NGOs and civil society are said to "institutionalize restraints on the power of the central government" (Woodward 2004). Some versions explicitly include references to women's NGOs such as Petras and Veltmeyer, Ghodsee, and Olsen while others make a blanket claim about NGOs which, by implication, include women's and feminist NGOs. In discussing Latin America, Asia, and Africa, Petras and Veltmeyer accuse women's NGOs of "pushing privatization from below," both by providing social services that substitute for state provided services, as well as by attacking public services, "using anti–statist rhetoric ... to reallocate state resources", and by repressing "criticisms of capitalism and a class analysis (Petras and Veltmeyer 2001, 128–30). Kristen Ghodsee makes a similar criticism of Bulgarian women's NGOs and NGOs in Central and East Europe in general (Ghodsee 2004, 740).

2. Intentionalist Arguments

The intentionalist version of the Imperialist Argument claims that civil society and local NGOs in Central and East Europe and the former Soviet Union are supported and created by "outside forces" who intend to realize policies and practices favorable to Western capital in the form of neoliberalism, to the detriment of the region. Petras and Veltmeyer characterized NGOs as "grass roots reactionaries," part of "imperialist strategies" (Petras and Veltmeyer 2001, 130; 138).

The intentionalist Imperialist Argument is often used to explain the funding of NGOs. Applied to local women's and feminist NGOs in the region, the argument implies that these NGOs are funded by Western governments and transnational institutions such as the UN and EU to promote Western imperial agendas and interests, especially the replacement of state socialism with neoliberal economies. Local women's and feminist NGOs are said to be "donor driven," that is, funders from outside the region determine local women's NGO agendas, and as the funder's understanding of their own interests change, so too, do their decisions on who and what they will fund.

The feminist version of this argument claims Western feminist NGOs only fund local NGOs to promote their own Western feminist agendas and their own NGO interests and are not in the interest of women in the region (Olsen, Ghodsee).

3. The Consequentialist Argument

This argument claims that the consequences of NGO activity, including that of local feminist and women's NGOs, Western women's and feminist NGOs, as well as the activity of Western funders, is to foster neoliberalism, weaken the former socialist state, and reduce social services. This is said not to promote gender, class, or transnational justice but to exacerbate these injustices. The consequences are said to benefit the West at the cost of those in the region. This argument will be discussed in detail below.

Cautionary Claims, Generalizations, and Reductionist Arguments

There are several ways to interpret any of these versions of the Imperialist Criticism as applied to local women's and feminist NGOs in the region. It could be a: 1) Cautionary Claim that there are limitations to the benefits of local women's and feminist NGOs because of the structural conditions under which they operate, and/or because some Western NGOs, funders, and local women's and feminist NGOs in the region contribute to neoliberalism or more to Western feminist agendas and interests than they do to those in the region; 2) a Generalization Argument that whatever else they do, most local women's and feminist NGOs are so constrained by the structural conditions in which they operate that generally what they do is promote neoliberal capitalism and increase class injustice. For example, they do so by taking over from the state the provision of social benefits; by redirecting attention away from a critique of neoliberalism; or by instilling capitalist attitudes and practices . The feminist version of this argument claims that NGOs generally foster Western feminist interests and agendas that do not help women in the region and ignore what is relevant. For these reasons it is said the NGOs deserve strong criticism. Because of these practices both forms of the argument draw the conclusion that it would be better if women's NGOs did not exist at all. A still stronger interpretation of the Imperialist Criticism is: 3) a Reductionist Claim that the only thing that local women's and feminist NGOs do is promote neoliberalism, or Western feminist and non–feminist interests, and are harmful to the region. It is also concluded that women's and feminist NGOs are therefore morally and politically unjustifiable on the grounds of gender, class, and transnational injustice and that it would be better if they did not exist.

It is certainly true that a deep bow must be made to charges of imperialism or neocolonialism and to feminist imperialism as in the Cautionary Claim, to which NGOs both east and west, and the NGOization of women's organizations are vulnerable. Julie Hemment, Sabine Lang, and Francis Olsen, among others, hint at such positions. I do not debate the empirical premises of the Cautionary Claim, in fact I affirm them. Fostering neoliberalism is sometimes part of the function of Western and local women's and feminist NGOs and, to some degree, and in some cases, they do contribute to the spread of neoliberalism. I also accept the assumptions that neoliberalism is not in the interest of women in the region or the region itself and even that the intention of some Western feminist and non–feminist funders of local women's and feminist NGOs is to promote neoliberalism. But I object to the generalization and to the moral and political criticisms that are said to follow from this claim. On the basis of the Cautionary Claim no conclusion follows about most women's NGOs or women's NGOs as a whole or that on balance their overriding impact is to promote neoliberalism. All that follows is the need for caution and for a case by case analysis, with sensitivity to the possible problems.

In contrast to the simple Cautionary Claim I hold a Compatibilist Cautionary Claim. By this I mean that I consider that the claim that local women's and feminist NGOs promote some neoliberal interests or interests of Western feminist NGOs to be compatible with the claim that they are also morally and politically justifiable, and promote gender and class justice in the region. In some cases the very thing that serves some Western interests also benefits the region and women in it. The simple Cautionary Claim does not seem to allow for this. Thus, participating in the creation of civil society may have helped to undermine a state socialist government that provided social benefits but it also helped to transform an anti–democratic or nationalist government, which opened up political space for some to foster gender, racial, and ethnic justice. This is not to deny that civil society also opened up space for nationalists and neoliberals. In other cases, women's NGO activity, either individually or collectively, is justifiable even if it does in some way contribute to neoliberalism so long as it only provides minimal support for neoliberalism, while producing sufficiently important benefits that would not be otherwise realized, and does nothing else that is significantly harmful. There are many women's NGOs that fall into that category. Thus, it may be true that accepting funding involves following budgeting practices, *de facto* adopting a small business approach to social problems, and developing business skills. But learning small business skills is not tantamount to promoting neoliberalism although it might minimally help to entrench neoliberal capitalism; but such an economy would have come to the region, whatever women's and feminist NGOs did. It is also certainly better that women also gained the know–how to operate in such an economy. In fact many women who were active in NGOs did not conclude that a small business approach was the only way to correct gender and social injustice and did not argue for the reduction of state services. Women's and feminist NGOs in the 1990s acted at a moment when there were urgent issues, of both individual survival, war, and traumatic economic transformations and there were only certain possibilities for women's political activity. Any minimal contribution women's and feminist NGOs in the region made to fostering neoliberalism was outweighed by the benefits, some of which will be discussed below.

The nonfeminist Imperialist Generalization and Reductionist Criticisms are more problematic than the simple Cautionary Claim. They make stronger empirical and normative claims. Both of the former claims oversimplify, overgeneralize, trade on vagueness at crucial points, and are in need of empirical proof. The Reductionist claim that women's and feminist NGOs in the region do nothing but promote neoliberalism is simply empirically false. There are many other consequences, functions, and intentions of local women's and feminist NGOs, as will be discussed below. This claim does a disservice to the actual practice of women's and feminist NGOs in the region and to some Western women's and feminist NGOs active on their behalf. It does not follow from women's and feminist NGOs' small contributions to neoliberalism in the region that local women's and feminist NGOs do no good at all, or that as Petras says, "they should stop being NGOs" (Petras and Veltmeyer 2001, 137). I therefore do not take the Reductionist Claim as a strong contender, and focus instead on the Imperialist Generalization Claim.

This leaves the Imperialist Generalization Claim as the version that might appear most persuasive. In what follows, I consider both the theoretical and empirical difficulties common to all versions of these arguments, but focus particularly on the Imperialist Generalization Claim, in its different versions.

General Problems of the Imperialist Criticisms

Several reasons for the persuasiveness of the Imperialist Argument are shared by all versions of the argument. These include 1) an implicit "dirty hands" argument, 2) oversimplification and overgeneralization, and 3) false empirical and theoretical assumptions.

The Dirty Hands Argument

By the "dirty hands argument" I mean the argument that assumes that any cooperation or acceptance of funding from any institution that promotes neoliberalism and hence is imperialist in the relevant sense, or any women's NGO that has any imperialist features, is morally and politically unjustifiable. But if this was a good argument it would mean that in the world of real politics and the exercise of power, where hardly anyone has clean hands, one should do nothing at all. This would eliminate any reform activity whatsoever, including most activities that are crucial to promoting gender justice and reducing other forms of injustice. For example, if the dirty hands argument were a good argument one would have to conclude that eliminating gender and racial injustice or sexual harassment in the military, in multinational corporations, or mainstream newspapers is unjustifiable because these institutions often promote harmful militarist and imperialist ends. One cannot demand "moral purism" and effect change in the real world, fraught with global injustice and power imbalances. This was especially true in the 1990s for women active in Central and East Europe and the former Soviet Union, and those in the West who were interested in supporting women in the region. These women did not generally have official political power and could not set basic state and institutional policies so that they fully conformed to feminist principles.

A political criticism of local women's and feminist NGOs on the grounds that they accept "dirty" money also misses the mark because what matters is not only what the funders intend the funds to be used for, but what the NGO actually does with it. The Imperialist Generalization Argument trades on the dirty hands argument in that it assumes that whatever else women's Eastern NGOs do, since they also cooperate with, support, or operate in conditions that promote neoliberalism they should be strongly criticized or even rejected as imperialist.

Oversimplification and Overgeneralization

Criticisms of "the West"

The Imperialist Argument also rests on claims about the agenda of "the West," including the function, consequences, or intention of "Western" funding of local women's and feminist NGOs. However, this assumes both that there is something called "the West" and that all NGOs are funded by it. Both claims are false. There is a very wide range of goals, interests, and objectives in "the West" and they sometimes conflict. Thus, the interests of the EU, increasingly important in the region, are not the same as those of the US. Western funding sources included the US, Canada, Japan, Australia, and many European countries, including Sweden and the Netherlands. It also included global and regional organizations such as the UN and the EU. Funders included not only government agencies for international development but also public and "private" foundations, small and large foundations, non–feminist and feminist foundations such as Kvinna till Kvinna of Sweden, The Global Fund for Women, the

Network of East–West Women, and MamaCash in the Netherlands. Foreign political parties such as the German Greens or Social Democrats, each with different interests and projects, also funded women's NGOs in the region. In the 1990s, the US was interested in establishing neoliberalism but in the early 1990s, the German Green Party was not and wanted to find political partners. They funded feminist organizations and ecology groups in Central and East Europe as potential political allies since there were no Green parties (Funk 1999a). The German Greens' FrauenAnstiftung [Women's Foundation] and later, their reorganized Böll Foundation (founded in 1998 and which incorporated the Women's Foundation), funded 20 women's and feminist NGOs concurrently in postsocialist countries in the years 1990–99. This included several of the most active women's and feminist NGOs in the region including Profem (Czech Republic), the Prague Women's Center, and the St. Petersburg Center for Gender Issues and the Independent Women's Forum (Russia) (Funk 1999a). Thus, an Imperialist Criticism based on the Western funding of women's NGOs needs a much more complex view of Western funders than that presumed by Imperialist Critics.

The Variety of women's NGOs in the region

Any argument that attempts to generalize about women's NGOs in Central and East Europe and the former Soviet Union is also bound to fail because of the diversity of women's NGOs within an individual country and between countries.

1. Non–Western funded women's and feminist NGOs. The Imperialist Generalization Argument assumes that local women's and feminist NGOs in the region were all funded by foreign Western states or Western dominated transnational bodies, but this is a gross oversimplification. There were also non–governmental and "quasi–NGOs" not sponsored by the West, but by local governments. These include the former communist party-based mass membership women's organizations such as the Organization of Women's Organizations in Macedonia and the Women's League or Democratic Women's Union in Poland, among others (Bagić 2002). In Russia many quasi–NGOs were funded by the Russian government, including the Women's Association of Russia and women's professional organizations. The Russian Women's Councils were transformed from state to non–state bodies and supported by the Russian government; women active in the Union of Russian Women often retained official positions in the government. In some cases, as in Russia, independent women's and feminist NGOs tried to work with these groups (Zdravomyslova 2000, 55). Eastern German women's activities were also almost all funded by local German governments.

There were also women's parties, women's subsidiaries of political parties, and unions in the region that supported women's and feminist NGOs such as in Hungary, Slovakia, and Russia (Schmedt 1997, 24–5; Fabian 1999, 213). These groups were active on different issues than those of Western funded NGOs. In addition, explicitly feminist organizations were only a small percentage of women's NGOs and some were anti–feminist. There were also networks of women's and feminist NGOs in many of the countries in the region. Women's and feminist NGOs were active both on gender and non–gender specific issues. In Bosnia–Herzegovina, women's and feminist NGOs worked on ethnic reconciliation after the war. In the former Yugoslavia many women's and feminist NGOs in the 1990s were peace activists during those wars. Some women's groups are ethnically defined and nationalist such as Rossija in Russia, the Hungarian Mothers' Party in Hungary, and the League of Albanian Women in Macedonia (Bagić 2002; Fabian 1999, 213).

2. *'Strong" vs. "weak" women's and feminist NGOs.* The Generalization Argument also does not distinguish between "strong" and "weak" or donor driven–women's and feminist NGOs in the region. By "strong" women's and feminist NGOs I mean those that had a strong sense of purpose prior to being funded or shortly thereafter, were in a position to insist on their own agendas, and were not donor-driven. Several such NGOs existed in the former Yugoslavia, eastern Germany, the Czech Republic, Poland, and Slovakia. Strong women's and feminist NGOs are also those that know how to navigate the foundation field, have extensive contacts with many different funders, and a proven record of accomplishment. In the 1990s this included women's and feminist NGOs led by women who had been self–identified feminists or activists within state socialism or shortly thereafter, such as Vesna Kesić, founder of Be Emancipated, Be Active [B.A.B.E], and cofounder of the Center for Women War Victims in Croatia; Lepa Mladenović of the S.O.S. Hotline in Serbia; and Marina Beyer of the Ost–West Europäisches FrauenNetzwerk [OWEN – East–West European Women's Network] in eastern Germany. Others had a self–defined interest in defending abortion rights, women's rights, and building women's studies centers in Poland, Russia, Serbia, Croatia, Slovenia, Slovakia, and the Czech Republic. In Croatia in 2002, B.A.B.E. had 19 different funders from several Scandinavian countries as well as the US. Such feminist NGOs as Women Against Domestic Violence [NaNE] in Hungary, and B.A.B.E. in Croatia rejected funders who wanted them to work on projects they were not interested in, such as trafficking, a project popular with many Western funders. Strong NGOs also had a better chance to challenge funders who engaged in unacceptable practices; they could publicize funders' bad practices, making their work more difficult. For example, one intermediary Western funder claimed credit for work done by a Croatian women's NGO before it had even received that funding. The local NGO made this public, shaming that funder into changing its practices (Funk 1999b). OWEN, in eastern Germany, always initiated their own projects based on support for women's dignity and self–respect in Ukraine, Russia, Poland, and eastern Germany. They received funding from the Berlin and Brandenburg governments in Germany. Critics such as Petras and Veltmeyer, and Ghodsee emphasize the weak women's and feminist NGOs, of which no doubt there are many, more in some countries than in others. These are more likely to carry out neoliberal agendas. But it is an overgeneralization to conclude, based on weak NGOs or those countries in which weak women's NGOs may predominate, that all

women's and feminist NGOs in the region or all those in a given country are likely to carry out imperial agendas and that it would be better if they did not exist at all.

False Empirical and Theoretical Assumptions

The Imperialist Generalization Argument also assumes that the West and Western policies wholly determine the nature, function, structure, and/or consequences of local women's and feminist NGOs, suggesting that they are "wholly immersed" in the pursuit of neoliberalism (Hardt and Negri 2000, 36). This reveals an arrogance and ignorance of the influence of cultural, historical, political, and economic contexts including the state socialist past, its organizations, and practices. It ignores the impact of local laws governing NGOs, especially tax laws and state laws governing NGOs, the agenda of active women in the region, as well as the influence of Western feminism. Some women's and feminist NGOs supported by Western funders, such as the Center for Women War Victims in Croatia, started by 12 women and organized by Vesna Kesić; the Feminist Network in Hungary; and the PSF Women's Center in Warsaw, studied and shared Western feminism's organizational principles including democratic decision making, participation, and shared leadership. Their functioning and impact was not solely determined by Western funders or the "conditionality" imposed by the IMF or World Bank. The Imperialist Generalization Argument also mistakenly assumes that local women's and feminist NGOs are passive, powerless victims who lack their own strategies to subvert the neoliberal agendas of their Western funders and who are not able to carry out their own agendas in spite of the conditions under which they act or the intentions of their funders.

Specific Problems in Nonfeminist Imperialist Generalization Arguments

The Intentional Version

This Imperialist Generalization Argument criticizes both donors as well as intermediary Western and local women's and feminist NGOs for accepting Western funding given the imperial or neoliberal motives and intentions behind the support. This Kantian-based moral criticism of motives may be relevant in assessing the moral virtue of the funders, but is not sufficient for a political assessment of those who accept their funds. Any reasonable political evaluation must take into account the actual and expectable consequences of the NGO's use of the funding. To assume that the consequences are imperialist or neoliberal, the intentionalist Imperialist Generalization Argument has to implicitly assume that local women's and feminist NGOs and Western feminist NGO intermediaries actually fulfill their funders' intentions, effectively contributing to the elimination and reduction of state welfare functions, and preventing the development of more critical grassroots groups. But not all intentions hit their mark. Not all local women's and feminist NGOs and their

Western feminist NGO supporters carry out what their Western funders intended or do so very successfully. Indeed, pragmatic critics have frequently claimed that many women's and feminist NGOs accomplish nothing or little at all, much less the agenda of "the West." Most women's and feminist NGOs in the region and Western researchers complained that accounting and budgeting requirements and the continuous search for grants seriously reduced local NGOs' ability to do much of what either they or their funders wanted; this fight for the limited sources of funding further undermined NGO success (Funk 1999c; Fabian 1999, 116; McMahon 2002; Richter 2002). Moreover, local adaptations, interpretations, and interests can also subvert funders' intended goals. Julie Hemment's study of crisis centers and centers for violence against women in Russia in the 1990s revealed that many Russian women's NGOs redefined the meaning of "crisis centers" that was intended by their Western funders in order to emphasize Russian women's "economic crisis" and their struggle for economic survival (Hemment 2004, 826). Hemment argued that the prior understanding of "crisis center" before "the arrival of foundation support" influenced this outcome (Hemment 2004, 828–9). Ghodsee herself argued that although Western funders wanted women to be active in formal politics, women in the region were more likely to support the "potential center or Left" and "an anti–World Bank or anti–EU government" position (Ghodsee 2004, 746). Thus, an argument based on intentions alone is insufficient and ultimately turns into an assessment of the consequences of funding and NGO activity, which will be discussed below.

In addition, Western government funders from agencies such as USAID in the 1990s who one can assume had a neoliberal agenda, sometimes depended on intermediary Western feminist NGOs to identify and work with local women's and feminist NGOs. But such intermediary NGOs as the Network for East–West Women [NEWW] in the US, the STAR Foundation, and the Global Fund for Women did not have neoliberal intentions. Nor did OWEN in eastern Germany, MamaCash in the Netherlands, and Kvinna till Kvinna in Sweden or the FrauenAnstiftung [Women's Foundation] of the German Greens. Such feminist and non–feminist intermediaries are not only interest driven but also "principle" or "value" driven. This is also true of some members of Western agencies and foundations such as Ford and Soros. Some funders genuinely wanted to promote gender justice in the region in the 1990s, such as Irena Grudzinska Gross of the Ford Foundation, Anastasia Posadsykaia and the staff of the Soros Women's Network Program, as well as others from the EU, UN, and even some in the US State Department.

This is not to deny that Western funders and activists in Western NGOs active in the region and local women's NGOs — both feminist and nonfeminist – often had mixed motives in their activities. These included self–interested motives for institutional and personal gain including: to promote neoliberal agendas; to enhance their personal and institutional power, status, and reputations; to gain recognition for their institution or organization as an effective agent in the region; to be invited worldwide to give lectures, build careers, earn good salaries, or any salary at all; to preserve their own Western feminist NGOs and run up a track record of getting grants, which would facilitate future funding. But self–interested motives are compatible with principled motives, which many had. Based on intentions alone most women's and feminist NGOs cannot be categorized as predominantly imperialist in the sense discussed above.

The Functionalist Version

In this version of the Imperialist Generalization Argument, the first problem is the assumption that the conditions under which NGOs operate are set by "the West" and that the function of women's and feminist NGOs in the region is to dismantle the socialist state. It is assumed that this function is generally fulfilled, serving Western interests and not those of the region. But, as stated above, many circumstances condition what NGOs will and can do: state tax laws and laws regulating NGOs; the past and present political culture; women's commitment to feminist principles; a sense of entitlement to health care and other social benefits; and women's institutions, politics, and economic circumstances in a country. Jointly these circumstances can subvert the intended "Western" function of women's and feminist NGOs in the region. In fact, some women's and feminist NGOs, rather than promoting neoliberalism, have been its strongest critics. The assumption that women's and feminist NGOs generally fulfill their "Western" function also belies the claims made by many pragmatic critics and members of local women's and feminist NGOs that many NGOs accomplished much less than was expected.

Secondly, even if it is a function of NGOs to create a new elite that promotes neoliberalism and replaces former communist elites this is also compatible with some of those elites serving citizens' interests in general, and women's interests in particular.

Thirdly, this version of the argument assumes that women's and feminist NGOs in the region have only one "function" and there are not any other functions that are determined by women in the region itself, such as to resist nationalist divisions and preserve contact between women of different nationalities, as women did in the states of the former Yugoslavia or to preserve abortion or introduce women's studies programs. Thus, the functionalist argument does not prove either that *the* function of women's and feminist NGOs is to serve imperial or "Western" interests, that the NGOs actually fulfill that function, or that it would be better if they did not exist.

The Consequentialist Version

This version of the Imperialist Generalization Argument (Petras and Veltmeyer, Rieff, Ghodsee) criticizes women's and feminist NGOs because of the neoliberal consequences of their activity. As stated above, it is claimed that Western funders supported local women's and feminist NGOs who provided services to women which enabled the state to disengage from providing services, thus further entrenching neoliberalism. In addition, local women's and feminist NGOs are accused of blocking the growth of more oppositional, grassroots women's organizations. The NGOs' purported focus on gender in the private sphere is also criticized for directing attention away from the construction of class. Yet, women's NGOs were, somewhat paradoxically, also accused of being "rarely effective" (Ghodsee 2004, 731).

First, it is important to note that the percentage of monies distributed by funders to women's and feminist NGOs was a very small percentage of total monies allocated. According to some reports from 1992–96 in Russia, USAID spent most of its Freedom Support Act budget "on market reform ... [and] at times as little as six percent for democracy assistance" (Mendelson 2002, 238). US democracy assistance to Eastern Europe was only 16.5 percent, according to Mendelson and Glenn (2002, 4). Support for women's and feminist NGOs was itself a very small part of those democracy assistance programs. Even if all women's NGO activity in the region successfully contributed to neoliberalism, unless they were wildly successful in proportion to their funding, their contribution to neoliberalism could at best be expected to be small. In addition, there are many positive consequences of their activity, as will be discussed below.

Secondly, some funders insisted that local women's and feminist NGOs were not to provide services but engage in activities that were more "political." Thus, the FrauenAnstiftung of the German Green Party in the 1990s criticized the Center for Women's Rights in Poland precisely on such grounds, much to the frustration of the Center. The German Green Party which in 1998 incorporated its more independent FrauenAnstiftung into its Böll Foundation, said they were not interested in doing "developmental work" and that such services are better provided by the state (Funk 1999a). In other cases, during the war in the former Yugoslavia, the Center for Women War Victims did provide services. But in no way did they substitute for a service the state would have provided, since the state would not have provided any services at all. It was sometimes these initial efforts that later persuaded the state to provide such services or incorporate women's centers started by NGOs into universities, as was done in Belgrade. In addition, the distinction between service and non–service providing activities is much less rigid than critics take it to be. For example, the Center for Women War Victims engaged in a kind of conscious–raising or political discussion with those they assisted, some of whom later became activists in the Center and on women's issues.

Thirdly, consequentialist Imperialist Generalization critics sometimes imply that it would have been better if Western and local women's and feminist NGOs in the region had not existed at all or were not active in the region. But such a conclusion involves the implicit counterfactual claim that neoliberalism would not have been as well entrenched in the region and/or that women in the region would have been better off and more constructively active if there had not been any women's and feminist NGOs in the region. Although it is true that women's activity in the region would have been different if there had not been women's and feminist NGOs funded in the ways they were, there is little way to know whether women in the region would have been better off if there had not been Western-funded NGOs. There are also some reasons to think women would have been worse off. Women would still have faced neoliberalism and the entrenchment of stark class distinctions in the region and many of the most important women's and feminist NGOs in the region would have had difficulty operating.

Fourthly, the consequentialist argument mistakenly assumes that if the activity of a local woman's and feminist NGO in the region, or of a Western NGO active in the region, has neoliberal consequences this is a sufficient political reason to reject that NGO, or women's and feminist NGOs in general, as imperialist. However, it is not *a priori* true that women's and feminist NGOs' contribution to neoliberalism overrides other more beneficial consequences of women's NGO activity, either individually or collectively. A consequentialist Generalization Claim is based on an assessment of women's and feminist NGO activities in the region and of Western women's and feminist NGOs working there. An adequate consequentialist argument has to consider all the short- and long-term consequences, including not only the neoliberal, but also the beneficial consequences of both individual NGOs and of women's and feminist NGOs in a region or in a given country collectively. The collective long-run significance of local women's and feminist NGOs in the region is as important as the immediate impact of any individual women's NGO. Yet, the consequentialist Generalization Claim usually focuses only on the short-run neoliberal consequences of a particular woman's NGO and from this makes a hasty generalization to NGOs and their consequences in general. Ghodsee, for example, often jumps from accounts of Bulgarian women's NGOs to claims about women's NGOs in Eastern Europe generally.

A more adequate consequentialist argument is one that considers the actually existing circumstances in the 1990s and what options were practically possible. If on balance the following conditions are met, then women's and feminist NGO activity in the region would be morally and politically justifiable: 1) the beneficial consequences in the long and short run of local women's and feminist NGOs in the region and of Western women's and feminist NGOs working with them were sufficiently important; 2) there is reason to believe that they would not have been otherwise accomplished; 3) the contribution to non–beneficent ends such as neoliberalism was not above an acceptable threshold; and 4) there are no inherently evil consequences, such as furthering racism or ethnic cleansing. It is, in fact, reasonable to believe the above conditions are satisfied, if one considers the impact of women's and feminist NGO activity in the region.

Among many of the not particularly neoliberal achievements of women's and feminist NGOs in the region are: new university gender and women's studies curriculums and the integration of gender into other courses in universities and law schools; freestanding women's centers; the writing of new text books for elementary and high schools that change gender stereotypes; the introduction of new language such as "sexual harassment" and "discrimination in employment" into public discourse; and proposals for antidiscrimination laws in Poland, eastern Germany, and Croatia.

Women's and feminist NGO attention to discrimination in employment and women's unemployment also belies the claim that women attended only to issues in the family, as Petras and Veltmeyer, and Ghodsee claimed. One writer claimed that 40 percent of Polish women's organizations were in fact concerned with employment, training, and retraining (Fuchs 1999).

Women's and feminist NGOs in the region also challenged gender-biased laws and legislation and played a major role in the development of conceptions of rights for both women and men. NGOs provided a voice that defended abortion rights in many countries in the region; challenged problematic family laws in Russia and Croatia; created ombudspersons; argued that the rape of women in war is a violation of women's human rights and a war crime (Croatia) and that violence against women is a violation of women's human rights; and fought against nationalism, corruption, and the cutting of social benefits. Izabela Jaruga–Nowacka stated that in Poland in 2003 her work as the Polish Governmental Plenipotentiary for Equal Status was strengthened by the existence of active feminist NGOs and non–feminist NGOs in Poland. Her office educated members of even the more liberal parties in Parliament in Poland who did not know that they were under a legal obligation to provide equality for men and women. This led to the gathering of gender disaggregated statistics to support arguments for the need for gender equality (Jaruga–Nowacka 2003). In Warsaw University women faculty applied to the Ford Foundation for a grant to introduce women's studies. Ford required the university to document the gender division of the faculty, bringing the practice of gender disaggregation to a university in a postsocialist state that had not previously done so (Funk 1999d).

The long-run general consequences of local women's and feminist NGO's activity included transforming public discourse and public consciousness in Poland, Slovakia, Serbia, Croatia, eastern Germany, and the Czech Republic, among others. Olga Pietruchova of the Slovakian NGO, ProChoice, stated that a politician who made disparaging comments about the possibility of Slovakian women serving in the chemical corps for Iraq was forced to publicly apologize because of women's demands in letters they wrote demanding such an apology; this reflects a major change in public consciousness (Pietruchova 2003). Women's and feminist NGOs' introduction of gender concepts such as "sexual harassment" and "discrimination" in employment made further political changes possible. In Poland by the early 2000s the latter term began to be used by all parties in Parliament, even conservatives, whereas the use of the term had previously been criticized as "aggressive" feminist confrontation (Grzybek 2003). Rather than simply replacing state services, women's NGO activity in Russia contributed to state officials becoming required to provide services for women (Hemment 2004, 822). Gender studies courses established by feminist NGOs in and out of universities were attended by future journalists, sensitizing them to gender issues (Grzybek 2003). Younger women educated in these courses and in the context of women and feminist NGO activity challenged NGOs as the primary form of women's political activity and engaged in new forms of public actions in support of abortion rights. By the early 2000s in Poland and Serbia women's activities and organizations got attention from the media (Graff 2003; Milic 2004, 73).

At the level of transnational organizations some women from women's and feminist NGOs in the region were able to enter the global feminist network and discourse. They were able to officially register with the UN, speak before UN bodies such as the Committee on the Status of Women [CSW], and challenge false official state accounts of the situation of women in their country. Women from NGOs participated in other transnational forums such as the UN's Fourth World Conference on Women in Beijing in 1995 and the UN's Beijing +5 and Beijing +10 Meetings in 2005. In 1995, women from the region made public the specific demands of women from their region in their "Statement from a Non–Region" at Hairou in an effort to influence the final NGO document of the conference to incorporate their concerns. Women learned how to appeal to international directions such as UN documents on human rights, International Labor Organization [ILO] conventions, international human rights agreements, the Convention on the Elimination of All Forms of Discrimination Against Women [CEDAW], as well as EU laws and policies that concern women. Women educated parliamentarians who either did not know about these documents, that their country had agreed to them or did not know that when a nation's law conflicts with such international agreements, the international agreement supervenes (Fuchs 1999, 13). According to the judgment of several women in the region all this provided women's and feminist NGOs in the region with the leverage and legal and political arguments to legitimate their activities and influence local politicians. Women networked with other women's and feminist NGOs, both in their own country, in the region, and with women from other regions. B.A.B.E. helped create a transnational NGO, the South Eastern Europe Legal Initiative [SEELINE], with 10 member countries from southeastern Europe, to monitor and influence laws from a gender perspective (B.A.B.E. 2005). KARAT, with 44 women's and feminist NGOs from 21 different countries in the region, formed after the 1995 Fourth Women's UN Meeting in Beijing (KARAT 2005). Women active in women's and feminist NGOs entered formal politics, parliaments, and are helping to start new parties, including Green parties. Through women's and feminist NGO activity, women thus gained support, experience, and became politically effective.

Given this panoply of examples it is reasonable to believe that the non–feminist Imperialist Generalization Claim is not true. Given the above – admittedly anecdotal account of women's and feminist NGO activity in the region – and considering all the long- and short-term effects of their activity, it is reasonable to believe that it was better that there was funding for women's and feminist NGOs in the region than if there had not been. Even if women's NGOs contributed to some extent to neoliberalism, neoliberalism would have come to the region in any case, to a greater or lesser extent depending on the country. This does not deny that some activities may have helped neoliberalism, such as the promotion of a small business mentality for NGO leaders, the development of a business based approach rather than a movement-based approach to political problems, the creation of competition rather than solidarity among women, and the fostering of hierarchical rather than democratically structured NGOs with grassroots-oriented activity. But, on balance, important inroads began to be made by local women's and feminist NGOs in the region.

This means that a Compatibilist Cautionary Claim is the most plausible position to adopt, and that participation in Western and local women's and feminist NGOs in Central and East Europe and the former Soviet Union, in important cases – though by no means all cases or even a majority of them – did provide valuable support for gender and ethnic justice and for peace, even if these NGOs also to some extent supported some imperial agendas. Of course, in any particular instance, any particular women's and feminist NGO in the region has to use political judgment to assess whether to accept the proffered funding or work with any particular Western NGO, feminist or otherwise, given the available options and whether what can be accomplished is worth the concessions. It is better to leave the decision to women in those NGOs, than to critics from outside the region deciding for these women what they should do. What is important is to identify how to make funding more constructive by attending to the voices of women in NGOs in the region on how and what to fund and the present problems in the nature of that funding.

Conclusion

Why does all this matter? Because, in the 1990s, NGOs in Central and East Europe and the former Soviet Union were an important arena in which women were able to be politically active. The state in the 1990s was gendered with most parliamentary positions and governmental ministers and official political and economic power held by men. For many reasons women who attempted to be agents in the transformation of the state, institutions, and social policy did so by creating and participating in women's, feminist, and non–women–specific NGOs. In the 1990s there were thousands of local women's NGOs throughout the region, although it is difficult to determine their exact number or the significance of those numbers. International funders and agencies sometimes tapped women's and feminist NGOs as the central agents for political change, such as for reconciliation and conflict resolution in the former Yugoslavia (Helms 2003). Many gender issues addressed by local women's and feminist NGOs in the 1990s had simply been ignored by the formal political institutions in postsocialist states or those bodies had taken very different positions, whether on economic issues or on abortion. The Imperialist Criticisms of women's and feminist NGOs tarnishes and condemns the public activity of some very brave, courageous, and creative women in Central and East Europe and the former Soviet Union.

Finally, the practice of NGOs is evolving and pragmatic criticisms are much more useful to determine how to change the practice. At a time when there is a debate on how and whether NGOs should have an increasing role in the UN and global governance it would be a shame to condemn and dismiss these women's and feminist NGOs in central and east Europe and the former Soviet Union as simply agents of imperialism and Western interests.

Note

[1]　I would like to thank all those in the region who have provided me with information and given generously of their time in discussion. I would particularly like to thank Marina Beyer and Vesna Kesić. I would also like to thank Bozena Chołuj for having invited me to the conference she held at Viadrina University in Frankfurt/Oder in 2003.

References

Abubikirova, N.I., T.A. Klimenkova, E.V. Kotchkina, and M.A. Regentova. 1998. Women's organizations in Russia today. In *Directory of women's non–governmental organizations in Russia & the NIS*, edited by N.I. Abubikirova, T.A. Klimenkova, E.V. Kotchkina, and M.A. Regentova. Moscow: Aslan Publishers.

B.A.B.E. 2005. [cited 06/06/05]. Available from <http://www.babe.hr/eng>.

Bagić, Aida. 2002. International assistance for women's organizing in south eastern Europe: From groups and initiatives to NGOs [cited 06/23/05]. Available from <http://www.policy.hu/bagic>.

Bebbington, Anthony, and Roger Riddell. 1997. Heavy hands, hidden hands, holding hands? Donors, intermediary NGOs and civil society organizations. In *NGOs, states and donors. Too close for comfort*, edited by David Hulme and Michael Edwards. New York: St. Martin's Press.

Clarke, Gerard. 1996. Non–governmental organizations (NGOs) and politics in the developing world. *Papers in international development*, no. 20. Swansea: Center for Development Studies.

Fabian, Katalin. 1999. Public nuisances: Women's groups and the significance of their activities in post–communist Hungary. Ph.D. diss., Syracuse University.

Fuchs, Gesine. 1999. Strategien polnischer Frauenorganisationen. *Berliner Osteuropa Info*. Osteuropa Institut der Freien Universität no.12. [Strategies of Polish Women's organizations. Berlin Institute for East European Studies Info, no.12].

Funk, Nanette. 1999a. Personal interview with Walter Kaufman, Böll Foundation. Berlin, Germany.

Funk, Nanette. 1999b. Personal interview with Vesna Kesić. Zagreb, Croatia.

Funk, Nanette. 1999c. Personal interviews in Poland, the Czech Republic, eastern Germany, and Croatia.

Funk, Nanette. 1999d. Personal interview with Malgorzata Fuszara, Warsaw, Poland.

Ghodsee, Kristen. 2004. Feminism–by–design: Emerging capitalisms, cultural feminism, and women's nongovernmental organizations in postsocialist Eastern Europe. *Signs* 29 (3):727–54.

Graff, Agnieszka. 2003. Lost between the waves? The paradoxes of feminist chronology and activism in contemporary Poland. *Journal of International Women's Studies* 4 (2).

Grzybek, Agnieszka. 2003. Gender Mainstreaming in Polen in der politischen Praxis der Gleichstellungsbeauftragten der polnischen Regierung. [Gender Mainstreaming in Poland in the Political Practice of Officers for Equal Opportunity in the Polish Government]. Panel discussion at the Conference on Gender Mainstreaming in der politischen Praxis der

Gleichstellungsbeauftragten, [Gender mainstreaming in the Political Practice of Officers for Equal Opportunity], at Europa Universität Viadrina Frankfurt/Oder, Germany.

Hardt, Michael, and Antonio Negri. 2000. *Empire*. Cambridge: Harvard University Press.

Helms, Elissa. 2003. Women as agents of ethnic reconciliation? Women's NGOs and international intervention in postwar Bosnia–Herzegovina. *Women's Studies International Forum* 26:15–33.

Hemment, Julie. 2004. Global civil society and the local costs of belonging: Defining violence against women in Russia. *Signs* 29 (3):815–40.

Hulme, David, and Michael Edwards. 1997. NGOs, states and donors: An overview. In *NGOS, states and donors. Too close for comfort*, edited by David Hulme and Michael Edwards. New York: St. Martin's Press.

Jaruga–Nowacka, Izabel. 2003. Gender Mainstreaming in Polen in der politischen Praxis der Geleichstellungsbeauftragten der polnischen Regierung. [Gender Mainstreaming in Poland in the Political Practice of Officers for Equal Opportunity in the Polish Government]. Paper presented at Conference on Gender Mainstreaming in der politischen Praxis der Gleichstellungsbeauftragten, [Gender mainstreaming in the political practice of Officers for Equal Opportunity], at Europa Universität Viadrina, Frankfurt/Oder, Germany.

KARAT. 2005. [cited 06/22/05]. Available from <http://www.karat.org>.

Lang, Sabine. 1997. The NGOization of feminism. In *Transitions, environments, translations. feminisms in international politics*, edited by Joan W. Scott, Cora Kaplan, and Debra Keates. New York: Routledge.

McMahon, Patrice C. 2002. International actors and women's NGOs in Poland and Hungary. In *The power and limits of NGOs. A critical look at building democracy in Eastern Europe and Eurasia*, edited by Sarah E. Mendelson and John K. Glenn. New York: Columbia University Press.

Mendelson, Sarah E. 2002. Conclusion: The power and limits of transitional democracy networks in postcommunist societies. In *The power and limits of NGOs. A critical look at building democracy in Eastern Europe and Eurasia*, edited by Sarah E. Mendelson and John K. Glenn. New York: Columbia University.

Milić, Anđelka. 2004. The women's movement in Serbia and Montenegro at the turn of the millennium: A sociological study of women's groups. *Feminist Review* 76:65–82.

Olsen, Francis. 1997. Feminism in Central and Eastern Europe: Risks and possibilities of American engagement. *Yale Law Review* 106 (7):2215–57.

Petras, James, and Henry Veltmeyer. 2001. *Globalization Unmasked: Imperialism in the 21st Century*, London: Fernwood Publishing.

Pietruchova, Olga. 2003. Gender Mainstreaming als neues Konfliktfeld der Geschlechter. [Gender Mainstreaming as a new Field of Gender Conflict]. Panel discussion at Conference on Gender Mainstreaming in der politischen Praxis der Gleichstellungsbeauftragten, [Gender mainstreaming in the political practice of Officers for Equal Opportunity], at Europa Universität Viadrina, Frankfurt/Oder, Germany.

Richter, James. 2002. Evaluating Western assistance to Russian women's organizations. In *The power and limits of NGOs. A critical look at building democracy in Eastern Europe and Eurasia*, edited by Sarah E. Mendelson and John K. Glenn. New York: Columbia University Press, 54–90.

Rieff, David. 2002. *A bed for the night: humanitarianism in crisis.* New York: Simon and Schuster.

Schittenhelm, Antja. 1995. Frauenpolitik in Russland unter besonderer Berücksichtigung der Entwicklung der Erwerbstätigkeit von Frauen. [Women's politics in Russia with special attention to the development of women's paid employment]. "Diplom" Thesis, Berlin, Germany.

Schmedt, Claudia. 1997. Die rolle des Dritten Sektors in Russland, Eine empirische Analyse. [The role of the third Sector in Russia. An empirical analysis]. Arbeitspapiere des Bereichs Politik und Gesellschaft, Osteuropa Institut der Freien Universität Berlin, [Working Papers in Politics and Society, Eastern Europe Institute of the Free University of Berlin], 13:1–43.

Stubbs, Paul. 1997. Croatia: NGO development, globalism, and conflict. In *NGOs and governments: A review of current practice for Southern and Eastern NGOs,* edited by Jon Bennett. Oxford: Intrac.

Wedel, Janine. 2001. *Collision and collusion: The strange case of aid to Eastern Europe.* New York: Palgrave.

Woodward, Susan. 2004. State–building operations: International vs. local legitimacy? Nation–Building, state–building, and international intervention: Between "liberation" and symptom relief. Paper presented at the Centre d'Etudes et Recherche Internationale and Critique Internationale, [The Center for International Study and Research and International Critique], Paris.

Zdravomyslova, Elena. 2000. Die feministinnen der ersten stunde im Heutigen Russland: Ein porträt vor dem hintergrund der Bewegung. [The feminists of the first hour in contemporary Russia. A portrait of the background of the movement]. *In Frauenbewegungen weltweit: Aufbrüche, Kontinuitäten, Veränderungen, [Women's movements worldwide: Outbreak, continuities, changes],* edited by Ilse Lenz, Michiko Mae, and Karin Klose. Opladen: Leske and Budrich.

Chapter 14

Cautionary Tales

Ann Snitow

As one of the founders of a small non-governmental organization called the Network of East-West Women, I was preoccupied in the early 1990s with keeping a little list of the difficulties facing the often isolated and beleaguered Central and East European feminist colleagues who made up half the Network membership. The list might have been named "Regional Reasons Why People Reject Feminism" and it grew and grew, including reasons I respected and reasons I hated, but above all including a variety of reasons, a richness of reasons from every quarter of both public and private life. Dissidents had their rationale for disliking feminism and so did former communists, and on and on.

Of course a shadow list of my own numerous difficulties as a feminist organizer in the United States was always running along parallel to my Central and East European one – but the differences were great and often illuminating, leading me to think at the time that an East-West conversation would give us all a new depth of understanding about our local and international situations. Different as we were, we were also all, precipitously, "post-communist," a state of confusion I for one wanted to experience in the company of others.

When it was published and translated, my catalogue of difficulties was sometimes read as an erasure of feminist initiatives in the former bloc – which were in fact fast growing from the early 1990s and are continuing now. But making the list was actually intended as an act of recognition of the knotty problems facing these fragile new movements. Feminists in the region had a discourse dilemma unfamiliar to their Western visitors: they couldn't start with a critique of the patriarchal family, because the family had been the bulwark of resistance to communism and was the often-beloved place of privacy, trust, and survival. Nor could they use the old language of communist "emancipation," because many remembered those old solutions to "the woman question" as crudely instrumental and hypocritical, not what women themselves had identified as their self-interest. Finally, they were tempted to embrace the general enthusiasm for new free markets, only to find that women's fate in these markets was often the dark side of the new dawn. But how were they to mount a popular critique of the very freedoms so many others were celebrating? Sour grapes – just when everyone seemed to be declaring a renaissance! These, then, were activists trying to use the category "women" against the grain. They were up against not only the new traditionalists in the post-communist countries, but also against many of the new free market democrats, who like their women to be free and flexible – as in flexible labor pool.

In a series of valuable and suggestive pieces, the Hungarian historian Maria Kovacs has tried to explain to her Western colleagues why all their assumptions about where to place "feminism" politically are unreliable when applied to the East. She has been building up a detailed diagnosis of the allergy to feminism so common in the region. In a description of the Hungarian political parties, she writes: "our liberals-turned-libertarians reject feminism for its close relationship with welfare egalitarianism, while our egalitarian nationalists reject feminism for its close historical and philosophical relationships with liberalism" (Kovacs, unpublished manuscript). In piece after piece she has identified particularities of timing and association that have rendered feminist discourses at best as wanderers, at worst as illiberal, racist, narrow, or Stalinist immigrants from some objectionable location on the political map. Like mine, Kovac's reasons-for-rejecting-feminism proliferated. As one piled the evidence up, the general result was clear enough: in Central and East Europe, resistance to feminism was over-determined. Feminism as a political movement was homeless.

Enter Western feminisms – or rather US feminisms to take the examples I know best. Each post-1989 East-West encounter has had its own dynamic, with successes and failures beyond the scope of this paper. But however different the two sides can sometimes seem to each other, the binary dissolves in the ironic fact that US feminisms have arrived – with whatever exotic fanfare – trailing their own increasing marginality and conceptual confusion from home. As disparate Western feminisms move across borders in the increasing round of international activity which I will damply abbreviate as "globalization," the likelihood of wasted effort, misunderstanding, and even of what I consider damaging uses of the categories of gender analysis multiply.

US feminist movements of the late 1960s and early 1970s were varied from the first but – without always being conscious of this – they were all deeply embedded in the Civil Rights movement and in the New Left. Though this ideological legacy was full of contradictions, both Civil Rights and New Left ideas were end points of long strings of ideological thought and political experience, which gave structure and coherence to feminist desires and demands. Even when in these 1960s movements we argued angrily about ideas or strategies, we often shared a basic aesthetic of politics and a sturdy, confident critique of the prevailing social order.

Now, not a sentence out of any of our mouths or an expectation – conscious or unconscious – is unchanged by the breaking up of the great structuring belief systems of the cold war period. Though some activists ignore the absence of a floor in the room in which they are toiling away at their former political tasks, and some are responding handily but abstractly with theories of hybridity, I want to pause a moment to discuss how odd US feminisms can be these days. I want to mark a serious break in discourse, not the end of ideology, but a loss of currently useable ideologies.

Like many other cultures of resistance that flourished before 1989, US feminisms are often, now, unmoored from the deeper structures that formerly attached directional arrows to their work. Feminist activists who relied on Left constructions of future possibilities now need to conceptualize what they want, and how to get it, in new terms, based on new conditions.

Indeed, feminism's Western "home" is breaking up, so that one might say that there is a parallel problem, East and West, with finding appealing, effective entry points for a feminist politics. In our homeless wanderings, there are many places where feminists may take refuge which can turn out to be no refuge at all, but places where feminism can lose its claim to being liberatory, socially innovative, or just. The potential illiberality of feminism can happen in big dramatic ways, or indirectly, in ways we are not expecting. The obvious cases are well known: a racist feminism; a class-bound, elitist, or careerist feminism; a narrow, single issue feminism without alliances; a puritanical, sexually repressive feminism, often advocating some form of censorship; a moralistic feminism; a feminism which asks merely for women's inclusion, not for more fundamental change. And the list could go on. I offer here, first, some examples of such limitations in the current diaspora of Western feminist ideas in Central and East European contexts and, second, a caveat against letting these weaknesses overwhelm the urgent project of finding newly vital entry points for feminism East and West.

In the catalogue below of ways in which Western feminisms circulate I do not mean to discount indigenous sources of feminism in Central and East Europe, or the former Soviet Union. On the contrary, there is a rich past that needs digging up. When one learns how, in 1948, the Czech communist party changed the locks on the door to the independent women's building, and how, in 1950, the party hanged the leading Czech feminist, Milada Horakova, one realizes a common heroic past, periods of mass mobilization, followed by defeat, that have been lost to memory, like the stories of so many other women's mass struggles. But, given this loss of memory about pre-communist feminist debates, and the stigma against Stalinist emancipation rhetoric in the East, the powerful engines that are Western ideas take up a lot of conceptual space, accompanied as they often are with glamour or with foundation money. Local traditions provide interpretative frameworks, of course, but the diaspora of Western feminisms gives rise to contradictions that deserve attention if feminism is to seem worth struggling for either in the United States or elsewhere.

Some Examples of How Western Feminist Fragments Circulate in East Central Europe and the former Soviet Union

Gender as a Convenient and Often Oversimple Explanation for Complex Problems

Sometimes in Central and East Europe, the category "gender" gains currency as a foreign import that holds out promise as an explanatory model. Often, though, it displaces other models or obscures them – most commonly "class," which in post-communism is still a much-discredited structure of explanation. For example, in Osh, Kyrgystan, women organizers identified the gendered character of the new poverty: where there had been 70 day care centers in 1992, in 1997 there were 20, as women were pushed out of the work force and back into unpaid care of children at home. But the gendered nature of the new unemployment was a local adaptation to events happening very far away. Gender inequality is a necessary but not a sufficient description of the new immiseration in Kyrgystan. As a category standing alone it is both weak and misleading.

As Carole S. Vance has argued, one might include current human rights work on the trafficking of women as yet another example of how class sometimes gets obscured by discussions of gender. The language of anti-trafficking campaigns often describes innocent or passive female victims who need rescuing. But one could describe the same phenomena very differently as a new form of poverty, as a new mobility of people and money, in which women make choices under terrible new economic pressures (Vance, unpublished manuscript).

Take for example this exemplary exchange between a Western feminist from the US and an Eastern feminist from the Czech Republic. The Western feminist bemoans the line of young Czech prostitutes along the road near the border with Germany. The Eastern feminist responds that yes, there's a terrible new problem with the currency differential between Germany and the Czech Republic. The Western feminist thinks, "What low feminist consciousness!" The Eastern feminist thinks, "Why do these Western feminists see sexuality as the key to oppression?" Yet this idea, that sexuality is at the center of the new disempowerment of women in the region, is the one that garners attention and support funds from Western advocates, and therefore often becomes the main issue for women in the region as well. Trafficking is indeed an alarming problem, but kidnapping is already illegal. What is flourishing without much censure is the economic manipulation of women in the new order. It is easier to arouse outrage by anti-prostitution campaigns than to construct a politics that criticizes the unregulated flow of capital and confronts women's further loss of social power both at work and at home. (Juliet Mitchell has described how the same displacement happened in England. When she first worked on women's issues in the early 1960s, she could not get labor figures disaggregated by gender. In the 1980s, after twenty years of feminism, the gender variable was everywhere and it was class that had become invisible in the statistics. She argues that feminist demands are often unself-consciously complicit in the developmental leaps of capitalism, so that feminists need to be aware how their work articulates with other categories of social analysis.) (See Mitchell 1986).

Related problems arise when the category displaced by "gender" is "race." Many Eastern feminists argue that racism is not a relevant issue for them, a familiar tragic error in the making. Many other Eastern feminists recognize that they may well be more like African-American feminists and feminists of the South in their priorities and interests than like the mostly white US feminists who seek contact with them.

"Which Western feminism?" is always a useful question as Eastern feminists sort through various imports, which offer quite varied interpretative frameworks.

Nonetheless, self-conscious as one may be in one's borrowings, issues of race and ethnicity are particularly hard to translate from context to context. For example, I suspect that racism and ethnic hatred are not precisely the same kind of phenomena and should not be mapped on top of one another. The kinds of phobic prejudice faced by African-Americans in the US and Jews and Roma in Central and East Europe and the former Soviet Union are similar to each other and different in kind from the intimate sibling rivalries of many of the ethnic conflicts in the region. In each situation, "gender," "race," and "ethnicity" have complex, changing relationships with each other, and there are no short cuts in the process of arriving at an inclusive politics. Western paradigms may or may not apply; though knowledge of past feminist failures to confront racism should sound a powerful warning bell.

Feminism as a Variable in Uneven Development

Western feminisms have produced long laundry lists of demands, but each item has its separate fate as it migrates into the discourses of other cultures. Take the liberal divorce law in Romania. One Romanian feminist lawyer expressed the wish to get rid of easy divorce in Romania. She observed that it was mainly men who wanted divorces, to escape their family responsibilities. Women rarely seek divorce, because a divorced woman is so disempowered in Romanian culture, so isolated, so ostracized that the freedom is rarely worth it. Some Western feminists got depressed at the idea of a Romanian feminist campaign against easy divorce, and in the long run they are probably right that a no-divorce law is hardly a solution to women's problems in the family. But what the Romanian feminist was expressing was the inadequacy of legal reforms without the cultural and economic revolutions that would support women's independence. New Right women in the US expressed similar criticisms of a feminism that they felt was stripping them of traditional protections without giving them enough in exchange. In Deirdre English's wonderful phrase, they "feared that feminism would free men first." Feminism is a social revolution. Without general social discussion, consciousness raising, a public expression of pain and dissatisfaction, the letter killeth.

Problematic or Powerless Structures Authorized by Feminist Ideas and Values

Both Eastern and Western feminist organizers often congratulate themselves and each other for the invention of grassroots political forms that are more accessible and democratic than traditional politics. Indeed, in the former communist countries, it is an urgent task to invent new forms for politics, to develop civil society, free associations, the idea of voluntary public participation. However, the rise of new forms of voluntarism, and specifically of female voluntarism, in the East coincides with the dismantling of social citizenship and the decay of social entitlements there. Now that the governments of Central and East Europe and the former Soviet Union are abdicating responsibility, the scene looks much more like the one in the United States, where private time and money are constantly filling in for government refusals to protect its citizens from ill health or poverty or old age. This situation leads to various distortions of the potential value of NGOs in the East. Powerless, local non-governmental structures are trying to compensate for the pain and chaos caused by failing governments. Since in the East there is little of the private money or the traditions of philanthropy that support this privatization of the social in the West, the small-scale women's NGOs so valued by Western feminists and Western funders often fail, reconfirming the general idea that women are politically and economically marginal and powerless.

To counter this trend, local feminisms would need to go against the current popular rhetoric of both the East and the West, that independence and small government are good, and that depending on the government is bad. Feminism would need to make what is in the East a counter-intuitive argument, that getting money and attention from government is necessary, that it is not a return to centralism, that resources from government can increase rather than decrease social freedoms. But such an argument is hard to make, given the so-recent totalitarian past. To avoid the failures they now face, some Eastern feminist NGOs construct themselves as enclaves, making bastions of safety against a larger exploitative situation. Or they build Western-authorized outposts, funded by Western sources. There is indeed useful work to be done in such outposts, but in general social supports for women's traditional tasks have received deathblows since 1989.

Gender as a Variable Emptied of Political Resonance

Central and East Europe and the former Soviet Union are ascriptive societies in which legitimization is a key value and a major theme of the transition from communism. Old structures of power and influence have fallen apart, but many of the formerly powerful have maintained their status regimes successfully under new names. One of the great sources of status is contact with the West, or with things Western. There is a (small) scramble to establish Western-style Women's Studies programs in universities. Though it is wonderful for feminist energy to establish new job pathways for women in the universities and in social policy agencies, Western feminisms can also function as the imported material that legitimizes static elite enclaves. Mass US women's movements were the initial source of energy and knowledge for American Women's Studies programs, and these programs claimed legitimization from those democratic roots for some years. But the East has much smaller, much more embattled movements. A university program could not currently gain legitimacy from the status of local movements alone. Added to this difficulty is another: the very idea of an intellectual enterprise linked to a locally active political movement is anathema to former dissidents who were kicked out of universities for their refusals to toe party lines. The fantasy of a university with no politics whatsoever is cherished, so that when feminist research ideas knock on the door for entry, they must leave their ties to social movements outside or stay outside themselves. In this situation, Western high theory is touted as pure philosophy; Western social research loses its social roots and is translated as pure science; and Women's Studies professors swear on bibles held by more established male colleagues that their work has absolutely no bias, no social commitments, no ambition to influence politics.

Gender Difference as a Way to Restructure the Workforce

Finding new entry points into the economy for women as professionals, as technicians, as freelance operators in charge of their own time are all examples of effective feminist organizing against women's poverty. But it is well to note some caveats: Veronica Schild has described how feminists who became professionals in Chile could sometimes weaken the poor women's grassroots movements they set out to serve (Schild 1998). And Juliet Mitchell warns that women are often allowed into new work situations first, just as they were the first in the textile factories of the nineteenth century. Like canaries in mines, they test the atmosphere, prepare the way for new work patterns. Mitchell argues that Western feminists have often been unaware of how their demands have supported larger, systemic changes in ways that were no part of their intent.

Like many other Western partners, the Network of East-West Women has raised money to give its members computers and computer training. Sometimes the power and freedom this gives is a delight to Western organizers' hearts. At other times, the same organizers might well feel a frisson of anxiety: have they merely offered a training program to prepare a new underpaid class for dreary office work to come?

As we seek new forms for work, we need to be aware of these larger patterns of change within which we shape our demands and desires. Women often want work that is part time, flexible, mobile. Be careful what you wish for. Mobility, without security or benefits, will surely be the prevailing form of exploitation for many workers in the future. The point is not to give up on the dream of mobility and flexibility – which are both values and work conditions that are already here to stay – but to recognize the need to bring these changes into politics, to establish new rights and protections under this new regime of fast-circulating capital.

Gender as a Grant

The English anthropologist Julie Hemment has been studying the early evolution of the Russian women's movement post-perestroika (Hemment 2004). Her work is rich and complex and I cannot summarize it here, but one central theme is the distortions introduced by Western granting organizations. Because of the general distrust of controlling bureaucracies, people also distrusted, a feminism clogged with the bureaucracy of foundations. One dispirited Russian feminist organizer told Hemment: "We used to live from party congress to party congress. Now we live from grant deadline to grant deadline." Once again, the point is not that Western grants are intrinsically bad or politically contaminated. There is no pure money from any source. The point rather is to arouse skepticism about the travels of "gender" across cultural lines. Local feminists deserve much support as they face the inevitable difficulties of making an unfamiliar set of "gender" concerns visible and meaningful in their own communities. In worst case scenarios, foundation support merely makes the mysterious and untranslatable term "gender" fashionable, bandied about as a new way of talking, as in one Russian health activist's remark: "Prostate cancer is a gender problem."

Conclusion

I intend no intrinsic insult to contemporary feminist activity by describing these moments of ill fit or illiberality in the current dispersion of feminist categories. Rather these are cautionary tales for committed feminists who hope feminist activism will prove agile enough, responsive enough to a changing situation, so as to last them a lifetime. Thirty years into this wave of the feminist project in the West, anomalies like the ones I have been describing are everywhere. It is no fault of feminist movements that their categories have often been descriptive and politically productive, so that bits and pieces of feminist analysis now crop up in unlikely combinations. In the US, for example, feminism floats around in the heads of right wing senators, who use it to modernize their old song of seduction and sin; now they say that Monica Lewinsky is the victim of sexual harassment! Such acts of appropriation are marks of feminist success. In the long run, the dispersion of feminism into many different locations, no longer visibly linked by a passionately loud, publically named "movement," may be another proof of the staying power of feminist sensibility.

All the same, feminists are right to worry about the after-life of their initiatives, the long journeys of their ideas. How often have we asked for autonomy – only to be left alone, without support; or asked for participation in the market – only to be instantly grabbed up (if we are young enough, pretty enough, without children); or asked for mobility – only to discover that we need to keep moving, changing our skills and our entire lives every few years in order to keep up. Critical hindsight is of great value in keeping feminism alive, a project under constant reconstruction.

Finally, though, I have an even more urgent reason for exploring feminist migrations that seem to me to be wasteful or wrong-headed, beyond the project of self-awareness and critique. I want to forestall a move I see coming: those political thinkers and activists with little personal stake in gender as a category on which to base thought and action will seize this time of dispersion and necessary rethinking as a chance to under-rate the importance of having independent feminist movement at all. Using its current weaknesses as an excuse, these often otherwise progressive voices will argue that political movements based on identity were always divisive and dreary and, now, thank heavens, they are dying. Let me take a detour to the couch and listen to the patient. Feminism whined. Feminism complained. Feminism was an unlovely form of special pleading. Feminist movements were limited, flawed, aggressive, grabby, and angry. In short, feminism was a mother who was less than perfect, so let her go home and be heard from no more. In this time of renegotiations of almost all post-cold war political relationships, this common willingness to let feminism disappear in both the East and West signals a dangerous absence, a failure of new political discourses to register women's aspirations for economic and social equality.

Like all movements seeking a post-1989 meaning and modus operandi, feminisms are vulnerable – not least of all to internal self-doubts. The best course for feminists is to embrace the doubts, to embrace the "homelessness" of feminism. In the US, I see the current feminist recognition of the differences among women, of our inevitable lack of unity, of feminism's fragmentation, as an advance. We are homeless in the positive sense that we are now out in the political world where no movement piety or automatic affiliation can be taken for granted. We now must construct our relationships with each other. Though women's movements have great potential for addressing basic problems facing the new market economies and for configuring strong new ways to demand social justice, economic equality, recognition of difference, etc., nonetheless, there is no reason to assume that a concern for women is automatically a basis for a powerful or useful politics. Feminism is not automatically a vanguard, an authority on what is to be done post-1989; if it is to contribute to a revitalization of politics, it will have to develop a worldview from which action can develop. Nor is there anything solid or eternal in a commitment to feminism alone, or feminism in the abstract. Incomplete and in process as feminist projects now are, those who choose to call themselves feminists must seek alliances with other groups which, like ours, are inventing themselves in response to a swiftly changing context. Feminists need skepticism about the long-term value of our actions, but, finally, our skepticism about our own foundations should not stop us from projecting tentative values as we move, case by case, decision by decision, to determine a political response to women's cumulative, multiple disadvantages.

Let me state the nature of the opportunity. "Gender" is not a nation to which anyone is required to migrate. It is, rather, a variable, a central one in the future ways in which labor, government power, and economic activity are all going to be structured – not to mention daily psychic life. Feminists have a long and distinguished history of debating the currently key issues of public and private, and feminist initiatives and political forms have great potential for widening democratic participation. In the current inflation of rhetoric about "the global," it is easy to lose sight of the future actors who might demand social justice or call for fundamental changes. Just now such ambitious movements are on the defensive, uncertain about their future course. But, to take the example at hand, the current weaknesses of some feminist movements are no good reason to turn away from politically confronting the specific problems of women or from building on feminist movements' world-wide accumulations of knowledge and power. Independent feminist movements can be of inestimable value. Are new forms of exploitation and political powerlessness to be contested – or not?

Notes

I have learned much from various works in progress: Maria Kovacs' evolving project on resistances to feminism; Carole S. Vance's conceptualization of her Rockefeller seminar, the Program on Sexuality, Gender, Health, and Human Rights, at Columbia University, 1998–2005; Shana Penn's unpublished work on Czechoslovakia where I first read about Horakova and other feminist histories from pre-communist Central and East Europe; Julie Hemment's book in progress, *Gendered Interventions: Action Research and Women's Activism in the Russian Provinces*; Victoria Hattam's forthcoming *Identification and Politics*, which has made me see the importance of the active choice of boundaries and alliances in the construction of any politics; Joanna Regulska's suggestive studies of local democracy in Poland and elsewhere, which explore the various vulnerabilities of women's NGOs (Regulska 1998, 2001). An earlier version of this article appeared in *Proceedings of the 93rd Annual Meeting* of the American Society of International Law, March 24–27, 1999: pp. 35–42.

Finally, my thanks to all the members of The Network of East-West Women who are facing the difficulties described here every day with wisdom, patience, and dedication.

References

Hemment, Julie. 1999. Report on her dissertation work in Tver, Russia at NYU's Center for European Studies.

Hemment, Julie. 2004. Global civil society and the local costs of belonging: Defining violence against women in Russia. *Signs* Spring 2004:815–840.

Kovacs, Maria. Ambiguities of emancipation: Women and the ethnic question in Hungary and The egalitarian appeal of nationalism. Unpublished manuscripts, on file with the author.

Mitchell, Juliet. 1986. Reflections on twenty years of feminism. In *What is feminism?*, edited by Juliet Mitchell and Ann Oakley. New York: Pantheon.

Regulska, J. 1998. The political and its meaning for women's transitional politics in Poland. In *Theorizing transition: The political economy of change in Central and Eastern Europe*, edited by J. Pickles and A. Smith. London: Routledge.

Regulska, J. 2001. Gendered integration of Europe: New boundaries of exclusion. In *Gender in transition in Eastern and Central Europe*, edited by G. Jahnert, J. Gohrisch, D. Hahn, H. Nickel, M.I. Peinl, and K. Schafgen. Berlin: Trafo Verlag.

Schild, Veronica. 1998. Market citizenship and the "New Democracies": The ambiguous legacies of contemporary Chilean women's movements. *Social Politics* Summer 1998: 232–249.

Vance, Carole S. Innocence and experience: Melodramatic narratives of sex trafficking and their consequences for health and human rights. Unpublished manuscript, on file with the author.

Epilogue

Persisting Struggles

Darja Zaviršek, Joanna Regulska and Jasmina Lukić

The idea of putting together an edited volume on contentions and controversies surrounding the gendered debates on citizenship in Central and East European countries originated from discussions among the participants of the Inter-Regional Seminar on Gender and Culture [IRSGC] (1994–1997), organized by the Program on Gender and Culture at the Central European University [CEU]. With funding from the Higher Education Support Program of the Open Society Institute in Budapest, Professor Nancy Leys Stepan, the program's director at that time, initiated this regular gathering of feminists from Central and East Europe, including countries of the former Soviet Union. As she explained:

> My thought was to work across national frontiers, in order to bring together in a regular fashion the women who were at the forefront of re-thinking issues surrounding gender. The seminar usually composed of 25 people at a time, met regularly over the course of each year in a series of workshops, each with its own agendas, shared readings, and passionate discussions. The idea was to address what we thought were some of the most crucial issues facing women living in eastern Europe: war, nationalism, the meaning of feminism, the legacies of the past, work, reproductive rights, the nature of the political (personal communication with Nancy L. Stepan 1998).

After Nancy Stepan left, the new co-directors of the Program (1996–98), Joanna Regulska and Kim L. Scheppele, and the associate director, Mindy Roseman, continued the program, including the IRSGC seminars, adding new themes and bringing in new participants.

The dialogues initiated at the CEU were eventually carried across the ocean to another feminist forum at Rutgers University, with which one of the editors is associated. During the 1996–1997 academic year, Joanna Regulska and her colleague, Barbara Balliet, became co-directors of the Ford Foundation sponsored project, "Integrating Area and Women's Studies," which was awarded to the Women's Studies Program (WST) at Rutgers University. The geographical focus chosen was Central and East Europe, and the yearlong seminar was run jointly by the WST and the Center for Russian, Central, and East European Studies (currently the Center for European Studies). Some of the participants of the IRSGC also became contributors to the Rutgers seminar and a two-day conference at Rutgers University, "Locations of Gender: Central and East Europe," which was held in the spring of 1997.

The present collection brings together several IRSGC seminar participants and contributors to the Ford Foundation sponsored seminar and conference, as well as feminist scholars whose writings came to our attention. The three co-editors, Jasmina, Joanna, and Darja, met during the IRSGC seminars and have since been collaborating in their commitment to challenge the barriers that divide women, and the systems that exclude them. In claiming our diverse identities, each of us, individually and collectively have been engaged, over the years, in advancing women's active and multi-layered citizenship at diverse sites, and through the diverse means of feminist activism, teaching, writing, research, mentoring, organizing, and policy-making.

This volume reflects the very contentious terrain of crafting the notion of citizenship in Central and East Europe. As contributors convincingly argue, struggles for women's citizenship rights, in the region (and for that matter across the world), made visible the underlying injustices, discriminations and exclusions that cut across all kinds of borders – cultural as well as political, social and economic; geographical and/or institutional. By claiming their agency, women engage in struggles and confrontations as well as in creative and productive mobilizations that allow them to become visible citizen-subjects. The chapters brought together in this volume attempt to understand the notion of citizenship, from diverse (inter)disciplinary and methodological perspectives, as well as within distinct cultural and historical contexts. Yet, the emphasis on recognizing diversity and difference did not minimize the core concept of the book – the notion of women's agency – which cuts across different topics and interpretative positions. The multidimensional and multi-layered concept of agency, as envisaged by the contributors, not only offers the common ground for accommodating these differences and diversities, but also enriches and signifies their critical role in citizen-subject formation processes. Agency, within such a context, connects different citizenship traditions, and acknowledges the very particular social conditions that characterized the transformative period in Central and East Europe, and that required from women a high level of social awareness and active involvement in the ongoing changes.

Authors, in the present volume, demonstrate the diversity of conditions under which women claimed their agency during the times of transformations. They have shown how women of different classes, ethnic backgrounds, ages, and bodily abilities have very different experiences when relating to and operating within gendered regimes of family or state institutions, and also how the subsequent changes of socialist regimes have implicated women's opportunities and struggles. While women (as well as other citizens) benefited from some of these adjustments, other changes challenged women's position in society in new and not always favorable ways.

Faced with both new opportunities and new challenges, women had to acquire new forms of political and social consciousness, and ascertain alternative ways of social organizing and involvement. From the perspective of their struggles to (re)frame their position as citizens within the new political and economic landscape, it is possible to argue that their agency was claimed within at least two new key domains. The first one was the domain of state institutions and the second that of civil society. Within the new political and social framework that reshaped party control and decentralized power, women had to re-define their attitudes towards institutions of the state (to make them more accountable), and learn how to use them as the locus of their own agency. At the same time, since these institutions were neither fully welcoming, nor sensitive towards women's concerns, (and in many cases, did not prove to be sufficiently supportive in addressing women's particular needs), women had to organize themselves parallel to the state, in the alternative spaces that were embedded within civil society.

The new roles of the state and its institutions within the enlarged Europe, and the expectations raised by these changes have been widely debated by scholars. Some writers have argued that the importance of the state will be diminished due to globalization and the emergence of supranational institutions such as the European Union. Yet, others have asserted the opposite, claiming that state power has increased because of the European integration. From women's perspectives, there was also a hope that regardless of the possible weakening of the state, the desire to embrace democratic practices would in fact enhance the probability that the state structures would become more responsive to women's concerns.

What the contributors to this volume repeatedly assert dispels these hopes. The positions of the new post-socialist states have not been weakened because of global transformations, "one economy," a single notion of "democracy," or some of the CEE countries' memberships in the EU. The state's powers have in fact become enhanced, while at the same time, state policies and actions have not become more women-friendly. Therefore, the post-socialist state, in its social, cultural, economic, and political capacities remains highly relevant for women.

This relevance can be equally observed in the countries that entered the European Union in May 2004, as well as in those which have not yet entered or who may never enter. New members of the EU, for example, had to rewrite and change most of their legislative frameworks in order to be accepted into the political space of the EU. They often found themselves with the need to erase and "rewrite" the collective memory that was linked not only to the period of state socialism, but also to the history of struggles for liberation and social justice across the globe (for example, 1 May, celebrated world-wide as International Workers Day, became, from the year 2004, the celebration of their official entrance to the EU by the nine CEE countries). The process of rewriting memories has produced new divisions, as states attempt to symbolically and materially eliminate the social and economic gains that had benefited their citizens, including women. For some, such an example shows how this time of transformations was not only a period of fast economic changes that resulted in the loss of everyday routines, welfare benefits, and job security, but also a period of transformations of cultural representations and changes of personal, collective, and public memories.

Faced with a complicated political and social dynamic, which often tended to erase some of women's acquired rights under the assumption that they were a part of an unwanted communist legacy, women had to be both strategic and persistent in arguing for their citizenship rights. As contributors demonstrated, women claimed their agency by becoming contributors, partners, lobbyists, and challengers of state decision-making processes. This was especially visible in the context of the newly established women's bureaus and offices for equal opportunities. These new governmental bodies that, at least for some years after the fall of socialism, were most often led by women, became an important part of the new governmental structures and a strong advocate of women's rights and gender equality. By working with and through these new state structures, women demanded gender visibility within the state statistics; they have challenged injustices such as violence, unequal pay for women, ethnocentrism, and able-bodism, and have attempted to reshape male-centrist language. They have shown the fallacy and the inefficiency of the so-called "gender-neutral socialist equalities," which controlled women's needs and rights in the past and have pointed out that, in the end, gender-neutrality only promoted a structural focus on men's needs, rights, and privileges.

Women's engagements in establishing non-governmental organizations have shown the importance of gender-reflexive democracies. As several authors pointed out, women's NGO work has focused on the lives of those women whose personal and collective stories were often silenced and denied, both in the past and under the new neoliberal regimes of the market economy. Women's groups have often focused on the everyday experiences of women and have shown that many so-called "democratic changes" in post-socialist countries were reflected neither in public policy nor in the new legal frameworks. There is no doubt that the agency that emerged, through women's activism, was remarkable. Some of the writers also suggest that when the NGO-ization of feminism began to take place, it underscored the fact that it was primarily through NGOs that different feminist activities and feminist orientations had found their locus.

For women who were working with and through NGOs, the most critical concern was that women and feminists' perspectives (which continued to remain marginal within state structures) come to the forefront of political agendas. Such NGOs served as critical vehicles that encouraged women to unfold personal experiences in order to demand equal participation in all spheres of social and political life. NGOs also facilitated the emergence of transnational and collective women's engagements and mobilizations, and therefore permitted the crossing of nation-state borders, in order for women to build new alliances and cross-border collective actions. The flow of ideas, skills, resources, and/or interpretations brought different dimensions of feminisms in the "East" and in the "West" closer; yet, it also resulted in the emergence of new tensions and misrepresentations.

Today it is obvious that women's and feminist NGOs, in post-socialist countries, have carried out democracy from below and have emerged as a way to mediate the relationships between the state, citizens, and supranational institutions. Yet, after the initial enthusiasm and struggles to build and strengthen women's and feminist

NGOs, it is also clear that new challenges have emerged. In many cases, for example, women's NGOs narrowed their focuses to singular issue such as counseling services, women's safe houses, and/or training. While these are, with no doubt, worthy and needed causes, this particularity of agenda prevented them from developing a long-term and wider platform of civil initiatives, or a political movement that could serve as a critical voice within patriarchal and male-dominated state institutions and policy climates. Contributors called then for women's and feminist NGOs to strengthen their capacity and to became more engaged politically.

Articles in this volume underscored the complex picture of women's agency as it has been forming over the last fifteen years in Central and East Europe. Authors mapped a number of positive changes, which resulted from the introduction of de-mocracy and signaled the hopes of what some policy initiatives would bring (such as gender mainstreaming). On the other hand, they also pointed to the "new" but old dangers of gender discrimination which continue to (re)appear in very different forms. They showed that there is always a danger of some form of the re-patriarcha-lization of state institutions and of societies in general. Several authors underscored that, despite being very active in all the processes that have led to the end of com-munist regimes in Europe, during the transformative period, women have had to face numerous challenges sooner then expected. Indeed, the fact that spaces of gender discrimination were expanding within the new social frameworks, which were sup-posed to bring benefits to all the citizens, proves this point. Expectations that, after 1989, women's citizenship rights would be strengthened across different spheres of their daily lives have not been fulfilled.

Several authors also called our attention to the numerous evidence of the his-torical repetition of "forgetting women" after times of turbulent changes and both violent, as well as non-violent revolutions. Just recently, in the fall of 2005, the newly elected Polish government, as one of its first public gestures, diminished the governmental office for equal opportunities, and reoriented their agenda towards family values. Thus, the Polish state reasserted its power and showed that mem-bership in the EU, even with its official gender mainstreaming policies, does not necessarily secure institutional protection for women, even in countries that joined the EU. Women in the EU and non-EU countries continue to experience increas-ingly precarious social conditions and jobs, and more often than ever before, they are being asked to take part time jobs. Several Central and East European countries legalized sex work, but at the same time left women who are involved in the sex in-dustry unprotected and stigmatized. Within the larger European context, the cultural representation of women from CEE countries often remains equated with that of a sex worker, "dirty cleaner," or an illegal worker who takes all the available jobs car-ing for the elderly and disabled.

It is obvious that the struggle for women's equality has not stopped with the end of state socialism or with the spread of "Western democratic values" across CEE countries. On the contrary, the new domination of neoliberal market relations across the world, the negative effects of globalization, which has increased the number of poor women workers and legal and illegal immigrants, and the creation of a new caste of working poor, all affect women on a daily basis. Women's citizenship therefore remains a dynamic and constantly changing concept, which includes a continuous struggle for women's agency, justice, and critical consciousness.

Name Index

Subject Index